ARNOLD KRAMISH

The Griffin

MACMILLAN
LONDON

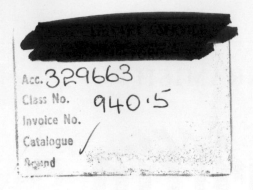
First published 1986 in the United States of America by
Houghton Mifflin Company, Boston

First published 1987 in the United Kingdom by
MACMILLAN LONDON LIMITED
4 Little Essex Street London WC2R 3LF
and Basingstoke

Associated companies in Auckland, Delhi, Dublin, Gaborone,
Hamburg, Harare, Hong Kong, Johannesburg, Kuala Lumpur,
Lagos, Manzini, Melbourne, Mexico City, Nairobi, New York,
Singapore and Tokyo

ISBN 0-333-45316-6

Printed in Hong Kong

CONTENTS

List of Illustrations vii

Prologue 1

1 *Graz* 3

2 *Metamorphosis* 8

3 *Contacts* 13

4 *The Strajner Deception* 19

5 *Private Lives* 22

6 *V.M.* 28

7 *The Man Who Wasn't There* 33

8 *Kapitza* 35

9 *The Exiles* 43

10 *Midwife to Fission* 50

11 *Departures* 56

12 *Beck's Book* 59

13 *The Oslo Report* 63

14 *Author, Author?* 69

15 *The Solution* 73

16 *Retreat* 81

17 *Cut-off* 86

18 *Theodor* 90

19 *The Forest of the Griffin* 97

20 *Sigurd* 103

21 *The Visit* 114

CONTENTS

22   *Return to Oslo*   122

23   *"The Heart of Your Enemies"*   133

24   *"The House Is on the Hill"*   137

25   *The French Connection*   146

26   *The Fox*   156

27   *"Juice"*   165

28   *The General Steps In*   171

29   *Ex-filtration*   179

30   *"Nicholas Baker"*   192

31   *Double-Cross*   199

32   *Cover*   206

33   *The Tears of the Oppressed*   216

34   *The Code of Codes*   223

35   *Victory*   230

36   *Conspiracy at Farm Hall*   242

Epilogue   249

Acknowledgments and Sources   253

Bibliography   265

Index   281

ILLUSTRATIONS

following page 150

Anna Rosbaud and Paul, 1896. (Photo by J. Tchinner)
Door to the apartment house at 8 Trauengauergasse, Graz. (Photo by Arnold Kramish)
The Heinnisser family villa in Waltendorf. (Courtesy Wilhelm Rosbaud)
Paul Rosbaud at 3 Quergasse, Graz, circa 1909. (Courtesy the Rosbaud family archives)
Johann Strajner, Paul's "father," as a spelunker. (Courtesy Max Tesimayer)
Karl Gaugl, Paul Rosbaud, and Anna Rosbaud. (Courtesy the Rosbaud family archives)
Sketch of Paul Rosbaud as an Austrian soldier on the Isonzo, 1918. (Courtesy the Rosbaud family archives)
Hans and Paul Rosbaud with Paul's daughter, Angela. Graz, 1936. (Courtesy the Rosbaud family archives)
Ruth Lange and fellow athletes in training in the early 1930s. (Courtesy Ruth Lange)
"Red Hilde" Benjamin, Ruth Lange's sister.
Ruth Lange. (Courtesy Ruth Lange)
Major Frank Foley in Oslo, autumn 1939. (Courtesy the Brotherton Library, University of Leeds)
Margaret Reid. (Courtesy the Brotherton Library, University of Leeds)
General Otto Ruge in colonel's uniform before his promotion. (Courtesy the Brotherton Library, University of Leeds)
"The Griffin." Paul Rosbaud in wartime. (Courtesy Hilde Rosbaud)
Beck's book. (Courtesy Metallgesellschaft A.G., Frankfurt, FRG)
Eric Welsh, in uniform. (Courtesy Sir Michael Perrin)
The hydroelectric plant at Rjukan at night. (Courtesy the Tronstad family)
The Vemork plant after the air raid on November 16, 1943. (Courtesy Jomar Brun)
The entrance to Farm Hall. (Photo by Arnold Kramish)

Door to the "listening room" at Farm Hall. (Photo by Arnold Kramish)

Sverre Bergh's passport. (Courtesy Sverre Bergh)

Dismantling the German atomic reactor at Haigerloch after the war. (Courtesy Sir Michael Perrin)

Otto Hahn. (Courtesy Hilde Rosbaud)

The Kaiser Wilhelm Institute in Dahlem, where Hahn and Strassman split the uranium nucleus. (Photo by Arnold Kramish)

Max von Laue. (Photo by Lotte Meitner-Graf)

Victor Goldschmidt. (Courtesy Professor K. H. Wedepohl)

Leif Tronstad as a major. (Courtesy the Tronstad family)

Henri Piatier, 1959. (Courtesy Henri Piatier)

Lise Meitner. (Photo by Lotte Meitner-Graf)

Odd Hassel. (Courtesy The Royal University Library, Oslo)

Hilde Rosbaud, Samuel Goudsmit, and Paul Rosbaud on the occasion of the Tate Medal award to Paul Rosbaud by the American Institute of Physics. (Courtesy American Institute of Physics)

Paul Rosbaud's body about to be buried at sea. (Courtesy the Rosbaud family archives)

For Bob

Prologue

THE SPY, a man who was not going to live much longer, leaned back against one of the intact walls of the old citadel of Graz. A French marshal by the name of Alexander MacDonald had blown up the fortress in 1809, but he had spared the bell tower and this piece of the ramparts. The man who stood there, meditating in the dusk, had once been a part of history himself, but he had commanded no troops, attacked no fortresses. His weapon had been secrecy, his victories had been silent, and there were only a very few people in the world who even knew his name, let alone his story. He had been, nevertheless, one of Adolf Hitler's great and formidable antagonists. Set in the parapet in front of him was an engraved steel plate with lines indicating the directions to Moscow, London, and Washington. Out there, along the stretch of those imaginary lines, was the world that his work had affected more than the world knew.

The Austrian city of Graz lay below him in the gathering darkness. It was a city he detested, the city where he had been born, and the city that still kept certain secrets from him, after all these years. Below him, lights flickered on in the apartments of the Khuenburg Palace. That was where the Archduke Franz Ferdinand was born in 1863, about a century ago. Franz Ferdinand, the bumbling heir apparent to the Austrian and Hungarian thrones, who died of a pistol shot at Sarajevo and thereby mightily changed the world of his time.

As the dusk deepened, the spy looked toward the slender Baroque spire of St. Andrä's and thought, perhaps, of the secret he had never been able to unearth there. Hidden below the other side of the rampart was the Dom, the great cathedral of Graz, with secrets of which the spy knew nothing.

There was another image, so much a part of him that it must have recurred once more as he looked down on his birthplace. This one was a mythical beast, a winged lion with the head and claws of an eagle. In mythology, it guarded ancient secrets and old treasures. In his own life, it was the figure on a family crest, a symbol, and a name that had become his talisman. The day that he had launched his deep, personal, silent war against Führer Adolf Hitler, he had given himself the pseudonym *der Greif* — the Griffin.

ONE

Graz

SOMEWHERE in northern Yugoslavia, there is a two-hundred-year-old document known as the *Zolchner Codex*. On its vellum cover is a drawing of the family coat of arms: a field of silver, a red hill in three parts at the bottom, and, on top, an upright griffin holding an iron pike. Surmounting the shield is a tournament helmet. And to emphasize the nobility of the beast, another griffin thrusts his pike forward. Originally, the codex, and the family for which it had been made, came from the old town of Graz, and here it was that an illegitimate child of Zolchner descent was born in 1896.

Anna Rosbaud, the mother of this boy, was a spinster. Old photographs show that she wore her hair close-cropped and that her face was chiefly notable for its strong chin. Yet her story shows her to have been a loving and spirited woman.

Anna always retained a certain pride in coming from a good family. On her mother's side there were the Zolchners, with their claim to minor nobility and their griffin crest. On her father's side were the Rosbauds from Bohemia. At some time in the Middle Ages, a Bohemian hunter had decided to give himself a last name, and choosing the most convenient object in sight, he called himself after his *rozbaud*, or thatched hut. (The word does not appear in modern dictionaries, and it would always fall with a foreign sound on German ears.) In the fifteenth century, some of the Rosbauds and some of the Zolchners were employed in the service of the Fugger merchant bankers, the former working in the silver mines in the Březové Mountains, southwest of Prague.

Both families were devoutly Catholic, but there was one odd incident in the Rosbaud past. In the early years of the eighteenth century, a Jewish girl named Judith Ginsburger was kidnapped from her wealthy banking family, was later baptized as a Christian, and married a Zolchner. This was considered merely a curious and interesting family anecdote until the year 1933.

The Rosbauds and the Zolchners joined when Wenzel Rosbaud married Ida Kockl, granddaughter of the last of the Zolchners. Wenzel came from the Bohemian town of Hořovice, known for its manufacture of fine musical instruments, and as a young man had gone to Vienna to study music. When his funds and his ambition ran out, he succeeded in getting a job as manager of the Kockl estate at Neu Künegg, on the Slovenian border, and soon stepped up in the world by marrying Ida, the daughter of the house. They became the parents of a son, Richard, and two daughters, Wilhelmina and Anna.

Before long, Wenzel's luck changed again, and a series of poor harvests—combined with his bad management—forced him to sell the estate. Impoverished now, he drifted back to Vienna and applied for a junior position with the Ministry of Finance. He was accepted and posted as a tax officer to the sleepy village of Eibiswald, also on the Slovenian border.

It so happened that while Wenzel was becoming a bureaucrat, a much younger man, a cobbler's apprentice, was hired by the revenue service of the same ministry. This Alois Schickelgruber was the bastard son of a serving maid and an unknown father. Later, he took the name of his foster father and became Alois Hitler. In 1889, he would have a son by his third wife and would christen the boy Adolf. There is no record that Alois and Wenzel ever knew each other, however.

The Rosbauds were not happy in Eibiswald. Ida went to faraway Graz as often as she could manage. Wenzel enjoyed playing the piano at noisy weekend parties in the home of the Heinnissers, friends in nearby Wies. When Anna was born to the Rosbauds in 1856, the parents thought it time for another change, and Wenzel used all the influence he could muster to get himself transferred to Graz. Here, they were convinced, they could be happy. There was still a little Zolchner money in the bank. There were friends. There was even one of the Heinnissers, who held an important position at the central city church and would welcome them.

As Anna grew, she began to show some talent for music. Her early triumph was a meeting with Clara Schumann, who had come to Graz to give a concert. She received Anna, even gave her a few piano lessons, and was impressed enough to predict that the young woman would have a great future. Instead, at the age of twenty-six Anna produced a great scandal in Graz.

Josef Heinnisser, as organist at the Grazer Stadtpfarrkirche, was an established figure in the town. His elder son, Josef, attained a high position in the administration of the province of Styria. Franz, the eighteen-year-old son, was, like his father, infatuated with church music. And it was through this interest that he met and became equally infatuated with Anna Rosbaud. Anna, usually a practical woman, every now and then during a holiday or celebration was likely to get carried away. The Weinachtsfest of 1881 must have been a particularly jubilant occasion, because shortly after the start of the year she discovered that she was pregnant by Franz. The Rosbauds were shocked; Anna's mother cast her out of the house. The Heinnissers, too, were shocked, but not so much as to neglect making the arrangement any prudent bourgeois family of the time would have made. In return for a promise that she would never demand anything else from them, they settled a little money on Anna, and she went off to live on the former Kockl estate, where her parents had begun their marriage. To put more distance between the lovers, the Heinnissers packed Franz off to Salzburg as an apprentice to a firm of organ makers.

The child born that September was baptized Bruno and was given—along with the remains of the Heinnisser gratuity—to the family of a master carpenter in Belgrade. In the years to come, Bruno was to become a musician and then a Yugoslav Partisan captain in the war against the Nazis.

Anna returned to Graz and supported herself by giving piano lessons to the children of the town's best families. After Ida died, Wenzel came to live with his daughter in her flat on the second floor of 8 Trauengauergasse (the Lane of Faith), near the tramway barns. Wenzel died there in September 1894, leaving Anna the sum of three hundred kroner, which paid his doctor's bill and bought the tombstone.

In November of the same year, the town of Graz was swept up by the modern age. It had been a tramway town for a long time, but now the city fathers made the decision to change from horse-drawn trams to electric ones. There was consternation in the neighborhood around the car barns at the end of Annenstrasse; it was here that conductors, drivers, ticket takers, and grooms lived and here that most of the shock was felt. On the twenty-fifth of the month, the new electric funicular railway to the top of the Schlossberg was inaugurated with a fireworks celebration in the Hauptplatz below. In the course of this auspicious event, Anna realized she was pregnant again.

Franz Heinnisser, in the twelve years since the scandal, had become a proper burgher. He had married and fathered three children; he had risen to the position of choirmaster at the Graz cathedral, the Dom. But he had not forgotten Anna. Shortly before the advent of electric transport in Graz, Franz came to 8 Trauengauergasse to express his condolences on the death of Wenzel—and managed to repeat the past.

The boy who was born from that reunion was named Johann; in later life he was known as Hans Rosbaud.

In mid February of 1896, there was another festive occasion in the Trauengauergasse. At number 6, a tram conductor named Johann Strajner was marrying a locksmith named Theresia Wesiak and, incidentally, legitimating their two daughters. It was a celebration that Franz Heinnisser could not bear to miss, so he came once more to see Anna. The result was inevitable.

The third son was born at half past nine in the evening of November 18, 1896. Because he was a frail infant, he was baptized at home eight days later, and Paul Wenzel Matteus Rosbaud, illegitimate son of Anna, was entered in register number 539 of St. Andrä's parish.

Shortly afterward, Anna fled the bill collectors, and the Graz police records show that a vain attempt was made to locate her. She had not gone far, however; in 1897 she was living with her infants Hans and Paul at Villa Ruckerlberg 101 in the affluent suburb of Waltendorf. That villa was the country home of the Heinnisser family. But the pattern repeated itself—another pregnancy and another move—and Anna was back in Graz at a new address, Quergasse 3, in the old neighborhood, when a daughter, Martha, was born. Unable to deal with three children, Anna found a foster home in the country for the new child.

One day in 1904, when Hans and Paul were home, Anna was visited by three "cousins," who were, in fact, her oldest son, Bruno, his fiancée, and her mother. Bruno, who had not seen his mother since infancy — and would not see her again — demanded to know who his father was. Anna did not lie, but all she said was "Your father came from a family of high station."

Legal records still in the Graz archives show that there was some attempt to cover up the paternity of all the children, and Anna did not clarify matters when she told the police that Martha's unnamed father had provided for her support — and later explained that she had no idea who Martha's father was.

Apparently Franz Heinnisser did arrange to provide for his children to some extent by giving them surrogate fathers. When Hans's musical talent began to manifest itself, Franz was able to interest Karl Ortner, an old family friend, a rich ironmonger, and a musical enthusiast who played the cello and the French horn. His dream was to create his own orchestra, and in Hans he seemed to have an ideal protégé.

Thus it was that one day in 1911 the fifteen-year-old Hans Rosbaud made his debut conducting the Orchesterrunde of Graz — an ensemble of twenty — at the ornate Graz Opera House.

Anna and Paul Rosbaud sat in the last tier of seats, which were the best that they could afford, and Anna wept with pride. With pride but also with a few tears for herself — the doctor had recently told her that she had breast cancer and that the prognosis was not good.

On the bright spring morning of May 6, 1913, as Anna lay dying, Paul came to her bedside and implored her to tell him the identity of his father.

She replied simply, "You will never need to know."

It was her final piece of bad judgment. Paul did need to know. In the years to come, that need would become a matter of life or death for him.

TWO

Metamorphosis

FRANZ HEINNISSER, the father whom Paul Rosbaud never knew, had separated from his wife a few years before Anna's death and eventually drifted to Vienna, where he died in 1944. Paul found his father substitute in the family's next-door neighbor, Johann Strajner, the tramway conductor during whose wedding celebration Paul had been conceived. Strajner was rather more interesting than his profession might suggest; he had an adventurous life apart from the trolley line. He was born in Ljubljana (then called Laibach) in the Austro-Hungarian province of Carniola, an area famous for its caves. As a boy, he became a spelunker, and cave exploration remained his passion for the rest of his life. Later, it seemed appropriate that Hans's father figure was the musical patron Karl Ortner, and Paul's a man whose great joy was the lonely exploration of subterranean darkness.

Despite the absence of a real father, the boys would remember a happy childhood in the squalid flat in Quergasse 3. Years afterward Paul recalled, "We did not miss our father at all—we did not know him and we did not want him. When one of us—usually I—was very naughty and tiresome, my mother used the stern warning that unless I was a good child, she would marry so that we would have a father who could better deal with us. This invariably had the desired effect, and in floods of tears I would promise to be a good boy."

It was music, however, that sustained the small family through hardships and disappointments. School records show that both brothers were excellent students with evident musical talent, but Paul was considered deficient in manual dexterity. Even though Anna spent most of the day giving piano lessons, she organized music for recreation in the evenings. The Rosbauds formed a chamber music ensemble, with Anna at the piano, Paul on the viola, Hans on cello or violin, and another older boy, Karl Gaugl, on the cello. When they could afford twenty kreutzer for tickets, Paul and Hans would stand at the rear of the Opera House to hear Casals, Hubermann, or Godowsky, or to marvel at a performance of *The Magic Flute*.

The boys were required to read Goethe, Schiller, and Shakespeare, but for thrills they read Conan Doyle and Jules Verne. Paul's favorite was the German author Karl May, who wrote about implausible adventures in the Wild West, with cowboys and Indians. Coincidentally, May was also admired by the young Adolf Hitler.

Despite Paul Rosbaud's later denial—"We did not miss our father . . . we did not want him"—there is evidence to show that the unknown father was not so easily dismissed. He had done a painful wrong to Anna and then had wronged them all by disappearing. After school, the boy would go into St. Andrä's where, above the altar, is a triangular representation of the Trinity with a disembodied eye in the center. To Paul, the eye seemed omniscient, for it was the eye of God. It knew the answer to the puzzle that would remain unsolved.

But there were good times for Paul and Hans. Graz was not a bad town to grow up in during the early years of the century. The two would wander down the Annenstrasse, cross the river Mur via the Franz Karl Bridge, then go up the Sackgasse past the fancy Erzherzog Johann Hotel. They would peer into the courtyard of the Khuenburg Palace, where the archduke was born, wishing that their cousin, Ottokar Uhlir, now the archduke's naval attaché, would appear and let them look inside. At number 20, the Reiner Hof, Hans would remember that it was here that Josef Haydn had once performed.

A few steps away from the Reiner Hof was the station of the funicular to the top of the Schlossberg, but riding it was a rare luxury for them, and they usually raced each other up the steep stairs and pathways. There was one time of the year when they always made it a point to be there. As Paul remembered it:

> We never failed to look 'round the Schlossberg on All Souls' Day, November 2, on the evening of which it was customary to light little wax lights on the graves. On a clear evening, one saw here and there on the hills near villages the glimmer of tiny little squares of the cemeteries,

and I remember that I was very quiet. Perhaps it was not only the sad beauty of an autumn evening that moved me but the first presentiment of another very quiet world, my first meeting with those who have preceded us. The thought of a warm light on the cool earth had something consoling for me.

After Anna passed on to that very quiet world in the May of Paul's seventeenth year, Hans was given the chance to enter the Hoch Conservatory in Frankfurt. There, he would soon establish a firm friendship with a fellow student, Paul Hindemith. As for Paul Rosbaud, he had one more year to finish at the trade school in Graz.

The summer of 1914 was one of yellow sun and radiant beauty. On the weekend of June 26, Paul took the train north to the Hochlantsch for a holiday weekend to celebrate his matriculation and his saint's name day. On Monday evening, he returned to Graz and heard the news that Graz's native son, the Archduke Franz Ferdinand and his wife, Sophie, had been assassinated in Sarajevo by a Serbian nationalist. It was a sad event but one that could scarcely affect Paul. He was intent on plans for his first trip to Germany to visit Hans in Frankfurt.

Hans had been playing the piano to accompany the silent films shown in a Frankfurt movie theater and had earned enough to pay Paul's fare. With him, Paul brought a little present for Hans—a program for a recital given by the Russian pianist Dimitri Agrenov in Graz twenty-seven years earlier. Anna had saved it.

Hans was very busy. Happy as he was to see his brother, he had no leisure time except late in the evening or on Sundays. Paul, left on his own, one sunny day decided to take a pleasant stroll to the nearby village of Vilbel to see the ruins of recently discovered Roman baths.

Because of the rumors of war, the Vilbel constabulary of four was being especially alert. The young stranger pretending an interest in the Roman masonry looked suspicious to them, so without hesitation they arrested him and took him off to the police station. When they strip-searched him, they found several incriminating documents. One was a sketch of Frankfurt's central railway station (where Hans had met Paul) included in a shorthand letter that none of the constables could read. Another was the concert program for Dimitri Agrenov. This fellow who said he was from Graz was clearly a Russian spy. It was to be Paul Rosbaud's single arrest on the charge of espionage.

In the end, he was saved by a compassionate—and literate—Vilbel citizer who could read shorthand and recognize a concert program, and ne was set free.

After the Frankfurt visit, Paul returned to Graz and the trade school. But on the ides of March 1915, he enlisted as a private in the Styrian Regiment K und K (Königlich und Kaiserlich) 27. He was eighteen.

In June, the Italian commander General Luigi Cadorna began a series of attacks along the Isonzo River on Italy's eastern frontier with Austria. The first was a bloody fiasco. Paul was with his regiment to defend against the second attack, launched in July and equally futile. Then came a third and finally a fourth, which lasted from November into December. During the last of these, Paul suffered a severe case of frostbite and was invalided to a hospital in Agram, now Zagreb.

It was an ideal place to recuperate, because Paul's aunt Wilhelmina, happily married and with a large family, lived in Agram. Paul fell madly in love with his beautiful cousin Anka. There were long walks along the Strossmayer Promenade at the edge of the upper town and ardent protestations from Paul—but Anka was only flirting. She rejected his offer of marriage, and he returned sadly to his regiment in May 1916. In August, the Italians struck again along the Isonzo, and the stubborn Austrian defenders were pushed back.

Thus it went, with bloody push and shove, through the seventh, eighth, ninth, tenth, and eleventh battles of the Isonzo. Paul contracted a severe case of typhoid and was hospitalized again. He rose from private to ensign to lieutenant and he won the bronze military cross with swords, the bronze and silver orders for bravery, and the Karl military cross. In October 1917 came the twelfth battle of the Isonzo—better known as the battle of Caporetto—when an Austro-German army inflicted a disastrous defeat on the Italians.

When an armistice was finally signed at the Villa Giusti, near Padua, on November 3, 1918, Paul's unit happened to be across from one of the eleven British regiments now on the line. Paul knew a little English, so he was sent with a flag of truce to arrange for the unit's surrender. But the British colonel had not heard of the armistice. He thanked Paul politely for his good intentions and returned him to the Austrian lines to carry on the war. Fortunately, Paul's unit by that time had been able to find another British force more amenable to accepting a surrender; thus, a little more than a week before the grand Armi-

stice, the war was over for Paul Rosbaud. That small, chance happening
—his becoming a British rather than an Italian POW—was to have
an effect on history twenty-one years later.

Long after the war's end, Paul wrote, "My first two days as a prisoner
under British guard were the origins of my long-time anglophilia.
For the British soldiers, war was over and forgotten. They did not
treat us as enemies but as unfortunate losers of the war. They did
not fraternize, but they were polite and correct."

The British transferred him to the Italians for an even more agreeable internment. He was sent to Castello Baia on the Amalfi coast,
where he enjoyed views of Pompeii in one direction and Capri in the
other. Baia had been the most sumptuous spa of ancient Rome. The
sixteenth-century castle had a faded grandeur of its own, and Paul
relished the surrounding park, with its ruined temples of Venus and
Diana. He was acquiring some knowledge of other languages, a liking
for foreign places, and a taste for Italian food and wine. At the end
of the year, when he was repatriated, he was no longer a simple
provincial from Graz.

THREE

Contacts

HANS ROSBAUD had escaped military service. While he was studying at the Hoch Conservatory, he had taken to an ill-planned vegetable diet, his health had deteriorated, and he had been given an exemption. About this time, he met and became a friend of Prince Alexander Friedrich, the Landgrave of Hesse. The prince, almost blind and a great lover of music, had formed an attachment to Hans. He was a gifted performer on the violin, and very soon Hans became his constant companion. Alexander Friedrich resided in Schloss Panker near the Baltic in the region that is called Holstein's Switzerland. "Come, come to Panker and abandon yourself to good work (but not too much work). Hurry!" pleaded the prince in a letter to Hans. Very well, replied Hans, but Paul must be with me.

The reunion of the brothers was warm. It was decided that Paul would live on at Schloss Panker while he oriented himself to the civilian world. He remained there for the next nine months, acquiring new poise and polish from palace life. In 1920, with the recommendation of the prince, Paul entered the Darmstadt Technische Hochschule (technical university) to study chemistry. At the same time, Hans was appointed director of the Municipal College of Music in nearby Mainz.

It was through Hans that Paul met Hildegard (Hilde) Martha Frank. Five years younger than Paul, the vivacious Hilde was the daughter of a prosperous Jewish timber merchant, Theodor Frank. Hilde's brother Rudolf recalled that Hans,

> introduced by his teacher Bernhard Sekles, became a frequent guest in the house of our musical uncle, the physician and town councilor

Dr. Edward Frank, and soon he brought his brother too. It was only a short distance from my father's house in Kaiserstrasse to the house of his brother Edward in Taunusstrasse. At one time when the brothers Rosbaud played music there, it happened that my sister Hilde entered the apartment. The younger brother was not inferior to the other one in playing a duet. I do not know which musical composition they performed, but I do know that the student Paul Rosbaud from Graz and Hilde from Mainz—hardly twenty years old—soon were in love and engaged. Hans had married in Mainz in the meanwhile. His bride [Edeltraud Shäfer] was not from Mainz, but her Munich personality soon took on a Mainz hue.

The fact was that the marriage of Hilde and Paul needed some assistance, for the Frank family was not entirely happy that Hilde was marrying outside her faith. Mainz is only twenty kilometers from Darmstadt, but French troops were still occupying the Saar and there were restrictions: one could cross during the day but had to return to Germany by midnight. On a certain evening, Paul and Hilde dined too late and Paul was unable to get to the occupation-zone border in time. The young couple spent the night together, creating a crisis that could be solved by marriage alone. So it was that he and Hilde were wed.

At about this time, Paul became friendly with a schoolmate named Walter Brecht, whose brother Bertolt was a promising young playwright. In a letter, Walter recollected his friend Paul this way:

Paul Rosbaud, called Bobby, was slender and a little taller than I, with a pale, vivacious, intelligent face. . . . His bearing was friendly, in an Austrian manner, [but] he maintained a clear distance from all people he did not like. Most Germans were in that category. . . . He never had any money. He would have liked to dress elegantly, but instead he had to wear clothes in the British manner, that is, with the assurance that something a bit odd and shabby does not reflect on one's personal taste. He spent his money on shoes—they could not be new and shiny enough for him. He liked to show off his unusually small feet. In a good mood, Bobby could be witty and he was assuredly talented, but he also possessed some amusing idiocies. He was always generous to his friends and surprised them with gifts he could not afford. He kept up relationships with several women at the same time, but he never let anyone know the details. He loved music and frequently attended operas and concerts.

After his graduation from the school at Darmstadt, Paul received a fellowship to study at the Kaiser Wilhelm Institute in Dahlem, a section of Berlin, where he did pioneering work on x-ray cinematography and earned his first advanced degree. After a brief stint as a research assistant at the Albertina University in Königsberg, the capital of East Prussia, Paul returned to Berlin, this time to earn his doctorate at the Technische Hochschule of Berlin-Charlottenburg. His thesis was written jointly with Hermann Mark, his professor. Professor Mark fondly remembers Paul: "He and I were very close friends . . . and so were our two wives. Also, after 1926, when my wife and I moved to Ludwigshafen, we worked together scientifically and met each other frequently. There was almost no political character in our friendship during these years."

X rays were the exciting tools for the physicists of that period, as nuclear particles were to become a decade later. But though his work was respected, Paul could not find a university post. He was, however, offered a well-paid position in a laboratory of the giant Metallgesellschaft A.G. in Frankfurt, though he always longed for the freedom and friendly exchange of the academic community. Besides, his boss was more than a little strange.

Paul's brother-in-law Rudolf Frank, well known in theatrical circles, was an expert on the early-nineteenth-century writer E. T. A. Hoffmann, who skillfully blended into his tales the type of fantasy, mystery, and romanticism that inspired Baudelaire and Poe. In his memoirs, Rudolf Frank told of one particular evening:

> Now appears the ghost of Hoffmann. At a banquet at the Metallgesellschaft A.G. in Frankfurt, my sister Hildegard sits next to a professor by the name of Ernst August Hauser. There are strange rumors current about him. He is supposed to have murdered his first and second wives. . . . My sister, gay as always, talked to Ernst August Hauser, who was at that time the boss of her husband, Dr. Paul Rosbaud. She mentioned me and said that I had proven [that a certain work] . . . was done by Hoffmann. Dr. Hauser's response: "Of course I have the manuscript; I inherited it from my wife."

There were other tales of Hauser reminiscent of the *Tales of Hoffmann*, and Paul and Hilde did not remain long in Frankfurt. The happiest event of that period was the birth of a daughter, who would be their only child. Angelika Anna Maria Mathilde Rosbaud — to be known as Angela or Anka — entered the world in August 1927. Her father adored her.

When Paul was offered a job in Berlin with *Metallwirtschaft*, a new

weekly magazine in the field of metallurgy, he took it without hesitation. Called a scientific adviser, he was really a sort of scout. It was
a unique position in scientific publishing, and it enabled him to travel
widely and meet scientists throughout Europe.

In this Weimar Republic period, the daily life of Germany was
becoming more and more politicized. So it was that Dr. Georg Lüttke,
the owner of *Metallwirtschaft*, was a secret member of the Nazi Party
and the patron of a Sturm Abteilung (storm trooper) unit in Saxony.
In the early years, the Rosbauds and the Lüttkes were close. Gertrud
Lüttke, like Hilde, was Jewish. She had Bavarian charm, along with
a talent for giving good parties.

Business was going well at 10 Mattäikirchstrasse, the office of the
journal. Paul reported there regularly after he made his rounds of
universities and institutes, getting promises for articles from scientists.
He visited not only German institutions but such centers of learning
as Oxford, Cambridge, Copenhagen, Groningen, and Oslo as well,
and after a while he was a familiar and accepted figure in the scientific
establishment. Even to a well-known professor, Rosbaud's persuasions
were flattering and his solicitations for contributions almost always
successful.

Paul also had a friendliness and enthusiasm that recommended him
to many of those scientists who would one day become the famous
names of our age — Albert Einstein, Peter Kapitza, Niels Bohr, Ernest
Rutherford, Leo Szilard, Otto Hahn, and Lise Meitner. It was they
who would bring physics into the nuclear era. Another acquaintance
was Frederick Lindemann (later Lord Cherwell), who was already
Winston Churchill's scientific adviser.

Rosbaud's position was a peculiar one. He was an adviser not only
to *Metallwirtschaft*, but to the European scientific and academic com-
munities. Although he was well known in those circles, he was professionally obscure because he had contributed little to research. He
described himself as "a pike in a pond full of carps." No one, however,
was better informed about overall scientific developments than he.

All the future would have looked promising for him had it not been
for German political developments, which were growing uglier by the
month. Rosbaud watched the rise of the Nazi Party until it was strong
enough to insert Adolf Hitler as chancellor of the Reich in 1933. Close
to home, Georg Lüttke began to show his Nazi colors openly. It was

at this time that Paul Rosbaud made a solemn and abiding pact with himself: he would do all in his power to destroy the man who was destroying the civilization so dear to Paul.

Hermann Mark has recalled:

> When I left Germany in 1932 because of the Nazis and went to Vienna, we maintained close contact. . . . Paul became more and more hostile to the regime in Germany; at several occasions when we met in Germany, England, or Austria he was full of criticism and justified antagonism toward the Nazis. He was one of the few who foresaw developments very clearly—we had long discussions what one could and should do about them. Several English friends—[the Marxist physicist] John Desmond Bernal, [the eccentric inventor] Geoffrey Pyke, [the physical chemist] Eric Rideal—participated at certain occasions.

Just about this time, Paul was relieved to have an offer of a new job. Dr. Ferdinand Springer, who, with his brother Julius, headed the prestigious publishing firm Springer Verlag, sought him out for the post of scientific adviser to all of the firm's publications. In this new position, Rosbaud soon achieved even greater access to the best minds of the European scientific community.

Some time in these early years of the 1930s, he made another acquaintance of a dramatically different kind. The knowledge of when, how, and under what circumstances the two men came together is still locked in some dusty official file.

Francis Edward Foley was one of those remarkable men who—like Raoul Wallenberg—saw the evil of their time, struck against it, and were almost forgotten. He was born in 1884 in Burnham-on-Sea in Somerset, was educated in France, and became an accomplished linguist. (Deputy Führer Rudolf Hess later observed that Foley "spoke German without an accent.") As a captain in the Hertshire Regiment, Foley had an impressive combat record and was mentioned in dispatches. But he was wounded in a German attack in March 1918 and reassigned to a desk job—in intelligence. After the war's end, Foley served as intelligence officer on the general staff of the British Army of the Rhine, then moved to the Secret Intelligence Service (known as SIS or MI6) and was posted to the British legation in Berlin with the usual—and transparent—cover of passport control officer.

After the Nazis came to power, Foley became more involved with the legitimate activities of his office, much to the annoyance of some of his fellow SIS officers back in London, for the deeply compassionate Foley began to spend more and more of his time helping Jews to leave the Third Reich. Rosbaud was also engaged in this activity, and it is probably in this connection that the two first met.

As the relationship between the two men grew more trusting, Paul began to pass along to Foley scraps of information, sometimes significant, sometimes not. But then came danger signals. For one thing, Foley's aid to refugees became somewhat more open and surely was known to the Gestapo at an early date. It was an activity the police watched closely. With Foley's agreement, Paul ceased most of the contact. Such developments as the suspension of civil rights, the Reichstag's loss of any power, and the establishment of the Gestapo — all in 1933 — made Paul re-evaluate his situation. An agent in place (or, in modern jargon, a mole) must have a deep burrow and an impenetrable cover.

In the Third Reich, a most important element of that cover was an "Aryan" family tree, and for Paul Rosbaud, bastard son of an unknown father, that posed a problem. He determined to conduct a thorough background investigation on himself before the idea occurred to someone else.

The notorious Gestapo Ahnentafel (Ancestry Register) required "racial purity" back to January 1, 1800. Judith Ginsburger, the only Jew in the Zolchner lineage of the Rosbaud family whom Paul could identify, was born in 1701. But though his mother's lineage would give no difficulty, the paternal mystery might hold something quite different.

FOUR

The Strajner Deception

THE CIVIL SERVICE LAW was promulgated on April 7, 1933, a few weeks after Hitler assumed power as chancellor. The new law required that every servant of the Third Reich complete a questionnaire (*Fragebogen*) to establish his or her ancestry. Hans Rosbaud was then chief conductor and head of the music department of Frankfurt Radio and, as such, was a civil servant. A strong advocate of modern music, he was already suspected of having non-Aryan tendencies. Paul, in his capacity as scientific adviser to *Metallwirtschaft*, was not a civil servant, but since he was a member of several government scientific committees, he was also required to fill out the questionnaire.

The part concerning Anna's ancestry was relatively easy, because there was an abundance of information. Paul completed that research in June 1933, finding that, indeed, Judith Ginsburger was the only Jewish forebear among the Rosbauds. His investigation filled in the actual details of the old family legend concerning the daughter of Moysis Ginsburger, court banker to Prince Karl Philip of the Palatinate in Graz. In 1710, the ten-year-old girl had been kidnapped. The motive — at least the one given in testimony — was a desire to remove the beautiful child from the heathen influences of her family rather than any hope for ransom. The judge had consulted Judith, who chose to stay with her Christian kidnappers because, she said, they treated her so well. The case then caught the attention of Emperor Karl VI, who directed Princess Elizabeth of the Palatinate to have Judith baptized. When she became Maria Augusta, she was no longer a threat to her descendants, Paul and Hans Rosbaud.

The paternal mystery was another matter. Lacking any clue from their mother and any documentary evidence, the brothers decided on a bold remedy. If no father existed, one must be invented. And who would seem to be plausible and, at the same time, amenable to the fraud?

The choice was obvious—the fatherly old Johann Strajner, tram conductor and neighbor in St. Andrä's parish. Paul's first step was to get copies of Strajner's records from the Graz police to study them for possible inconsistencies. When he had satisfied himself, in the spring of 1933, he set out for Graz.

Johann was the Johann of old, quite as willing to be the father of record—if the new times required such—as a father in spirit. He could not claim that he came from a family of "high station," as had Franz Heinnisser, but Strajner's values were undoubtedly higher. And his own free spirit also rebelled against the Nazi dictatorship. With Paul's help, he composed an affidavit that read, in part:

> I [Johann Strajner] was born in Laibach [Krain], now Yugoslavia, on December 21, 1860, the son of the couple Mathaeus and Maria, née Piuck, Strajner, and I was baptized in the Roman Catholic rite in St. Jacob's at Laibach. I attended the German school there, learned baking, and left Laibach because of the unpleasant national situation.... In 1899, I went to Graz and took a job with the Tramway Company.
>
> I had two children with Fräulein Anna Aloisia Rosbaud, Hans and Paul.... The paternity was not publicly acknowledged at court because I accepted it right away. At that time, I was married to Theresia Wesiak.... Therefore, the mother of the Rosbaud children did not wish to make my paternity public or to acknowledge it to the children. Only after the mother's death was it revealed [to them]. My parents were innkeepers and came from Unterkrain. They were German.... It is impossible that there could have been a Jew among my ancestors.

The document was certified and signed on May 29, 1933. It was, of course, a close weaving of truth and falsehood.

A very determined Gestapo investigator might have discovered that Strajner was not married to Theresia when Hans was born. He might have found out that the virile Strajner was, at the time, also having an affair with a knitter, by whom he fathered three children. And the investigator might have wondered why the knitter's illegitimate children, even when they were very young, knew that their father was Johann Strajner. If the investigator had found Hans's scholarship application, completed by Strajner after the death of Anna, it would have been damning, for the city file clerk had made the notation "Father dead."

But there was no such Gestapo investigator.

The brothers made a great show of the manufactured relationship. In July 1936, Paul attended a scientific conference in Graz and brought Hilde, Angela, and Hans with him. Together with Strajner and his daughters (Theresia had died in 1919, so there was no disrespect to her), they laid flowers on Anna's grave. At the same time, Paul, worried about the inconsistencies in Strajner's 1933 declaration, helped him write an amended statement for the authorities. In it, Strajner professed to have been intimate with Anna Rosbaud over a period of years. There is no mention of Strajner's legal wife and children or of his open relationship with the knitter and her three children — not a hint that he ever had a relationship with anyone but Anna Rosbaud.

On December 17, 1938, Hans conducted his second concert in Graz. Rather ostentatiously, the front row of the theater was reserved for Johann Strajner, his legitimate children, and his grandchildren. If anyone inquired about the special guests, they were told that these were Hans Rosbaud's closest relatives in Graz. On the program was a Haydn composition, in remembrance of the great composer's 1782 concert in Graz. There was also Beethoven's "Ah, Perfidio." Was that an ironic choice by Hans? The proceeds of the concert were earmarked for Hitler's favorite charity, Winterhilfe (Winter Aid), for the benefit of soldiers, and Hans was as stoutly anti-Nazi as his brother.

Hans and Paul bought a new tombstone for their mother's grave. For two years, Strajner put fresh flowers there from time to time to buttress the lie. After he died, in 1940, there was no one in Graz to care. The brothers allowed the tombstone to be removed in 1943, and Anna was reburied. Some distance away there leans the tombstone of Johann Strajner, the father of record. It is in bad condition and has been neglected for years.

FIVE

Private Lives

AFTER the catastrophic inflation of 1923, Germany began a slow economic recovery. By the year 1928, optimism about the future produced an explosion of artistic expression and of sophisticated vulgarity in and near the capital. Experimentation was the catchword, and it was often difficult to separate the flashy from the truly new and worthwhile. There was Brecht in the theater, Gropius with his Bauhaus style in architecture and design, Marlene Dietrich in the night club, Schoenberg in the concert hall, Georg Grosz and the art of mordant caricature, and *The Cabinet of Dr. Caligari* on the motion picture screen.

There was also a passion for speed and for sports. Wernher von Braun was experimenting with miniature rockets from the family villa's garden on the Tiergartenstrasse. Josephine Baker promoted ostrich races. Fritz von Opel got his rocket car to a speed of almost two hundred kilometers per hour. Athleticism was the vogue for everybody.

The social results of all this flux were quite unexpected and quite un-German: a new kind of morality and a newly emancipated woman.

Paul and Hilde had taken a flat in Ruhleben, the first of a succession of flats and houses in Berlin. It was near the racetrack and Spandau Prison, and life was agreeable enough there. On Sundays, Paul would go jogging around the perimeters of fairy-tale lakes in the Grunewald Forest, would pass the stadium track, where a certain athletic girl friend might stop practicing to chat with him, then would turn toward home.

Hilde was an avid gymnast; her small body was full of energy. That helped to make the Rosbauds popular in the elite scientific community of Berlin. Liselotte Schorsch has recalled that while Rosbaud, Hermann Mark, Michael Polanyi, and others were gathered for intellectual lunches at the Institute for Physical Chemistry, "in the adjoining Otto Hahn Institute, the wives participated in the gymnastic sessions under the direction of Hilde Rosbaud. . . . Lise Meitner also took part."

Things were not quite what they seemed, though. The Rosbaud marriage, which had begun with the ill luck or contrivance of the broken curfew, had become a permissive affair. Hilde, it was said, had some difficulty in communicating with her lover, and the frequent joke was that she "was sleeping with a German-English dictionary under her pillow and an Englishman on top."

Paul, for his part, had Ruth Lange—Ruthilein, to him—for his amusement and companionship. Although stocky when they first met, Ruthilein slimmed down nicely at Paul's direction, and she was comely and vivacious. Not only that; she held the women's world championship in shot put and the national women's championship in discus throwing. But the attraction seemed to lie in other qualities: Ruth was much younger than Paul; he dominated her and treated her like a 1920s Galatea to his Pygmalion; she was—and would be in the years to come—comforting and supportive. For the present, he was happy to show her off in the cabarets of afterdark Berlin.

At a higher, cultural level, Hans Rosbaud was being noticed both by Josef Goebbels, the minister of propaganda and popular enlightenment, and by his peers in the musical world. Igor Stravinsky recorded in his autobiography "enlightened activity in the realm of music of such organizations as the Rundfunk [Radio] in Berlin and that of Frankfurt-on-Main, and to note particularly the sustained efforts of the latter's admirable conductor, Rosbaud, who, by his energy, his taste, his experience, and devotion, succeeded very quickly in bringing that organization to a very high artistic pitch."

It was not only Stravinsky who took note of Hans Rosbaud. Hans fostered contemporary music and was honored when his old friend Paul Hindemith played his viola concerto with the Frankfurt Radio orchestra. With Rosbaud conducting, Béla Bartók played the world première of his Second Piano Concerto, and Arnold Schoenberg heard for the first time a performance of his Variations, Opus 31. Several times, Goebbels was in the audience, seeming to enjoy the contemporary music, although officially he had to denounce it.

Paul's world did not lack interesting people. Ruth's sister Hilde was interesting in a different way. She had joined the Communist Party (KPD) in 1927, had obtained a law degree, and had married Georg Benjamin, a prominent sports doctor and also a Communist. Georg's brother Walter was a brilliant eccentric, writer, and Marxist literary theorist. On January 14, 1926, Walter Benjamin wrote to a friend that his brother Georg would in a few days marry "a sympathetic young maiden, a friend of my sister, whom he has indoctrinated in Communism. That has been for his Christian in-laws . . . a bitter pill for them to swallow."

In January 1930 there was a sensational murder. Horst Wessel, a student and the son of a Protestant chaplain, had joined the Sturm Abteilung Brown Shirts and had gone to live in the slums in order to spread the Nazi doctrine there. He became a street fighter and a pimp. It so happened that he quarreled with a man named Ali Höhler over a prostitute named Erna Jaeneke, and Höhler shot him. When he died, five weeks later, the Nazis claimed him as a martyr murdered by Communists. Hilde Benjamin served as defense attorney for Höhler's landlady. As for Horst Wessel, he left behind a song that was adopted as an official anthem by the Nazis.

By coincidence or not, Paul Rosbaud probably crossed paths with Wessel, because Paul and Ruth were frequent visitors to Haus Mexico near the Alexanderplatz. "Haus Mexico, the Stranger's Abode for Everyman," as it was advertised, was Wessel's headquarters. Here could be found such professional ladies as Black Sonja and Fat Edith.

For there was this darker side to Paul's nature — though it was quite in keeping with the decadent Berlin of the time. The respected scientific adviser of the day could become by night the frequenter of notorious streets in the east end of the city — or, again by night, could dine with his wife and the Gropiuses. Or they could be seen in the company of Paul Hindemith or perhaps attending opening night of *The Threepenny Opera*, the bizarre new musical by Kurt Weill and Walter Brecht's brother.

Times were changing swiftly, however, and as the republic gave way to Hitler in 1933, Nazification of the country became intense.

The so-called Nuremberg Laws of 1935 — and later supplements —
succeeded in destroying all Jewish legal, cultural, and human rights.
This was dramatized — for the Rosbauds especially — when Hitler an-
nexed Austria in the Anschluss of March 11, 1938. The Nazis organized an orgy of sadism against the Jews of Vienna; and one of their
first decisions was to set up a concentration camp at Mauthausen, near
Hitler's hometown of Linz. Paul's hometown of Graz, incidentally,
had been the first to welcome Hitler and to be named a "hero city."

The Rosbauds' status was altered drastically, because they were no
longer Austrian nationals. When Paul slipped information to a trusted
friend in England, he was now — as a citizen of the Reich — a traitor
as well as a spy. Without Austrian citizenship to protect her, Hilde
was, like any other Jew, subject to official persecution. For some years
now, she had wanted a divorce, but Paul's Catholicism made him
hesitate. After the Anschluss, their marriage was the only thing saving
Hilde and Angela — for the time being. It was probably at this point
that Paul thought of his old contact Frank Foley, now a major at the
British legation in Berlin.

He had known Foley for the past five years, but the two had not
seen each other for some time. One of the reasons was that London
was interested primarily in political, military, and economic intelligence. The occasional tidbit of technological information passed by
Rosbaud was judged to be of minor interest. Also, Rosbaud had ample
opportunity to pass information directly to scientists in England, which
he visited frequently.

Whether much of that information found its way into the SIS was
doubtful, only because the service lacked interest. When the SIS required an insight into German air force research, they dispatched
Captain Frederick W. Winterbotham to Berlin. Winterbotham was
chief of the Air Section of SIS in London and he carried on his
observations openly, mingling with the highest levels of Nazi officialdom.

The other reason was that Foley had done much to compromise
himself as the SIS head of station. His passport duties were the official
cover for his intelligence work, but Foley, a man of great humanity,
could not bear to see what was happening to Germany's Jews and was
using his passport office to help Jews leave the country.

One April morning in 1938, a worried Paul Rosbaud set out for

Foley's office at 17 Tiergartenstrasse—nine-thirty to twelve-thirty were passport hours.

The Tiergarten had begun as a hunting preserve for princes and electors. In the 1930s, it was a leafy and lovely public park in the center of Berlin. (Even so, the 1930 Baedeker warned that "the remoter sections of the park should be shunned after dark" because of thieves.) Rosbaud made his way from the Springer offices on Linkstrasse to the street on the southern boundary, lined with the mansions and villas of wealthy Berliners. It was a tranquil street of Silesian sandstone and tan stucco.

Rosbaud paused for an instant at the Wagner monument directly across from Foley's office windows. Here was Gustav Eberlein's grandiose affair of marble, showing the composer surrounded by Tannhäuser, Brünnhilde, Siegfried, and a Rhine maiden. Then he crossed the street to number 17, hoping that no one from the Gestapo was on surveillance.

Foley was, of course, delighted to be of assistance, and Hilde received her visa for Britain without formality. Paul wanted one for Angela, as well, because she now had the status of a *Mischling*, or one of mixed blood, and thus could be in danger. But, he explained, Angela wanted to remain in Berlin with him for the time being. A few days later, Paul and Hilde boarded a Deutsche Lufthansa plane at Tempelhof Airfield and landed at Croydon four and a half hours later. They were met by Robert Atkinson, chief assistant at the Royal Observatory in Greenwich, and his wife, Irmin, a gymnastics enthusiast like Hilde. The Atkinsons had already found a small flat on Maze Hill, near the observatory, for Hilde. She and Irmin proceeded to establish their own little enterprise, a gymnastics school. Professor Robert Salmon Hutton, a close friend of Paul's and later a conduit for his information, helped Hilde with the formalities of completing immigration procedures and obtaining a work permit. In September, Angela joined her mother—less from anxiety about the situation in Berlin than because Ruth Lange had moved into the Rosbaud house on Waltraudstrasse in Zehlendorf.

Paul would make trips to London every four or five weeks, bringing money and some small family belongings. In addition, he posted ten marks—the legal limit—to Hilde every day from Germany. He was facing a grave decision. It was still possible for him to move to England, even up to the end of August 1939. Air travel had stopped shortly before that, but the land routes were open. In England were Hilde, for whom he felt an obligation and a certain compassion in those years of trial, and Angela, whose absence truly pained him. England would have offered for him a good living, no doubt, and a refuge from Nazi savagery. In Germany, there was Ruth. Beyond that, there was the opportunity to inflict a few wounds on the Nazi state and on Adolf Hitler. And the desire to wound had become an obsession.

SIX

V.M.

MAY 17 is the national day of Norway, commemorating the adoption of the constitution in 1814. The founding fathers, assembled in Eidsvold, also showed their nationalism in a disagreeable way, decreeing that both Jews and Jesuits should be barred from the country as people utterly alien to the Nordic race.

Thirty-seven years later, after a long crusade, the poet and patriot Henrik Arnold Wergeland succeeded in convincing his countrymen that the ban against Jews displayed very little sense of justice and Christian charity, and so it was that Jews became eligible for Norwegian citizenship.

In 1905, a very capable Norwegian-Jewish scientist, Heinrich Jacob Goldschmidt, was appointed professor of physical chemistry at Norway's only university in Kristiania, which was named Oslo in 1925. In the same year, his seventeen-year-old son, Victor Moritz, matriculated at the university and began studies in his father's subject as well as in mineralogy and geology.

Young Victor had grown up in a free, tolerant, and intellectual household. His mother, Amelie, encouraged his bent toward expressing himself frankly and honestly. A favorite family anecdote told of Victor, then a child of six just entering a private school, having his first encounter with the headmaster. Herr Göckel, a large, bearded figure of alarming appearance, asked Victor if they might become good friends. Victor stared up at him and replied, "Not particularly, sir."

Victor showed little more respect for some of his professors at the university, but he got away with this because he was a brilliant student.

Within six years, he served apprenticeships to distinguished scientists in both Vienna and Munich, finished his studies, and was awarded his doctorate. At twenty-six, V.M., as he was called, became a full professor at his university and director of its Mineralogical Institute. It was the beginning of a notable career that would contribute much to Norway and to science elsewhere.

The same year, 1914, marked the beginning of the First World War, during which Norway maintained a steadfast neutrality. The country, cut off from some vital materials, created the Government Commission for Raw Materials, and Victor Goldschmidt became head of its raw materials laboratory as well as chairman of the commission.

In the ensuing years, he developed the science of modern geochemistry, which relates chemistry and geology and is the basis for all present exploration for minerals. This led Goldschmidt to more fundamental research into the laws that determine the relative amounts of the different chemical elements that compose the earth. From that knowledge, he and others developed the laws of abundances of elements in the universe, giving us an understanding of the composition of stars.

He did pioneer work in the exploration of the atomic nucleus, although other scientists gained greater renown when they carried forward Goldschmidt's work. He developed a hypothesis about the properties of what he called superuranium and what is now called plutonium. In 1942, in occupied Norway, he was to publish a paper on that element. Luckily, the paper, printed in Norwegian, was not noticed by German scientists.

It was inevitable that the brilliant, eccentric geochemist and the canny, unconventional science editor should meet. They became warm friends, and during the 1920s Goldschmidt got into the habit of making trips to Berlin to talk with Paul Rosbaud.

The year 1929 marked a crisis in V.M.'s life; he got into one of those stormy academic-promotion disputes that occur in every university. Goldschmidt's candidate for the newly created professorship of chemistry was a brilliant protégé. The competitor was Ellen Gleditsch, nine years older, a respected teacher, an early collaborator of Marie Curie, an honorary Ph.D. from Yale, president of the International Federation of University Women, and an activist for women's rights. But what weighed most heavily was that her father had been rector of the University of Oslo. Gleditsch got the post.

V.M. resigned in anger and took a long-standing offer of a professorship at the University of Göttingen in Germany.

By then, there were already signs of anti-Semitism in German academic life. Five years earlier, Goldschmidt had been offered the chair of chemistry by the University of Munich, but the faculty had voted him down with the words "We already have one Jew on the faculty." (That Jew was Richard Willstätter, scion of an upper-class Karlsruhe family, pioneer researcher in the structure of cocaine, and winner of the 1915 Nobel Prize in chemistry for his studies on chlorophyll and photosynthesis.)

In spite of that, and because the Prussian minister of education was genuinely welcoming, V.M. brought his household to Göttingen — his aged father, his mother Amelie, and his splendid Norwegian housekeeper, Frøken Marie Brendigen. She was a woman of Norwegian country stock, proud of her title of Frøken, or Miss — and woe to the caller who addressed her as Marie. She was a combination of housekeeper, substitute mother, and nurse for the ailing Amelie. Goldschmidt's students remember her as "the best cook in Göttingen." She was to stay with V.M. for many years.

Frøken Brendigen established the Goldschmidt household at 8 Wagnerstrasse, from which V.M. could stroll along the outside wall of the old city to the chemical laboratory and the university's institutes, where there worked or had worked such men as Enrico Fermi, Walther Bothe, Otto Hahn, Werner Heisenberg, Max von Laue, and a galaxy of other Nobel laureates and laureates-to-be. Göttingen in those days was an intellectual treat. When V.M. was not at his office in the Mineralogical Institute, he was usually on his way from one office to another for stimulating talk with such great mathematicians as Richard Courant and David Hilbert, Nobel physicists Max Born and James Franck, or the astronomers, chemists, and zoologists of equal stature. This was such an Eden for the mind that V.M. forsook his Norwegian citizenship.

Naturally, Goldschmidt saw a great deal of Paul Rosbaud, and Rosbaud has left this profile of him at that time:

> In those prewar days, Goldschmidt was a heavily built, stout man, shy and often difficult to approach. He had an old-fashioned courtesy which could change to an outspoken but equally courteous frankness in scientific and other arguments. As well . . . he had a grim and sarcastic

sense of humor and was very quick-witted. In all scientific and personal affairs, he was completely sincere, honest, and incorruptible. . . . He had a certain naïve streak of vanity, and he was easily hurt if insufficient credit was given to his work. He was by nature a pessimist and, partly because of his Jewish origin and anti-Semitism he had experienced from childhood on, he occasionally suffered from a feeling of persecution. This was why he did not trust people until he knew them well and also why he was so responsive to genuine overtures of friendship. His kindness and generosity were unfailing.

Göttingen became Nazified soon after 1933, but this paradoxical man stayed on. This pessimist retained a persistent optimism that things would change again for the better. And this Jew and liberal intellectual collaborated—there is no better word for it—with Hermann Goering's Luftwaffe, which often called on his expertise in strategic minerals. One of his best students, F. K. Drescher-Kaden, was a member of the Nazi Party. Another student from Leningrad, V. V. Schcherbina, remembered those turbulent days:

> I was a witness to the occurrences of the several days after the fascist coup, when a group of Brown Shirts with red bands and swastikas on the sleeves surrounded the institute and demanded to take over. "We don't fight with you," answered Goldschmidt's deputy. [V.M. at that time was not in the institute.] The fascists wanted to hang their flag on the institute. . . . Goldschmidt returned and took the fascist flag as a personal offense. "How glad I am for you, dear colleague," he told me, "that after a few days you will return to your comfortable Leningrad."

V.M. stayed for two more years. Schcherbina and other acquaintances were convinced that Goldschmidt had a card certifying him as a "gifted Jew" (*begabter Jude*). His services were essential to the Luftwaffe, and the card would have given him immunity as a Jew who worked for the Reich.

None of this made him covert or servile. He was so moved by the news of persecution of his fellow Jews that he and his father—previously nonpracticing—both joined the synagogue of the small Jewish community in Göttingen. Hilde Rosbaud has said that V.M. even had himself circumcised at the age of forty-six.

It could not last. V.M. became more morose and withdrawn. In 1933, Berlin students burned twenty thousand books on Unter den Linden; in 1934, *Vossische Zeitung*, the *New York Times* of Germany, was forced out of business; in 1935 came the Nuremberg racial laws.

At last, Goldschmidt told Rosbaud that it seemed time to leave, and he asked for Rosbaud's help.

Paul acted swiftly. He approached the Norwegian legation in Berlin and requested a full restoration of citizenship and academic posts to Goldschmidt and citizenship for his father. Norway was only too happy to welcome back V.M. Goldschmidt, a national asset. The Royal Norwegian Ministry of Justice issued documents of naturalization on August 29, 1935, to be picked up when the Goldschmidts arrived in Berlin.

On September 6, there was a grand send-off for Victor and Heinrich at the Göttingen railway station. Co-workers and students, Nazi and non-Nazi, turned up to wish them farewell. The Nazi government, however, was a little slower to note that one of its first-rate scientific assets was about to depart.

When the Goldschmidts arrived in Berlin, they were met by Paul and Hilde Rosbaud and were bundled into a car, with Hilde at the wheel. It was best, Paul thought, that they drive around for an hour or so until Paul was able to get the passports from the Norwegian legation. Paul rushed off on his errand and Hilde fired up the Opel.

Those who have ridden in a car driven by Hilde have always survived, but with considerable cost to their nerves. Having outlasted both Hilde's driving and the threat of traffic police, the Goldschmidts arrived at the Stettiner Banhof, were handed their passports by Paul, and thereupon became Norwegian citizens. They had no trouble passing through the Gestapo control, and very soon they were in their native land.

It should be noted that today on the new campus of the University of Göttingen, far to the north of the old Mineralogical Institute, there is a short street named Goldschmidtstrasse. It is one of the few tributes to this remarkable man.

SEVEN

The Man Who Wasn't There

AT THE BEGINNING of one academic year in the late 1920s, while he was still in Oslo, Victor Goldschmidt heard the news that there was a new instructor in physical chemistry at the university—and, according to rumor, that he was exceptionally intelligent. V.M. sat down at once and dashed off a note, inviting the young man to come round for a cup of tea or a drink one afternoon.

The instructor replied, by another note, that he would prefer to have V.M. make a visit to his rooms. Very audacious, Goldschmidt thought—to request a senior professor to make the trip from the Mineralogical Institute. The response only served to pique V.M.'s curiosity still more.

When Goldschmidt entered the dimly lit room, he saw a death's head figure, like the one in Edvard Munch's *Evening on Karl Johannsgade* made real. The hair was almost luminescent in its whiteness; when the man came nearer, Goldschmidt looked into fiery red pupils surrounded by pink irises. This was Odd Hassel, a man who preferred to live in shadows because the light troubled his eyes. They sat down and began to talk. The talk turned into a rousing argument—the first of many they would have over the years to come—and Goldschmidt was delighted. This strange young albino, he saw, was very bright indeed.

Once, a close associate of Hassel's described him as "the man who wasn't there," and the tag stuck. Kenneth Hedberg—now a professor at Oregon State University and once a student of Hassel's—viewed him as "a rather difficult person. He could be very kind and helpful, as he always was with me. On the other hand, he was easily offended and could be biting and sarcastic with those he didn't like." In other words, a perfect match for Victor Goldschmidt. But Professor Hedberg added, "There is no doubt that he was a man of considerable courage." Hassel demonstrated that when the war came.

Hassel was from a rich shipping family. He was eight when his father died, and in time the boy had a great urge to escape from Oslo. He went abroad as soon as he could and studied in Berlin and Dresden. It was shortly after he returned to Oslo that he had that first encounter with V.M. Then, in 1929, Goldschmidt backed him for the chemistry professorship and made his thunderous exit when Hassel lost. But Odd Hassel stayed on.

Quite unexpectedly, the parting turned out to be a benefit for both men. No longer able to turn to Hassel for certain kinds of research, Goldschmidt began to think more about the principles of the behavior of matter and less about the substance of matter. Following this direction, he was able to make contributions to science that were more fundamental than his earlier work had been. Hassel, freed from V.M.'s strong personality, began to investigate new areas — how carbon and hydrogen are bonded in molecules, for example. He discovered techniques for studying the passage of electrons through gases and, from the results, for determining the molecular structure of the gases.

It was this work that twenty-four years later, in 1969, would be recognized by the award of a Nobel Prize in physics, shared with Sir Derek Barton. Like many other scientists who knew Hassel, Sir Derek could find almost nothing sympathetic in him. He said, "Hassel's character . . . was negative, as if he were not there. He was also an albino, and no doubt this influenced his behavior."

There was one man, however, who could understand Hassel as a human being, and there was a happy reunion when Victor Goldschmidt returned to Oslo in 1935. All had turned out well in spite of the Gleditsch affair, although Professor Gleditsch herself hardly ever spoke to the two men again. V.M. had spent some productive years at Göttingen, and Odd Hassel had attained his professorship at the university.

EIGHT

Kapitza

THE SOVIET EMBASSY on Berlin's Unter den Linden was a drab, uninviting sandstone building. But inside were reception salons as grand as might be found in a czarist palace. As well they might, for the furnishings had been looted from one. On an evening in the second year of the Third Reich, Soviet Ambassador Jacob Suritz served as co-host to a stellar gathering of top scientists. The other host was Paul Rosbaud.

One of the guests was Paul Ewald, a pioneer in x-ray crystallography, and the event remained vivid for the rest of his life. In a letter, he recalled:

> At that time Lise Meitner had received an invitation to come to the Russian embassy to see a modern Russian film and to have supper. Lise was doubtful to go or not and asked me to accompany her. I agreed and she obtained a second ticket from Rosbaud, who distributed the tickets.
>
> The first screening was Gulliver's Travel to Lilliput, an interesting film demonstrating a new technique of combining two orders of magnitude: the one for Gulliver and the second for the much smaller Lilliputs [*sic*]. After a short interval came the second, more important, film, showing Russian soldiers jumping from airplanes in full flight, falling for a considerable time before releasing their parachutes, and landing safely on earth, ready to go into combat. This film made a shudder run down our spines by the daring of each man, and the hundreds of soldiers taking part.
>
> It took Lise and me some time to recover and to go to the large table loaded with caviar, smoked fish, roasts, unknown vegetables and fruit. There were about fifty guests, among them heads of other Dahlem Kaiser Wilhelm Institutes. Several of them excused their presence by

telling us that they were there only to report on the films to their formations of the SS or of the Hitler Youth, etc. Lise Meitner and I returned to Dahlem rather taciturn and deeply impressed.

The assembled guests had seen Alexander Ptushko's *The New Gulliver*, the world's first feature-length puppet film, with its extraordinary special effects. The second film was Alexander Dovzhenko's *Aerograd*, again with special effects by Ptushko. The climax of *Aerograd*, which is set in a Siberian border town, is a massive military parade, as only Stalin or Hitler might stage one, showered with paratroopers from above. It is, indeed, a frightening film, and in 1935 it was meant to impress the Nazi regime with the Soviet might.

Paul and the distinguished scientists from the Kaiser Wilhelm Institutes were not at the Soviet embassy that evening to be exposed to blatant Soviet propaganda. They were there to show their support for the plight of a distinguished scientist, Peter Kapitza.

Rosbaud had complete freedom in selecting his own assignments from the moment he became scientific adviser to *Metallwirtschaft* on New Year's Day, 1928. His first trip abroad took him to the Cavendish Laboratory of Ernest Rutherford in Cambridge. There, the New Zealander had built the world's foremost nuclear physics laboratory, complementing the theoretical work over which Niels Bohr presided in Copenhagen. Seven years before Rosbaud's visit, an experimental genius had come to Cambridge from the new Soviet paradise. Peter Kapitza was an applied physicist, not a theoretician. But Lord Rutherford was certainly the former, and he found Kapitza indispensable in devising special equipment for his experiments. Kapitza became the favorite of other physicists at the Cavendish and was elected a fellow of Trinity College, of which Lord Rutherford was a senior fellow.

A great raconteur and gourmet, Kapitza hit it off with Rosbaud at their first meeting, and Rosbaud asked him to be one of the regular contributors to *Metallwirtschaft*. The two began to meet in Britain and in Berlin.

On April 8, 1931, Nikolai Bukharin, the prime motivator for scientific reconstruction in the Soviet Union, declared in Moscow: "So-called pure science, that is, science devoid of contact with practical life, is a figment. The whole fabric of scientific investigational work in capitalistic countries is a weapon in the hands of capitalist magnates and governments and their industrial and military organizations."

In other words, what was a good socialist and illustrious native son like Kapitza doing in England, aiding her industrial and military organizations? Bukharin, after attending a London conference, repeated his message to Kapitza in Cambridge in July and invited him to return to Moscow permanently. Kapitza balked.

Rosbaud was in Cambridge at the same time, and it is probable that Kapitza introduced him to Bukharin, who was proficient in English and German. He and Rosbaud would have been drawn to each other. In appearance and habit, Bukharin was very similar to Lenin, brawny in build, balding, and with a reddish complexion. Although an ideologue, he had courage and principles, characteristics that would later cost him his life.

From someone, most likely Bukharin, Rosbaud received at that time an unprecedented invitation to visit the Soviet Union's major research and industrial laboratories. The intention was to make the Germans aware, through Rosbaud, of the progress being made by the scientific and industrial cadres in the socialist state. Rosbaud accepted.

It required a year to find an opportune moment, and in November 1932 Kapitza came to Berlin to brief Rosbaud on what he could expect and what he should ask. The visit was timed to coincide with a metallurgical conference. Paul took some nice photos of Kapitza and sent them to Lise Meitner, with a note concluding, "I am leaving today for Russia for 10 to 14 days."

They were crowded days, and the visit was extended. Rosbaud was given the most extraordinary privileges, including visits to sensitive facilities like the Materials Testing Laboratory of the Aviation Trust in Moscow and the Metallurgical Institute in Leningrad. There, he visited Kapitza's old mentor, Abram Ioffe, who showed Paul around the Physico-Technical Institute and gave him a comprehensive briefing on what was going on in physics in Russia. And it seems likely that Paul met Bukharin again, for in his report he gave the commissar due credit for his contributions to Soviet technology.

When Paul returned, he found awaiting him an invitation from Kapitza to be his honored guest at the opening of the new Mond Laboratory in Cambridge. Endowed by the Ludwig Mond nickel industries through the Royal Society, the laboratory would enable Kapitza to use his skills for what would prove to be truly pioneering work on very strong magnetic fields and the physics of low temper-

atures. It was this work that was recognized with the Nobel Prize in
1978.

The occasion was festive. Prime Minister Stanley Baldwin dedicated
the building on February 3, 1933, and the physicist Geoffrey I. Taylor
and his wife, Stephanie, held a reception at their home, where Rosbaud was a house guest. But the celebration was marred by grim news
from Germany. Only four days earlier, President Paul von Hindenburg had appointed Adolf Hitler chancellor. Rosbaud hurried back
to Berlin to see what was happening and to write reports of the
laboratory dedication and of his Russian visit for *Metallwirtschaft*.

Another guest at the dedication of the Mond Laboratory had been
Samuel Borisovich Cahan, a counselor at the Soviet embassy. In fact,
Cahan was seldom to be found in the chancery, at 13 Kensington
Palace Gardens in London. He was Kapitza's contact man, for Kapitza
had been sent to England to advise on the acquisition of technical
equipment and to establish scientific contacts for the new Soviet state.
He was not exactly a spy, but rather a high-level information collector.
Sammy Cahan, however, was a genuine spy. In fact, he was the res-
ident director of the entire Soviet spy apparatus in Britain.

There was other business in Cambridge for Cahan in those days,
rewarding business. Hitler was the best recruiter Communism ever
had. A decade after the First World War, Marxist discussion groups
became active in Cambridge, particularly at Trinity College. Students
like Kim Philby, Donald Maclean, and Guy Burgess, dons like Anthony
Blunt, and others were believed to have been recruited by Sammy
Cahan to penetrate the Foreign Office and other establishments. Some,
like Alan Nunn May, were chosen to be moles in the future. May
became an atom spy.

Cahan would have preferred that Kapitza remain in England to
continue his information-gathering activities, but Kapitza, not antic-
ipating difficulties, accepted an invitation to celebrate the hundredth
anniversary of the birth of the inventor of the periodic table of the
elements, Dimitri Mendeleev. The celebration was in Leningrad, and
Peter and Anna Kapitza decided to motor there via Newcastle, Bergen,
and Oslo. It was never a good idea to return to the Soviet Union, but
the summer of 1934 turned out to be the worst of times.

Stalin had just decided to reconstitute the secret police in anticipation of another blood purge. In July, he formed the new NKVD,
(which absorbed the old OGPU and preceded the present KGB) and

to head it appointed Genrikh Grigorievich Yagoda, known to be a ruthless and bloodthirsty man. Yagoda thereby became Sammy Cahan's new boss and the arbiter of the fate of Peter Kapitza.

To make matters worse, just before Kapitza departed for Leningrad two Russian visitors came to the Mond Laboratory and demanded to be shown around. The busy and often brusque Kapitza refused their request. When they reported the incident to Moscow, they added that Kapitza must have been working on some secret project for the British military.

After the Kapitzas arrived in Russia, Peter was informed that he could not leave the country again, but his wife was permitted to return to Cambridge to fetch their two sons and their household effects. She stayed a year, however, in a vain effort to bring Peter back to Britain. Lord Rutherford mounted a quiet campaign for petitions on behalf of Kapitza, and most of the scientific elite of Europe rallied round, but with no effect on the Soviets. Paul Rosbaud, perturbed not only by Kapitza's plight but by the potential damage to scientific research, decided with some misgivings to enter the fray. Public advertisement was not Paul's style, but he had an idea for a direct approach.

At the beginning of March 1935, Paul went to London for a scientific congress and spent considerable time with Anna Kapitza in Cambridge. At first, she was not receptive to his idea, but on March 18 she wrote to Paul (and the wording and spelling are hers).

> I certainly agree with you that it would be a good thing to let the representative of C & T [Soviet Commerce and Trade Delegation] know and talk to the USSR ambassador in Berlin. But you must remember when writing the letter that even if you put in strong expressions, you must always bear in mind, that the Russian Government has complete legal right to do exactly, what they want with K., as he is a Russian citizen. And that the only ground in which you can approach him [the ambassador] is the moral one, and also the regretation of the R. Gov. abroad in the scientific circles. K., himself, is known to be greatly opposed to anything like a political scandal, and who certainly will do his best to prevent any kind of quarel. . . .
>
> The other one is you must have behind you the support of all the German scientists, so your voice is echoed by them, and make this clear to the Ambassador.

When Rutherford's approach failed, Paul decided to make this appeal known to the German scientists he was planning to enlist and to Niels Bohr. Lise Meitner happened to be visiting Copenhagen

at the time, so *Durch Eilboten* (By express courier) Paul wrote to Lise
of what he had learned from Anna Kapitza and asked her to relate
the circumstances to Bohr. Kapitza was living in the Hotel Metropol
in Moscow, and, Paul remarked, had decided that "he was in an
impossible situation, that there was no way to create a work environ-
ment equivalent to that in Cambridge. That goes without further
saying. He has a plan: if he is forced to remain in Russia, he will
completely abandon physics and turn to physiology. Professor Pavlov
is very happy to have him work in his institute . . . unless the Russians
forbid it. He has been denounced as working for the British War
Ministry. Not a word of that is true." The thought that physics would
lose Kapitza pained Paul as much as Kapitza's loss of his freedom.

The Soviet Commerce and Trade Delegation in Berlin, the Handelsvertretung, had offices at 11 Lietzenburger Strasse. Its legitimate
operations were massive, involving hundreds of millions of marks
yearly in arms and industrial equipment transfers. In the pre-Hitler
era, the Handelsvertretung had been an arrangement of convenience,
for it was in Russia that Germany tested the aircraft and armaments
that the Treaty of Versailles prohibited her from building. Gradually,
the Handelsvertretung became the center of military and industrial
espionage for the Soviets. The "representative of C & T" that Rosbaud
turned to was Hilde Benjamin, sister of Ruth Lange.

Hilde Benjamin, having achieved some notoriety as one of the defenders of those accused in the Horst Wessel case, after 1933 was
forbidden to practice privately. But she was allowed to become legal
adviser to the Handelsvertretung. Paul knew that the Benjamin household was under constant Gestapo observation. Hilde's husband, Dr.
Georg Benjamin, much respected by Paul, had just been released from
a year in a concentration camp and was enjoying a brief respite from
what was to become a series of arrests. This was not the time for Hilde
Benjamin to risk further exposure by trying to help Peter Kapitza.

She arranged for Paul to contact the Soviet ambassador, Jacob Suritz, through an engineer named A. Trettler, who was director of the
Deutsch-Russiesche Gesellschaft Kultur und Technik, the German-
Russian Society of Culture and Technique. From his modest office
on Steierstrasse in Berlin-Friedenau, near the research institutes in
Dahlem, Herr Trettler distributed pamphlets praising the commu-
nality of spirit of Russian and German science. Actually the Deutsch-

Russiesche Gesellschaft existed to complement the espionage activities of the Handelsvertretung. The latter penetrated German military and industrial establishments; Herr Trettler and his staff pried into the scientific research institutions in search of interesting developments.

Rosbaud, of course, was aware of Trettler's true purpose in Berlin and was increasingly uncomfortable about his mission on behalf of Peter Kapitza, but he had made promises to Anna Kapitza. On March 22, 1935, Rosbaud wrote Trettler a long letter, giving him the background of the Kapitza case, with which Trettler was already acquainted. Paul pointed out that Lord Rutherford and Niels Bohr had made strong representations for Kapitza's return and added, "I also believe that every scientist in Germany would deplore it extremely if the valuable work of Kapitza should come to such an unpleasant end." If this affair was of interest to Herr Trettler, Rosbaud would be happy to supply more details about the attitudes of the academic community.

Herr Trettler was not in the slightest interested in Peter Kapitza at this point, for he knew that Kapitza's fate was sealed. But he was always interested in making more friends in the German academic community. So he suggested to Rosbaud that a reception or dinner might be arranged at the Soviet embassy, where Rosbaud and his scientific colleagues could meet Ambassador Suritz and present their petition on behalf of Peter Kapitza. Would Rosbaud like to take care of the invitations?

Rosbaud was trapped and he knew it, but there was no alternative. He had tickets printed at Springer Verlag and sent them to the most eminent scientists in Berlin. A good number attended, interested in the fate of Kapitza and curious about Paul Rosbaud's role in this affair.

Paul was in agony as he and his friends were subjected to the blatant and frightening propaganda of Dovzhenko's *Aerograd*. But the food was excellent and the ambassador gracious. He appeared to be sympathetic to the plea of the German scientists, some of whom, as Paul Ewald noted, later reported the event to the SS.

In August, Anna Kapitza and Geoffrey Taylor made one final try by visiting Sammy Cahan in Kensington Gardens. Cahan's charming façade disappeared. Showering Anna and Taylor with abuse, he threw them out of the chancery. But he did purchase the Mond Laboratory, every nut and bolt, and shipped it off to Moscow to create a new institute for Peter Kapitza.

Paul Rosbaud had heedlessly fallen into a trap and exposed himself to the Gestapo. The consequences were not as dire as he had feared, but he learned never again to take such overt risks. In retrospect, it was a gamble worth the risk.

NINE

The Exiles

As KAPITZA was learning to accept the enforced hospitality of his native land, other scientists were departing from theirs. The act of leaving behind Germany and their colleagues was painful and often disorienting. Among the émigrés were two of Paul Rosbaud's close friends, Victor Goldschmidt and Max Born.

In 1925, Born's brilliant student Werner Heisenberg, staying on the rocky North Sea island of Helgoland to cure his hay fever, had an inspiration that became an important contribution to quantum mechanics, the analytical method used for describing the behavior of atomic and nuclear particles. In 1933 (when the awards for both 1932 and 1933 were announced) Heisenberg was granted the Nobel Prize in physics—in the very year that Hitler came to power and Heisenberg's teacher, Max Born, fled to Cambridge.

Heisenberg was indebted to Born for more than just his tutelage. Born had had the mathematical insight that enabled Heisenberg to develop the quantum theory. With another student, Pascual Jordan, Born and Heisenberg, beginning in 1925, published what became classical papers on modern atomic theory. It saddened Born that Jordan soon became a member of the Nazi Party—but what grieved him more was the behavior of Heisenberg.

Early in his youth, Heisenberg showed signs of a sudden, violent cutting outburst of rage. For example, in 1925, when the dean of atomic theory, Wolfgang Pauli, dared question Heisenberg's early results, the student replied that the distinguished theoretician was a "big jackass." Through the years, made arrogant by his Nobel Prize and the conviction that he alone was destined to lead and preserve the glory of German physics, Heisenberg and his choler became even more intolerable.

By 1934, Born had settled in Cambridge, and Heisenberg came to bring an official message from the Nazi government, the first of many official missions Heisenberg would carry out for the Nazis. He had obtained permission for Born to return to Göttingen. As Born recorded the incident in his memoirs, "I would not be allowed to teach but could do research. I was rather bewildered by this sudden offer, which to a homesick immigrant sounded quite attractive. After a few moments of consideration I asked, 'And this offer would include my wife and children?' Then Heisenberg became embarrassed and answered: 'No, I think your family is not included in the invitation.' This made me very angry."

Subsequently, Born did go back in an unsuccessful attempt to retrieve some of his possessions. One of his associates has vividly recalled Born's brief return to Göttingen:

> H. was by then a professor in Göttingen, and when the Borns went to visit him, they were met with anti-Jewish sneers and obscenities, and in the end H. spat on the floor at Max Born's feet! . . . When the Borns returned [to England] and . . . I warmly inquired about their trip and how they had fared, very reluctantly Max Born confided in me about this great shock. . . . I was both horrified and profoundly angered. . . . Later Mrs. Born gave me her version and ended with a statement that I have never forgotten. She said simply at the end, "And my poor Max wept."

When Paul Rosbaud heard the story soon after, it enraged him and deepened his contempt for those scientists who had begun to serve the aims of Adolf Hitler.

In his vulnerable state, Born started to correspond about his future with Peter Kapitza, who was by now adjusted to Soviet repatriation. The Russian scientist wrote, in his English, "Now that Anna and the children are with me, I feel much happier. . . . After all, our Bolshies are angels compared with your Nazis, and what is more, they have a true case to fight for. I agree with you they are the only ones who keep the right line, and endeed a winning line. . . . Your letter gave me the idea of playing a nasty trick to you and make your state of mind a little more perturbed then it is at present, and to suggest to you that you could include our ⅙ of the world in a possible choise of a place where you could settle."

Born took Kapitza's wry proposal seriously and replied that he was interested. Kapitza answered with a letter full of Marxist conviction:

> The capitalisme tries to increase its stregth organising the middle class, and has no better slogan to throw out than the extreme nationalisme, the victim of which you are. . . . The socialisme bases itself on broad internationalisme. . . . History requires catastrophy to change from one system to another. It is absolutely naive to think about a gradual and peaceful change. . . . No, there is no hope whatever to avoid the catastrophy. The question is only the question of time 1 or 5 years. . . . And it is quite hopeless to think that facisme will change its face or its attitude to the Soviet Union, as it is hopeless that the two systems can come to a friendly existence side by side in the future. . . . I like very much English people they have been very nice and kind to me, and I have the most happy recollection of my 14 years in Cambridge, but even then spiritually I belonged to the new growing system in Russia. . . . I see its power and correctness. . . . You must clear up your mind and come to the Union with sincer desire to help as a scientist in a new political system, which is at the moment opposed to the one adopted by your country, which is the last hope of the capitalist world.

When Max Born turned to Rosbaud for advice "to clear up" his mind, Rosbaud advised him to stay in England, the "last hope of the capitalist world."

The experiences of Kapitza and Born are representative of the troubles scientists were undergoing everywhere in Central and Eastern Europe in the 1930s. They could no longer enjoy the isolation of their university laboratories; most stayed, some became collaborators, and others hoped not to be noticed. Many made the decision to escape westward. One of these was the Hungarian-born Leo Spitz. He had served as a junior officer in the Austro-Hungarian army in the First World War (although he never suffered the kind of hardship Paul Rosbaud experienced on the Isonzo). After the war, he attended the University of Berlin when Rosbaud was a student in Berlin-Charlottenberg and the two became acquainted. Leo received his degree in physics in 1922 and was given a teaching post at his university, a recognition of his marked talents.

As a young man, Spitz (which means "sharp" in German) changed his name to Szilard (which means "solid" in Hungarian), but to no avail. He remained sharp, but for many years his life was never solid. He was always fearful and usually mobile. He dreaded imagined enemies and catastrophes yet to come. He lived in hotel rooms and out of suitcases most of his life. His sensitivity to danger signals led him to decide to leave Germany in 1932, shortly before Hitler became chancellor, and he went to England to work at the Clarendon Laboratory at Oxford.

Szilard's other notable activity was to help in the foundation of the Academic Assistance Council, under the chairmanship of Lord Rutherford. As Rosbaud later described it, "Many hundreds of German and, later, Austrian scientists owe their lives and the continuation of their work to organizations like the Academic Assistance Council and to men like Ernest Rutherford, A. V. Hill, Sir Henry Dale, R. S. Hutton, and to Esther Simpson, who devoted her whole life to the support of refugees. In spite of all the difficulties — financial and the lack of academic positions — most of the refugee scientists settled down in England — to the advantage of their hosts and to the great disadvantage of Germany, which never recovered from the irretrievable loss of a great part of her scientific elite."

Rosbaud had been active in helping the council in its early days, but in 1935 he was more cautious about how the association might affect his position in Germany, and thereafter his contacts with it were indirect. There is a thumbnail portrait of him at that time as remembered by Esther Simpson, the moving spirit of the council: "He had a soft voice with just a trace of an accent. In repose, he was melancholy. In speaking, animated. Humility was an outstanding characteristic. He was scrupulously moral in his dealings with others. He was always well tailored in a subdued way — and very British." What Esther Simpson did not know was that Rosbaud, through certain members of the Academic Assistance Council, had established important contacts with the British Secret Service.

As for Szilard, he was on the threshold of the accomplishments that would make him famous. In 1914, H. G. Wells had predicted in his book *The World Set Free* that atomic energy would first provide unlimited industrial power and then end by destroying the world in 1956. When Szilard read the book in 1932, the predictions seemed likely to him. All around him were revolutionary scientific discoveries, like the neutron and artificial radioactivity, which made Wells's forecasts all ring true. Szilard would remember

> very clearly that the first thought that liberation of atomic energy might in fact be possible came to me in October 1933, as I waited for the change of a traffic light in Southampton Row in London. The thought did not come entirely out of the clear sky. A week or two earlier there had been the annual meeting of the British Association and Lord Rutherford was reported to have said at the meeting that whoever talks of the large-scale liberation of atomic energy is talking moonshine. I was wondering whether Rutherford was right. . . . If we could now find an element which captures neutrons, and in the process of doing so, emits further neutrons, we might have something like a chain reaction.

In 1933, the year that H. G. Wells wrote *The Shape of Things to Come*, his thoughts of two decades earlier were becoming substance at a traffic light in Southampton Row.

In that year another refugee came to work with Lord Rutherford and Peter Kapitza in Cambridge, helped by Esther Simpson and the Academic Assistance Council. He was Rudolf Peierls, a Berliner who had spent his student years wandering from Munich to Leipzig to Zürich to Leningrad — wherever the exciting new world of physics might entice him. (He still likes to think of himself as a "bird of passage.") He settled temporarily in Birmingham, where he was given a professorship. Soon he encountered another refugee, Otto Frisch, and the two began to understand how Szilard's idea of a chain reaction, with fast neutrons, might be made to work — as an atomic bomb.

Otto Robert Frisch, a child prodigy and the grandson of a Polish Jew from Galicia, was Viennese-born. He started his professional career at the Physicalishe Technische Reichsanstalt, Germany's bureau of standards. Although Frisch knew the academic community in Berlin, he remained somewhat out of the mainstream for three years. Another three years as an assistant at the University of Hamburg afforded him the opportunity to do some interesting experimental work, but he was still removed from the exciting sphere of the new physics. Although he was an Austrian citizen, and presumably legally immune from Nazi persecution, Frisch did not pass up the offer of the Academic Assistance Council. But he did not stay long in Cambridge. An invitation to join Niels Bohr in Copenhagen was irresistible.

Here, at the Mecca for all physicists, Bohr's Institute of Theoretical Physics, Frisch found his métier, the physics of the nucleus.

With the Anschluss in 1938, Frisch became a German citizen — an honor he was happy to decline — and began to think of returning to England. There, within a year, he joined up with Rudolf Peierls at Birmingham for that fateful collaboration which would lead to the atomic bomb. But first he had an equally fateful encounter with his aunt, Lise Meitner.

Paul Rosbaud was drawn to Lise Meitner, intellectually if not physically. Shy and withdrawn, Meitner was respected by most of the men with whom she worked, but though she was not unattractive, none ever seemed to be sexually attracted to her, nor she to them. Probably her drive to be considered equal in a Prussian academic society, which regarded the female researcher as an aberration, caused her to adopt a demeanor that evoked respect but not love. Even Hilde Rosbaud, who taught Meitner in gymnastics classes at Otto Hahn's institute, sought a closeness that never came.

Meitner's friendship with Otto Hahn lasted over fifty years, but cooled toward the end. In the beginning, she was his constant collaborator and the interpreter of his results. For, although Hahn was one of the most competent chemists of that era, his imagination was sometimes limited, and he often failed to grasp the broader significance of what he had observed. But in discovery he was unsurpassed. Lord Rutherford once wrote to him, "You seem to have a special smell for discovering new radioactive elements." And if Hahn did not always immediately recognize what he was smelling, Lise Meitner's perception made up for that.

In 1917, in collaboration with Hahn, Meitner had discovered a new element, protactinium. She became a professor at the University of Berlin in 1926, when women professors of science were exceptionally rare. More recently, she had been participating in Hahn's experimental research in bombarding the uranium nucleus with slow-speed neutrons. Now, she had to find a new life elsewhere, but she planned to keep in close touch with Otto Hahn.

The Anschluss imperiled Meitner, as it did all Austrians of Jewish extraction. Although she had been baptized as a child, that was no salvation in the Nazi era. Rosbaud took swift action through his Dutch friends. Peter Debye, the Dutch director of the Kaiser Wilhelm Institute of Physics in Dahlem, made the first move; he asked Dirk Coster at the University of Groningen to obtain permission from the Dutch government for Meitner to cross the border. Leaving nothing to chance, Coster went to Berlin to escort Meitner out of Germany, going directly to Meitner's flat on the night of July 12, 1938.

Hahn recalled, "Aided by our old friend Paul Rosbaud, we spent the night packing the clothes she most needed and some of her valuables. I gave her a beautiful diamond ring that I had inherited from my mother and which I had never worn myself but always treasured; I wanted her to be provided for in an emergency." Paul Rosbaud then took Meitner to Hahn's house to stay overnight. Hahn had no automobile at that time, so Paul picked up Lise the next day in his Opel and drove her to the station. Meitner was tense, fearful, and Rosbaud had to use all his persuasive talents to get her aboard the train. Dirk Coster was waiting for her in a first-class compartment and got Lise safely across the border. She stayed briefly in Holland and then left for Stockholm, where she remained, in misery, until the end of the war.

After the war, Meitner and Rosbaud quarreled, but Lise moved to heal the rift. She wrote:

> I have a bad conscience and would like to relieve it a bit in this letter. . . .
> I personally remember gratefully the last evening in Dahlem, when you
> went through my rooms with great friendly understanding and put all
> sorts of things into my trunks. Also I have not forgotten the shipment
> of books which you so carefully selected. So please be sure that nobody,
> and certainly not I, has any doubts about you in this respect. . . . I do
> hope that this letter eliminated what might have gone wrong in our
> discussion.

There never had been any breach of faith on the part of Paul Rosbaud, for Lise Meitner, more than she herself realized, became of inestimable value to Rosbaud and the British Secret Service. Although no one could accurately foresee the consequences of the event of 1938 in which Rosbaud played so vital a role, he knew that he was doing something more than helping friends escape from the Third Reich. In a few weeks, Paul became midwife to an event that changed forever the history of the world.

TEN

Midwife to Fission

ON THE NIGHT of December 22, 1938, five months after they had conspired to save Lise Meitner from arrest by the Gestapo, Professor Otto Hahn, of the Kaiser Wilhelm Institute of Chemistry in Berlin-Dahlem, and Dr. Paul Rosbaud, scientific adviser to Springer Verlag, both prominent citizens of Hitler's Reich, joined to transform the course of human events.

That evening, Hahn phoned Paul Rosbaud with the news that he had just finished writing a paper describing the experiments that he and Fritz Strassmann had performed. These experiments verified beyond a doubt that new elements were created when a slow neutron struck a uranium atom. Although the men did not recognize that they had split the atom, they understood that they had discovered an important nuclear process.

Paul was electrified. In the world of physics, this was headline news. He went to fetch the paper and immediately called Fritz Süffert, the editor of the Springer publication *Naturwissenschaften*, and got him to pull one of the articles already being typeset for the next issue in order to make room for the Hahn and Strassmann paper.

Hahn would probably have been slower to arrive at some of his startling conclusions had it not been for the stream of criticism and interpretation he was getting from Meitner in Stockholm. Of course, he sent her a carbon copy of the *Naturwissenschaften* paper at the same time he sent the original to Rosbaud.

The astonishing thing was that Hahn had not realized that he had split the atom. He had explored the long path to the great secret and then failed to see what lay before his eyes. But Lise Meitner, who was spending Christmas in a small town near Gothenburg with her nephew, saw what Hahn had not seen. Sitting on a tree trunk in the woods and discussing Hahn's paper, Meitner and Frisch suddenly understood that Hahn and Strassman had split the atom. They made a quick calculation showing that Hahn's experiments had released more energy than any other process in history. The power inherent in the nucleus of an atom had been revealed.

As it happened, Niels Bohr was about to leave for the Institute for Advanced Study in Princeton and then attend a conference in Washington, D.C., so Frisch hurried back to home base in Copenhagen to share the news with the Danish Nobel laureate. Bohr enthusiastically carried the word abroad. The conference, sponsored by the Carnegie Institution of Washington and George Washington University, was on the physics of low temperatures, at that time a field considered unrelated to nuclear energy. But in attendance were Enrico Fermi, Eugene Wigner, Edward Teller, and others very much interested in what happened when a neutron encountered a uranium atom. After Bohr announced the discovery of Hahn and Strassmann to the conference, a number of physicists left to try to repeat the experiments in their own laboratories. They did, and a new age began.

Rosbaud, of course, was playing a strategic game in all this. Probably earlier than any of the scientists, he realized the vast destructive potential of what Hahn, Strassman, and Meitner had discovered, and he was acutely conscious that the fundamental research had been done in Germany. He wanted the rest of the world to know of the significance of the work at least as soon as Nazi planners did. By rushing into print with Hahn's manuscript, he was able to alert the world community of physicists.

At the moment when fission was discovered, Britain's Secret Intelligence Service had no scientific officer and was not the least bit interested in such esoteric subjects as atomic energy. But a number of British scientists were. It had long been a tradition that some university don would recruit for the SIS a promising student and send him off, say, to Germany on the pretext of studying chemistry in Munich. Another might go to Arabia as an archeologist. But such agents were expected to obtain political and military information. Rarely, if ever, did the SIS ask for scientific intelligence. Many eminent academicians, if they were not in some sort of direct contact with the SIS, knew precisely who was. And they also knew what the SIS wished to be informed about.

One of those eminent scientists was John Douglas Cockcroft of Cambridge's Mond Laboratory. He had been trained as an electrical engineer, and when Peter Kapitza came to Cambridge, Rutherford asked Cockcroft to assist Kapitza in the construction of his equipment for experiments with low temperatures and high magnetic fields. Kapitza owed much of the success of his famous experiments to Cockcroft, but he rarely admitted that in his later years. When Kapitza left the Mond Laboratory, it was Cockcroft who prepared for shipment to Russia the equipment Cahan had bought, and took on the task of rebuilding the stripped laboratory.

Cockcroft's own claim to fame was the high-voltage accelerating machine, which he built with Ernest Walton in 1931. It was the first atom-smashing machine in the world. Consequently, Cockcroft had a proprietary interest in the new work on smashing the heaviest element known — uranium. He entered into correspondence with Lise Meitner soon after she and Otto Frisch published the correct interpretation of Otto Hahn's results. In a letter to Cockcroft, dated February 13, 1939, Meitner gave a detailed account of the interpretations to date, but Cockcroft wanted to know more, especially about what was happening in Germany. And Otto Hahn wanted him to know more. On March 2, Hahn wrote to Meitner, "The day before yesterday, I have spoken with Rosbaud in detail, who will again travel to England and meet with Cockcroft. . . ." Rosbaud was a willing courier, and quite possibly, Otto Hahn had sensed his deeper purposes.

The men met for lunch at the Athenæum at twelve-thirty on Friday, March 10, 1939. Rosbaud's masterly summary of the experimental results on nuclear fission in the Reich impressed Cockcroft. Along with Hahn's yet unpublished findings, Paul relayed accounts of the more practical experimentation of such scientists as Siegfried Flügge at the Kaiser Wilhelm Institute of Physics in Dahlem, aimed at determining whether atomic energy was practical. The experiments of Willibald Jentschke and Friedrich Prankl at the Institute for Radioactivity in Vienna were beginning to demonstrate how the energy of the split atom might be harnessed. Fascinated, Cockcroft asked Rosbaud to report frequently. Of course, Paul agreed, knowing well that the atomic bomb was the one weapon that had to be denied to Hitler.

But compared to the university research in Britain, France, and the United States, the German investigations on atomic energy were not moving fast enough to satisfy some professors. Paul Harteck, who had worked with Kapitza and Cockcroft, recalled in a letter that "Groth and a few other members of my institute in [the University of] Hamburg came formally into my office and asked me to propose a research project — since war seemed imminent — that would prevent them from being drafted." With that wholly nonscientific aim, Wilhelm Groth and Harteck drafted a letter to the Reich Ministry of War. Sent from Harteck's office on April 24, 1939, it read, in part:

> We permit ourselves to direct your attention to the newest development in the field of nuclear physics, for in our estimation it holds a possibility for the creation of explosives whose effect would be many times greater than those presently in use. . . . In America and in other Anglo-Saxon countries as well as in France pure atomic physics is presently much more intensively pursued than here, where no particular interest is shown in such investigations, which are regarded as purely theoretical. We deem it our duty to call this to your attention. . . . It is obvious that in case the means for creating energy in the manner sketched above became a reality, which is entirely within the realm of the possible, the country that first makes use of it would, in relation to other nations, possess a well-nigh irretrievable advantage.

The final sentence caught the eye of the War Ministry, as had a simultaneous suggestion by other physicists to the Ministry of Education. Five days later, the government called a closed-door conference at which it was recommended that secrecy be imposed on atomic research and that all uranium stocks in Germany be secured. Present at that conference was Josef Mattauch, who had taken Lise Meitner's place in Hahn's laboratory and had even rented her former apartment.

On August 5, 1945, the day before the Hiroshima bomb was dropped and before very many in the world were privy to the secret, Rosbaud summarized a few of his activities for Allied intelligence authorities. This is part of his report about the meeting that inaugurated the German atomic program:

> The idea how to make use of this energy either under the assumption of the mechanism of a chain reaction for an enormous bomb or for a big source of energy . . . was first put forward by a man with the name Hanle (the diminutive form of Hahn's name). . . . At that time [Education Minister] Rust's expert for physics was a young physicist . . . Dr.

Dames. Hanle . . . was glad to have an opportunity to report to this
mighty man and laid before him this idea of a bomb which should be
able to destroy a town, a province, even the whole of an island. Dames
immediately called all the nuclear physicists to Berlin to a most confidential gathering; the plan was discussed and a research association
founded which later, in the jargon of physicists, was called "Uran-
Verein." . . . I do not deny that I was somehow alarmed when Mattauch
who was present at this meeting told me the next day everything about
it. . . . Professor R. S. Hutton of Cambridge, who came the following
week from London for a couple of hours, had the kindness to transmit
the information to Dr. J. D. Cockcroft, F.R.S.; this was in May or June
1939.

Whether it was for deferments from military service, for research
money, for the excitement of the research, or for the quest for the
"irretrievable advantage" for the Reich, those involved in the German
atomic program, backed by two ministries, forged ahead. Through
Rosbaud, the British knew everything they wanted to know about the
German atomic program—from its inception and throughout the
war—except during a year and a half hiatus in his reporting from
the end of 1939.

Rosbaud was in England several more times before the outbreak
of war. In his memoirs, Hutton, a professor of metallurgy at Cambridge, described one of their last meetings:

He asked me to meet him in London, as he had some important news.
We found a safe spot on a seat in the Mall and he asked me to convey
the valuable information to those most concerned with it. Apparently
Hitler had considered the possibility of an atomic bomb as his secret
weapon number 1, but this had to be put aside, because the only German
physicists who could have given effective help refused to cooperate. In
this and many other ways Rosbaud was of great service to the Allies.

Hutton's memory was faulty, reflecting the postwar myths about
the German atomic effort. At that moment in time, the German program was officially endorsed, well organized, and well ahead of programs elsewhere. It was only in August, four months after Harteck's
letter to the War Ministry, that Albert Einstein, prodded by Leo Szilard and another Hungarian physicist, Eugene Wigner, wrote his famous letter to President Roosevelt. Roosevelt did not read the letter
until October, a month after the war in Europe had begun, and the
American nuclear research effort did not get started until the day

before Pearl Harbor, over two years later. Even then, it came about only because of persistent urging by the British.

At that meeting on the Mall, Hutton told Rosbaud that his own government had not taken seriously Paul's warning. Angered, Paul returned to Berlin to start preparing something that even the British would notice.

ELEVEN

Departures

ON THE NIGHT of August 21, 1939, the Soviet news agency Tass announced that Germany's foreign minister, Joachim von Ribbentrop, was going to Moscow to meet his Russian counterpart, Vyacheslav Molotov, and to sign a nonaggression pact with the USSR. The die for the invasion of Poland was cast.

Rosbaud at once got in touch with the British legation in an attempt to reach Frank Foley, but Foley had already left for England. Rosbaud, nevertheless, seemed to have some private knowledge that Foley soon might be in Oslo, so it was there that Rosbaud went on August 26.

He arrived on Victor Goldschmidt's doorstep in Holmenkollen unannounced but warmly welcomed by Frøken Brendigen and V.M., who was able to offer him for his stay the side of the duplex usually occupied by V.M.'s colleague and friend Tom Barth and his family. Barth was spending a few months at the Geophysical Laboratory of the Carnegie Institution in Washington, D.C. Again, Paul was faced with a fundamental decision in his life: whether to join Hilde in England, move to Oslo, or remain in Germany. He would let his strongest motivations make the choice for him. Now, he simply had to await the appearance of Frank Foley.

Foley had hastily departed from Berlin by automobile with his wife, Katherine, his daughter, Ursular, and his secretary and cipher clerk, Margaret Reid. The Foleys had maintained a home in Stourbridge, a glass-manufacturing town near Birmingham. One of their neighbors recalls that "the Foleys were on leave here when the war broke out and had nothing but their car, which they had brought out for the holiday. All that they possessed in Berlin, they lost." Margaret Reid didn't have much, either, so she shopped for warm clothes at Simpson's. She wrote to her mother that on August 26,

> I was to meet my chief on the train at L'pool Street, but he missed it. There was a first-class traffic jam. . . . I was not perturbed about Mr. F. missing his train. I guessed what had happened but was pleased to get a radiogram from him saying, "Flying Copenhagen tomorrow." The train journey to Copenhagen was tedious, but we had good company in the carriage, including the new Naval Attaché [Admiral Hector Boyes].

Margaret got a heavy exposure to Copenhagen's night life in the company of Foley and assorted companions, including SIS agents and British newspapermen. At seven A.M. on Monday, August 28, they took the ferry to Sweden and thence a salon car to Oslo, their new post. Foley was once again a passport control officer.

There were several American visitors to Oslo at that time; one of them was Professor Karl Lark-Horovitz of Purdue University. Lark-Horovitz was a distinguished solid-state physicist who would make important contributions to the technique of radar. Before he moved to the United States from Austria, he and V.M. had become friends. Now, he was staying at the Holmenkollen Tourist Hotel and enjoying a reunion with V.M. and Odd Hassel. In the natural course of things, he met Paul Rosbaud.

Rosbaud for years had held an unlimited visa to visit England, but the state of war between Germany and Britain had invalidated that. Paul explained that he had a family in England and required a one-time visa in order to go there now. But because he was a German citizen, he was reluctant to visit the British legation openly. Hearing this, Lark-Horovitz volunteered to act as intermediary.

One morning in the first week of September, Norman Vorley, the British consul, brought Professor Lark-Horovitz to Foley's office. After the introduction, Lark-Horovitz made his request on behalf of his new acquaintance, Paul Rosbaud.

Rather difficult under the circumstances, Foley said. A German national, wartime, and all that. Nothing could be done really until London had been queried and the matter decided at Whitehall. Would Professor Lark-Horovitz be kind enough to return in two days?

He would, of course, but the delay was annoying, because he had planned to spend some time with his sister in Stockholm before sailing for America.

When Lark-Horovitz called at the legation again, Foley expressed his regrets with official politeness. Whitehall had not seen fit to grant a visa to the professor's friend. He was very sorry, but that was it.

Rosbaud received the news with no show of emotion. Lark-Horovitz went off for a hurried visit with his sister and returned to Oslo on September 16, but Rosbaud had departed a day earlier for Berlin.

It had all happened exactly as Rosbaud and Foley had planned it. Both Hilde and the Gestapo — if it were ever to inquire — would learn that Paul Rosbaud was considered persona non grata in England.

TWELVE

Beck's Book

IN SEPTEMBER 1939, the war lightning struck and the Polish army was overwhelmed in eighteen days. In the last two of those days, the Russian jackal came in for its share of the kill. The victory had to be memorialized in a speech by Adolf Hitler; what would make a better stage than the old Hanseatic port of Danzig, now restored to the German flag? On Tuesday, September 19, in front of the ornate guildhall, he gave an oration that combined a small bid for peace with a mighty threat of further attack. He said that he had "no war aims against Britain and France" and wished that other peoples would realize "how useless this war would be" and think of "the blessings of peace."

He then went on to boast that the time would arrive quite soon when "we will employ a weapon [*waffe*] with which we could not be attacked." As for defenseless women and children, too bad, for "naturally, if a column marches across the market square and is attacked by aircraft, it can happen that someone else is unfortunately sacrificed."

That sent an alarm through the Allied nations. They had just seen an awesome demonstration of German technological superiority. Newspapers throughout the world began to speculate on a secret "death ray" and other imagined weaponry. Prime Minister Neville Chamberlain grew nervous and called in Admiral Hugh Sinclair, head of the SIS and known as C, to find out all he could about Hitler's hidden arsenal.

The assignment came down the line of command and ended on

the desk of Dr. Reginald V. Jones, only a few days in SIS employment. Jones, a remarkable young Oxonian with a good scientific background, had been assigned to Frederick Winterbotham, now a wing commander, at the Air Intelligence Section. (There was no Scientific Section of the SIS at that time.) It became Jones's job to find out exactly what Hitler had meant by his Danzig threats.

After he had gone through SIS files for weeks, Jones was "impressed by the paucity of information." Knowing almost no German and finding that Winterbotham's was very poor, Jones asked for a new translation of the speech, which was duly made by Frederick (Bimbo) Norman, a professor of German. Norman pointed out that *waffe* could mean a single weapon or could refer to an armed service, as, for example, the Luftwaffe, which was the weapon of the air. This must have been what Hitler was referring to. Jones concluded that there were no secret weapons, at least at the present time, and he was rather pleased with himself for making this the central point of his report. "Hitler had done me a great service by securing my base in the very heart of Intelligence," he later wrote.

There were few more agreeable neighborhoods in Berlin than the Wannsee district. At Bismarckstrasse 11, on the water's edge, was the comfortable villa of Dr. Ing. Adolf Beck, director of magnesium operations for the giant I. G. Farben complex at Bitterfeld. Bitterfeld was a grim industrial town eighty miles to the south, and Dr. Beck much preferred to spend his time in Wannsee working on a book with his co-editor, Paul Rosbaud.

It was to be a definitive work on, as the title stated, *Technology of Magnesium and Its Alloys*. Eighteen experts would write on their specialties, covering the extraction of magnesium from raw materials such as olivine, its production as a metal and in alloys, its full physical properties, the techniques for shaping and casting it, and all of its applications — including its use in explosives.

Rosbaud knew a great deal about olivine, because his friend Victor Goldschmidt was the world's greatest authority on the subject. He was haunted by the beauty of peridot, a yellowish-green gemstone that is one of the forms, but he was much interested in its practical values. Olivine is one of the most common materials in the earth's crust, and there are large deposits of it on the west coast of Norway. In 1925,

Goldschmidt had discovered the refractory value of olivine, that is, its ability to hold other substances being melted at very high temperatures. He patented the use of olivine as refractory material and licensed his patents to the Harbison-Walker Company of Pittsburgh. (And he was paid a good income until 1941, when the U.S. government—in the worst of ironies—seized his royalties as enemy alien property.)

Paul Rosbaud was not so entranced as Goldschmidt with olivine, but he had long dealt professionally with its magnesium derivative. When he was scientific adviser to *Metallwirtschaft*, his priorities, judging from his published commentaries, were mainly the lighter metals, aluminum and magnesium. They were destined to become key strategic materials during the Second World War for aircraft and rocket construction and for filling the fearsome aerial incendiary bombs. Thus, after Rosbaud moved to Springer Verlag, he conceived the notion for a comprehensive book on magnesium and its alloys.

In Berlin, Paul Rosbaud had reason to take Hitler's Danzig speech far more seriously than did the inexperienced R. V. Jones. He knew quite well that Hitler used the word *flugzeug*, not *waffe*, when he spoke of aircraft in general. And Rosbaud also knew well that Hitler had more in his laboratories and arsenals than was ever shown in the easy Polish campaign.

October 15, 1939, was a lovely Indian summer day in Berlin. If Rosbaud had been lured to take a stroll in the Zoological Gardens and the Tiergarten, he would have seen the crowds of Berliners taking the air that Sunday morning. It was the first autumn weekend of the Winterhilfe drive. Everyone seemed in a good mood because the news was good. Only yesterday, Lieutenant Commander Gunther Prien's U-47 had sunk the mighty battleship *Royal Oak* in Britain's safest harbor, Scapa Flow.

Anyone fortunate enough to find a table at Café Kranzler on Unter den Linden could have watched children scrambling playfully among the piles of captured Polish cannon. Suddenly, a bizarre scene materialized in front of the sidewalk patrons of the cafés. A large black limousine pulled up to the curb and out of it jumped a German shepherd, accompanied by its master, the actor Harry Piel, and a photographer.

This was Hitler's favorite dog, Germany's answer to Rin-Tin-Tin.

For a donation of fifty pfennigs to Winterhilfe, one could pose with it for a picture. Rosbaud declined, though he noted the beast's name. Der Greif — the Griffin — was part of his family crest.

Returning to his study, Rosbaud probably sat down once more to examine the advance copy of Beck's *Magnesium and Its Alloys*, at last in finished form. He foresaw what Beck did not — that very shortly after its publication, the Luftwaffe would order that it be withdrawn from sale. But before that could happen, Rosbaud hoped to carry out his special plans for this copy.

The Oslo Report

ONE OF THE BEST WAYS to see Oslo in the late 1930s was to take the tram. Beginning at the western end of the Stortingsgate, the line snaked down the Drammensveien, a drab thoroughfare that gradually changed to become one of the city's more handsome promenades. On your right would appear the Royal Palace, a plain oblong atop a hill in the beautiful, wooded Slottspark. On your left would be the Victoria Terrace offices of the government. Then would come the Nobel Peace Institute, just before the line veered southwest into a fashionable quarter. Here were the leafy estates of Kristiania's old, rich families, and, beginning at Leiv Erikssons Gate, an embassy row.

The passenger could view the German legation on his left at Drammensveien 74. Just to the right and on a small rise would be number 79, the former mansion of Thomas Fearnly, master of the hunt, which now housed the British legation. It was easy for lookouts in either building to identify callers at the front door across the street.

Next to the Germans were two houses that were the headquarters of the Norwegian Academy of Sciences, among whose members were Victor Goldschmidt and Odd Hassel.

On a crisp November day in 1939, a man turned in at number 79 and took the uphill path to the British legation entrance. After making an inquiry, he was received by a legation officer on duty, a man who introduced himself in Oxonian accents as Harold Freese-Pennefather. The visitor asked for a legation officer by name. He wished to deliver a package to him.

Freese-Pennefather replied that Mr. So-and-So was not on duty at the moment. The visitor began to show signs of annoyance — he was, he said, simply doing an errand for a friend. At this moment, Freese-Pennefather suddenly recalled a recent directive that could solve the small problem: "Discreet cooperation [can] take place between naval attachés and representatives of the SIS." An extraordinary wartime measure, it seemed. The legation officer the stranger had asked to see was an SIS man, and, Freese-Pennefather knew, Rear Admiral Hector Boyes, the naval attaché, was in his office. Although Mr. So-and-So had colleagues and secretaries, they were in another building, and it was simply more convenient to take the package to the naval attaché in the main building.

When the twelve-by-six-by-two-inch package arrived at his desk, Boyes sighed and began to open it. As a young officer, he had seen action in the Boxer Rebellion and had commanded gunboats on the China Station. Now, reactivated at fifty-eight, he had been given this outpost of the navy, largely because his wife came from a rich and social Norwegian family.

Inside the wrappings were a German technical book and a smaller package. When the admiral opened the book, bound in black cloth, he found inserted in it a folded technical report, also in German. The first part of the report, consisting of five pages typed with blue ribbon on thin bluish paper, was untitled and contained two diagrams. Boyes's attention was particularly drawn to the second diagram, for it contained a sketch of a ship, and just above it were words identifying a new type of torpedo, which, he translated, "is probably the type that sank the *Royal Oak*." Here was something for a naval attaché!

The second part of the report was titled "Electric Fuses for Bombs and Shells" and contained three diagrams, which took most of the space. On unwrapping the smaller package, Boyes found a sealed glass tube; it looked something like a radio valve, and its description seemed to coincide with what was written in the second part of the report now on his desk.

Boyes initially had been unimpressed — this seemed to be some sort of information relating to presumed German secret weapons. Often enough, some well-wisher — naïve or unbalanced — would offer His Majesty's Government unsolicited advice on how to win the war. Boyes disposed discreetly of all such communications. But after he had looked a little closer at what he held in his hands, instinct told him it was not the work of a crank; it seemed to be serious enough to warrant full translation, in any case. Admiral Boyes decided to have that work done in the legation and, if anything of interest appeared, to send the lot to London.

The exact date of these events has never been determined. On one copy of an early translation, however, there is written "November 4, 1939." Whatever that may have to do with the report, it was an important date in the history of the SIS, because on that day Admiral Sinclair died. He was succeeded as C, head of the Secret Service, by Graham Stewart Menzies (pronounced "*ming*-iss"), and it was he who gave the report and glass tube to Frederick Winterbotham.

The Oslo material, sans the Beck book, ended up on the desk of R. V. Jones, who at the moment was finishing his report on secret weapons. His own report was to be dated November 11, 1939, which is of some help in fixing an approximate date for the Oslo Report, as the mysterious gift came to be called.

Part of the persistent lore of the Oslo Report is the story of the preliminary communications. As the story goes, Admiral Boyes received an anonymous letter, posted in Oslo, asking whether the British would like to know of certain German scientific and technical developments. If so, they should alter the preamble of the BBC evening broadcast of the German service from its usual form to "*Hullo, hier ist London*." R. V. Jones has written, "We duly altered the preamble and the information arrived." One problem with this version is that it requires the report's courier, or his surrogate, to have been in Oslo twice in a few months — once to mail the letter of inquiry and a second time, weeks later, to pass along the report. This would have constituted a double risk for the informer. On the other hand, if there is substance to the story, it narrows the list of the report's possible authors.

When the tale of the Oslo Report was told in 1947, Hector Boyes wrote to Jones that the BBC preamble was to be altered if *more* information was required. Boyes was of the opinion that this had been done, but no other mysterious packages came to the legation, and Boyes assumed that the author had been "liquidated." A message from the SIS to the sender affirming receipt and requesting more information would seem to have been a likely follow-up. But apparently, and incredibly, nobody concerned with the analysis of the Oslo Report ever requested more information from the same source.

It seems probable, however, that the special signal was never transmitted by the BBC, before or after the report was received. Leonard

Miall, who was in charge of the BBC's German news talks from March 1939 to October 1942, has reported in a letter, "With regard to what was usually said at the start of the German news and news talks program, my recollection is that it was invariably *'Hier ist der Londoner Rundfunk.'* " Miall verified this with Maurice Latey, his assistant at that time, and concluded that "a special message altering the nature of the newscast in an obvious way is something that we would have noticed." Sir Hugh Greene, who became the German news editor in the fall of 1940, recalled that special messages were broadcast only later in the war. Indeed, Paul Rosbaud received many special messages that way after the autumn of 1941.

Winterbotham has said, "I never heard of the request for the BBC broadcast. The jacket [containing the Oslo Report] was handed to me by Menzies. . . . He asked me to let him know what I thought about it. I handed it to Jones—no mention of a BBC reply. I later informed Menzies that it appeared to be genuine."

Jones was fascinated when he viewed the translation. In front of his eyes was a rundown of new weapons or novel applications possessed by the Germans. "The report was obviously written by someone with a good scientific and technical background, and was quite different from anything I had so far seen in intelligence," Jones later wrote.

Oddly, the document began with an assertion that seemed almost crackpot: the Germans were producing five thousand Junker-88 bombers per month and would increase the rate to twenty-five thousand to thirty thousand by April 1940. Even someone not an expert would have viewed that as an exaggeration. In fact, it was to take the Germans three years and five months more to reach a total of five thousand JU-88s. Either the author of the report was trying to scare the British or he was a person with little knowledge of production realities. But the report did reveal to the British, accurately, that the JU-88 "has the advantage of being able to be used also as a dive bomber."

And there followed a number of other items within the realm of possibility and almost equally shocking:

• A remote-controlled, rocket-propelled glider launched from aircraft against enemy ships. (Later in the war, this FZ-21—afterward renamed HS-293—would inflict severe damage on the British fleet.)
• Other rocket projectiles (of 80-cm caliber, still not perfected).

• An experimental station at Peenemünde, "at the mouth of the Peene, near Wolgast, near Greifswald," where this rocket work was being done. This was the first mention of Peenemünde in an intelligence report.
• The FZ-10 pilotless aircraft.
• A new acoustic-homing torpedo; a new magnetic fuse for another type of torpedo and countermeasures against it.
• An effective infantry tactic, combining smoke screens and flame throwers, for use against bunkers.
• Two types of radar systems.

And there were several more. Like any good empiricist, Jones took the glass tube to the Admiralty Research Laboratory and found that it was exactly as described in the text — an electronic triggering device that activated a proximity fuse in antiaircraft shells. This was enough to convince him of the unknown author's veracity, at least in part.

But not the British armed services. All three branches rejected the report as a hoax, and a senior official at the Admiralty suggested that Jones was naïve to take any stock in it. This official had two good reasons for his skepticism. First, he said, it seemed improbable that any one man in Germany could have learned so much about developments in so many different fields. Second — in reply to Jones's point that at least some of the evidence was demonstrably correct — one always tries to trick the enemy by giving him a salting of truth over the body of falsehood, and this is what the Germans had done. None of the services troubled to retain its copy of the translation.

Other arguments against authenticity were less convincing. Some said that the writing style was too good to be that of a scientist — but the document is not known to have been read by anyone who combined technical expertise with a thorough knowledge of German. And good style in scientific writing was not unknown, even in those days. Others insisted that the report was a piece of propaganda meant to intimidate the British.

Some months later, probably after the middle of 1940, the report was sent to SIS Section V, which was charged, along with other duties, with authenticating documents. The top Section V expert on the German military intelligence organization, the Abwehr, and on Norwegian matters was none other than Frank Foley. That Section V did not label the report a fraud was most probably the consequence of Foley's knowing it to be authentic even before he examined it. Jones later wrote, "As the war progressed and one development after another actually appeared, it was obvious that the report was largely correct; and in the few dull moments of the war, I used to look up the Oslo Report to see what should be coming along next."

And this was the tragic side of the story. Jones might amuse himself by using the report as a forecaster of German technological nastiness, but the services failed to take heed of its obvious lessons. Jones himself had joined the SIS on the strength of Hitler's "secret weapon" speech. The Oslo Report, which was replete with mentions of secret weapons, came into his hands days before he submitted his own report. Yet, as he wrote, "My secret weapon report was issued on 11th November, and did not have much about the Oslo Report in it — indeed nothing at all." Only rarely was the Oslo Report used as a basis for instructing intelligence collectors. Curiously, Jones's November 11, 1939, report (AIR 20/8535) had been missing from his files in the Air Historical Branch of the Ministry of Defence for decades until the branch obtained a copy in May 1982 — from R. V. Jones.

In the report, Jones apologized:

> It should be mentioned that any conclusions in this paper are made solely on the evidence of the S.I.S. files and may be biased by the fact that the writer is a physicist.
> The S.I.S. reports do indicate that some specific new means of warfare are envisaged by Germany, although it is difficult to assess the merit of the majority of the individual reports, because of their distorted nature.

But, as it turned out, very little in the Oslo Report proved to have been distorted, and only rarely was the Oslo Report used as a basis for instructing the collectors of intelligence.

FOURTEEN

Author, Author?

IN THE WHOLE HISTORY of espionage, there are few documents as renowned as the Oslo Report. The official SIS historian, Professor F. H. Hinsley, has stated that the "Oslo Report first lifted the veil of ignorance which surrounded Germany's most important scientific and technological advances." It is therefore astonishing that no one in British intelligence tried to discover the identity of the author. That lack of inquiry is testified to by all those living who had anything to do with the report. It appears that Frank Foley alone, and later a single successor, knew the source, and both held this information very closely.

After the war, there was a new, historical kind of curiosity. R. V. Jones was, of course, particularly interested, and he attempted to flush the author into the open by revealing the existence of the Oslo Report in a lecture at London's Royal United Services Institution on February 19, 1947. But the effect was the opposite: instead of revealing himself, the author remained stubbornly in the shadows.

Jones persisted. By the time he wrote *The Wizard War: British Scientific Intelligence, 1939–1945*, he said he believed he knew the name of the author, adding, "But the way in which his identity was revealed to me was so extraordinary that it may well not be credited."

This in itself is an extraordinary statement—not so much that the author still had to be protected but that the manner of his or her revelation to Jones had to be hidden.

Jones was not the only searcher, however, and there have been a good many attempts. The distinguished historian Walter Laqueur has long sought the solution and has recently written: "The identity of the author of this most astonishing intelligence document of the Second World War is still a secret." On the basis of a conversation with Jones, Laqueur wrote: "The family of the author of the Oslo document has so far opposed publication of his name, but it seems likely that his identity will become known soon." Prophetic words, perhaps. Then there is the case of the Danish journalist.

The Monaco Bar in the Latin Quarter is a small, nondescript place, hardly a likely setting for a discussion of World War II mysteries. It is a hangout for Foreign Legionnaires, but they do not gather there in the morning, so the place is fairly quiet then. But the traffic noise from the nearby Carrefour de l'Odéon can drown out all conversation at times. The Danish journalist told the writer-physicist to whom he was talking that he had been investigating the Oslo Report for more than a decade and had finally come to focus on Dr. Hans Kummerow. Kummerow, in loose alliance with the famed Soviet spy ring the Rote Kapelle (Red Orchestra), may have been sufficiently disillusioned by the August 1939 Hitler-Stalin pact to furnish information to the British. The physicist thought that there was at least a hint of logic in that notion.

But the theory was not new to him. In the late 1960s, scores of Eastern European newspaper articles, magazines, and books attempted to deify the members of the Rote Kapelle, Kummerow among them. Arrested in a Gestapo roundup of the Rote Kapelle in September 1942, Kummerow hung himself in his cell in February 1944 on hearing that he had received the death sentence. The Kummerow story, as it became further elaborated, had some obvious fallacies. Kummerow had traveled to Oslo by way of Stavanger, on the west coast of Norway. It is an unlikely way to enter the country unless one is coming from England — which was an unlikely place for Kummerow to be after the declaration of war. In Stavanger, he is supposed to have telephoned a member of the Movement to Free Germany to say that he was en route to the capital.

As the story continues, the spy arrives at the British legation at Drammensveien 79 early one rainy morning. He does not notice that he is now across the street from the German legation, and he is surprised to learn that the British office does not open until ten in the morning. The spy is carrying a yellow envelope, but he keeps it rather than putting it into the legation's mail slot — because just at this moment, he notices a gray limousine cruising along the street. It has Trondheim license plates, and inside is a Gestapo man who just happens to be known to the spy as a man called Reinhard. Kummerow boards a tram and flees to the home of a friend in the affluent suburb of Bygdøy.

That evening, a woman in evening gown and fur coat—no doubt a disguise to fool the Gestapo—arrives at the British legation and slips the yellow envelope into the mail slot. Her chauffeur, standing smartly by her limousine, opens the door for the lovely lady to re-enter, returns to the wheel, and speeds away. A legation secretary finds the envelope the next day—and the rest is what we know.

There are other fantasies about the Oslo Report—some of them advanced by well-known intelligence historians—but none quite as unfortunate as that of Anthony Cave Brown, described in his *Bodyguard of Lies*, published in 1975. Brown conjures up a picture of a British legation guard making his rounds in a snowstorm on that fateful November 4, 1939. On the stone ledge by the porter's lodge, he finds a half-covered parcel "about three inches thick, the size and shape of a block of legal-size pads," addressed to the British naval attaché. Brown surmises that if the guard had not chanced across it then, the package might have lain hidden by the snow for weeks.

It is quite peculiar that the British legation had its private snowstorm that day, because the records of the Royal Norwegian Meteorological Office show that the first snowstorm of the winter did not arrive in Oslo until November 24, twenty days later.

Anthony Cave Brown also may be the origin of another legend. He wrote that when the naval attaché opened the parcel, he "found a note signed by a 'well-wishing German scientist.' " The author of the report may indeed have been that, but those who were associated with the early history of the Oslo Report, including R. V. Jones, have never referred to such a note.

Professor Jones—recently retired from the University of Aberdeen—has been for four decades the leading authority on the Oslo Report; thus, his opinion on the authorship must be heeded. Indisputably, Jones invented the analysis of technical intelligence, and the author of the Oslo Report was the "father" of the collection of technical intelligence. Early in my investigation for this book, I found circum-

stantial evidence indicating that Paul Rosbaud ought to be considered
among the possible candidates. Jones commented, "Your conjecture
. . . is a most interesting one, but it will probably be some time before
I am able to comment." In a recent conversation, however, he firmly
rejected the possibility that Rosbaud was the author of the Oslo
Report.

FIFTEEN

The Solution

WITH ALL DUE RESPECT to R. V. Jones, there were others who had a closer contact with the original of the Oslo Report during the war and there were others who were obliged to consult it in the course of official business after the war.

Foremost among the latter was Sir Harry Hinsley, now Master of St. John's College, Cambridge, and wartime member of the Ultra signals intercept team. He is the author of *British Intelligence in the Second World War*, the official history, in which the full English text of the report (but without the diagrams) is given as appendix 5 of volume 1. A decade or so ago, Professor Hinsley ran across a transcribed copy of the report in German, without the diagrams. He prepared a new translation, which turned out to be much superior to the 1939 version used by Jones. Recently Hinsley located another German copy that apparently predated his first find. This may even have been the original of the report, because it contained diagrams. But when the professor requested the release of his discovery, Her Majesty's Government consigned it to a deep vault of the Ministry of Defence.

Although hardly in a class with the crown jewels, the report is a forty-seven-year-old treasure with an established place in history. It deserves to be displayed in the British Museum. The only conceivable reason it is not there may be that the document bears some clue to its authorship, and its author, dead for decades, possessed certain other secrets that should have been buried with him and the Oslo Report.

F. W. Winterbotham of course read the report before handing it to Jones in 1939. Winterbotham's only recollection of it is a "document

together with a small phial . . . a typed report interspersed with hand
drawings, e.g., the acoustic mine, etc." But neither he nor Jones saw
the German original.

At this point, certain distinctions should be made. There may have
been several contributors, witting or unwitting, to the report, and
thus, by the strictest definition, the authorship may have been a mul-
tiple one. It was nevertheless clear to all who analyzed the report that
the text was assembled and edited by a single hand. It is also possible
that the author was not the person who brought the document to
Oslo — or, indeed, the man who carried it to the British legation.

Another small curiosity lies in the fact that Jones, writing about
atomic energy intelligence, has noted, "Our knowledge was, incidentally, largely due to Paul Rosbaud." Charles Frank (now Sir Charles),
who served as Jones's assistant in the SIS, as it happened had known
Rosbaud well in Berlin before the war. He has said that neither he
nor Jones heard of Rosbaud as a source during the war.

Witnesses are rare at this late date, and the remaining testimony
and evidence must come from Norway. In 1939, Norway possessed
no intelligence service, so there could be no record of anything per-
taining to the report. But after the Oslo Report became known in
1947, it was natural that a few Norwegian officials and former members of the Resistance would become curious about its authorship.
One of the latter made discreet inquiries of the personnel who had
served in the British legation at the beginning of the war. Did they
recall any peculiar visit during November 1939? The only recollection
was that an albino had delivered some sort of package about that time.
When this story was relayed recently to a senior Norwegian intelligence official still in service, he replied, "Odd Hassel is your man."
But he would not say more.

General Leif Rolstad was a liaison officer with the Norwegian army
at the time of the German invasion of Norway in April 1940. It was
then that he met Frank Foley and his cipher clerk, Margaret Reid.
He accompanied them back to England and remained their good
friend. General Rolstad has had access to Margaret Reid's personal
papers. He wrote:

> Regarding the "Oslo report" (or "Oslo papers" as I know the matter)
> of November 1939, I have understood that these papers seemingly were
> intended for Mr. Foley, but were by mischance handed to the only
> British forces attaché on the spot, Rear Admiral Boyes, who presumably

did not know what it was all about and did not inform Foley. The papers therefore took a very long time in reaching their proper destination via the British Admiralty.

In a subsequent letter, General Rolstad wrote, "I gained the *impression* that Foley was waiting for something—possibly this. Margaret Reid may have been alluding to it when she wrote, 'We had to keep going for eight months with little enough to justify our presence [in Oslo].' " Oslo was an odd assignment for the top SIS expert on Germany. Foley would have been far more useful in London. Instead, he was sent to a post already staffed by two men equal in rank and old hands in Scandinavian affairs, Commander J. B. Newill and Major Leslie H. Mitchell. Margaret Reid's actual words were:

> Frank would have liked to give this story to the world; he suffered, as small men do, from an inferiority complex about himself and his work. He was not always Persona Grata in Norway; we came into a situation [from Germany] where there was already an officer in charge, Commander Newill. We had to jog along for eight months with little enough to justify our existence.

The story that Reid thought should be told was of Foley's retreat with the Norwegian forces after the German invasion, but perhaps she also meant, as General Rolstad thinks she did, the "little enough to justify our existence"—the Oslo Report.

Thus, the strong impression in Norwegian official and semiofficial circles is that both Odd Hassel and Frank Foley were somehow connected with the Oslo Report. Both men are long gone; being the silent men they were, they never spoke of the report.

Had any of the British intelligence officers involved any recollection of other circumstances of the report? The question was referred to R. V. Jones, Sir Charles Frank, and F. W. Winterbotham. Now, although Odd Hassel became a Nobel Prize winner, his name is unknown to most scientists. It proved unknown to Jones and Frank, both of them scientists, but they had come to know Foley during the war. Winterbotham, not a scientist, recollected that he had heard the name of Hassel in connection with the Oslo Report. That must have been in the early wartime period, because after the invasion of Norway, Winterbotham became preoccupied with Ultra work, the interception and decoding of German signals traffic.

When Foley returned to the legation in that November of 1939, he undoubtedly inquired about the package he was expecting. When he heard of its delivery, he must have been curious about who had brought it. If he did not know the courier from Freese-Pennefather's description, he would have been able to identify him easily by asking a few questions in Oslo—perhaps even by glancing across the street to see who was entering the Norwegian Academy of Sciences.

In November 1939, the Oslo newspapers reported the opening of a German book exhibition at the KNA Hotel on the evening of the twenty-seventh. In preparation for it, leading German publishers—such as Springer Verlag—would have sent their representatives in advance to arrange for the display of their publications. This show was sponsored by the cultural section of the German legation in Oslo, in collaboration with Dr. Ulrich Noack.

Noack, a man of some polish, was a historian engaged in writing a book on Norway and Nordic history, a subject dear to the heart of SS chief Heinrich Himmler. This enterprise also was warmly supported by Noack's superior in Berlin, Dr. Josef Goebbels, who cherished the idea of unity between the Nordic and Aryan races. One of Noack's friends in Oslo was Vidkun Quisling; the two shared the idea that Russia—despite the Hitler-Stalin pact—was the real enemy. Another of Noack's friends was Dr. Gulbrand Lunde, Quisling's chief philosopher. Lunde would become Goebbels's counterpart in the Quisling government after the invasion of Norway. Neither the Germans nor Norwegians were ever completely comfortable with Noack. He had a Norwegian wife and years earlier had come to Norway as a "refugee." Yet after the Anschluss, he established connections with the German legation. He was recalled to Germany after the invasion of Norway because of his opposition to Quisling. There is much yet to be known about Ulrich Noack.

Lunde was a scientist of no small reputation. In his early career, he had been affiliated with the geochemist Tom Barth, and they had written some papers together. A few years later, Lunde and Victor Goldschmidt became friends and associates in research. Lunde was a contributor to *Metallwirtschaft* and in 1929 had collaborated with Rosbaud on a paper on crystalline structures, which they later published.

One side of the house at Holmenkollen, where Frøken Brendigen presided over the Goldschmidt ménage, including assorted animals, was occupied by the Barths. In the summer of 1939, when Ulrich Noack arrived to take up his diplomatic post, he at once ingratiated himself among the university faculty. Not only did he and Barth have a mutual friend in Lunde, but Barth found the German quite charming.

Barth, having been invited for a few months to Washington, D.C., had suggested that Noack take over his half of the house while he was away. This invitation displayed a large amount of insensitivity. In fact, when he heard that a German official was about to move in, V.M. was furious. After the dust had settled a bit, it was agreed that Goldschmidt would pay Barth's share of the rent and that Noack would find shelter elsewhere.

Thus it was that Paul Rosbaud, visiting Oslo from the end of August to mid September 1939, was installed in Barth's quarters by V.M. In all probability — and this is the speculative part — Paul Rosbaud would have called at the German legation during his stay in Oslo, and because he was a publisher's representative, his contact would have been Dr. Noack. It may even have been Rosbaud who suggested the book exhibition. It would, he may have said, be helpful to cement Norwegian-German cultural relations; this was the kind of idea Noack was looking for.

One of the books later on display at the KNA Hotel was an advance copy of *Vitamine in frischen und konservierten Nahrungsmitteln* (*Vitamins in Fresh and Preserved Foodstuffs*). The author was Gulbrand Lunde, who concluded in the foreword, "The book appears at one of the most difficult times for the European people." The publisher was Springer Verlag of Berlin — and the editorial supervisor was Paul Rosbaud.

Assume this problem: a spy finds it essential to smuggle some materials to a foreign country — a bound book, some manuscript pages, and a small phial. War has been declared, however, and the secret police are more suspicious than ever about the luggage of passengers going abroad and about packages mailed to other countries. In addition, the spy knows there is even a danger that his country's secret service will be watching addressees in the foreign country. The materials must be slipped through this invisible mesh of surveillance — but how?

Assume also that the spy is in the publishing business. What is more effective, then, than to get the Propaganda Ministry itself to sponsor a large shipment of books for an exhibition in the foreign country? The secret police will not inspect it. The nation's embassy will have no reason to be suspicious of it. And the publisher's representative will see to the unpacking of his own company's part of the shipment.

The book exhibition was less than a success. The German ambassador, Kurt Bräuer, was present, as were a good number of Norwegians, led by Vidkun Quisling. There were toasts to a lasting friendship between the two nations and the German display was admired. But on the following morning the Russians announced a new nonaggression pact with Finland. The Soviets were pushing into Scandinavia, and the Nazi-Soviet partition of Poland was still a fresh lesson. Amicable feelings toward the Third Reich had cooled considerably by nightfall.

It remains to be verified that Paul Rosbaud was, in fact, in Oslo again on or just before the crucial November 4. He himself seemed to contradict it many years later when he noted that his next wartime contact with Goldschmidt and Hassel came in December 1939. But Rosbaud was always careless about dates and could have made an error about the month.

That he did make such an error is suggested by some circumstances of the time. Rosbaud visited Oslo from August 26 to September 16. That is firmly documented. The finished copy of Beck's *Technology of Magnesium and Its Alloys* was not available until mid October. Metallgesellschaft A.G. of Frankfurt, Rosbaud's old employer and a Luftwaffe contractor, logged in its copy on October 23. Years later, in 1961, Rosbaud was awarded the Tate Medal of the American Institute of Physics in New York. He made a small confession appropriate to the occasion. It was he, Rosbaud said, who had transmitted Beck's book to Oslo.

There is a strong hint in Lise Meitner's correspondence with Hilde Rosbaud of Rosbaud's whereabouts in November 1939. It suggests that Rosbaud visited Meitner in Stockholm about the first week of the month. From there, it would have been an easy trip—blessed by a semiofficial excuse—to Oslo.

On September 7, Hilde wrote to Lise, "My husband is staying with V.M. in Oslo." On October 11, she again wrote to say, "He [Paul] hopes to come back soon to see V.M." So Hilde knew that Paul planned a second fall trip to Oslo. She added doubtfully, "I do not think it possible." But she was hopeful and asked, "When you see Paul, please give him this letter"—apparently a reference to an enclosure.

Hilde wrote to Lise in December, "If only I would know whether

Paul will see V.M. soon; perhaps you will ask Paul when you see him next." But the most telling piece of paper is a letter from Paul to Lise without his address. Almost invariably, Rosbaud put his address on his letters so that his friends could keep track of his movements. On November 3, 1939, from his unknown location, Paul sent Lise birthday wishes and "an informative book." With the generous supply of books he had imported for the exhibition in Oslo, what present could be closer at hand?

Hilde wrote to Lise on January 8, 1940, "I know that you see Paul from time to time. I am terribly worried about him." It seems reasonably certain, then, that Lise Meitner saw Paul Rosbaud between mid October and the first of the year, probably as he was going to or returning from Oslo.

In addition, Rosbaud insisted after the war that at about this time he had warned his Norwegian friends of German plans to invade their country. Such warning could not have been transmitted before October 10, when the navy chief, Admiral Eric Raeder, presented his plans for the invasion of Norway to Adolf Hitler and a few senior officers.

It seems that Rosbaud was in the right place at the right time, and it seems indisputable that the mysterious messenger who delivered the report to the British legation was Odd Hassel. But corroboration from Norwegian sources is important. Almost all surviving Norwegians who had some connection with Rosbaud's wartime activities have proved to have exact memories. Their recollections have time and time again checked out when compared with other sources and documents—and the best of these memories belong to the professionals who are still active.

Professor Brynulf Ottar is at present the director of the Norwegian Institute for Air Research at Lillestrom. During the war, he was one of the three people who organized the special Resistance intelligence organization, XU, through which Rosbaud channeled much of his information to Britain. In the fall of 1939, Ottar had been a student of Hassel's. His observations on the Oslo Report question were these:

One day Hassel told me that a Professor Rosbaud had come to see him. He worked in Springer Verlag and I had the impression that Hassel knew him from the time he had studied on a Rockefeller grant in Germany before the war. . . . Professor Rosbaud told him that Germany was going to attack Norway and he urged Hassel to warn the Norwegian authorities. Also, he asked Hassel to deliver a book of some scientific papers to the English Embassy [sic].

My impression was that there was nothing special about these papers but simply that Rosbaud did not want to be seen entering the English Embassy. I don't think either of us believed too much in the [German] attack plan, but Hassel delivered the papers and told the Ministry of Foreign Affairs that he had been informed from presumptively reliable sources that Germany planned to invade Norway.

We did not talk much about it, but when the Germans came in 1940, it did of course come up again, and attention focused on the fact that Norwegian authorities had not taken his warning of half a year earlier seriously. On this basis, I believe that Rosbaud's visit in Oslo must have been some time in October or November 1939.

But Professor Ottar had a better basis for fixing the date of Rosbaud's visit to Oslo: "I did not know Hassel well in August and September 1939. The visit Hassel mentioned to me must have taken place in November. . . . I also remember there was a book exhibition."

Although it seemed clear that Odd Hassel delivered a package for Paul Rosbaud that November of 1939, its contents had to be more conclusively verified. So in 1985 the full text of the Oslo Report was sent to Professor Ottar, who, having served in the Norwegian Defense Research Establishment from 1947 to 1969, could appreciate it fully. He wrote once more:

> Things now seem to fall in place, and to me it seems evident that Hassel received the book, the Oslo Report, and the "radio valve" from Rosbaud, which he delivered to the British Embassy [sic]. As mentioned before, Hassel told me he had delivered a book on light metal alloys and some papers. When you mentioned a radio valve, I seemed to remember this also. My impression at the time was that Hassel found it somewhat untimely of Rosbaud to bother him to travel downtown to the British Embassy with an ordinary book, some scientific papers, and the radio valve. But, as Rosbaud had said that he had little time because of some meeting (I think with Professor Goldschmidt), Hassel had consented to do the errand for him. I therefore believe that Hassel had no idea of the real value of the material he was delivering at the embassy.

There it is: Beck's book, the Oslo Report, the "radio valve" (in reality the proximity fuse), and the warning about a German invasion. Beyond doubt, the Griffin's first great contribution to British intelligence came out of Germany in a shipment approved by Josef Goebbels himself.

SIXTEEN

Retreat

JUST BEFORE FIVE A.M. on April 9, 1940, people in Oslo awoke to the sound of heavy guns from the Oslofjord, and the news came that a German naval task force was trading fire with the Norwegian forts on the coast. The Cabinet met in emergency session. They had scarcely begun the meeting when Kurt Bräuer, the German ambassador, arrived with Hitler's demand for immediate surrender. The Cabinet rejected it at once and at 5:52 Bräuer was back in his legation, cabling Berlin that the Norwegians had told him that "the struggle has just begun." He then went down to the harbor with a festive group of legation people to welcome the invading fleet and troops.

They waited a long time in the chilly darkness, but the task force did not arrive. The guns of the old fortress of Oscarsborg, fifteen miles down the fjord, had sunk one German cruiser and severely damaged another. The task force turned back. That bought enough time for the Norwegian government and the royal family to board a train for the town of Hamar, eighty miles to the north.

At about the time Bräuer was en route to the palace, Frank Foley telephoned Margaret Reid and told her to come to the passport office at once. When she got there, she found Foley and Commander Newill emptying all the sensitive files — and the cash from the safe — into wastepaper baskets. When they had finished, they managed to find a taxi that took them to the legation by a back way. As Margaret Reid described it, "We saw a great bonfire before we reached the grounds. The men there were already at work. We struggled up the muddy slope with our precious wastepaper baskets and were soon frantically rending code books and files to feed the flames. . . . The fire brigade, unconscious of what was afoot, appeared on the scene shortly and wanted to put the fire out. We laughed and told them to bring us some petrol for the blaze."

Into that fire went registry receipts, appointment records, and every other scrap of paper that could have documented the receipt of the Oslo Report.

Foley and Reid then drove to Hamar and were on hand at the railway station to greet the train bearing the king and what was left of the government of Norway. The English pair had thoughtfully brought along their wireless equipment. Reid wrote:

> It was undoubtedly our wireless which saved the situation then, as it did again later. An aerial was soon rigged to a flagstaff and within a very short time we were in communication with London using the Foreign Office emergency code. Messages to and from the Norwegian Government were sent and among them came the assurance from H.M.G. that we would support the Norwegians in their resistance against the aggressor to the utmost of our power.

In the meantime, a small force of German paratroopers had taken Oslo, and efforts were under way to persuade the king to surrender. The next day, Foley and Reid drove up the somber Gudbrandsdal to Dombas and then to Åndalsnes on the coast, a hundred miles south of Trondheim, to await British troop landings.

Very shortly, however, Major General Otto Ruge, the Norwegian commander, requested them to come back to his headquarters in the Gudbrandsdal, where they took control of the communications link with Britain. Messages went to Lillehammer, thence to Ålesund, then to Wick at the tip of Scotland. Foley and Reid used a "book code," which was very secure, providing the enemy did not know the title of the book. The book they used was *Sesame and Lilies*, a collection of essays by John Ruskin published in 1865. Churchill himself was in frequent communication with Ruge, and the link was so important that the general once remarked to Foley, "Your name will go down in history!"

At this time — and, indeed, throughout the war — the subject of heavy water was a prime intelligence concern. To Frank Foley, with his day-to-day problems as intermediary between HMG and the Norwegian army, it was more an annoyance than anything else. Foley and his staff had just settled down at the headquarters in Oier when an argument broke out among the Allies.

On April 21, there appeared on the scene the French military attachés from Oslo, headed by a fierce-looking type with a patch over one eye. He was the senior attaché, a major named Bertrand-Vignes, whom the British secretaries soon nicknamed "the Pirate." He argued that the British had an *idée fixe* about preserving their iron-ore supply route through Narvik, but that they were overlooking something far more important. In Telemark, seventy-five miles west of Oslo, was the dam at Rjukan and the heavy-water production plant. The British should make its defense a priority. The major cited the recent French interest in the facilities at Rjukan.

Foley argued that there was no way that British troops could make their way inland over treacherous territory and hold the installation. Much to the disgust of Bertrand-Vignes, Foley would not change his mind.

Although heavy water had been discovered by the American chemist Harold Urey in 1932, there was still only one producer in the world, Norsk Hydro at Rjukan. After Otto Hahn split the atom with slow neutron "bullets," heavy water assumed importance. It is important in harnessing atomic power, because it is a convenient substance for slowing down the neutron bullets to split the atom.

The Rjukanfoss, or "foaming waterfall," had been one of the more imposing sights of southern Norway, but in the first decade of the century, its beauty was diminished by the construction of a hydroelectric plant that fed electricity a short distance to a factory at Vemork. This factory manufactured explosives and ammonia for conversion to nitrates for fertilizer, and the processes required huge amounts of hydrogen produced by electrolysis. In ordinary water there is a very small amount of heavy water, which can be extracted by staging the electrolytic cells in a certain way.

There were foreign shareholders in Norsk Hydro, and toward the end of 1939, two of them began to contend for purchase of the entire heavy-water stock and control over future production as well. One of the shareholders was I. G. Farben, the giant German chemical combine, and the other was the Banque de Paris et de Pays Bas. French scientists were well aware that even small quantities of heavy water might speed German research on its way to the atomic bomb.

The episode that Bertrand-Vignes had been referring to was this: a month before the invasion of Norway, Jacques Allier, an official of the French bank and a reserve officer in the Deuxième Bureau, France's secret service, met with the general manager of Norsk Hydro in his Oslo office at Solligaten 7. Dr. Axel Aubert told Allier that the Germans had just made a bid for his entire stock of heavy water. But, said Aubert, if Allier took the water with him, France could have use of it for the duration of the war as well as an option on future production. The deal was struck at once.

The Allies, with the help of the Deuxième Bureau (intelligence) station chief in Oslo and two associates, managed to get the twenty-six canisters past the German agents on watch and onto a plane for Edinburgh. Foley had arranged for clearance at the airport and special handling of the 410 pounds of water. The three agents loaded the shipment into two first-class compartments of the train and escorted it down the length of England and across the Channel to Paris.

Although he had played a minor part in this operation, Foley knew and cared nothing about heavy water. Until April of that year, it had no mention in SIS requirements for agents. But in April, the British had developed a sudden interest, of which Foley had not been informed.

Just one day after the invasion of Norway, the British atomic energy committee met on the premises of the Royal Society in Burlington House to listen to a special guest. It was the first meeting of the group of four, which was composed of George Thompson, son of the discoverer of the electron and himself a noted researcher at Imperial College in London; John Cockcroft, who had succeeded Kapitza at the Cavendish Laboratory at Cambridge; and Mark Oliphant and Philip Moon of Birmingham University. They were there to discuss the subject of heavy water with the French intelligence officer Jacques Allier.

Allier's subsequent report to Paris included promises by Cockcroft to furnish information on Belgian uranium supplies and the production of heavy water in Canada and the United States. In turn, Allier undertook to furnish any information the French had about Belgian uranium. There was also to be a list, compiled by the British, of the German scientists with an interest in heavy water.

The last part was easy. Paul Rosbaud had given such a list to Cockcroft via R. S. Hutton the year before.

In Norway, in the meantime, the situation had been quickly deteriorating. The king and the governmental party had pushed on up the rugged valley toward Åndalsnes on the northwest coast. The Germans and British had fought a day-long battle at Lillehammer on April 21, and the outgunned British and Norwegians had been forced to retreat northward. Foley's party came under attack by a German fighter plane the next day, and he decided to follow the general movement toward Åndalsnes in an attempt to link up with British forces there.

Foley was present at the meeting when General Ruge handed over command to the British, and Margaret Reid described the scene in her diary, mentioning "the worn general in his shabby uniform . . . and the natty British general [in his] perfect turn-out."

As the embassy party finally approached Åndalsnes they saw, as Reid put it, "a warm glow in the distance, illuminating the snow." She was sure that the town was on fire, but Foley insisted that it was the rising sun. He convinced nobody, for the red glow remained on the horizon — and it seemed unlikely that the sun would rise in the west that day, no matter how confused the world seemed to be.

The town, which they reached at daybreak, was indeed a burning shambles from Luftwaffe bombing. But the Årfarnes ferry was still running, and they managed to cross the fjord to Molde. The charming little town, known for its roses, honeysuckle, and cherry trees, had also been badly hit by the German planes.

Before long, however, they had a welcome sight. A gray leviathan came slowly to the quay — it was the Irish ferry steamer, the *Ulster Prince*, part of the evacuation fleet.

The king and his party had already embarked on the cruiser *Glasgow* and had left Molde for Tromsö far in the north. General Ruge decided to stay and fight his way northward to Narvik — where he had to surrender at last on June 8.

As for Foley, Reid, and their embassy party, they awoke aboard the *Ulster Prince* on May 3 to find themselves in the midst of the British fleet at Scapa Flow, and two days later they were home in London. Shortly afterward, the Norwegian government awarded Frank Foley the Order of St. Olav for his communications feat in keeping Norway in touch with the world during those disastrous days.

SEVENTEEN

Cut-off

ON THE MORNING that Hitler launched his invasion of Denmark
and Norway, April 9, Niels Bohr was asleep on the night ferry from
Oslo. He had dined with King Haakon at the royal palace the night
before. Lise Meitner had just arrived in Copenhagen the night before
the Germans invaded, on a visit to the Bohr Institute. As Meitner later
described it:

> We were all much relieved, as you may imagine, when [Niels] came.
> We had been awakened by the noise of plenty of aeroplanes at about
> a quarter to six in the morning and there was nothing to do but await
> what might happen next. The central post office, the offices of news-
> papers, radio stations and police stations, were occupied almost im-
> mediately, but you saw very few soldiers on the street and they all—
> *mirabile dictu*—were speaking Danish. They did not interfere officially
> with anything as long as I was there. . . . Of course, Niels and Margrethe
> are very unhappy about the events, but he does not have it in view to
> give up his work.

It was the end of April before Bohr was able to contrive a way to
slip Meitner across the Öresund and back to Sweden. The Gestapo,
that model of ruthless efficiency in books and movies, had failed for
nearly a month to pick up a Jewish escapee from the Reich who was
also one of the world's eminent physicists.

Once back in Stockholm, Meitner began to try to reassure worried
friends. Hilde Rosbaud had written from London, "Please tell Paul
that Anka and I are perfectly all right and he must not worry in the
least about us. I am very much longing for him, but on the other
hand, I am terribly worried. Do you think they have enough to eat? . . .

I am so terribly depressed and everything seems hopeless. Do you know where Prof. Goldschmidt has gone? I do hope that he could leave Oslo in time."

Lise wrote back to say that she had heard from Otto Hahn in Germany. Paul had enough to eat, "though they do not have many provisions, as you can imagine," and as for V.M., he was "working in his usual place and was all right so far."

Another friend in England had been worried about the Bohrs in Nazi-occupied Copenhagen, and Meitner cabled MET NIELS AND MAR-GRETHE RECENTLY BOTH WELL BUT UNHAPPY ABOUT EVENTS PLEASE IN-FORM COCKCROFT AND MAUD RAY KENT.

When this message was passed on to Cockcroft, his atomic energy committee was in consternation. What vital news was Meitner trying to convey in this impromptu code? James Chadwick, the discoverer of the neutron, was sure that the message was a warning about German secret work on some sort of deadly ray. Cockcroft, trained in cryptography from doing the *Times* crossword puzzles, perceived an anagram that read "radium taken" and concluded that the Germans had seized Bohr's supply. An amateur code expert was brought in and he divined the ominous signal "Make Ur Day Nt." Because there seemed to be no verifiable solution, the expanded committee christened itself the MAUD Committee in honor of the puzzle that baffled science.

Wilfrid Basil Mann joined the committee not long after and was able to enlighten it. Mann had met Maud Ray in Copenhagen in 1932. She was the Bohr governess and now lived in Kent.

In the meantime, German armies had swept through Holland, Belgium, and northern France. On June 4, the British evacuation of Dunkirk was complete. On June 10, the Reynaud government fled Paris for Bordeaux, and the defeat of France seemed inevitable. Aside from all this, the MAUD Committee's chief worry was the heavy water Jacques Allier had transported from Norway.

The twentieth Earl of Suffolk was also worried about that heavy water, and he had been wiring London about it. The earl was a derring-do character whose cover in the Paris embassy was that of science attaché but whose real assignment was the intelligence service. Now he was in charge of bringing out whatever could be salvaged from the French chaos—industrial diamonds, machine tools, even a personal supply of champagne. Allier was able to advise Lord Suffolk that the heavy water had been moved from the Collège de France in Paris to a prison at Riom in the Auvergne. They agreed that it should be taken to Bordeaux immediately and embarked for England.

Allier drove his Simca to Riom at top speed and appeared at the prison gates, demanding the heavy water. The warden refused. Allier drew his revolver. The warden saw the point and agreed to release the imprisoned canisters.

At this point, Foley decided to direct the evacuation himself; after all he was getting adept at evacuation from invaded countries. Once he arrived at the French port, he began to organize the hasty exodus of the cargo: assorted French atomic scientists, industrial diamonds, and heavy water. Foley provided the quiet guidance and Suffolk the piracy. Lew Kowarski, one of the scientists who played bodyguard to the heavy water, has left an account:

> We were brought on board the ship *Broompark*, a Scottish collier which had been commandeered by Lord Suffolk. We arrived there, I think, soon after midnight, the night of June 17th to 18th. All sorts of officials of the Ministry of Armament — fairly high rank, shall we say, colonels or so — were carrying not only the cans of heavy water but also our household belongings. They knew enough about our connection with this new force of nature and they obviously wished that we should continue in England . . . and that would be a valuable French contribution to the Allied effort. . . .
>
> In the morning, things got organized. There was a captain of the ship, but Lord Suffolk was obviously in charge — a very picturesque personality looking like an unkempt pirate. . . . He was dressed in rags, with a beard. . . . He was limping around the ship with two secretaries, one blonde and one brunette.

The *Broompark* left the estuary on the nineteenth and arrived in Falmouth on June 21. Most of the passengers were seasick, but not Lord Suffolk and his two secretaries, who were feeling just fine. They had brought aboard an ample supply of champagne, which, the noble lord explained, was absolutely the best remedy for *mal-de-mer*.

Frank Foley was not aboard to share a glass. He had stayed to have another look around as the German advance motorized units headed for Bordeaux. They arrived soon enough, and, barely managing to evade the Gestapo, Foley escaped to the safety of the Spanish Pyrenees. On Sunday, June 23, when Adolf Hitler went sightseeing in Paris, Frank Foley was back in London.

EIGHTEEN

Theodor

THURSDAY, MARCH 6, in the second year of the war was an "exacting day" for Winston Churchill. His foreign secretary, Anthony Eden, had just arrived in Athens, and Churchill wired him that WE MUST LIBERATE GREEKS FROM FEELING BOUND TO REJECT A GERMAN ULTIMATUM. The reply from Athens was that there was no question of that, for the Greeks HAVE DECIDED TO FIGHT GERMANY ALONE IF NECESSARY. THE QUESTION IS WHETHER WE HELP OR ABANDON THEM. Churchill was losing his own battle to preserve his forces for engagement elsewhere. Staying in Greece, he feared, would bring about "another Norway, Dunkirk, and Dakar rolled into one." At lunchtime, the prime minister harangued his chiefs of staff over Greece and the question of permitting American naval bases in the West Indies. The final straw that day was the calling of a strike at John Brown's Shipyards at Clydeside.

"Very anxious decisions have been in the air, making the P.M. impatient, the atmosphere electric and the pace tremendous," recorded his private secretary, John Colville. At the end of that day, Churchill relaxed by drafting his directive on "The Battle of the Atlantic," the objective of which was to loosen the German stranglehold on Britain's food supplies and her connection with the United States. The prime minister did not realize that his directive would also reactivate the Griffin for the next four years.

The next morning, Sir Stewart Menzies, C, showed up at 10 Downing Street with Queen Victoria's battered dispatch box. Churchill took great delight in reading the intercepts of German coded wireless traffic. The reading of these Enigma-coded messages was the single pleasure the prime minister looked forward to every morning throughout the war. After reading the intercepts that Friday, Churchill handed C his battle of the Atlantic directive of the evening before and requested Menzies to put the resources of the SIS behind it. This day did not pass without more satisfaction for the prime minister. HMS *Wolverine* sank Commander Gunther Prien's U-47, the submarine that had sunk the *Royal Oak*.

But there were other U-boats creating havoc with British ships, and German battle cruisers were having a field day. The *Scheer*, the *Hipper*, the *Gneisenau*, and the *Scharnhorst* had complete freedom of the seas. Soon, the mighty *Bismarck* and her consort, the *Tirpitz*, would come into service. As Churchill brooded, "In no way could Hitler have used his two giant battleships more effectively than by keeping them in full readiness in the Baltic and allow rumours of an impending sortie to leak out from time to time." The task given to C was: Help the Royal Navy sink the *Bismarck* and the *Tirpitz*!

C found the ideal officer in Naval Intelligence and arranged to have him transferred to the Norwegian Section of the Secret Intelligence Service, which was then headed by Commander J. B. Newill, Frank Foley's colleague in Oslo. Newill was an old Norwegian hand, well qualified but not so devious and clever as the man who came to work for him on March 15.

He was Lieutenant Commander Eric Welsh, whose Most Secret SIS dossier records that

> together with Major Nagell of the Norwegian "E" Office, he established a joint Anglo-Norwegian Intelligence Service on Norway, the primary object of which was to be an attempt to hold control over the movements of the major units of the German battle-fleet on the Norwegian coast.

The SIS evaluated Eric Welsh as "a little man with a big head and an excellent operational organizer." This "little man" was a deceiver, a secret agent, and a British mole almost all of his life, which began on August 31, 1897, at Newbiggen by the Sea. As a child, one of eight boys, Eric looked out on the North Sea toward Norway — and never ceased looking in that direction. He joined the navy as an ordinary seaman in World War I and was commissioned at sea for gallantry in action.

Someone noticed Eric Welsh, and the young officer did not return to sea. He was taken into Naval Intelligence and cultivated as a long-term mole, something usually considered to be more in the tradition of the Soviet KGB than of the gentlemanly British Secret Service.

A "legend," that is, full-length cover story, had to be created. Welsh began to be recorded as having taken a degree in chemistry from the University of Durham. Yet a careful search of the university's records shows that Welsh was never even enrolled there. Armed with his fictitious degree, and helped by someone with influence in the Holzapfel firm, Welsh was placed with that paint company in Felling-Newcastle.

After steel hulls were introduced on ships, about 1840, corrosion and fouling by barnacles became a problem and an opportunity for enterprising chemists. Max Holzapfel, a young emigrant from Germany, and two other chemists started a plant to manufacture a compound that protected ships' hulls. The firm prospered and formed subsidiaries in Sebastapol, Odessa, Genoa, New York, Hamburg, Nagasaki, and elsewhere — all before World War I. Because the firm delivered its product not only to civil shipping but to navies, the Holzapfel order books were an accurate index of what was happening throughout the world. The big German firm of Blohm and Voss in Hamburg was one of their clients. The naval construction at Blohm and Voss was considered so critical by the British that they had their master spy Sidney Reilly report on its operations through an organization in St. Petersburg. And because ships had to be protected against barnacles, the British could check on German naval vessels by watching the various international operations of Holzapfel.

With the coming of the First World War, Max Holzapfel, although a naturalized British citizen, thought it prudent to move to Holland, which remained neutral throughout the war. And by 1918 there was at least one British spy on the premises of Holzapfel. That man was Eric Welsh. When the war ended, British Naval Intelligence shifted priorities. Scandinavia, neutral in the past war, would not, the British thought, be neglected by a resurgent Germany in the next one. There should be someone there, watching. That someone, Eric Welsh, debarked at Bergen on June 21, 1919. His mission was to cultivate academic and professional people in Scandinavian universities and industries and to report, especially, on German activities in those circles. In Bergen, of course, he was to keep an eye on ships that would be using Max Holzapfel's antifouling compounds.

By this time, the Holzapfel firm had been renamed International Paints and Compositions Ltd., which was the forerunner of today's global International Paints Ltd. But even then, it was a worldwide operation, and a major facility was International Farvefabrik A.S. in Bergen. Welsh was warmly received by the founder of the Norwegian branch, Lars Pihl-Johannessen, who helped him to find a house at Nubbekken 15. Welsh had been a good on-the-job learner at Holzapfel, and by the time he started working in Bergen, he was a reasonably adept chemist. He soon rose to be technical manager of the firm.

Conrad Pihl-Johannessen, the son of the founder and a friend of Eric Welsh, recalled in a letter that "he cooperated very well with my father, was a hard worker, and was given a lot of responsibility. He was put in charge of buying raw materials and running the technical side of all production. He was tough, very demanding with workers and staff, but fair and respected by most."

Welsh also thrived in the social milieu of Bergen. A hard-drinking man, he enjoyed the parties, particularly during winters. One evening a friend, Christopher Brun, introduced Welsh to his enchanting cousin Johanne Brun Svendsen. Johanne was distantly related to the composer Edvard Grieg and was a second cousin of the contemporary heroic poet Nordahl Grieg. Whether Eric Welsh was really in love with Johanne, or whether he thought it politic to enter into an alliance with a Norwegian family of such distinction, is uncertain. But he proposed to Johanne, married, and sired two daughters and one son. For an Englishman, he became as Norwegian as one could become.

Because he was technical manager and in charge of raw materials for the paint company, Welsh soon became acquainted with Victor Goldschmidt, who, besides being the ultimate authority on raw materials, held a number of paint patents. One of Goldschmidt's closest collaborators was Gulbrand Lunde, who years later would become a collaborator of a different sort.

Then Gulbrand Lunde met Eric Welsh. It happened shortly after the year of turmoil, 1929, when Goldschmidt quarreled with Ellen Gleditsch over the university appointment. Lunde got a job with the Norwegian Canning Industry in Stavanger, where a handsome new research laboratory was built for him. The laboratory needed special chemical-resistant floor tile and wall paint. By this time, Eric Welsh was the outstanding authority on such materials. The spy and the future Nazi collaborator came together.

They began to collaborate on other problems. Fish was canned in olive oil, and the combination of olive oil and fish oils corroded the cans, creating odors and destroying vitamins. Lunde, who was becoming a world authority on vitamins, thought that if the interior of a fish can were coated with a special lacquer, the fish would remain edible and the vitamins would survive. Eric Welsh helped Lunde develop basic lacquers needed to solve the problem. In fact, Welsh delivered several papers on the process, even as far away as Los Angeles.

It seems highly likely that through his connections with Victor Goldschmidt and Gulbrand Lunde, and because of his overall interest in European technology, Eric Welsh would have met Paul Rosbaud before the Second World War, but that cannot be documented. It is also possible that Rosbaud furnished Welsh with information at that time, although this also cannot be established. There were many matters that interested Welsh in Berlin, among them its night life, and he went there incognito sometimes. Once, he sent his family a passport photograph from Berlin, with his hair parted in an unusual way. On the back was the inscription "How do you like Mr. Smith?"

Eric Welsh's floor-tile expertise drew him into the technology that would occupy his time in later years. Soon after heavy hydrogen was discovered in the rare form of heavy water, Norsk Hydro began to produce small quantities of the substance for atomic research. A very caustic chemical was associated with the process, and Eric Welsh was asked by the plant's chief engineer, Jomar Brun, to come to Vemork to help solve the problem. He was able to do so by developing and producing at Bergen a special floor tile for the high concentration heavy-water facility. Welsh became intimately familiar with heavy water, its possible uses, and, of course, the layout of the production plant where it was produced. Brun and Welsh formed a friendship that would have important consequences during the war.

That was only one of the secrets that Welsh did not divulge to his colleagues in the SIS. Anyone, including his closest associates, who felt that Welsh was ever completely candid was very much mistaken.

The battle for heavy water would come soon enough. Conrad Pihl-

Johannessen remembered that at "six o'clock in the morning, April 9, 1940 the Germans had just landed in Bergen. Shooting was going on and I drove to the factory where I met an exceptionally nervous Mr. Welsh picking up some mail or whatever and asking me immediately to drive him south and eastward out of Bergen. I dropped him in the hands of some Norwegian officers at area outside Bergen, and never saw or heard anything of him until after the war."

The memory is slightly inexact, for Welsh first was dropped off at the British consulate with the "mail or whatever." Ridding himself of the sensitive papers was his first priority; his family was second. He was then taken by Pihl-Johannessen, at the request of Norwegian Commander Just Olsen, to Norheimsund, where he arranged for the safety of two British officers and their families. Afterward, Welsh reported to the Norwegian government that he had returned at eleven A.M. to Bergen to collect his own family. He was lying about his gallantry, for someone else had come to fetch his family. Welsh was afraid of capture. One of his daughters recalled in a letter:

> At about five in the morning there was a lot of aeroplanes over Bergen. Father was very nervous and he thought they were English planes until we saw the swastikas on the wings. Father had been listening to the wireless a great deal during the preceding days. . . . Father left to go to the British consulate. . . . Later that morning a young man came with Father's car—a Dodge, it was, and quite new—and told us to come and meet Father outside of Bergen at Lars Phil-Johannessen's house. . . . Mother threw some things together and we got into the car. . . . We were all frightened. There were German soldiers all over but they did not try to stop us. . . . There was a German roadblock. The young man swung into a gas station and turned around and took another route out to Lars Phil's house. Father was there and he took over the car and we drove to Norheimsund, expecting to meet Germans everywhere. But we didn't.

On April 21, Eric Welsh left his family in occupied Norway. He wanted to take them to England, but Johanne refused to go. Welsh was not particularly saddened by her decision. He was a pragmatic man, and Johanne just might be more useful to him in Norway than in England. And, indeed, she became so. The official SIS history laconically notes that "he even left his wife and family in Norway with false papers. They became an asset to SIS."

The "asset" survived harrowing German attacks during the following days while Eric traveled toward the Norwegian Dunkirk, Åndalsnes and Molde, where he met up with Frank Foley and Margaret Reid. A navy man, Welsh managed to get a berth on a submarine, which left Åndalsnes on the twenty-ninth, the day before the bombed-out port was permanently abandoned by the British. On the first of May, he reported for further duty at three separate offices in London, the Admiralty, the War Office, and the Foreign Office. All were eager to hear what he had to report. On the basis of that, he was assigned to a "deep cover" operation.

On the fifth of May, Eric Welsh dropped out of sight for nine months. It is the only period during which his movements cannot be traced. He said afterward that he had been posted as "a scientific worker," but did not explain where or why. Nobody believed that. He suddenly surfaced again in His Majesty's Minesweeping Flotilla at Newcastle, the city where his spying career began with the Holzapfel firm. Once again, he was looking eastward to Norway, whence German aircraft and U-boats were menacing north coast shipping. The battle of the Atlantic became more pressing. A British naval base was being built on the western coast of Iceland, at Hvalfjord, to protect shipping passing through the Denmark strait off Greenland. An intelligence liaison man was needed, and Welsh seemed to be the right man for the post. He arrived aboard HMS *Baldur*, but in less than two weeks' time, C called him back to London. The assignment: to set up an intelligence-reporting system on the German battleships hugging the coast of Norway. Welsh's network soon developed into much more than that. And an early order of business for him was using the network to re-establish contact with Paul Rosbaud. Welsh adopted the operational code name Theodor, and under that name he became the new spymaster of the Griffin.

NINETEEN

The Forest of the Griffin

NINETEEN FORTY was the year of silence. Lise Meitner was the communications link between Paul and Hilde Rosbaud, but Paul had no way of communicating directly with London. He listened for hours every evening to his powerful Philips 990X receiver, but no messages were broadcast to him. The prefix code number for Germany was twelve. Foley's code number had been 12001, and Rosbaud's number was something like 120XX, so Rosbaud would have recognized any special messages directed to him. Such messages to any agent in Germany or occupied Europe were rare, however, at this stage of the war.

Frank Foley and his wife, Katherine, were happy to be back in England. Moreover, Frank was given one of the more exciting assignments in the SIS. An SIS colleague has said, "Shortly after his return, Foley joined Section V, where his exceptional knowledge of the workings of and personalities in the Abwehr, acquired during fifteen years' service in Berlin, made him a tower of strength in an expanding section."

Kim Philby, the Soviet mole in Section V, described its work as follows:

> The counterespionage section of SIS, known as Section V, and MI5 [the British equivalent of the FBI] were in fact two sides of the same medal. The primary function of Section V was to obtain advance information of espionage operations mounted against British territory from foreign soil. It was clear that effective advance warning from Section V would go far to help MI5 in its task of safeguarding British security.

Thus, Frank Foley was preoccupied with matters far removed from technical intelligence. And the Oslo Report was still only an object of amusement for Reginald Jones, because the SIS had no collection capability for technical intelligence. That is not to say that the Griffin was not gathering information. When Eric Welsh was given the task of garnering technical intelligence, Rosbaud was prepared with old information and was collecting new.

Paul Rosbaud had been ready for high-level British contact for a year and a half. He had no way of knowing whether the Oslo Report was useful, no way of knowing who would read his reports and whether they were competent to analyze them. Competence was not lacking; the extraordinary R. V. Jones had joined the SIS just before the Oslo Report was received. But an operational link to Rosbaud was still lacking. Welsh would forge that link.

Rosbaud, confident that any military information would in time be useful, was not idle. It may be that he found a channel to London before Welsh came on board, but as far as is known, London received nothing of substance from Rosbaud between the time of the Oslo Report and the autumn of 1941. Some time after Eric Welsh joined the SIS and before August 1941, the communications link was re-established. Lise Meitner's letters to Paul and Hilde never mentioned last names, and she did not forward the actual letters she received. Then, on August 24, 1941, Paul joyously wrote to Hans, "As to myself I can report that—touch wood!—I have received very favorable news and very dear and touching letters."

To establish himself as the credible and reliable taskmaster, Eric Welsh had transmitted to Paul letters from his family and, with them, information on a Norwegian student, Sverre Bergh, who would be contacting him. Touch wood, the Griffin was reactivated!

In anticipation of the contact, Rosbaud decided to augment the Peenemünde information from the Oslo Report. In his opinion, what was being done there posed the most important new technical threat. As always, some of what Rosbaud learned came from the publishing world. But he had a better link, an old school tie. After the outbreak of war, Wernher von Braun got the idea of inviting "the best brains in the country" to come to Peenemünde. He proposed to enlist them in what he considered the most challenging technical problem of the time. So they came, all of the best technical and engineering brains of Germany, to what jocularly became known as *Der Tag der Weisheit*, the day of wisdom.

It became the day of wisdom for Paul Rosbaud, who was not there but had many friends who were. Von Braun might just as well have invited Rosbaud personally. As it was, von Braun performed a great service for British intelligence by organizing Der Tag.

Actually, it was three days: September 28 to 30, 1939. Dr. Hermann Kurzweg, who had come to Peenemünde in 1937 and was the deputy in charge of wind-tunnel experiments, described Der Tag in a recent conversation. According to his account, von Braun welcomed the scientists, as did the commanding officer, Major General Walter Dornberger. A number of the professors present were already contract researchers to Peenemünde, and many more were enlisted before the end of Der Tag. Although the weapons they developed would kill and maim thousands in Britain five years hence, it may well be that Der Tag saved the Allies from even greater catastrophe. In Britain, engineers of Imperial Chemical Industries (ICI) had been working side by side with the physicists during their MAUD Committee considerations on tapping the energy from the nucleus of the atom. One of the reasons the Germans never achieved the atomic bomb was that very few engineers with applied industrial experience were called in to ask the hard questions. The best were working for Peenemünde or for its many contractors. Keeping them occupied was another service that Wernher von Braun unwittingly performed for the Allies.

One of the Peenemünde staff who spoke was Dr. Eric Steinhoff, who had come to Peenemünde that spring. He was a capable man who would eventually head the Department of Instruments, Guidance, and Measurement. Steinhoff was a plane and glider pilot, a graduate of Darmstadt, Paul's alma mater. Steinhoff's favorite professor at Darmstadt was A. Walther of the mathematics department, and of course Walther was also present at Der Tag. Not surprisingly, he, too, was a friend of Paul Rosbaud; whenever Rosbaud returned to Darmstadt, he would drop in at Fichtestrasse 21 to chat. At the gathering were other Darmstadt professors whom Rosbaud knew, including Carl Wagner from the physical chemistry department and a man named Thum from the materials testing laboratory. And there were acquaintances from other technische Hochschulen throughout Germany. None of the professors was an active collaborator in Rosbaud's spying. They were innocent "resources" whom he had expertly tapped ever since the Oslo Report was sent. And when the opportunity to report to Britain was about to be renewed, Paul decided to see something of Peenemünde himself.

Paul was welcome in many homes throughout Germany. Before Der Tag, he had hinted to a certain professor that he would like to spend a week or so, that August of 1941, in the medieval town of Greifswald, close to the beaches of the Baltic. Professor Gerhard Jander of the university and his wife, Johanna, were only too happy to invite him. Their daughter Anneliese had died a few years earlier, and Paul could have her room.

The river Ryck empties into the Baltic near Greifswald. Even though it was wartime, the city was celebrating its five-hundredth anniversary, which was another excuse for Rosbaud to visit. Children of Greifswald are told a tale of early times, when a small village stood where their town stands now. A deep, dark forest surrounded the village, and in the forest dwelled the griffin, a fearsome beast with the body of a lion and the head and wings of an eagle. One day, the beast seized a child from the village, brought it into the forest, and devoured it. The griffin demanded a sacrifice once in a while—that was to be expected—but on that particular day, the griffin returned to seize another child and fed it to his hungry brood.

That was too much. The furious villagers pulled down the beast's nest, killed the brood, and drove the beast eastward to the island of Usedom, where, in an even deeper and darker forest, the beast took refuge. He was no more welcome there, and a brave cowherd set fire to the forest, leaving nothing but ashes. The beast did not die, but he did vanish. So today, the children of Greifswald are comforted when they read in their books that "since then, the griffin has nevermore been seen."

But in mid August 1941 a griffin did return to Greifswald, not to be seen but to see. Paul Rosbaud wanted to have a look at the place where the forest once grew on the island of Usedom. The name of the place was Peenemünde.

It was a good time to be away from Berlin. On June 22, Hitler had turned against his Soviet ally and launched Operation Barbarossa. Paul's military sources were too preoccupied to speak with him. On the night of August 12, the RAF carried out its first large-scale raid on Berlin, which unroofed three hundred houses in the Waltraud-strasse near Paul, although his house suffered no damage at that time.

As the house guest of Gerhard Jander, Paul, as often before, was accepting the hospitality of a Nazi. In 1933, Otto Hahn had been asked to assume the directorship of the Kaiser Wilhelm Institute of Physical Chemistry. He accepted, but the authorities pushed him aside in favor of Jander, who was a Nazi Party member; Hahn was not.

Professor Jander, however, was a man of considerable academic accomplishment. Before he went to Berlin, he had been a professor at Göttingen, and two years after he had displaced Hahn, he had come to Greifswald. In that same year, 1935, a young native of that region began to look for an isolated place to conduct his rocket experiments in secret. The site Wernher von Braun selected was at the tip of the island of Usedom.

In the bay, between Greifswald and Peenemünde, was a barren islet called Greifswalder Oie, about a thousand yards long and three hundred yards wide. In 1929, Johannes Winkler had tested the earliest liquid-fueled rockets on the Oie. In 1937, von Braun began to test there his A-3 rocket, the forerunner of the V 2. By the time of Paul's visit, the vapor trails from the test rockets were commonplace items of chat in Greifswald, in Ihlenfeld's restaurant, and in Bartens' wine rooms. A casual visitor to the ruins of Hilda, the Cisterian monastery at the mouth of the Ryck, could himself view the vapor trails on a testing day. The forest of the griffin was a good vantage point for a spy.

The activities at Greifswalder Oie and Peenemünde were a part of Germany's evasion of the Treaty of Versailles. Prohibited from maintaining more than a certain number of conventional weapons, the army had sought weapons that were never imagined by the treaty makers. In 1923, Adolf Hitler wrote in *Mein Kampf*, "We will have arms again!" but even before he grabbed power, the German military were rearming. In 1929, Professor Karl Emil Becker, a colonel and chief of the Army Weapons Board, suggested to the minister of national defense that rocket research could provide Germany with weapons that would not violate treaty obligations. By 1932, a secret rocket-development and -testing station had been established at the artillery proving ground of Kummersdorf West, seventeen miles south of Berlin, under the direction of Colonel Walter Dornberger. Its first civilian employee was Wernher von Braun. All rocket researchers elsewhere were given three choices: quit work and turn over their patents, be put in jail, or work on the government rocket program (if they were good enough). Most chose the last course. The scope of work expanded, and in 1936 the army took over the area on the island of Usedom known as Peenemünde East. It was there that the V-2 terror rocket was developed and tested. The air force took over Peenemünde West and developed the V-1 pilotless winged rocket, predecessor of the rockets directed at Britain in World War II and precursor of today's cruise missiles. The Oslo Report had described a remote-controlled glider-type weapon, the FZ-21 (later termed Hs293), which could be directed against ships. It was developed at Peenemünde West. Now, Rosbaud had become interested in what was happening at Peenemünde East, the rocket-development site.

The information that Paul gathered in Greifswald included a general description of Greifswalder Oie and Peenemünde. He noted the frequency of tests and gained a fragmentary description of the V-2 rocket and some of its components. On his return to Berlin, he first penned a note to his brother Hans in Strasbourg: "Came back yesterday [August 23] from a ten-day vacation, which I spent as [Jander's] guest on the Baltic Sea." The second item of business was his Peenemünde report, which would be picked up by Eric Welsh's contact in Berlin a month later.

TWENTY

Sigurd

WITH GOOD REASON, Eric Welsh fancied himself the ultimate spy. After all, for two decades he had mastered the craft of a mole and was now, in 1941, running his own vast Norwegian network. The short, owlish, and slightly rotund Welsh also fancied himself a ladies' man. If he was close-mouthed about his actual deeds, he was garrulous about his romantic conquests, which, by and large, were a tribute to his vivid imagination. He was always trying.

One morning, shortly after Eric Welsh had taken over the SIS Norwegian Section, he was waiting in the outer office of Stewart Menzies, head of the SIS. Welsh made a nuisance of himself by commenting on the typing of Menzies's secretary—a form of his flirting. As he later told the story to Rudolf Peierls, Welsh said, "You have misspelled this name, and that man is not at X, but at Y." At that point Menzies appeared and asked how Welsh knew so much about these people. Welsh answered, "It's my hobby; I have always been interested in scientists and their work." Welsh went on to tell Peierls that he was immediately chosen to work on atomic energy intelligence. Welsh did so with great ability.

Although at that particular moment C was mainly concerned with atomic bombs, Welsh's charter included the operational aspects of all scientific and technical intelligence, as defined at that time by the Oslo Report. His assignment was to parallel and support the analytical efforts of R. V. Jones. But Welsh's task, being operational, was covert, and the "customers" were to know as little as possible about the sources. Jones did not learn of Welsh's principal source, Paul Rosbaud, until after the war.

It is easy to understand why, at this particular moment, Menzies was so interested in atomic intelligence. The MAUD Committee was drafting its final report, recommending a full-scale push toward the atomic bomb. The initial impetus for the report had been a memorandum by Otto Frisch and Rudolf Peierls, showing that it was possible to make a bomb by using a reasonably small amount of fissionable material. The Germans never achieved the understanding that Frisch and Peierls did, and that, basically, is why they never created the bomb.

While the MAUD report was being drafted and Eric Welsh failed to pick up Menzies's secretary but got himself an additional job, another German refugee scientist was given full clearance to work with Peierls on the atomic bomb. His name was Klaus Fuchs.

As a physics student in Berlin, Fuchs joined the Communist Party in 1932, and on October 3, 1933, the rector of Berlin University addressed this letter to the student's address at Holtenauerstrasse 82: "You are expelled from the university because you are engaged in Communist activities." Fuchs went to Birmingham to work with Max Born, who wrote that Fuchs "never concealed that he was a convinced Communist." Fuchs was interned as an enemy alien on the Isle of Man when war broke out, was transferred to a camp in Canada, and was then cleared by British MI5 to work on one of the most sensitive projects of the war.

Eric Welsh had in mind an even more sensitive project for him. Peierls had made a suggestion for monitoring the Germans: he would review the German scientific literature for clues. Peierls later wrote, "I suggested keeping an eye on the movements of certain people who would probably be involved in any atomic-energy work, and checking whether they were away from their normal places of work, travelled to unlikely places, and so on." He also consulted Fuchs.

One of the names on Peierls's list was that of Werner Heisenberg, then politicking to get his own atomic energy program in Germany. MI5 (the British equivalent of the FBI) had been just as diligent in following Heisenberg as it had been in investigating Fuchs. The reply came back: "It is very interesting that you should mention this name [Heisenberg], because he visited Cambridge shortly before the war, and we have no record that he ever left the country." Years afterward Peierls said, "I was shocked by this reaction and reflected that if this was a fair sample of British intelligence, the outlook seemed grim."

The outlook, in fact, was even grimmer than Peierls suspected. In

1950, Klaus Fuchs confessed, "When I learned about the purpose of the work [atomic bomb], I decided to inform Russia and establish contact through another member of the Communist Party. Since that time I have had continuous contact with persons unknown to me, and whatever information I gave was communicated to the Russian authorities." One of the "persons unknown" was Simon Kremer, who had replaced Sammy Cahan, the nemesis of Peter Kapitza, at the Russian embassy in London.

What the Germans were doing was of no less interest to the Russians than to the British. Thus, it is more than likely that the wages paid for the survey task to Rudolf Peierls and Klaus Fuchs also supported the intelligence objectives of the Soviets. This may not have been the only instance where Welsh's intelligence found its way to the Soviet Union.

Peierls was shocked by the apparent state of British intelligence about the German atomic project, but that situation was about to be corrected.

There was a source of technical information in the Reich. He was the author of the Oslo Report, known to Frank Foley and to Margaret Reid. Foley might have been given Welsh's position had not Deputy Führer Rudolf Hess decided to parachute into the Scottish Highlands on May 10, 1941, for reasons that are still obscure. Winston Churchill told C that he wanted his best expert on Nazi officialdom to interrogate Hess. That man was Frank Foley. At the time Welsh was appointed director of scientific operations for SIS, Foley was occupied with Hess in a high-security camp forty miles outside London. Whether or not he was aware of Welsh's new post, Foley would not have had the time to chat with him.

Welsh did not need Foley to learn about the Oslo Report, because when Foley went away on his new assignment, Welsh inherited Margaret Reid. He was astounded by the saga of the Oslo Report. If he did not personally know Paul Rosbaud, he certainly knew of him, through Gulbrand Lunde and other acquaintances. The author of the Oslo Report was already an agent in place; not only that, there could be none better. Only one problem remained: how to tap the Rosbaud resource.

At the outbreak of the war, there were several hundred Norwegian students studying at various technische Hochschulen. A number returned to their homeland as soon as possible before Norway was invaded in April 1940. Others stayed to complete their degrees. Some were sympathetic to the Nazi cause, and it was to cultivate them that the German government adopted very liberal policies with respect to the movements of Norwegian students. A few new students came to Germany after April 1940 to take advantage of the excellent academic facilities. And several students took full benefit of their freedom, not to acquaint themselves with the cultural splendor of Nazism but to undermine it. One of those students was Sverre Bergh.

The Technische Hochschule of Dresden was one of the best. It was situated south of the main railway terminal on the left bank of the Elbe in a section that did not reflect the charm and elegance of a city long famed for its fine buildings and art treasures. But a raucous student life made up in pleasure what the suburb lacked. Sverre Bergh came to Dresden in August 1940 to enjoy the good life, to acquire an education, and to do what he could to harm the Reich.

The twenty-year-old student was born in Tönsberg, the oldest town in Norway, due south of Oslo on the Oslofjord. In the fourteenth century it had been the most important town in Norway, famous for its seafarers. Now, it was an anchorage for seal-hunting vessels.

Theo Findahl, Berlin correspondent for Oslo's *Aftenposten*, was an uncle of Sverre Bergh's. Findahl had devised a telephone code with his editor in Oslo. They spoke frequently, and Findahl managed to impart a fair amount of sensitive political information to this editor, who was linked to the intelligence operations of the Norwegian government-in-exile in Stockholm. It was understandable that Findahl's nephew should want to engage in the same type of activity.

Bergh had enrolled at Dresden in structural engineering, and if he displayed an interest in various types of structures throughout Germany, that, of course, was only in connection with his studies. He heard from a Swedish friend that there were interesting structures at Schweinfurt, some distance away to the southwest. Schweinfurt was all the more interesting because it was, for its size, the best-defended area in all of Germany.

It should have been, for its three factories produced half of Germany's supply of ball bearings, vital to aircraft and other military equipment. The industry was old, having been founded in 1906, but it had been supplemented by two factories of the Swedish-owned Vereinigte Kuggellagerfabriken A.G. The VKF factory number one was in a residential district at the southern edge of town. Its buildings and the antiaircraft emplacements guarding it could be observed at leisure from the garden of any of several nearby inns. Never one to spurn the pleasures of an inn, Sverre Bergh took his time watching the activities and studying the layout of VKF-1.

He brought the information back to Oslo during the summer break of 1941 and contacted a close friend of his uncle's, Arvid Brodersen, a researcher in sociology at the University of Oslo. Brodersen's position in the Norwegian Resistance was unique. He was the contact man with Lieutenant Colonel Theodor Steltzer, an officer in the transport command of the Wehrmacht in Oslo. Steltzer gave Brodersen information on the internal affairs of German organizations in Oslo, particularly advance warning of actions to be taken against students and professors at the university. Because of his special position as Steltzer's confidant, a position that the Norwegian underground did not wish to see weakened, Brodersen generally refrained from other Resistance activities, which might have compromised him. He therefore referred Sverre Bergh to Øivind Strømnes, the head of the newly established XU underground intelligence group in southern Norway, which was master of itself but effectively responded to the priorities of Eric Welsh.

Strømnes, code-named Øle, remained Bergh's Norwegian taskmaster for the remainder of the war. Aided by his charming bride, Anne-Sofie, Øivind Strømnes created and directed the most efficient underground intelligence organization to serve the Allied cause. The Americans never knew its name. In 1943, the chief of U.S. Army Intelligence, Major General George V. Strong, sent an officer to the SIS to obtain its assessment of the various underground intelligence organizations. The officer reported: "The Norwegians have one of the best intelligence systems operating on the continent. The British have been willing to cooperate more with the Norwegians than with any of the other governments-in-exile. . . . The Norwegian intelligence is without a doubt furnishing the British and American headquarters with the most complete and most accurate intelligence of any occupied country." That was an anonymous tribute to the Strømnes couple, Brynulf Ottar, and many others in XU, who after the war accepted no decorations for their services.

The XU group was certainly the most organized and productive intelligence organization to operate in World War II. Brynulf Ottar, who had heard from Odd Hassel the details of how the Oslo Report was delivered to the British legation, and who was a founder of XU, later wrote:

> The XU was organized shortly after the fighting ended in 1940. The initiative was taken by Mr. Arvid Storsveen, a civil engineer from the technical school in Trondheim. . . . He and my friend from the University of Oslo, Ivan Th. Rosenqvist . . . were both sergeants in the engineer corps. When the fighting in southern Norway ended, Ivan went to northern Norway and continued fighting there until the end. Arvid went to Stockholm and made arrangements with the Norwegian military attaché to establish an intelligence service in Norway. Back in Oslo he managed, in cooperation with senior officers and others who had started to plan a secret military organization (MILORG), to establish an intelligence service in the Oslo area. A courier service between Oslo and Stockholm was set up in cooperation with Ivan, who had returned from the fighting in northern Norway, and some of his comrades in arms.

MILORG, from *Militaerorganisasjonen*, military organization, was just that, the means through which the Norwegian government-in-exile carried on its battle against the Nazis under the British High Command and, later, under the Allied Supreme Command. (It had begun as an independent organization.) MILORG's intelligence arm initially provided some useful information on German installations, but the group was not well organized. When Norway capitulated, General Ruge had appealed, "Wait, trust, and be prepared!" By the beginning of the new year, 1941, Norwegians had waited enough and reorganized their intelligence activities into highly efficient operations.

Sverre Bergh's information on Schweinfurt reached Welsh in London. He was impressed with its detail and the daring of the student from Dresden. Welsh needed a reliable contact with the Griffin, and Sverre Bergh seemed just the man. The overall XU effort was controlled by Welsh through the exiled government's military attaché and director of intelligence, Alfred R. Roscher Lund, who worked out of Stockholm. Roscher Lund was hard-drinking and hard-driving, and Eric Welsh, being the same, considered him essential. Walter Ettinghausen, who was working at decoding German naval signals with F. H. Hinsley, later became Walter Eytan and an Israeli ambassador. He once jested that "Roscher Lund would like nothing better, I believe, than to be commander-in-chief of the Haganah."

Roscher Lund himself had obtained his degree from the Dresden

Technische Hochschule in 1937. He was helping Welsh in setting up the wireless stations, which were reporting on the German fleet. It was natural that Roscher Lund would attempt to recruit agents in Germany at his alma mater. And several of those students would be "running" messages for the only agent in place Britain had in Germany — Paul Rosbaud. Already, one of Roscher Lund's classmates at Dresden, Einar Borch, was working for him. But Borch, the scion of a rich landowner from Jevnaker, was aging, a perpetual student. He had first enrolled in chemistry at Dresden in 1929 and was still there, lounging around, sometimes attending classes but often not. Borch was too well known, too conspicuous. He was not the ideal intermediary between Welsh and Rosbaud. But it was probably Borch who brought Hilde's and Angela's letters to Paul and reactivated the Griffin.

Roscher Lund, at this point, was a crucial element in establishing the links. But he was being reassigned to London by the Norwegian government. Welsh panicked and went to C, informing him that the transfer of Roscher Lund would threaten the collection of vital technical information from a citizen of the Reich who had already demonstrated his value and dedication to the defeat of Hitler. Menzies forthwith took the problem to Winston Churchill. Just one week earlier, Churchill had met with his chiefs of staff, who urged "that no time, labour, materials or money should be spared in pushing forward the development of this project [the atomic bomb]." Churchill feared that Hitler's chiefs of staff would be giving him similar advice, and the prime minister wanted to know about that.

From number 10 Downing Street, a message was dispatched that very Wednesday, September 10, 1941, to the prime minister of Norway and his foreign minister:

I shall be much obliged if your Excellency and Mr. [Trygve] Lie will help me in a matter to which I have been giving my personal attention.

I am told that it is the intention of the Norwegian Government to withdraw from Stockholm their Military Attaché, Captain Roscher Lund. This officer has been of great service to the British Intelligence organization in Sweden, and his presence there is of special value to His Majesty's Government, and to the Allied cause as a whole.

I realize that the case presents difficulties. Nevertheless, since this is a question which affects not only the Norwegian Government, but the general war effort, I sincerely hope that your excellency and your colleagues may feel able to reverse the decision which has been taken. It is·a matter to which I attach great importance.

Yours sincerely,
Winston S. Churchill

The decision was reversed that afternoon.

Sverre Bergh's specific assignment from Welsh, via Roscher Lund and Welsh's man John Whistondale, was "to assist Paul Rosbaud in every way, to collect information from him, and transmit to Welsh by existing and new means such information." Bergh was not given an independent intelligence assignment, but being the independent person he was, he provided throughout the war valuable information that he gathered alone or with other students at Dresden.

The train journey from Oslo to Gothenburg was only five hours in peacetime but double that in 1941. The glimpses of the fjords were pleasant enough, but the concentration of SS troops increased as the border town of Kornsjø was approached. Bergh's papers were quite in order. This time he was going to Germany not as a casual agent but as a spy with a mission to help a spy. After examination of papers, a tedious process, the train passed through a no man's land until it reached the Swedish customs house at Mon, and only then was Bergh able to breathe freely for one more day, until he entered Germany again.

The railway terminal had cubicles with cots and wash basins where weary travelers could rest and sleep between trains. Bergh was to meet someone in the morning, so after visiting a few dives along the Gotha River, he retired to his cubicle. The visitor who gave Bergh the proper password the next morning at Gothenburg's central station was Whistondale, the SIS man posted by Eric Welsh to Stockholm to handle the operations of the Griffin. Sverre Bergh was fair, well over six feet tall. Whistondale was about five feet seven and, as an SIS colleague described him, "dapper, dark, and athletically built, a good athlete and a very steady worker. He spoke Norwegian well." That was an essential attribute for the job he would be doing, but on that day he and Bergh spoke English.

Whistondale was frank with Bergh, holding back little, for Bergh deserved nothing less. Whistondale was sending the man to help steal some of the most vital secrets of the Reich. If he was caught, the penalty would be the maximum. Whistondale told Bergh that he would be under the direction of Roscher Lund and one Eric Welsh—an extraordinary revelation. Bergh was given a password with which to contact Dr. Paul Rosbaud, code name Der Greif, at Springer Verlag in Berlin. Rosbaud would be providing Bergh, on a continuing basis, information on the German atomic program and other technical intelligence and one of Sverre Bergh's code names would be Sigurd. Bergh and Whistondale had met on Monday, September 29, 1941. After the war, Werner Heisenberg confessed, "It was from September 1941 that we saw an open road ahead of us, leading to the atomic bomb." He was wrong, but Eric Welsh's timing for watching Heisenberg had been perfect.

As soon as he arrived in Berlin, Sigurd put through a call to 21–81–11 from a kiosk in Stettiner Bahnhof. A rather beguiling voice answered. It was Annemarie Belz, Rosbaud's secretary (and a rival of Ruth Lange for his affections). Yes, Dr. Rosbaud was available. "Can you state your business?" "A student from Dresden." "Oh, yes, Dr. Rosbaud was expecting a call."

They agreed to meet that afternoon in the Tiergarten at one of the tent restaurants for a beer. The man Bergh met was of moderate stature and with sharp features. He was carrying a pipe. His fingers were tactile, perhaps those of a concert artist, and his Austrian voice was forceful if soft.

They liked each other, and each sensed almost immediately the other's fascination with clandestine activity. Rosbaud told Bergh that he had something very important for him already. It was passed, folded into a book, when they met the next day in another tent café in the Tiergarten. What Bergh read later made him delay transmission until he himself could travel to the place where Rosbaud had been a month earlier.

The Oder flows northward from the Carpathian Mountains of Czechoslovakia; nowadays it defines the border between East Germany and Poland. It widens at Stettin, some seventy miles from Berlin, and then empties into the Baltic Sea by means of three branches. To the east, the Dievenow contributes its flow to a strong tide that flows eastward along a straight coast. To the west, the Swine and Peene rivers carve out the island of Usedom, shaped like a tyrannosaur. The head of that dinosaur was Peenemünde.

On the east side of the dinosaur's neck was Zinnowitz, a pleasant beach resort. The western part of the neck was the terminus of the ferryboat to Wolgast, across the Peene. To the north of Zinnowitz was Karlshagen, a housing estate for the workers at Peenemünde, and farther on were the V-2 rocket production and experimental works, capped by the main rocket-testing area, all on the east coast of Use-dom. At the very tip of the island was the launching area for the V-1 flying bombs. Some of the buildings of the Peenemünde complex were quite tall and could be seen from the area between Zinnowitz and the Wolgast ferry station.

Sverre Bergh, after hearing from Rosbaud what he had learned at Greifswald, decided to journey northward to see what he could see. He spent the night in Swinemünde with a girl he had picked up in a bar and set off early the next morning toward the Peenemünde pen-insula, hiking north along minor roads and catching lifts from truck drivers, not riding with any one for too long. Bergh headed toward the area between Wolgast and Zinnowitz and somewhat to the north. Four tall buildings began to loom from the Peenemünde area, and Bergh sketched them in his mind and, being a structural engineer, guessed well their functions. They were two workshops, the assembly building, and what looked like a power plant. Although he could have proceeded much farther north before reaching the guarded security area, Bergh decided not to press his luck. Hiking back to Swinemünde, he decided, after some hesitation, to forgo the pleasures of the evening before and caught a train back to Berlin.

The following evening, Rosbaud and Bergh prepared their first substantial report for Eric Welsh. It included a rough description of the V-2 ("cigar-shaped") and its approximate dimensions. The co-ordinates of Peenemünde were given precisely, and the locations of the four buildings identified by Bergh were pinpointed.

One of the attachés at the Swedish legation in Berlin had a Nor-wegian relative, and Theo Findahl had developed a friendship with the family. The attaché also had access to the diplomatic bags that were sent daily to Stockholm. There, another Swedish accomplice, according to Bergh, passed the material to Roscher Lund, who in turn passed it to John Whistondale. A 1943 summary, prepared for Win-ston Churchill, of presumably all intelligence reports on the German rocket program, gives not a hint of the 1941 reports. When, after the war, Bergh asked Roscher Lund what had happened to the 1941 report, the latter replied that it wasn't believed and was therefore scrapped. Anne-Sofie Strømnes recalls that her husband, Øivind, received a signal from Britain at the end of 1941, saying that the latest transmittal from Sigurd on Peenemünde matters simply didn't make sense. There is no record of who rendered that judgment.

To be sure, that was the first report of any substance that Welsh had received from the Griffin since his elevation as chief of SIS scientific operations. And Welsh was probably annoyed. Beyond doubt, in that particular period the main intelligence collection priority was supposed to be the atomic bomb, as far as Rosbaud and Bergh were concerned. Yet the two had risked much to collect information about some missiles that neither Welsh nor anyone else cared about. The 1941 report did not correlate with any other information received up to that time, and although it was about Peenemünde, it did not seem to describe the type of activity mentioned in the Oslo Report. Welsh was always suspicious of any agent, and Rosbaud was no exception. Foley was still cloistered with Rudolf Hess, so he was unavailable to assure Welsh once more that Rosbaud was genuine in every respect.

No matter whether he was genuine; the report from Bergh and Rosbaud reached Welsh when there were more important priorities. The battle of the Atlantic was in full force. Ultra signal intercept 1712 of August 31 had indicated that the *Admiral Scheer* was moving toward Oslo, Welsh's territory, with a "special task." Welsh concentrated all of his resources, including his coastal radio stations, on the mighty pocket battleship. On Friday, September 5, and the following Monday, RAF Flying Fortresses carried out abortive raids on the *Scheer*, which then sailed southward to Swinemünde, to the southeast of Peenemünde. One would think that this circumstance, which occurred just before Welsh received the report on rocket-research activity in the same area, would have catalyzed intensive reconnaissance activity, but it did not.

The Ultra intercepts indicated that the *Scheer* was preparing for major forays, and all intelligence had to be focused on blunting that objective. Welsh's networks could not be compromised for missile threats, which appeared to be neither real nor imminent. That may be one plausible explanation of the puzzle of why the 1941 report on Peenemünde went unheeded. It may be that Welsh simply did not pass it on for fear of compromising not only his coastal reporting networks, but his most valuable source in the Reich—for whom he had other tasks. If Eric Welsh did transmit the 1941 report to someone, then another explanation is needed.

TWENTY-ONE

The Visit

BY MID 1941, both Britain and Germany had made the decision to proceed with research on the atomic bomb, and each had become curious about what the other country was doing. The United States, though uneasy about German progress, was unable to mount any atomic intelligence effort until very late in the war. In Russia, the situation was different.

When Hitler launched Operation Barbarossa in June 1941, Soviet scientists had to drop their work on the atomic bomb. It was precisely at that time that Klaus Fuchs began to report on the British program, in particular the conclusions being reached in the final MAUD report, then being drafted. Thus, just when the Soviets might have started to forge ahead in the race for the bomb, the invasion forced them to drop out.

Until that time, they had kept apace with the German program, though they were behind the British. Recently, Rudolf Peierls, who with Otto Frisch gave the British their head start, was asked to evaluate a November 1940 paper by the leading Soviet atomic scientist, Igor Kurchatov. Peierls wrote: "He [Kurchatov] had certainly a good knowledge of the literature . . . [but] missed the idea of a bomb. . . . In other words, they were in November 1940 well behind in points that by that time were well understood both in England and in America."

In July 1941, Kurchatov was sent to the Black Sea to research the problem of countering the German magnetic mines fitted with the type of fuse described in the Oslo Report. In the Berlin trials of the members of the Rote Kapelle Soviet spy group, after it had been exposed in September and October 1941, there was no mention of Soviet interest in the German atomic energy program, although the ring had sought information on many other advanced weapons' technologies. This is certainly strange, for the German program was the primary target of other intelligence services and must have been a Soviet target, especially after Hitler attacked. Furthermore, Klaus Fuchs, the major (but not the only) Soviet atomic spy in Britain, passed on the work he was doing, as well as the MAUD report. If Rote Kapelle was not providing information on the atomic effort from inside Germany, then who was? That mystery remains to be solved.

There is another mystery dating from precisely the same time the members of the Rote Kapelle, including Hans Kummerow, were being arrested by the Gestapo. And it too had to do with intelligence gathering. In October, Werner Heisenberg and another physicist, Carl Friedrich von Weizsäcker, contrived a special visit to Copenhagen to visit the doyen of all atomic scientists, Niels Bohr. After the war, Heisenberg's admirers invented a theory that their idol had come to the "pope" of physicists to implore him to ask all the scientists of the world not to work on the atomic bomb. The actual purpose of that visit is one of the most vexing mysteries in the history of the atomic bomb. It can now be solved with the help of official records and documents relating to Paul Rosbaud.

Carl von Weizsäcker came to believe that had Rosbaud been aware of Heisenberg's supposed intent, Rosbaud might have reported differently. In 1983, von Weizsäcker wrote (in translation):

> I knew Paul Rosbaud only a little. I had the impression that he did not trust me and therefore did not talk to me openly. Hence I was not informed about his activities during the war. I would certainly not have condemned those activities, even though I myself acted differently.

Von Weizsäcker seems to feel that if Rosbaud had been more open to him, Rosbaud would not have misunderstood Heisenberg's intentions when he talked with Bohr. But Rosbaud had a different assessment of the visit.

In 1941, the Nazis established their own university in Strasbourg, the city where Hans Rosbaud had been appointed conductor. And Carl von Weizsäcker was appointed to the faculty of the university,

which was inaugurated in the same month as the visit to Bohr. While
Rosbaud at that time warned his brother against becoming too friendly
with some of the faculty, in the same letter he mentioned von Weizsäcker in a not unfriendly tone. But in January 1944 Paul Rosbaud,
in another letter to Hans about the Strasbourg faculty, wrote:

> The physicist is by far the most cunning and diplomatic. His father is
> the well-known Herr v.W. Give him my best regards. He is a pure
> theoretician with a strong philosophical inclination, a good friend of
> Heisenberg. But here too, I keep my distance. . . . I recommend to you
> to restrict yourself to very objective things, and even there a certain
> reticence is desirable. Probably it would become known within two days
> if you were to say something commendable about the great Gustav.

Hans and Paul had their own code, based on music and their childhood readings of Schiller and Goethe. King Gustavus Adolphus of
Sweden, the Lion of the North, was immortalized in Schiller's epic
Wallenstein trilogy. The king intervened in the Thirty Years' War to
oppose the Hapsburgs, whose traditions were revered by Hans and
Paul, so Gustavus Adolphus had been something of a personal enemy
and an object of jokes in their childhood. In 1941, Paul Rosbaud was
reminded of the Lion of the North, for in June 1630 the Swedish
expeditionary force had landed at, of all places, Peenemünde. Of
course, the "great Gustav" was a cynical reference to the other
"Adolphus" — Hitler — whom the brothers fervently wished another
Wallenstein would come along to slay.

Rosbaud's changed attitudes toward Werner Heisenberg and Carl
von Weizsäcker had much to do with their visit to Copenhagen in
October 1941. Von Weizsäcker's belief that Rosbaud "did not trust
me and therefore did not talk to me openly" is doubtlessly correct.

And von Weizsäcker's judgment is basically sound, since Rosbaud
did indeed have a different idea about the purpose of the visit. But
he was wrong to think that if Rosbaud's impression had been otherwise, he "would not have sent other reports to England." Rosbaud
had more than an impression; he knew much about the visit, and he
perceived its aims as completely different from those of Heisenberg
and von Weizsäcker.

Paul's primary battle was against Hitler. His fear was that the attitudes
that had allowed Hitler to come to power might never be changed

and that later dictators would also hold sway. That is why Heisenberg and von Weizsäcker's visit to Copenhagen explains many of the Griffin's motivations and actions.

Rosbaud and von Weizsäcker shared deep inner moral convictions against war but took different paths. Rosbaud's crusade was a most private one, but von Weizsäcker took the more open, missionarylike way. As the prefix to his surname connotes, Carl F. Freiherr von Weizsäcker was born into a family of some substance, his grandfather having been the last prime minister of the kingdom of Wurttemberg, once the land of the Swabians. An uncle pioneered the science of anthropological medicine, and his father, Ernst, became Hitler's state secretary in Joachim von Ribbentrop's Foreign Ministry. His brother Richard is today the president of the Federal Republic of Germany.

As a child, Carl F. von Weizsäcker became fascinated by astronomy, which was the basis for his lifelong quest for the mystical forces underlying physical order and the meaning of life. His spiritual quest intensified when he married into the Lutheran Bodelschwingh family, which had founded the Bethel colony for epileptics. Today, von Weizsäcker is devoted to church work and to the quest for world peace. He is candid about those events of yesteryear; it is sad that he and Rosbaud never reached a common understanding.

As a student of Werner Heisenberg's, von Weizsäcker perhaps felt much at home with Heisenberg's fundamental discovery of the uncertainty principle, which may have another, spiritual interpretation, to the effect that man himself is not all-knowing about the exactitude of physical measurements. Certainly, that is how one of the co-discoverers, Pascual Jordan, felt, and he came to believe in psychic phenomena.

Heisenberg himself was uncertain in his personal life. He was, as von Weizsäcker has said of him, "a spontaneous person" who had "a competitive, fair, uncontrollable ambition for achievement." The word von Weizsäcker used for "ambition" is *Ehrgeiz*, which means more exactly "greed for honor." Rosbaud respected Heisenberg for his sharp mind, but the uncontrollable ambition and the greed for honor were the qualities that Rosbaud detested in Heisenberg.

The greed for honor for himself and for the Reich motivated Heisenberg to extremes that lost him the respect of many scientists who

otherwise held him in high esteem. Even after Heisenberg spat at
Max Born in 1933 and humiliated the future Nobel laureate and his
wife, Born never failed to extend to Heisenberg the greatest cour-
tesies. Rosbaud knew of that episode and found it difficult.to act with
similar tolerance.

Heisenberg was not a scientist who made concessions to the regime
in order to survive, as many scientists had to; he was a loyal servant.
His attitude was recorded precisely while he was visiting Holland
during the week of October 18, 1943. He declared:

> History legitimizes Germany to rule Europe and later the world. Only
> a nation that rules ruthlessly can maintain itself. Democracy cannot
> develop sufficient energy to rule Europe. There are, therefore, only
> two possibilities: Germany and Russia, and perhaps a Europe under
> German leadership is the lesser evil.

The eminent scientist Hendrik B. G. Casimir, whom Rosbaud visited
during the war, remembered those precise words.

And he had heard about the visit of Heisenberg and von Weizsäcker
to Copenhagen in October 1941. This is the way it came about. In
1941, German academic research on atomic energy was controlled by
Bernhard Rust, the minister of education. He was a Nazi with no
discernible talent or administrative skills. He had been gauleiter of
Hanover, and thus had a certain immunity from criticism. But even
Josef Goebbels had complained, "Rust has nothing to say. His ministry
is in a complete shambles." Usually inebriated, boorish, and with a
reputation in the diplomatic community as someone to avoid inviting,
Rust understood even less about atomic energy than he did about
education.

Carl F. von Weizsäcker came to Rust's office at the end of July 1941
to discuss the atomic energy program. Rust requested von Weizsäcker
to find out how far advanced the United States was. On September
5, 1941, von Weizsäcker forwarded his report, attached to this letter:

> Honorable Reichsminister!
>
> In an attached paper I am sending you the report on America's
> advantage over Germany in nuclear physics, which report you asked
> for during the course of the interview you granted me in the latter part
> of July. It is unfortunate that there were long delays in completing the
> report, caused by the investigations which I had to set up and by duties
> of military importance.

I again express my respect and my thanks for the support which you, Herr Reichsminister, have given to the advancement of science.

Heil Hitler!

C. F. von Weizsäcker

The investigations that von Weizsäcker "set up" were arranged through his father's Ministry of Foreign Affairs. In that post, Ernst von Weizsäcker had supported early expansionism, yet he later became disenchanted with Hitler's lieutenants and became ambassador to the Vatican and contacted Resistance figures. He remains enigmatic.

Only a day before he sent his report to Rust, Carl F. von Weizsäcker transmitted to the army high command a Swedish press report on experiments in the United States that could be interpreted as leading to an atomic bomb. A 5-kilogram bomb, it was said, would create a crater one kilometer deep and forty kilometers in radius. Even after the report for Rust was completed, the elder von Weizsäcker sought more information. On October 6, he asked the Foreign Ministry press branch for any reports, especially from the American press, "on the use of uranium for explosive purposes."

At the same time, according to Heisenberg's postwar account, Carl F. von Weizsäcker came up with the proposition that the two of them visit Niels Bohr in Copenhagen to discuss atomic matters. Heisenberg agreed, as he usually agreed to von Weizsäcker's suggestions, but Bohr refused to invite the two to his institute. Through his connections, von Weizsäcker arranged that Heisenberg be invited by the Danish-German Society to give a lecture at Deutsches Haus, a Copenhagen restaurant taken over by Propaganda Minister Josef Goebbels to disseminate Aryan culture. It stood at number 5 Axeltorv, sandwiched between Shellhus and Dagmarhus, the Gestapo's torture chambers. Today, 5 Axeltorv is New Daddy's, a discothèque.

Niels Bohr did not dance with glee when he heard that Heisenberg and von Weizsäcker had found an excuse to come to Copenhagen, and he still refused to receive them at his institute, nor would Bohr set foot in Deutsches Haus. The two German physicists thought it prudent that Heisenberg alone should meet Bohr. Bohr had already brought much honor to Denmark, and in recognition the Carlsberg Brewery had given him the house of its founder. Heisenberg met Bohr one evening in the garden of the House of Honor.

After the war, as noted earlier, Heisenberg, his wife, and most biographers insisted that Heisenberg had come to Bohr in 1941 to ask his good offices in making the physicists of the world refuse to work on the atomic bomb. That presumes that Heisenberg was naïve enough to believe that the physicists of this world resided on a higher moral plane than the leaders of nations who had declared war and the soldiers who were fighting and dying. Bohr himself remembered the visit differently.

Aage Bohr, Niels's son and himself a Nobel laureate, believes that such assertions have "no basis in the actual events, since there was no mention of any such plan during Heisenberg's visit. . . . On the contrary, the very scanty contact with the German physicists during the occupation contributed . . . to strengthen the impression that the German authorities attributed great military importance to atomic energy."

Heisenberg's widow, Elisabeth, claims that Bohr misunderstood her husband, and that "German intelligence did not have the slightest inkling" regarding the American atomic effort. What with von Weizsäcker's curiosity about the U.S. program at that time, and Elisabeth's connecting German intelligence and her husband's higher purpose, it seems clear that a major reason for the visit to Copenhagen was for the gathering of information. Of all physicists in Germany and occupied Europe, Bohr was the person most likely to have heard rumors of what was happening elsewhere. If Bohr misunderstood Heisenberg, as the latter's defenders have insisted, it would have been owing to the delicacy of Heisenberg's mission and the manner in which he sought the intelligence. But Bohr did not misunderstand at all.

He told his son and others at the institute about Heisenberg's visit, and word soon got around to Lise Meitner in Stockholm and to Rosbaud's closest confidant in the German physics community, Max von Laue. The following March, Meitner was visited by a young associate of Bohr's, Christian Møller. (Møller had been the first to suggest to Lise Meitner and Otto Frisch that neutrons might be freed in fission and that a chain reaction was therefore possible.) Meitner wrote to von Laue in Berlin,

> I had Dr. M. with me one evening and that was very nice and pleasing. He told me much about Niels and the institute, and most was comforting and satisfactory. Half amusing and half depressing was his report about a visit of Werner [Heisenberg] and Carl Friedrich [von Weizsäcker].

Among other noteworthy matters C.F. appears to have his own peculiar thoughts, particularly about "Constellations" [that is, astrology], but I beg you to keep this confidential. I became very melancholy on hearing this; at one time I had held them to be decent human beings. They have gone astray.

Von Laue tried to ameliorate her distress, but Meitner could not accept his reassurance and never forgave the two for their visit. In June 1945, she wrote to von Laue, after hearing of the horrors discovered in the concentration camps, "One should force a man like Heisenberg and many millions with him to go to these camps and see the martyred victims. His visit to Denmark in 1941 is unforgivable."

What Paul Rosbaud could not forgive was that Heisenberg and some of his admirers distorted the purpose of the visit, trying to create the myth that Germany's scientists were on a higher moral plane than other scientists. In a 1959 magazine article Rosbaud wrote that "Heisenberg's statement, in 1946, that 'external circumstances' had relieved the German atomic experts from the need 'to take the difficult decision whether or not to produce atom bombs' may be regarded as correct — if ignorance of how to do so is taken to be synonymous with 'external circumstances.' "

C. P. Snow's views coincided with those of Rosbaud, who had written to him in 1958, deploring the "complete vindication of the German scientists by implying that they knew exactly how to make not only an A- but also an H-bomb, but that they were silent in order to keep this weapon from Hitler's use. In fact, they did not know how to make either bomb. This will now be the new legend and, of course, a deliberate distortion of the truth."

Snow, the pre-eminent British scientist, writer, and humanist, replied, "I agree with you that this could be dangerous," and several months later he wrote again to Rosbaud, "I agree with almost everything you say. I wish you would write a book on the subject." Unfortunately, the person who knew more than anybody else about the morality and politics of the German atomic project never lived to write that book.

TWENTY-TWO

Return to Oslo

THE ONE PERSON under Hitler's control who might have put the German atomic program on the right track was the Norwegian Jew Victor M. Goldschmidt, still in occupied Norway. Had Heisenberg and his colleagues come to a proper appreciation of the man-made element plutonium, Germany might have had an atomic bomb in early 1945, and Hitler might have won the war.

The only physicist within the Reich who had a reasonable perception of plutonium was Fritz Houtermans, who, like any true Viennese, worked only in cafés. In those times, coffee cups were never refilled; they were replaced. The waiters would not remove the cups until they were requested to present the bill. Houtermans had achieved some fame in his student days at Göttingen by setting records for the number of coffee cups piled at his table. The brilliant student moved to Berlin and began to collaborate with a young Welshman, Robert d'Escourt Atkinson, a protégé of Frederick Lindemann's. Lindemann even then was a close friend to Churchill, and as world war neared, he became his intimate adviser on many matters, including science. It was Irmin and Robert Atkinson who, in 1938, found the flat in Greenwich for Hilde and Angela Rosbaud.

At the coffee tables of Berlin in 1929 there had been a fusion of friendship between Atkinson, Houtermans, and Paul Rosbaud. The scientific subject Houtermans and Atkinson were interested in at the time was the fusion of elements that created thermonuclear reactions in the sun and stars, the same thermonuclear reactions that man would create in bombs decades later. The imaginative papers that the two physicists published caught the attention of Carl F. von Weizsäcker, always attracted to anything concerning stars, and that of Hans Bethe, who later won the Nobel Prize for his work on the same subject. Also attracted to the theories was Victor Goldschmidt.

In 1933, Fritz Houtermans fled to Russia, where his free spirit soon ran afoul of the secret police; the Austrian had a prolonged opportunity to explore the theory of numbers in the cells of the NKVD. After the Hitler-Stalin pact of 1939, Houtermans returned to Germany, tainted by his stay in the Soviet Union, mistrusted and shunned by many of his peers. He took rooms at Uhlandstrasse 189 at the eastern end of the Kurfürstendamm, where the cafés suddenly began to experience a shortage of coffee cups. Fritz Houtermans was not alone to blame, for Paul Rosbaud was often with him.

It was certainly over a cup of coffee that Houtermans had his brainstorm about plutonium. He reasoned that if the more common component in uranium were to capture a neutron, it would be transformed into a new element that could be made to explode just as easily as the rare component of uranium. And it would be easier to separate the new element by chemical means than to separate the rarer explosive form of uranium by physical means. Fortunately nobody paid any attention to Houtermans's report. Later, Heisenberg and von Weizsäcker vaguely mentioned new elements that might be built on uranium, but they had no clear idea of their usefulness.

In fact, Houtermans returned to Russia, this time attached to Hitler's Luftwaffe. Curiously, he was not on a mission for the air force but on an intelligence mission for the navy. The army and the Reich Research Council were the entities charged with atomic research, but Houtermans was suspect by both organizations. Somehow, possibly through Paul Rosbaud's introduction, Admiral Carl Witzell, head of the navy's ordnance department (which had developed the magnetic fuses and the degaussing method described in the Oslo Report), had taken a fancy to Fritz Houtermans. After Houtermans had completed his plutonium report, Admiral Witzell asked him to go to the occupied parts of Russia to "evaluate the quality, political inclination, and present situation of physicists, engineers, and technically trained aides in the Soviet Union."

Based at field post L–23–1–33 in Breslau, Houtermans made forays to Kiev and Kharkov in October and November 1941. There he saw

old friends and inspected their laboratories. But what he felt he had
to report was not what Berlin wanted to hear:

> The only desire of these people is to live in peace with their families
> so that they can work in peace. . . . It would be wrong to believe that
> hatred of the Soviet system exists in these circles, though one might
> expect this. On the contrary, most, especially the younger and capable
> intellectuals, are fully convinced that the Soviet system is correct.

Admiral Witzell, himself a reasonable fellow, sent Houtermans's
report off to Professor Rudolf Mentzel, the director of the Reich
Research Council. Mentzel replied on March 31, 1942:

> The situation in the scientific sector in Germany is such at the present
> time that all research work is directed almost exclusively toward im-
> portant objectives for the government and war, and all this work must
> be kept secret. For this reason, the use of Russian personnel is ques-
> tionable.

Thus, at a time when he might have been promoting his findings
about plutonium, Houtermans was in Russia. And the tone of Mentzel's letter made it clear that he not only mistrusted scientists still in
Russia but certainly a scientist who had just come from Russia. Plutonium never again received serious consideration in wartime Germany.

Paul Rosbaud knew about plutonium, but he was more worried
about a friend who was curious about plutonium. Victor Goldschmidt
was wondering whether that element, the one he called superuranium,
was present in extremely small quantities in nature, and he began to
speculate on the chemical characteristics of the substance, going far
deeper into its chemistry than anyone in Germany, including Houtermans. Goldschmidt's thoughts paralleled the secret work of Glenn
Seaborg and his associates in the United States, the work that preceded
the large-scale chemical separation process used for producing the
plutonium for the Nagasaki bomb. Recently, Nobel laureate Seaborg
wrote, "I have been familiar with the work of Goldschmidt for a long
time and, on the basis of this, have been one of his admirers."

Fortunately, the German scientists were not among Goldschmidt's
admirers, and Goldschmidt's publishing in Norwegian did not help
them. Until January 1942, when he completed his superuranium paper, Goldschmidt worked without interference from the occupying

authorities. In February, every one of the fifteen hundred Jews in Norway was required to fill out a *Fragebogen*, similar to the question-naire that Goldschmidt had had to complete years earlier in Göttingen. The letter J was stamped in passports and identity papers of Jews. In March, Vidkun Quisling reversed the 1851 constitutional reforms sought by Henrik Wergeland and declared all Jews in Norway to be illegal immigrants.

V.M.'s home in Holmenkollen had a fine view, which made it a strategic asset, so it was confiscated to become a German army command post. The cats, Frøken Brendigen, and all the clutter were forced to move to a flat on Holmendammen Terrase in Smestad. Tom Barth did not go with Goldschmidt, but took a rather ordinary white painted house in Sogn Hageby. They were now kilometers apart, much to their mutual satisfaction, but Goldschmidt was still in passage.

To rally all Norwegians to his new order, Quisling called on Gulbrand Lunde, his minister of propaganda. The same Gulbrand Lunde whom Eric Welsh had helped to can fish without odor. Now Lunde had a different odor, attached to himself, much to the disgust of his former friends Victor Goldschmidt and Paul Rosbaud. For a time, even after the invasion of Norway, Rosbaud had tolerated Lunde. In November, Quisling published a book in imitation of Hitler's *Mein Kampf*. *Quisling Has Said* was a collection of his speeches over the preceding decade. The introduction was written by Gulbrand Lunde, who proclaimed that it was providence that had sent Quisling to the Norwegian people when they needed him most.

At one time Rosbaud had needed Lunde, whose book on vitamins had helped smooth the transmission of the Oslo Report. Recently, Lunde had become obsessed with a new vitamin, B-X, which he claimed would prevent hair from graying. To remain in Lunde's good graces, Rosbaud placed several of his papers on that questionable subject in *Naturwissenschaften*; but after Lunde was royally received by Josef Goebbels, in March 1941, Rosbaud could no longer stomach him. Goebbels wrote in his diary that Lunde was "a very clever man, for a Norwegian." Rosbaud told Meitner in a letter that Lunde had "sent me an invitation, but I did not go to see him."

A year later, Paul wanted to go to Norway. Concerned about his friend Victor Goldschmidt, Paul asked one of his influential Nazi friends, Professor F. K. Drescher-Kaden, for a letter that he could use to promote a trip to Oslo. Drescher-Kaden, always willing to do anything for Rosbaud, obliged with this letter, dated June 9, 1942:

Highly esteemed Dr. Rosbaud!

As you have belonged to our Raw Materials Working Group for some time, I should like to ask you to place your great experience at our service by rendering us more advice.

The acquisition of beryllium metal has become more and more urgent, as you know from your former relationship with us and with the Reich's office for non-ferrous metals. We must make an urgent attempt to obtain a clear picture of the quantities that are available in Norway. The Research Department of Reichsminister Goering deems this question most important. . . . The chairman of the Norwegian Raw Materials Commission and the professors of raw materials research at the University of Oslo, Barth and V. M. Goldschmidt, should know more about it. . . . It is *absolutely necessary* that you make contact with these gentlemen as quickly as possible and fly to Oslo for this purpose, if necessary, using the help of Lunde. Please give the report of your results directly to the Research Department of the Ministerial Office of Reichsmarschall Goering. Do everything necessary to obtain permission for this trip as soon as possible.

> With kindest regards,
> Heil Hitler!
> Your most faithful servant,
> F. K. Drescher-Kaden

It was most audacious of Drescher-Kaden to describe Victor Goldschmidt as a "gentleman" just after Vidkun Quisling had declared him an illegal immigrant. And it was quite as strange to recommend visits to both Commission Chairman Lunde and Goldschmidt. Drescher-Kaden was clearly no orthodox Nazi.

On June 4, in Berlin, there had been a meeting that changed the history of the world. On that date, Albert Speer, Hitler's minister of armaments and war production, and his staff met with the scientists who were doing atomic bomb research. The place was Harnack House in Dahlem (near the Kaiser Wilhelm Institutes), and the array of top brass was impressive. Representing the navy was Admiral Carl Witzell; the army, General Ernst Fromm; and the air force, Field Marshal Erhard Milch.

Werner Heisenberg, spokesman for the contingent of scientists, began with an explanation of how to make an atomic bomb. He knew that Speer and the military had stayed away from a similar meeting a month earlier on the grounds that the agenda seemed too technical. Now, Heisenberg tried to be as elementary as possible. He led off with a description of how two pieces of fissionable material could somehow be assembled to produce an atomic explosion. But he may have made the lecture too elementary, because it gradually began to dawn on the decision makers that Heisenberg hadn't the slightest idea of how to obtain sufficient amounts of the fissionable materials or how to bring them together to explode. When Field Marshal Milch asked him how large the bomb would be, Heisenberg replied, "As large as a pineapple."

(After the war, Heisenberg's defenders cited that phrase to prove that he knew what he was talking about. Not so. Meitner and Frisch had calculated how much energy is released from a split atom, and from their findings any physicist could have estimated the size of a bomb. *The Saturday Evening Post* of September 7, 1940, had carried an article noting that one pound of uranium "would have the explosive power of 15,000 tons of TNT." Given a bomb made of the very dense uranium, its size would be about that of a pineapple, and most scientists knew that it also would have a very low percentage of efficiency. When the German atomic scientists were interned in England after the collapse of Germany, they began to formulate their positions. Before the atomic bomb was dropped on Hiroshima, Karl Wirtz suggested a tactic, recalled by Eric Bagge: "We must tell the Americans that Heisenberg is the only man in the world who is able to make the bomb." When the ten scientists listened to the BBC on the night of August 6, 1945, Heisenberg exclaimed, "It's a swindle!" and repeatedly mumbled that he did not believe the announcement that an atomic bomb had been used over Hiroshima. He argued that it was an improved conventional explosive, but the other internees finally convinced him that the bomb was atomic. Even so, all of the scientists thought the bomb was fabricated from uranium. Not even von Weizsäcker, who was credited after the war with being fully aware of plutonium, suggested that the bomb might have been made from that substance.)

Even though Heisenberg had demonstrated no special knowledge of how he would build a bomb, he went on to press for support. How much money did he want? Speer asked. Heisenberg said that 100,000 marks would do — and Carl von Weizsäcker asked for an additional 10,000 for construction.

Requests for such pittances left Speer and the brass even less impressed. At that time, Milch's Luftwaffe was spending the equivalent of two billion dollars every three months (equivalent to the total cost of the future Manhattan Project). But giving Heisenberg the benefit of the doubt, Speer offered to raise the sum to a few million marks, and General Fromm agreed to release several hundred scientific assistants from army duty to help on the project. Much to the chagrin of Speer and the officers, Heisenberg replied that he didn't know how to use resources of that magnitude. He was being quite honest. He had no idea how to create his deadly pineapple.

With that meeting, the chances for a Nazi atomic bomb vanished for good. The country where Hahn and Strassmann had first split the uranium nucleus, where Albert Einstein, Lise Meitner, Leo Szilard, and Otto Frisch had worked, now effectively dropped out of the race.

Milch departed to his job of supervising a secret weapon in which he had more confidence, the V-1 glider weapon for use against England. A few weeks later, Speer reported briefly to Hitler on the Harnack House meeting. The dictator merely nodded. He too had nearer-term weapons on his mind.

Had Hitler known of the item on President Roosevelt's agenda of the previous week, he would have questioned Speer's presentation harshly. On June 17, 1942, the president's scientific adviser, Vannevar Bush, presented him with the comprehensive plan to proceed with the making of atomic bombs. Said Bush, "This report and program have been approved by those with whom you instructed me to take up matters of policy on this subject. . . . If you also approve, we will proceed along these lines immediately." The President wrote on the report "VB. OK. FDR."

Within one fortnight, the American (and British) and the German atomic bomb programs moved in completely opposite directions. Heisenberg and his scientists went back to their laboratories to work on a small, simple "uranium machine" to produce, by design, zero amount of power and no plutonium. The German atomic bomb program died on June 4, 1942.

The German program suffered another severe setback just a few

days later. In May 1942, the American and German knowledge of a
nuclear reactor, but not a bomb, was about the same. With his experimental reactor at Columbia University, Enrico Fermi had achieved
a multiplication of neutrons that was 5 percent short of the goal of
producing more neutrons than were injected into the assembly. To
their credit, at the same time Werner Heisenberg and R. Döpel achieved,
in their experimental assembly at Leipzig, 13 percent in excess of the
same goal. That was the single great triumph of the German atomic
program and the only part of the atomic race the Germans won.

But the triumph of Heisenberg and Döpel was short-lived. Their
reactor was designed as two concentric shells of uranium metal powder
separated from the heavy water. Uranium powder and water, heavy
or light, are not chemically compatible substances, and when a leak
brought them together on that same June day of 1942 when Speer
spoke to Hitler of his meeting with Heisenberg, fate dealt Heisenberg
another blow — the destruction of his reactor.

After the war, Paul Rosbaud described the quandary of the German
scientists:

> One can appreciate their exquisite dilemma now. What are they to say
> to their countrymen of the part they played? Did they deliberately keep
> from the Nazi government the possibilities of a bomb, and so contribute
> to their country's defeat? Would they have done this if they had known
> their country stood in serious danger of atomic attack? Did they simply
> judge that the bomb couldn't be made with the resources and organi-
> zation available ... or were they just bad physicists who did a sum
> wrong?

Of course, Paul Rosbaud had some friends at Harnack House that
day, and he soon learned of Speer's decision. After a Physical Society
meeting one evening a few days later, some scientists gathered at a
café on the Ku'damm and professed their relief at not having to build
the bomb. Rosbaud listened silently, but he needed drink to steel
himself. Finally, he burst out, "Nonsense! If you knew how to build
it, you'd present it to your Führer on a silver platter!" Stunned by
Rosbaud's uncharacteristic outburst, the gathering broke up — everyone scared, some thinking Rosbaud's exclamation might be a prov-
ocation. By replying, they would implicate themselves and be reported
to the Gestapo. After all, they had been indiscreet enough.

Rosbaud flew to Oslo by military aircraft on June 10, carrying the momentous news of the meeting between Heisenberg and the military men. He had hoped to stop off in Copenhagen to visit Niels Bohr on his return trip, but permission was denied, so he spent his entire visit—eight days; longer than he had planned—in Victor Goldschmidt's flat. He gained a few needed pounds, thanks to Frøken Brendigen's cooking. But he was annoyed by V.M.'s optimism. After the J stamp was put in Goldschmidt's identity card, he had been called to the Sicherheitsdienst (SD) headquarters. The SD was the intelligence arm of Heinrich Himmler's SS, and Rosbaud found the summons ominous. Goldschmidt had been interrogated intensely on his background, current activities, and so forth, to the extent that he was convinced that his interrogators had had no dossier on him. Rosbaud feared otherwise. V.M. had been getting money transfers from Germany—royalties on his patents. In April the transfers stopped. Rosbaud checked with his contacts in the Norwegian Resistance, who told him that several times they had offered Goldschmidt safe passage to Sweden but that he had refused. No amount of cajoling by Rosbaud could persuade V.M. to change his mind.

Then, there was that grim sense of humor, which also worried Paul. Goldschmidt carried a capsule of hydrocyanic acid in his pocket in the event—unlikely, he thought—that he would be tortured. A colleague at the university asked V.M. for a capsule. "This poison," answered Goldschmidt, "is for professors of chemistry only. You, a professor of mechanics, will have to use the rope."

Rosbaud also visited Goldschmidt's former friend Tom Barth. Barth's son recalled:

> In 1942 . . . my sister, who was then eighteen years old and worked fairly full time in the civil secretariat of the Resistance, returned home to find Father in conversation with a German officer in uniform: Paul R. She became entirely disoriented by this, and reacted with coldness and rejection, though she recognized him as a family friend. My father felt compelled to hint to her afterwards that P.R. was indeed active on the right side.

Rosbaud was on the right side, but in uniform he was on the wrong side. It was probably a Luftwaffe uniform, since that was the organization that was sponsoring his trip. And being in uniform, with a military pass, he could go wherever he wished in Oslo. Some of the friends he met actually benefited from being seen with a German officer, but others suffered unkind remarks about collaborating. It depended on the circle one belonged to in Oslo. But all friends were eager to know about German progress in atomic research.

Paul's main mission, of course, was to pass on a mass of information about that research to Welsh via the XU, but it is also likely that he gave a circumspect version of the news to a few trusted friends.

Having learned definitely that he would not get permission for a stopover in Copenhagen, he wrote to Bohr, on July 3, "It would have been very important for me to see you again in order to discuss several questions that probably interest you as well as myself." He extended greetings from the physicist Harald Wergeland, Victor Goldschmidt, and Odd Hassel. So Bohr, hearing nothing to the contrary, continued to think that the Germans were on the track to a nuclear weapon.

An odd thing happened in Oslo a short time after Rosbaud's visit. A German scientist named J. Hans D. Jensen turned up in August and held a "colloquium" for a select group of Norwegian scientists. Jensen had been a professor at the University of Hamburg and had collaborated with the Austrian Hans Suess on the "magic numbers" that define the structure of the atom's nucleus. (For this work, Jensen won the Nobel Prize in physics in 1963. Suess recently noted that the magic numbers were first discussed in a paper by Victor Goldschmidt in 1938 — and that he and Jensen had appropriated the idea without giving credit.) Jensen often came to Norway during the war in connection with heavy-water production.

Harald Wergeland later gave this account of the colloquium to Professor Brynulf Ottar, who reported:

> Wergeland attended . . . together with Prof. Hylleras, Prof. Tom Barth, Dr. Romberg, and others. . . . Dr. Jensen asked the audience not to take notes, because he was afraid that this could be dangerous. But Wergeland remembered Barth giving him a sign not to bother about this. I believe that all persons present . . . had some connection with the underground organizations.
>
> Heisenberg's opinion was, according to Jensen, that Germany would be unable to make the bomb. Wergeland made a detailed report from this meeting and what Jensen told him privately. The next day or so, one of my co-workers in the XU organization . . . told me I had to go and see Wergeland, because he had some important papers which had to be sent to England as soon as possible. I visited Wergeland in his house . . . and I think Jensen was there, too.

Being there was foolish of Jensen and he was lucky to get away with it, but it did give Eric Welsh a good confirmation when he heard what

Jensen had said. He now had two reports from reliable sources. Cautiously, he requested further verification from Rosbaud, and once he had that, by the summer of 1943, the SIS was able to state—or, in a properly British way, understate—that the German atomic program "was ceasing to be a source of grave anxiety."

Because they did not have the benefit of word from the Griffin, the Americans believed the opposite.

TWENTY-THREE

"The Heart of Your Enemies"

VICTOR GOLDSCHMIDT was not only a Jew but a prominent Norwegian citizen. He would not remain undisturbed long. On October 22, 1942, his former secretary, Bodil Lonna, herself getting ready to flee, telephoned V.M. that she had heard that his arrest was imminent, but he ignored her warning, as he had ignored others. On the twenty-fifth, two Norwegian policemen came with a confiscation order for all of his property and money, allowed him some warm clothing, and then put him to Oslo's Bredtvedt Prison overnight.

V.M. might have appealed to Gulbrand Lunde, but by curious coincidence Lunde died in an "accident" the day after Goldschmidt's arrest. He and his wife, Maria, were driving onto a ferry at Ålesund when the craft moved forward and their black Mercedes plunged to the bottom of the bay. Whether accident or design, it was just retribution for the arrest of his friend and mentor. At the moment of the accident, Goldschmidt was being taken to the notorious concentration camp of Berg, an improvised prison for Jews. The conditions there were abominable. Goldschmidt was suffering from kidney disease and other ailments, and the camp physician, Dr. Jervell, obtained permission to take him to the hospital at nearby Tönsberg.

In the hospital, Goldschmidt encountered two Jews who completely transformed the brief remainder of his life. He shared his hospital room with Moses Katz, a well-known hosiery peddler on the streets of Oslo, and with Lesser Rosenblum, an umbrella-handle maker, whose establishment at Dronningsgate 28 was popular with the diplomatic community. Katz was an Orthodox Jew. Rosenblum was just the opposite, an atheist and a militant socialist.

When Goldschmidt first met them, he was seething with rage, and he swore he would never forget his tormenters. To his amazement, Moses Katz calmly replied, "Revenge is not for us; that must be left to the Almighty." "Well, what should we ask God to do then?" asked Goldschmidt. Katz replied, "You may pray that the heart of your enemies will be enlightened."

And to V.M.'s greater astonishment, the socialist and atheist Lesser Rosenblum interjected, "We must terminate the evil circle of retribution; else there can never be an end of evil." Goldschmidt's conversion must have been immediate and complete, for little else can explain his actions in the following month.

Goldschmidt's friends complained to the authorities that no one else could solve certain immediate and critical problems relating to fertilizers, and V.M. was released to return to Oslo early in November. He was calm, confident, and assured that no harm could come to him, for he had indeed prayed that the hearts of his enemies would be enlightened. But his prayers were not answered. The second week in November, his name was published in a newspaper in a list of Jews whose remaining property was to be confiscated. For V.M. that meant his precious microscopes, x-ray equipment, and measuring instruments. He decided not to pray for them but to make a vigorous protest, and he was promised that he could keep his precious instruments. But on November 26, he was arrested again and brought to Bredtvedt Prison for a second time. Moses Katz was already there. The next day, the two were taken with 531 other Norwegian Jews to the "Amerika Pier" to await the boarding of the *Donau* for transport to Auschwitz.

This is Goldschmidt's account, given to Norwegian authorities in Sweden a few weeks later:

> At 10:50 came a state policeman, seemingly the same who had arrested me the previous day, and called out to see whether Victor Moritz Goldschmidt was present. When I answered yes, he told me to walk forward toward the ship and said I was free and could return home. He added that he was glad to give me this message. I drove home in a taxi, which was paid by the state police, as I had had to hand in all my money at Bredtvedt the day before. . . . As I learned, my release had been engineered by Professor Halvor Solberg, the dean of our faculty, and protector [of the university] Rector Adolf Hoel, who . . . had gone to the chief of the state police, Marthinsen, and impressed on him that I had to be set free for work vital to the state.

This time, Goldschmidt knew his time was limited. That evening, Hans Suess, in Norway on another heavy-water mission, had dinner with V.M. in his Smestad flat. Sissy Feinsilber, Goldschmidt's woman friend, was there, but nothing could dispel his gloom. Canned goods had become rare in the Reich, so V.M. pressed a supply of them on Suess, saying he would not need them.

The *Donau* sailed without Goldschmidt but with Moses Katz and Lesser Rosenblum among the crowded passengers. They eventually perished at Auschwitz. Goldschmidt, three weeks later, was loaded into a hay wagon by the Resistance and transported, protesting all the way, to Sweden. At one point, German soldiers prodded the load of hay, but they missed Goldschmidt. V.M., however, had already suffered from the prods of his drivers, who had difficulty keeping him hidden in the hay.

Others had problems with Goldschmidt after he arrived in Stockholm. The kidney infection he had contracted in the Berg concentration camp was still with him, and when he checked into the Ersta Hospital, the doctors found he had a serious blood disease as well. Lise Meitner and other friends visited V.M. in the hospital, and word got to Eric Welsh that Goldschmidt was being too talkative about Rosbaud, XU, and other sensitive matters. It became vital to transport V.M. to London if only to shut him up.

But Goldschmidt insisted that he would not leave Sweden without Sissy, who had also found her way to Stockholm. In early March 1943, Sissy and V.M. stepped onto British soil at an SIS airfield in Huntingdonshire. That evening, V.M. was in a Kensington hotel under guard while Sissy went nearby to room with Goldschmidt's niece, Erika Schulhof. Often under escort, Goldschmidt and Sissy sampled whatever of the good life was left in London, but when they saw friends, Goldschmidt was still entirely too talkative for Eric Welsh's peace of mind.

Welsh decided to take the problem to Sir John Anderson, lord president of Churchill's Privy Council and supreme arbiter of all matters concerned with atomic energy. Anderson, an experienced physicist, had obtained his doctorate in Leipzig, and he knew Goldschmidt. The witness to the meeting was Michael Perrin (now Sir Michael), who was Eric Welsh's link to the technical side of the British atomic energy program. Welsh tended to bring intelligence matters relating to atomic energy to Perrin rather than to R.V. Jones for evaluation. Perrin has a vivid recollection of how Welsh placed the problem before the Lord President. Anderson, who wore a permanent enigmatic smile and would listen with his hands clasped together and thumbs pulling on his vest, heard Welsh out and then asked what he proposed to do. Welsh made a menacing gesture. Sir John, not usually a man of temper, erupted: "What! You are asking me, a former home secretary, to do this?"—and he mimicked the gesture. Welsh backed off and suggested that V.M. be exiled from London, to some place where fewer German agents might be lurking but that was convenient to the SIS. An interim solution was the Macaulay Institute for Soil Research in Craigebuckler, near Aberdeen. A while later, V.M. transferred to the Rothamsted Experimental Station near St. Albans—the SIS station where Section V conspired to foil German spies. But those places were too rural for Sissy Feinsilber, and she ran off to marry a Norwegian politician.

TWENTY-FOUR

"The House Is on the Hill"

AN AGENT IN PLACE and linked to London once again, Rosbaud had need of frequent and timely communications to learn the current collection requirements. The Norwegian students and a friendly Swedish diplomat did not travel frequently enough to handle the volume Welsh demanded and Rosbaud wanted to give.

Sverre Bergh then thought of a new means of communicating. Every night at nine P.M., Paul would listen on his Philips 990X to the BBC service, as would Bergh in Dresden. They became particularly attentive if the broadcast began with the code phrase *"Das Haus steht am Hügel"* ("The house is on the hill"). That meant there was a special message for the Griffin and Sigurd. Bergh always formed his messages in ten paragraphs, sometimes by subject, sometimes by sections of a subject. If London, for example, desired more information on paragraphs two, five, and seven of a message previously transmitted through Stockholm or XU, the BBC announcer would continue: "The house has two doors, five windows, and seven chimneys." Rosbaud and Bergh would then know their next collection requirement; more information was required on paragraphs two, five, and seven of the previous report. The system made possible the transmission of very detailed instructions and replies. Often, by the time Bergh came to Berlin, Rosbaud would have the information ready.

With the help of the new code, Bergh reported to Norwegian intelligence in 1945, ten to fifteen messages on atomic energy had been sent to London between 1942 and 1945, or an average of three to five a year. The average for all subjects was substantially greater.

Bergh estimates that he traveled from Dresden to Berlin to see Rosbaud some fifty to sixty times, that is, once or twice a month. All other British informants were casual sources, each sending a single report or two and then lapsing into silence. Considering all of Rosbaud's activities with Sverre Bergh and his other contacts, the Griffin could be said to have invented the business of industrial espionage.

At the end of 1942, information began to come in concerning the rocket threat. There had been a casual air reconnaissance of Peenemünde on May 15, 1942, but nobody seems to have correlated the photographs with the earlier reports from Sigurd and the Griffin. One of the wartime photo-interpretation experts, Ursula Powys-Lybbe, commented recently:

> Nobody . . . knew what the things [rockets] looked like or where they were based, and it was only by a stroke of luck that one was identified at the experimental base.
> If photo reconnaissance sorties had been laid on earlier, the interpreters would certainly have noticed "winged objects" either outside aircraft factory buildings or on their launching ramps, and as a result of their reports a bomber attack would have been carried out, if bomber aircraft at that time were sufficiently long range to reach the target. One can only guess at what transpired at higher echelons, but I would think that probably those who had access to the Oslo Report decided to sit on it for political reasons. Some scientists did not think it wise to pass on useful information, on the grounds of security.

Not until January 1943 were reconnaissance aircraft sent over Peenemünde again. It was because of reports received from "a Danish chemical engineer." He was agent "R.34," Aage C. Holger Andreasen, an importer and exporter of machinery. Andreasen had overheard or somehow had been privy to a conversation between a "Professor Fauner of the Berlin Technische Hochschule and an Engineer Stephan Szenassy." On November 30, 1942, Fauner or Szenassy had witnessed trials near Swinemünde of a rocket containing five tons of high explosive with a range of two hundred kilometers.

The two German scientists were not known to the SIS by those names, but R. V. Jones had speculated that "Fauner" might be a Professor Volmer at the Berlin Technische Hochschule and that "Szenassy" might be his son-in-law Stranski. Both of them would be credible sources. What Jones did not know was that both Volmer and Stranski often confided in Paul Rosbaud.

Zehlendorf is a quiet suburb next to Dahlem, where a substantial part of Berlin's scientists worked. Rosbaud, Ruth Lange, and Henri Piatier, a French physicist and POW, lived in the house of Magda and Michael Polanyi in the Waltraudstrasse, and not far away, in the Reiherbeizestrasse, lived the gregarious Bulgarian Iwan A. Stranski. Stranski and Rosbaud drank and jogged together. Stranski had a bad leg, but a mutual friend has said that "Stranski could outrun Paul Rosbaud any time."

Stranski specialized in crystallography. Immensely prolific, he became internationally known as the father of crystal growth. The Sofia-born man had come to Berlin in 1930 as a postgraduate student to study under Max Volmer. A pragmatic experimentalist, Volmer had patented in 1918 the basic design for a mercury-vapor vacuum pump. Known as the Volmer pump, it is even today a familiar piece of laboratory and industrial equipment. With royalties from his various inventions, Max and Lotte Volmer had the well-known architect Emil Ruester build them a delightful villa in Babelsberg, just southeast of Zehlendorf. Nearby, spanning the Havel, is the Glienicke Bridge where nowadays east and west exchange their spies. In the Volmer greenhouse was a collection of orchids from all over the world. There, at Jaegersteig 8, one might have found on an evening Albert Einstein playing the violin and Max Volmer at the piano. Volmer resembled Paul Rosbaud a little, and they shared an old world charm, a love of music, and a preference for bow ties. They also may have shared some secrets.

The "chemical engineer" was supposed to have sent three reports dated December 22, 1942, January 1, 1943, and March 31, 1943. Churchill was told in June that the three reports "describe the conversation in the first report." That is a most curious statement since the total length of the reports is only a moderate paragraph. It is even more curious that by the end of 1942 Max Volmer was in a Gestapo prison. And in an adjoining cell was none other than Hans Kummerow, one of the purported authors of the Oslo Report.

Volmer had helped hide one of his Jewish students, Hans Briske, and his family. Briske also was in contact with the husband of one of Volmer's closest research collaborators, Gertrud Zimmerman Tohmfor. Erhard Tohmfor was associated in some way with the Rote Kapelle. In the Kummerow–Oslo Report legend, it was Tohmfor who made all of the arrangements for Kummerow to go to Oslo, but Tohmfor's widow is emphatic that "there was no connection with Kummerow in 1939." Only at the end of 1941 or early 1942 did Kummerow ask Erhard Tohmfor for a job "that would relieve him for active service in the war." But in 1942 Tohmfor was associated with Kummerow, and Kummerow was associated with the Soviet spy ring.

The Gestapo roundup of the Rote Kapelle had begun in July. On September 17, Gestapo agents at Potsdammer Bahnhof arrested two men who were passing information. One was a Soviet agent who had recently parachuted into Germany. The other was Kummerow. Andreasen was supposed to have obtained his information on December 18, but by then Volmer was either in prison or very close to being arrested. If still free, he would have been excessively cautious.

Thus, the idea of a commercial traveler like R.34 as a *primary* source at that particular moment has to be questioned. Perhaps Volmer and R.34 met on a matter like the licensing of a patent, and Volmer, in the company of Stranski, gave away some Peenemünde secrets, but that does not seem likely. In Stockholm, R.34 reported to Victor Hampton, who was an associate of Sverre Bergh's contact. Possibly Andreasen, whose courage cannot be understated, was the courier of information that originated with Rosbaud.

Rosbaud knew Andreasen. Sverre Bergh recalls the name and believes he heard it from Rosbaud; he associates the name with Christmastime of 1942. But Bergh had nothing to do with the transmission of any information in which Andreasen was involved.

After the war, when Bergh was discussing with Welsh and Roscher Lund the reasons that his and Rosbaud's Peenemünde reports of the autumn of 1941 had been ignored, he learned about the Danish reports of 1942–1943. Roscher Lund and Eric Welsh must have felt some compulsion to assure Bergh that his and Rosbaud's efforts had not been in vain.

Bergh did transmit a V-2 item from Rosbaud to Eric Welsh through XU channels during that period. Askania Werke produced the gyroscopes for the guidance of the V-2, and Rosbaud had obtained full technical details of the system. The only item of consequence in the three reports presumed to have been transmitted by Andreasen concerns the gyroscopic guidance.

The probable explanation for there being three reports that finally ignited interest in Peenemünde is that only the first report came through Andreasen, who may have obtained it himself from Volmer and Stranski—or from Rosbaud. At least one overlapping report was received from Bergh and Rosbaud after Volmer was arrested. As he had done before and would do again, Welsh protected his most sensitive sources by attributing some of their information to other sources less sensitive. Welsh held the Danish sources, not directly controlled by himself, to be less sensitive than his Norwegian networks. And for Welsh's purposes, the fewer sources cited, the better. Thus, he attributed all three reports to "the Danish chemical engineer."

A year later, Andreasen was arrested by the Gestapo and incarcerated in a concentration camp until the end of the war. With both Volmer and Andreasen immobilized, it was convenient for Welsh to perpetuate the attribution to them.

Whatever the explanation, what are called the chemical engineer reports are significant in that they finally catalyzed interest in Peenemünde, three years after the Oslo Report identified the testing site and a winged object being developed there. But the three reports only complicate the Rosbaud mystery. It cannot be coincidence that the Rote Kapelle keeps cropping up in the Rosbaud story.

There is the inescapable fact that Hilde Benjamin was the legal adviser to the Soviet Commerce and Trade Delegation in Berlin, that her brother-in-law Walter was a prominent Marxist philosopher, that Paul Rosbaud was fond of Hilde and Georg Benjamin and once even risked visiting a concentration camp with Hilde to give food and clothing to her husband, and that Hilde's sister Ruth was Paul's mistress and lived with him throughout the war. And why, just when the Gestapo was rounding up the Rote Kapelle, did Paul manage to be away from Berlin more than at any other time during the war? He traveled to Budapest, Kolozsvár, Zagreb, Vienna, Salzburg, Holland, and elsewhere in the last six months of 1942. And he wrote to his brother, rather injudiciously, "I want to be a little less visible here."

But not a shred of evidence has thus far come to light that Paul Rosbaud was a member of Rote Kapelle or that he was ever a Soviet spy. What is evident is that before, during, and after the war Rosbaud sought the company of the exciting and the unusual people of his time, and politics was no barrier in that quest.

Most of all, he fantasized about the return of the Hapsburgs and the Austro-Hungarian Empire. Some of his Jewish friends shared those fantasies. Many had left Austria after 1933, but Paul continued to correspond with them. Josef Roth, a novelist from Galicia, had converted to Catholicism, and until he died in Paris, in 1939, he continued to evoke the vanished Danube monarchy in *The Radetzky March* and other writings. So did Stefan Zweig, who, in Rio de Janeiro a few days after Carnival in February 1942, had taken a massive dose of veronal after finishing his retrospective work, *The World of Yesterday*. Ruth Lange and a French friend remember Paul mourning for Zweig. Perhaps that is why Paul went to Budapest in October to promenade along the Ferenc Jozsef Rakpart, with its fashionable hotels and cafés, and to drink in the Transylvania wine rooms of Erdélyi Borozo.

At Kolozsvár, Paul stayed with the mathematician Samu Borbely and listened to the Gypsy bands playing in the gardens on the banks of the Szamos. But the journey to the world of yesterday had to end, and Paul returned to Berlin—to the harsh reality of the present. He still had one important mission to carry out before the end of 1942.

In December, he went to Holland, ostensibly to arrange for some publications. His actual purpose was to contact the Dutch underground. Perhaps, for the time being, he was a bit uneasy about transmission from Berlin. He wanted to pass on information about preparations for chemical warfare and suspected that Dr. Jan Hendrik de Boer of Philips Eindhoven was now working on that problem in Britain.

That, indeed, was true. De Boer had departed for England on May 14, 1940, the day the Luftwaffe utterly flattened Rotterdam. An organic chemist, de Boer was highly versatile, his research ranging from biochemistry to infrared imaging. He was the right man to receive the information Rosbaud had. The only problem was how to get it to him. Once again, Rosbaud displayed a trait that annoyed Eric Welsh mightily. For "Theodor" was not the exclusive taskmaster of the Griffin. If Rosbaud thought something should go directly to a someone other than Welsh, he would send it to that person. Of course, Paul had no idea how his information was used and analyzed in Britain. He did not know of R. V. Jones until after the war, so he directed his information to where he thought it would be most useful.

That is why Paul went to Leyden to see some of de Boer's associates, particularly Hendrik B. G. Casimir and Anton Eduard van Arkel. Paul also met a cousin of van Arkel's, Hille Ris Lambers, a botanist, and entrusted to him some information about a new toxic material that could pass through gas masks. This was iron pentacarbonyl, which would decompose under the action of the carbon in a gas mask and asphyxiate the wearer. Rosbaud mentioned that the German experts on this technique were Professor Walter Hieber (another friend!) of the Institute of Inorganic Chemistry at the Technische Hochschule in Munich and a Dr. Eisenhut at the I. G. Farben works near Oppau. Lambers told Rosbaud that he had a way to reach de Boer, but Rosbaud thought the information so important that he also gave it to Sverre Bergh after returning from Holland.

Rosbaud saw many people, including Casimir and Hajo Bruining, at Philips in Eindhoven. Of Bruining, Casimir later wrote that he "remembers Rosbaud's visit during the war. He trusted Rosbaud completely, but apart from listening to the BBC together, they did not discuss illegal work. Bruining tells me that he heard later—but he does not recall the source—that R. had played an extremely dangerous game, collecting information under the cloak of Springer activities and passing it on to the Allies."

Rosbaud collected information in Holland as well as transmitting it. A hint as to what he was after is given by Professor R. Kronig, who recalled:

> During the last war Rosbaud visited me several times in Delft at my house. Although I had an inkling that the real object of his visits to Holland in wartime might not be purely personal or editorial, he never revealed to me anything about other purposes, nor did I ask him directly about this. Only later, after the war, some light was cast on these aspects: he probably endeavored to gather information about research going on in Europe that might lead to the realization of the German side of the atomic bomb.
>
> Now in Holland the government had purchased shortly before the war in Belgium several tons of uranium oxide, stored at Delft, while in Norway, Norsk Hydro could produce heavy water in considerable quantities, both substances being relevant, after Hahn's discovery, in connection with the possibility of constructing a fission bomb.

Some of the information that Rosbaud did not transmit through Sverre Bergh went out directly from Holland, where he had several direct contacts with British intelligence. One of them was Professor A. M. J. Michels, who had taken the position of de Boer at the Van del Waals Laboratory of the University of Amsterdam. Michels was one of the very few and one of the most important British agents in Holland. In the dedication to his 1978 book, *The Wizard War*, R. V. Jones paid tribute to several members of the Resistance groups, among them an "A. A. Michels," whom Jones now acknowledges to have been A. M. J. Michels.

Paul also saw in Eindhoven someone dearer to him, a Graz school-mate, Herbert Stifter. Stifter's daughter Susanne has written that Paul Rosbaud "is one of the two sons of Mrs. Rosbaud, who gave piano lessons to my father at Graz, long before W. W. I." Old friends were Paul's most trusted friends. Through the Stifter connection, Paul may have had a line to Allen Dulles, who directed the American Office of Strategic Services in Switzerland. But the Central Intelligence Agency (successor of the OSS) is firm in its assertion that there is nothing at all in the OSS archives about Paul Rosbaud. If Rosbaud had any contact at all with American intelligence, it probably was indirect and in connection with the Resistance rather than for the passing of technical information.

In 1938, Stifter had fled Austria, where he had been the editor of several popular journals, to accept an editorial job with Philips in Eindhoven. Holland was a poor choice for a refugee, but he had friends there. One of Allen Dulles's contacts in Holland, W. E. A. De Groot, was prepared for the Nazis:

> When in May 1940 the Netherlands was ... invaded, I began doing the work which had earlier been agreed on with the authorities and for which it was felt I was fitted because of particular circumstances. I was personally acquainted, in fact, with a man in the headquarters of the State Security Service in Berlin whose responsibilities included editing confidential reports made out by Himmler and taken to Hitler in person. This man, who was totally opposed to the Nazis, was of course an extremely important contact. He enabled me, for instance, to inspect very recent reports, of the kind referred to above, which I learned by heart and two days later dictated at the house of Allen Dulles, who was then special assistant to the American minister in Bern. . . .
>
> I involved Dr. Stifter, whose tact and intelligence I greatly respected, in my Resistance activities by pretending that what he did in relation to the German authorities was done at my request. . . . The upshot of this was that both Dr. Stifter and I were regarded as people who were perhaps conducting secret negotiations with the Allies in consultation with the highest circles in Berlin. The fear of assuming responsibility was so great among the Nazi authorities in the occupied areas that the

verification of things was not even considered. . . . Dr. Stifter had a number of contacts among Resistance groups which were extremely useful and which consisted of persons other than my contacts. He had a line to the Vatican, for instance, via a Catholic priest in Essen.

And so did Rosbaud. His Vatican contacts were Father Alois Gatterer, S.J., born in Linz of an old Grazer family, and Father Joseph Junkes, S.J., the son of a postal assistant at Goch in the Rheinland. (Gatterer was a distant relative, himself descended from Judith Ginsburger, whose granddaughter married a Gatterer in 1801.) Both priests were astrophysicists at the Vatican Observatory at the pope's summer home, Castel Gandolfo. Brother Karl Treusch, S.J., who helped the two priests to construct experimental equipment, has recalled hearing Rosbaud's name during the war, but he could not remember in what connection. Nevertheless, Paul's relationship with Fathers Gatterer and Junkes was close, and they were among the very few who knew how devout Paul was. In 1946, Father Gatterer came to London to give him a personal message from Pope Pius XII and a rosary blessed by His Holiness, according to a letter Paul wrote to Hans. But he did not tell Hans what the message was, and the Vatican archives do not reveal it, either.

Yes, 1942 was a productive and busy year for the Griffin. The war would rage for two and a half more years; they would be even more crowded with danger.

TWENTY-FIVE

The French Connection

A SON was born to Juliette Grenier Piatier in 1918, in a cave at Bar-le-Duc, France, where death was far more usual than birth. In February two years earlier, the German armies had launched a surprise attack against the fortresses of Verdun. A new French commander, General Henri Pétain, promised, "They shall not pass," and he held the ground in a long-drawn-out battle in which a million men died. The lifeline that saved the French defenders was a fifty-mile stretch of hell called the Sacred Road, kept open for supplies and reinforcements from Bar-le-Duc by a monumental effort.

Juliette's son Henri must have breathed in some gunpowder at birth because, after he had grown, he graduated from the École Polytechnique in Paris and became an artillery reserve officer. At the beginning of the 1939 war, he was posted to the front lines. One of his best friends at the Polytechnique had been his classmate Charles Peyrou, who was also commissioned in the artillery and sent to the Maginot Line. Neither, however, had any ambitions for an army career—both intended to finish their advanced degrees in physics after the war was over.

In that fearful spring of 1940, the Germans took Verdun with no trouble, bypassed the Maginot Line, and rolled up the French army —including Henri Piatier and Charles Peyrou. Marshal Pétain, the World War I hero of Verdun, became premier in a new government sympathetic to the Nazis. When the two classmates met again, it was in Germany, at a Hitler Youth camp that had been converted to a POW stockade.

Meanwhile, even in these trying times, Frédéric Joliot-Curie—with his wife, Irène, co-holder of the Nobel Prize in chemistry—continued his research at the Collège de France. He was employing his cyclotron for further investigation of the problem of nuclear fission. In September, he had a visit from a German delegation headed by General Eric Schumann of the Army Weapons Office. Schumann demanded that Joliot-Curie turn over the heavy water that Allier had smuggled out of Norway.

Impossible, said Joliot-Curie. The heavy water was at the bottom of the Atlantic. Which ship? asked Schumann. Why, it was the — and here Joliot-Curie named a ship known to have been sunk in the Bordeaux evacuation, not the *Broompark*. The German general was not happy at the news. He announced that there were to be some changes in authority in Joliot-Curie's lab.

Schumann's interpreter during this exchange was a man named Wolfgang Gentner, a friend of Paul Rosbaud's and secretly a determined anti-Nazi. Gentner had worked in Paris with Joliot-Curie for some years and then in Berkeley with Ernest Lawrence, the inventor of the cyclotron. More recently, he had been assisting Walther Bothe to design his cyclotron in Heidelberg. The result of the Schumann visit was an edict that Gentner would assume control of the Paris cyclotron operations.

Before research reactors became available, cyclotrons were the essential tools in nuclear research, and the best way to observe the nuclear reaction produced by the cyclotron beam was by means of a cloud chamber. The path of a bombarding particle and its collisions could be nicely viewed and photographed by this means. Bothe, Gentner, and Meier-Leibnitz had just completed a beautiful atlas of cloud-chamber photographs, with the encouragement of Paul Rosbaud.

After Gentner had taken charge, the thought struck him that it might be useful to have a French edition of the atlas to guide the work of his newly acquired staff at the Collège de France. He mentioned this to the distinguished physicist Louis LePrince-Ringuet. Not only was LePrince-Ringuet receptive but he had a suggestion for the translators. He had two bilingual students who would be ideal for the job. Unfortunately, they were now in a prisoner-of-war camp in Germany. Paul Rosbaud later told the rest:

> In 1942, I heard from Gentner that he had been approached by two French POWs, asking for permission to translate this atlas into French. . . . I felt sorry for these two physicists — neither of whom had his degree yet — and I tried to think of how to salvage something from their years

of captivity. I phoned some of my reliable friends and soon achieved my purpose.... Dr. Michael Schön was delighted to apply for permission for both to continue their work on pure physics, first with Schön and later with Timofeev-Ressovsky, on biophysics. I was even able to arrange for Piatier to live with me for a year.

Although Peyrou did not live in the Rosbaud household, his life was profoundly affected by Paul's intervention and Paul's personality. He wrote:

> Even if I try to control my French superlatives when I write in English, I think I can say that Rosbaud was a superior man and a fascinating personality. He had a great influence on me and my life. Even the simple fact that he took the initiative of calling both Piatier and me to Berlin to start in physics changed all my life from the point of view of my physics, of my conception of the world (political or other), and even from a family point of view, since I met my wife in Berlin.... I owe to him a part of my musical and above all my political education.

Piatier and Peyrou found some rooms in Schöneberg at Apostel Paulestrasse 18. After Rosbaud was bombed out of the Polanyi house early in 1943, he and Ruth found a nice villa in Teltow, and Piatier moved in with them, having obtained permission to wear civilian clothes. Ruth and Henri saluted Paul as the Skipper, but Rosbaud ran a loose ship. All that was prohibited was gloom. In bringing Henri Piatier into his house, Rosbaud had connected with the major French Resistance network, Noah's Ark, led by Marie-Madeleine Foucarde, a thirty-two-year-old mother of two. Her agents took animals as their code names. Marie-Madeleine's major contact in the SIS has described her as having "Nefertiti-like beauty and charm." There was a more secret subnetwork, Druid, which did not take the code names of animals, and that was the network which was in indirect contact with Rosbaud through Henri Piatier. But much of what Piatier reported was independent of Rosbaud.

In fact, Peyrou and Piatier probably were selected not just because they were bilingual but because Rosbaud needed at least one of them for other purposes. Piatier had become agent Rhein-1202 of the Druid network. Rhein is an anagram of Henri, and 1202 was the postal code of his brother's office.

André Piatier, three years older than Henri, was an economist and had been a French intelligence agent before the war. The Institut de

France had an office in Berlin, a private mansion next to the Reich War Office. André worked at the institute for a while, and through a brilliant analysis of unclassified documents obtained next door was able to work out the secret German army budget. In June 1940, artillery officer André Piatier laid down his arms along with thirteen thousand other French soldiers in the Pyrenees. But he escaped the fate of his brother.

André made contact at Bordeaux with the new Vichy government and joined its Merchant Marine Administration in a cover job for his activities in the Druid network. In September 1940, he contacted British intelligence in Geneva at 41 Quai Wilson, where Frederick (Fanny) van den Heuvel was chief of the SIS station. He also was a papal count and a director of Eno's Fruit Salts — very good for the digestion. And shortly, he would be smoothing Paul Rosbaud's channels in Switzerland.

André's organization had unlimited access to French prisoners of war. Only five words on a postcard per week were allowed each POW, but with a number of prisoners participating in the scheme, substantial coded messages were sent from the camps. POWs labored at the most sensitive war facilities, and they were good observers. If necessary, a POW with important information could be brought out of camp or separated from a work force. All that was necessary was an injection of atropine to increase the heart rate and a bar of soap to induce foaming at the mouth. A camp commandant was quick to discharge someone with such a pernicious disease to a civilian hospital. Vichy representatives, some of them Resistance agents, roamed Germany in the camps to look after the welfare of prisoners and to gather information.

Naturally, the Griffin could not resist tapping such a resource, especially when one of the key agents, Rhein-1202, was living with him.

In August 1945, Rosbaud submitted this report to Allied intelligence:

> I am very glad that I met Piatier, he became an intimate friend of mine and did his best to get all sorts of information about the new weapons, the Nazi war industry. He was all the time in connection with the leaders of French camps of prisoners of war, who were informed by him about every phase of the war, according to information given by the French service of the BBC; he organized small groups of active prisoners and

he came in contact with other prisoners in the concentration camp of Oranienburg (branch in Lichterfeld Sud). He arranged [for] the clandestine communications of the French prisoners to be sent to their parents in France and he gave me a great deal of the contents of the food parcels sent to him from his mother—and for his compatriots in the concentration camp. . . . I am grateful that I found in Piatier such a gallant ally and I dare say that the friendship with this *chevalier sans peur et reproche* is the only thing I owe to Hitler.

Piatier did not see this report until recently, and he has responded, "The confidence which we had in one another was such that Paul Rosbaud kept me current concerning his intelligence activities for Great Britain." But Rosbaud did not tell Piatier of everything he and Sverre Bergh were channeling through each other. On occasion, Rosbaud orchestrated what may have been the only occasions of collaboration of the Norwegian and French Resistances.

Now, Rosbaud had two inside men in a war plant. Michael Schön, an upright, very devout Catholic nicknamed Der Heilige Vater (the Holy Father), directed a research laboratory at Osram, which in peacetime was known for its electric light bulbs. In wartime, it conducted research for the Luftwaffe. Schön's own speciality was phosphorescent materials. Schön, Piatier, and Peyrou wrote secret papers on the subject, and the results were reported not only to the Luftwaffe but to foreign eyes as well.

In the adjoining laboratory at Osram was a ceramic research facility that developed the special material, called cermet, an experimental substance, for the motors of the new jet aircraft, the Me-262. It was the plane that could have restored air supremacy to Germany, and it performed beautifully when it finally came into service. Fortunately, it had problems that delayed its operational capability until it was too late; the Me-262 never became an important factor in the war.

Piatier and Peyrou knew that cermet would be of interest to the British, so Henri stole a small sliver of the material, about the diameter of a pencil and two centimeters long. But how to get the sample to England?

Sverre Bergh knew a friendly Swedish journalist, Olle Ollen, well known in Berlin for his passion for tennis. Once in a while, he would send his racquets back to Stockholm to have them restrung. Sacrificing one of his precious racquets for a good cause, Ollen allowed Bergh to hollow out part of the handle, insert the cermet sample, and cap it. In a few days, the tennis racquet reached the home of Oddvar Aas, the Norwegian press attaché in Stockholm and one of the liaison staff with Eric Welsh's representative in that city. Neither Aas nor his wife had any idea as to why they had been sent Ollen's tennis racquet. And so it remained in their home—until the thought occurred to Mrs. Aas that perhaps John Whistondale might be interested in it. The cermet thus found its way to Eric Welsh. But that was not all that Rosbaud provided on the Me-262.

The Griffin found that Osram was producing cermet for Hermann Goering's research establishment, near Braunschweig, known as LFA. As he had almost everywhere else, Rosbaud had a friend at LFA. He was Ernst Schmidt, the director of research. Since Rosbaud had come to Springer Verlag, the firm had been publishing successive editions of Schmidt's popular *Introduction to Technical Thermodynamics*. One day, Paul rang up Schmidt to discuss a forthcoming edition. Would Schmidt mind his coming over one evening to chat for a few hours?

Of course not. So Paul spent a delightful evening at Schmidt's Fasanenstrasse home and learned something about the Me-262. Within the week the information was on its way to Stockholm via Sverre Bergh's channel. This was how Rosbaud used his French and Norwegian connections to inform the British on German jet production.

Collecting intelligence was pleasure, and the tricks they played on Nazi officials afterward made for many hilarious evenings for Henri and Paul. Ruth laughed along with them, but she rarely was let in on the actual details of the information they had purloined. But the Skipper's crew were concerned about Paul's state of health. He was anemic and weak. Peyrou and Piatier shared canned foods from the packages they received, as POWs, from France. Peyrou's brother was stationed at the Suez Canal and was able to send Charles packages of better items to share with Paul.

A friend of Piatier's who worked in an abattoir stole a ham and sold it to him, even though for both it was a crime punishable by death. On the S-Bahn, Piatier, with the ham under his jacket, looked like a frightened heavyweight wrestler. Later, the ham was divided into four pieces, and Rosbaud gained great satisfaction from selling a quarter to one of the directors of Springer Verlag for the price of the whole ham. The household ate well for weeks.

Paul got more satisfaction out of other pranks. Michael Schön, the boss of Peyrou and Piatier at Osram, was always experimenting with chemical additives to stretch his gas mileage. One day he poured carbon tetrachloride into the gas tank of his little DKW. The tank corroded, and Schön lost the use of his automobile for the rest of the war. But the experiment was instructive and useful. Piatier prepared capsules of the chemical for other POWs, who would drop them into the tanks of the military vehicles they had to service. They also added salt and sand to the grease boxes.

The trick that brought the most joy to Rosbaud, however, was the explosion of the Telefunken plant in north Berlin. Inspired by an accidental explosion in prewar France, Piatier and his friends introduced compressed air into the plant's gas supply. The authorities never did comprehend why a hit by a small bomb in the next air raid caused the entire plant to explode.

Rosbaud and Piatier had different spymasters, and with all the antics they were enjoying, they never neglected their primary tasks. Since the beginning of 1943, Eric Welsh finally had signaled Rosbaud to concentrate on what was going on at Peenemünde. Often Rosbaud did not have to try very hard for such information. At the end of July 1943, he received a letter from a well-known Nazi scientist whom he detested and regarded as a buffoon but nevertheless had been cultivating for information. The letter was from Pascual Jordan, and the return address was Neue Feldpostanschrift: Heimat-Artillerie-Park 11, Karlshagen/Pommern, Aerodynamisches Institut. Jordan's new address was the professional workers' barracks at Peenemünde. Rosbaud now had an inside man, or perhaps just another inside man.

Jordan complained about an officer and added, "I have no idea when and how I might come to Berlin." But he was eager to get away, and he succeeded within a week's time.

Pascual Jordan's great-grandfather, for whom he was named, had been a Spanish soldier in Napoleon's army who settled down in Germany. Himself the son of an artist who became a professor at the Technische Hochschule in Hanover, Jordan rebelled at an early age against the evangelistic Lutheranism practiced by his family. He was a child prodigy who questioned everything and found some of the answers in adventures into the occult. In later years, he was drawn to psychic phenomena, and he corresponded with Carl Jung about dreams.

Physics held some of the other answers Jordan was seeking, and after graduating from his father's Technische Hochschule, Jordan had the good fortune to become "the best pupil" of Max Born in Göttingen. This was at the time when classical physics underwent a revolution because of the invention of the quantum theory. The three inventors were Werner Heisenberg, Max Born, and Pascual Jordan. Two became Nobel laureates. The third became a member of the Nazi Party.

The membership card of Nazi Party member number 2810642 has a photograph of a bespectacled, slim, and well-groomed man who was accepted by the party on May 1, 1933, the day that Hitler ordered a halt to the avalanche of membership applications that followed his accession to power. Eager to show his allegiance to the New Order, Jordan joined a Jew-baiting SA unit that November. By that time, he had attained his professorship at the university in the Hanseatic city of Rostock. His former colleagues at Göttingen, Nazi and non-Nazi, could no longer abide him. At the beginning of the war, Jordan obtained an army commission and divided his time between Rostock and an air defense research establishment at Bremen's Neuenland Airfield.

That Paul Rosbaud could associate with this Nazi fanatic is but one more illustration of Rosbaud's attraction to anything bizarre. Besides, Jordan undeniably was intellectually stimulating and sometimes amusing. He had a severe handicap that made a conversation with him difficult—even painful; he was a stutterer and almost incomprehensible when sober. Rosbaud knew how to correct this and looked forward to Pascual's visit, especially since the Nazi scientist was now at Peenemünde.

Jordan's impressions of the work at Peenemünde were fresh but somewhat random. It helped that he was working with measurement techniques similar to those used for the phosphor problems that Henri Piatier was researching in Michael Schön's laboratory at Osram. Dr. Hermann Kurzweg, one of the senior research staff, has recalled that Jordan was generally useful on all theoretical problems at Peenemünde and had access to everything. Ruth Lange played the seductive role, and the rest of the Rosbaud ménage began to ply Jordan with drink and questions about Peenemünde. It was an uproarious evening that still remains a vivid memory for Henri Piatier and Ruth Lange.

Jordan was hardly in condition to notice that Piatier was taking notes. The report, mainly about V-2 rocket research at Peenemünde East, was transmitted the next day by Henri Piatier through the Druid channel, in which André was a crucial link.

Henri Piatier recalls that the Allied attacks on Peenemünde happened just after this transmission, so that dates the Jordan episode as early August 1943. There was another transmission concerning Peenemünde through Druid at the same time, but it concerned the V-1 winged weapon developed at Peenemünde West. On August 16, Commandant Leon Faye (Eagle) and Marie-Madeleine Fourcade (Hedgehog) were in a cottage near Chichester sorting out reports that had come in on Operation Dürer the night before. The packet had been loaded on a Lysander at Bouilhancy, forty kilometers from Paris. The pilot was Vaughan Fowler, and the flight was smooth, without incident.

One of the reports brought back was "out of the ordinary." It was a detailed description of the V-1 weapon developed at Peenemünde West, along with plans for its deployment. The report was said to have come from a source known as Amniarix, the code name for the pixieish Jeannie Rousseau, whose profession, then as now, was interpreter. She had coaxed the information from a German captain who was attached to the new V-1 deployment group headed by Colonel Max Wachtel.

Marie-Madeleine Fourcade confirms that both Amniarix and Rhein-1202 operated in the Druid network. Each performed valiantly, but Rhein-1202 was in the Reich itself throughout the war, a situation somewhat unusual for French Resistance operatives. As a result, the 1943 V-1 report has become very well known, but the equally informative companion report on the V-2, taken to Winston Churchill at the same time, remains quite unknown.

On the afternoon of Tuesday, August 17, 1943, the senior staff of Peenemünde assembled in the office of General Walter Dornberger to discuss production delays. Wernher von Braun, who after the war always maintained he was at Peenemünde for the thrill of future space travel, was the most vehement, complaining that "we first of all have to develop in peace and quiet a prototype we can mass-produce and then go on to blueprints for production." The windows of the office faced westward, and the brightly colored curtains displayed cathedrals and griffins.

That night, the curse of the Griffin shattered von Braun's peace and quiet. Five hundred and sixty RAF four-engine aircraft found their targets at Peenemünde, dropping 1528 tons of explosives and 267 tons of incendiaries. The V-2 facilities that the Griffin, Sigurd, and Rhein-1202 had described were completely destroyed. A month later, Marie-Madeleine's Noah's Ark network was taken apart by the Gestapo.

The V-1 "flying bomb" facilities reported by Amniarix were untouched. The first V-1 fell at Swanscombe, Kent, at 4:18 A.M. on June 13, 1944, just a week after the Allied assault on the Normandy beaches. The first V-2 killed three people and injured seventeen at Chiswick in West London at 6:30 P.M. on September 8. In the remaining months of the war, six thousand British civilians were killed by the V-1 flying bombs, and twenty-seven hundred were killed by the V-2 rockets. "I aimed for the stars," said Wernher von Braun. He missed. He hit London.

TWENTY-SIX

The Fox

ALTHOUGH BY 1943 the atomic bomb had ceased to be Eric Welsh's first priority in technical intelligence, it remained high on his list of collection requirements. Politically, it was becoming more important, and Welsh was never one to ignore the preferences of high political figures. And though some of his colleagues in the SIS may have thought at the time that Welsh was open with them, he decidedly was not. R. V. Jones has written, "I suspect in retrospect that Welsh was beginning to use me, as he ultimately used others in more eminent positions, as a puppet."

There were serious technical questions still to be solved by the British and Americans and uncertainties about the best routes to the bomb. The Germans might take an unanticipated route, so they had to be watched carefully. For the Norwegians, the atomic bomb remained the top intelligence-gathering requirement, for they felt a special responsibility. Norway was the only producer of the heavy water that might provide the key to success. No one perceived that more acutely than Leif Hans Larsen Tronstad.

The heavy burdens of life were imposed upon him before he was a year old. His father, a farmer in Baerum, just outside of Kristiania, died then, and from a young age, Leif had to labor hard to help support a sister and his widowed mother. He saved enough money to study at the Norwegian Technical University in Trondheim and, because of his fine record, was recommended by his professors to colleagues in Berlin. Any student thought to have promise by his professors was soon discovered by that impresario of talent, Paul

Rosbaud. Tronstad, with his blond hair, laughing blue eyes, sharp mind, and irrepressibly blithe spirit, attracted Rosbaud. Soon Tronstad was in Rosbaud's stable of *Metallwirtschaft* authors, writing articles on plasticity of metals and metallic films.

After studying in Berlin, Stockholm, and Cambridge, Tronstad returned to Trondheim as one of the youngest professors in Norway. He had become intrigued by the energy possibilities inherent in the atom. Already, heavy water seemed to hold the key to unlocking that energy. The first person in Norway to be become interested in the production of heavy water had been Odd Hassel, Rosbaud's silent albino friend. In 1933, immediately after the discovery of heavy water, Hassel approached Norsk Hydro about using their facilities at Rjukan and Vemork to produce heavy water, but he could not arouse any interest.

Jomar Brun, chief engineer of the plant, has said:

> Later on, in the summer of 1933, Tronstad and I presented a proposal to Norsk Hydro to take up technical heavy water production. We had been puzzled by the interest of the German firm I. G. Farbenindustrie in getting samples of electrolyte from the Vemork plant. . . . Our proposal was accepted, and after some experimental work we were able to present the layout of a commercial plant, still on a very small scale. This plant was started early in 1934.

That was the year when Brun called in Eric Welsh, of the International Paint Company in Bergen, to make the special floor tiles that would resist the caustic fluid and prevent the loss of the precious heavy water. From that moment on, the British spy learned everything there was to know about the production of heavy water and its possible uses. The nexus of the spymaster Welsh, his master spy Rosbaud, and the Norwegian heavy-water creator and destroyer, Leif Tronstad, had begun to form at the same moment that the discovery of the neutron and heavy water made the unleashing of the energy within the atom seem feasible.

In September 1940, two young artillery officers, Erik Welle-Strand and Sverre Midtsku, had come to England after the occupation of Norway but then returned to set up clandestine radio stations. Midtsku's group operated out of Oslo; Welle-Strand was in Trondheim ostensibly to resume his studies. Welle-Strand's operation was code-named Skylark, but because he could not operate a radio, he recruited a fellow student, Bjørn Rørholt, to run it. A sergeant, Rørholt had been captured in the Gulbrandsdal fighting and had served some time in the Grini Prison. He was a nephew of Alfred Roscher Lund, then in Stockholm as military attaché and chief of intelligence for the exiled Norwegian government.

The peculiar geography of Trondheim made it an ideal port of call, shipyard, and arsenal for the German navy. The Nid River empties into a harbor that is ice-free all year around, thanks to the Gulf Stream. But before it meets the sea, the Nid surrounds the city. Central Trondheim is the shape of a foot kicking northward. The Gestapo could easily close off the old city at the ankle and at the few bridges to the mainland. Rørholt and his companion, Egil Reksten, had digs at 5 Brinken, just outside the old city bridge, a safe location with easy access to their transmitting posts in the woods and later at Bymarka, a ski area west of Trondheim. With many German warships calling at Trondheim, it was a fertile location for the collection of intelligence.

Skylark made its first radio contact with England early in February 1941. The messages in both directions were always in coded English. About May 1941, just as Eric Welsh entered the technical intelligence picture, Rørholt and Reksten received message number 65 for Skylark:

FOR HEAVENS SAKE KEEP THIS UNDER YOUR HAT STOP TRY TO FIND OUT WHAT THE GERMANS ARE DOING WITH THE HEAVY WATER THEY PRODUCE AT RJUKAN STOP PARTICULARLY FIND OUT WHAT ADDRESS THEY SENT IT TO IN GERMANY STOP GUD SIGNE NORGE MESSAGE ENDS.

The two operators understood GUD SIGNE NORGE—God bless Norway—but hadn't the foggiest notion of what was meant by heavy water. They found out later that GUD SIGNE NORGE was Eric Welsh's personal mark to indicate "strictly limited" distribution on the British side. Rørholt had a friend who had been shot down by the British after he had escaped from Norway in a naval aircraft. The late friend's father was a director of Norsk Hydro. Given the son's fate, would the father, Sverre Bernhard Brænne still help the British? Rørholt thought so.

The audacious Rørholt went to see Brænne in Oslo. Brænne educated Rørholt about heavy water, but gave him a warning. He said that Imperial Chemical Industries was a competitor of Norsk Hydro in the world marketplace for chemicals and that in peacetime ICI was one of the major clients of the SIS. Brænne suspected that the inquiry about heavy water might be a probe by ICI for industrial intelligence under the guise of military necessity.

Returning to Trondheim, Rørholt, together with Reksten, composed a message in which was included one of the more famed and widely quoted phrases of the war:

MESSAGE NO 87 STOP YOUR NO 65 STOP IF YOU CAN ASSURE US THAT IT IS OF IMMEDIATE IMPORTANCE TO THE PRESENT WAR WE WILL GET THE INFORMATION YOU REQUEST AT ONCE STOP IF IT IS ONLY FOR THE ICI THEN PLEASE REMEMBER THAT BLOOD IS THICKER EVEN THAN HEAVY WATER STOP GOD SHAVE THE QUEEN STOP MESSAGE ENDS.

Eric Welsh did not pass the irreverent message to the queen, but he gave the censored version to R. V. Jones, whose account, however, diverges from Rørholt's.

As he had done for the Oslo Report in 1947, Jones in 1967 immortalized in his writings the phrase "Blood is thicker than heavy water" in the annals of intelligence. By Jones's account, he had received a telegram from Norway saying that the Germans were stepping up heavy-water production, and the sender of the telegram would be happy to supply more information if London wished. Jones then contacted Eric Welsh, who is said to have replied, "Bloody silly telegram! Who ever heard of heavy water?" But Welsh had; indeed he knew more about Norwegian heavy water than did Jones. The "bloody silly" response would have been typical of Welsh, a practiced deceiver for over two decades, who would hardly make an exception for R. V. Jones.

Skylark could not have sent the original telegram of inquiry because at the time the team knew nothing about heavy water, so Jones was mistaken. The content of message number 65 to Skylark from London indicates that it was sent in reaction to intelligence originating elsewhere, possibly Berlin or Stockholm — possibly Rosbaud. Message number 65 was apparently sent by someone who spoke Norwegian; hence the GUD SIGNE NORGE conclusion. Welsh spoke Norwegian. Jones would not have received a telegram directly from an agent, but Welsh might have. Thus it seems that Welsh, typically, "laundered" the messages and compounded the deception by claiming never to have heard of heavy water.

Jones also attributes "Blood is thicker than heavy water" to Leif

Tronstad, but Rørholt's memory is quite clear that Tronstad came into the Skylark operation after he and Reksten sent message number 87 to London. In fact, Rørholt is certain that when Tronstad was shown Welsh's request, "he did not immediately see the significance." From then on, every message from London on the subject of heavy water ended with "God bless Norway" and every reply from Skylark concluded with "God shave the queen."

That September, the remarkable and audacious Skylark team was broken by the Gestapo, and Rørholt had to flee to London via Sweden, where he consulted with Norwegian intelligence. A month later, Sverre Bergh passed through Gothenburg and linked up with John Whistondale for the Griffin operation.

In London, Rørholt finally set eyes on the mythical Eric Welsh. They met at the corner of Broadway and Birdcage Walk near the SIS headquarters and proceeded toward the Admiralty annex. There, Rørholt was briefed on the *Tirpitz*, which was lying at anchor in Trondheim fjord. He was to return to Norway to monitor the *Tirpitz*, a task that superseded intelligence on heavy water and earned him the first British DSO to be awarded to a Norwegian. The German atomic bomb was never again to be a collection priority for Rørholt, but he did hear about it, and about Paul Rosbaud, during later trips to London. For example, in mid 1942, Tronstad told Rørholt a detailed story of a chemical explosion that had destroyed an experimental assembly at Heisenberg's institute in Leipzig. The report had come through Rørholt's uncle, Roscher Lund. A while later, at the right moment, Rørholt made inquiries about the source of that report. It was, of course, a certain "Dr. Paul Rosbaud, chief editor of Nazi Germany's leading scientific periodical."

After the exposure of Skylark, Tronstad was forced to escape to Britain. Early in October, Rørholt and one of Welsh's deputies, John Turner, met Tronstad at King's Cross Station to escort him to Eric Welsh. The first order of business was heavy water. Welsh told Tronstad that stopping the heavy-water production at Vemork was a top war objective. Welsh said that he needed the most minute details about the production plant and that concerns about Imperial Chemical Industries' stealing the industrial secrets of Norsk Hydro were completely unfounded. Tronstad then visited ICI at Billingham and concluded that it was in his and Norway's best interest to cooperate

fully with Eric Welsh in providing detailed information about Vemork.

There is more mythology about Norwegian heavy water than about
any other aspect of the wartime German atomic project. Motion pic-
tures, authors, and even former SIS members practice their creativity
on the subject. Sir William Stephenson, alias Intrepid, the wartime
SIS representative in New York, recounted to his biographer how,
just before the invasion of Norway, he met Leif Tronstad on a train.
Tronstad happened to have all of the heavy-water blueprints in his
satchel, and of all people, it was Sir William who told the very competent physicist Leif Tronstad about atomic energy. Apparently Tronstad had not been reading the newspapers or his scientific journals
for over two years. Frightened, Tronstad pulled out the blueprints
and handed them over to Intrepid without concern about Imperial
Chemical Industries. Intrepid was also prescient in describing to
Tronstad the work of the "British Uranium Committee," which was
not to hold its first meeting for another six months. (It is no wonder
that the latest British edition of *A Man Called Intrepid* carries the
publisher's warning: "This novel is a work of fiction. Names, char-
acters, places, and incidents are . . . products of the author's imagination.")

By now, Tronstad really was uninhibited about sharing information
with the British and spent many an evening at the Thatched House
Club discussing politics. In November he met R. V. Jones and came
away with a very favorable impression, which endured. For Tronstad,
"Dr. J. is the prototype 100% honest thinking and working British
man."

It was not until the spring of 1942 that heavy-water intelligence
became well organized. Tronstad took the operational code name
Mikkel—the Fox. Mikkel established frequent contact with Jomar
Brun. At first, Welsh had hoped to find a means to transport the
heavy water to Britain, but the plan was abandoned as being impossible. So Brun, code name Master, began to sabotage the heavy-water
production cells by adding castor oil, which caused the water to foam
and the process to be interrupted. What Brun did not know was that
others in the plant were also feeding castor oil to the cells. There was
so much foaming that Brun thought it prudent to cease his little
sabotage effort temporarily.

The increased German interest in heavy water, Rosbaud's June report, and the visits of scientists directly concerned with the uranium program in Germany excited official interest in Britain and intensified the pressure on Welsh to get better intelligence and to do something about stopping the Norwegian heavy-water production. In July the War Cabinet ordered that the Vemork heavy-water plant be destroyed. For the moment, the atomic bomb once again became Welsh's top technical priority, as well as Tronstad's. Welsh arranged for Tronstad to dine with John Cockcroft on the evening of Thursday, August 6, so that Cockcroft could let him know how the atomic bomb project was proceeding. The full go-ahead had been given by President Roosevelt only a few weeks earlier. As far as the Allies were concerned, the "race" with the Germans was on, but the race had just been abandoned in Germany. Full confidence in Rosbaud's reports was not to be achieved until the next year.

Cockcroft gave Tronstad an overview of the Allied decisions and a technical briefing. An exuberant Tronstad left the dinner feeling that "this means it will be the scientists who will command the officers," a view not uncommon among many scientists when they first encountered the awesome new force. Leo Szilard had been frantic about it for years, and at the University of Chicago Metallurgical Laboratory (the cover name for nuclear research at the university) had already earned the sobriquet of Commissar for his constant talk of the German atomic threat.

Late that spring, the Commissar received a telegram that Houtermans had managed to send from Switzerland. The message is lost, but Eugene Wigner, one of the Hungarians who went to Einstein three years earlier to induce him to write to President Roosevelt, recalled the wording as very general — something like "They are getting organized." That was true. For the perpetually frightened man, this meant the worst, and Szilard spread the word around, thus creating huge excitement and eventually contributing to a rift between Britain and the United States.

Houtermans's telegram can be reconstructed from other documents from the metallurgical laboratory. He informed Szilard simply that Werner Heisenberg had been put in charge of atomic research. He then added a sentence about the paper he himself was writing at the time, in which he concluded that a nuclear chain reaction was a better

route than the separation of isotopes. From this scanty bit of information, Szilard built his own Potemkin village and convinced the
director of the laboratory, Arthur Compton, that he should inform
James Conant, chairman of the National Defense Research Council,
of the "threat." Wrote Compton in July, "We have become convinced
that there is real danger of bombardment by the Germans within the
next few months using bombs designed to spread radio-active material
in lethal quantities. . . . Apparently reliable information has reached
us to the effect that the Germans have succeeded in making the chain
reaction work. Our rough guess is that they may have had the reaction
operating for two or three months."

Houtermans would have been amused by this interpretation of his
telegram, for he knew full well that his German colleagues were nowhere near achieving a chain reaction. And he might have had another cup of coffee with Paul Rosbaud to toast the fertile imagination
of their frightened friend.

On July 23, the American embassy in London transmitted to the
British scientific authorities a paraphrase of a cable received from
Conant, containing Szilard's warning about the Germans. By this time,
Szilard and the entire American atomic hierarchy had transformed
Houtermans's vague telegram into firm intelligence that the Germans
were already operating a large-scale nuclear power plant and that an
attack on the United States by radioactive fission products was imminent. The British demurred and informed Conant on August 18,
1942, that "information which has just come to us indicates that research is still in progress." The source was not identified.

The source again, of course, was Paul Rosbaud, and this was one
of his very few reports, and probably the only one of that period,
given to the Americans.

The Szilard report brought to the surface the American fear that
the Germans might be building nuclear reactors not for bomb making
but for producing deadly radioactive materials, and it inflated that
fear out of all reasonable proportion. The United States hypothesized
a German nuclear reactor program many times larger than the pro-
jected American program. The result was a fearsome scenario, which
they passed to the British, who then put one of their best scientific
analysts, Alan Nunn May, on the problem.

The ultimate irony was that this analyst was one of two (at least) top Soviet spies working for the British to find out what the Germans were doing, Klaus Fuchs and Alan Nunn May. May, a friend and Trinity College classmate of the Soviet spy Donald Maclean, who had never made a secret of his Communist sympathies before the war, had been enlisted to help the MAUD Committee. Though normally based in Bristol, May was working with James Chadwick at Liverpool on bomb design. Altogether, it can be said with fair certainty that the Soviet Union was very well informed not only about Allied atomic bomb research but about the Allies' information on the German research.

May's technical analyses, like Fuchs's, had been objective, however, and contributed to the British rejection of the American fears about radioactive warfare. After all, if there was a German nuclear threat to Britain, the Russians would have been similarly threatened and would have wanted the truth. There are situations in which even spies must be objective. It is impossible to say how much this particular assessment contributed to the widening of the rift between the entire British and United States atomic programs. At Hyde Park in June, Churchill and Roosevelt had agreed on close cooperation, but by the end of the year Roosevelt's advisers were actively pushing aside the British. Perhaps, with their resources and immune location, the Americans would forge ahead of the British, but what the Americans did not realize was that by dealing out the British on technical matters, the United States also isolated itself from the excellent intelligence Britain was receiving on the German atomic program. Until the end of 1943, the British did not pass atomic intelligence of any importance to the United States.

TWENTY-SEVEN

"Juice"

FOR THE MOMENT, Welsh had more pressing matters on his mind than Anglo-American relations. He was set to destroy the Vemork heavy-water facilities. The Secret Intelligence Service had no operational capabilities for that kind of mission, so Welsh turned to the Special Operations Executive. Winston Churchill had created the SOE on July 22, 1940, with the words "And now set Europe ablaze!" Most of the epics of brave men and women engaged in covert activities during World War II are stories of the SOE, and they are known because they involved patriots of countries other than Britain, where the archives of the SOE, as of the SIS, are still sealed. In the course of its activities, the SOE collected information from Resistance groups that also conducted sabotage and otherwise disrupted the German war machine. Only one Resistance group in Europe devoted itself exclusively to general intelligence collection and reported not to the SOE, but exclusively to the SIS. That was XU, through which Rosbaud channeled many of his reports.

The first head of the Scandinavian Section of the SOE was Sir Charles Hambro, a member of a distinguished line of bankers that had come to Norway from Denmark. One of his wartime associates has described him as "enormously tall and athletic, with broad shoulders, broad eyes, and a broad smile." Harry Sporberg, Hambro's deputy, has said:

> Although I was not familiar with the Rosbaud operation, I certainly heard of him. I do not believe that Welsh and Hambro were close enough to have shared such a source. It would have been quite out of

character for any permanent member of SIS such as Welsh was to share such a source, but I do know that he kept Charles Hambro fairly regularly informed.

Other sources affirm Sporberg's impressions. Two of the foremost experts on the Resistance, Olav Riste and Berit Nøkleby, wrote:

> The agents sent in by SOE and SIS were all Norwegians but trained by the British. SIS was not involved in any activity of the home organizations; its sole interest was military intelligence from Norway, and its agents had strict orders to avoid unnecessary contact with people at home. These agents worked in utter secrecy, and little is known and less written about them.

That is one of the reasons that Rosbaud himself is so little known. Although Hambro knew of him, he never suggested that Rosbaud be tasked for the SOE. In 1941, Hambro took over direction of the entire SOE, and John Skinner Wilson replaced him as head of the Scandinavian Section. Rosbaud was never identified to Wilson. In 1942, there was a shuffling of positions in the SOE, and Hambro left the organization and shortly afterward went to Washington as part of a group for allocating uranium ores. (He did retain an interest in Rosbaud, however, and assisted him in Berlin after the war.)

Wilson was born into a religious family and in his earlier career had served for many years as deputy commissioner of police in Calcutta. At the time he came to the SOE, he was director of the Boy Scouts Association. A colleague of his in the Scouts has described Colonel Wilson as having "the appearance of being a rather shy and retiring person, but those of us who were privileged to know him soon realized this only concealed his kindness and generosity." In other words, he was the antithesis of Eric Welsh. On the other hand, one of Wilson's Norwegian contacts remembers him as "an ambitious social climber who constantly worried staff members of the Norwegian High Command about recommending him for the Order of St. Olav. I think of Wilson as being at least as devious as Eric Welsh, in his outwardly pious way."

But Wilson was a copy of Leif Tronstad, who had been a Boy Scout in Trondheim. And the men were allied in a mission — to destroy the facilities that were producing heavy water for the Germans. In their communications to the Norwegian underground, heavy water first was coded as IMI — the question mark in International Morse Code. The substance was mysterious, but IMI did result in some confusion, so other code names for heavy water were adopted. XY and Soup were two of them, but the Fox preferred Juice.

Vemork, where the Juice was being produced, was close to the electricity-generating facilities and nitrate plant at Rjukan. Western Norway and much of southern Norway lie on a great barren plateau known as the Hardangervidda, near the region of Telemark. River valleys and lakes abound in Telemark, as do waterfalls, the natural source of energy for the plants at Vemork and Rjukan. The windswept Hardangervidda, particularly in winter, is not at all hospitable, but any sabotage party would have to land there, some distance from the well-guarded Vemork plant.

Close to midnight of October 18, 1942, an advance scouting party, Rype (Grouse, in English) — was dropped on the Hardangervidda to reconnoiter the German security positions around the plant. They radioed the information back to England, where Eric Welsh and Leif Tronstad, with the help of Jomar Brun's information, built mock-ups of the heavy-water plant. The security points were highlighted for a sabotage team. Winston Churchill was briefed about the plans by Eric Welsh, and when he learned that Jomar Brun was still in Norway, insisted that Master be brought to Britain at once to protect him from any possible retaliation after the sabotage operations. Grouse would remain in Norway for a long time to support a number of anti-Nazi operations.

The first of those, Operation Freshman, was badly conceived, against the advice of Norwegians attached to the SIS, and resulted in total disaster. Thirty specially trained British Commandos took off from Wick, Scotland, on November 19, 1942, for the Hardangervidda. One aircraft and two gliders were lost. The few captured survivors were shot by order of the Führer. It was a heavy blow, for Tronstad particularly. Another attempt was made in January, but mist obscured all the landmarks, and the party returned to Scotland.

The object of Freshman had been to blow up the entire heavy-water plant at Vemork. Now, with Brun in London, under his new code name, Sverre Hagen, it seemed possible to plan a more delicate sabotage operation — to penetrate the Vemork plant itself and blow up the equipment. The Gunnerside team was staged for this venture at Farm Hall, from the outside an unimposing mansion on West Street in Godmanchester, near Cambridge. Inside, the Georgian rooms imparted a sense of calm in contrast to the tense nerves of its transient occupants, who were usually about to depart on missions of intrigue and danger. Farm Hall belonged to the SOE; it was Special Training School Number 61. So it was not Eric Welsh's exclusive domain, but it was his favorite one. One member of the Gunnerside team, Knut Haukelid, has described the place:

> It was a station for people who were going to Europe on secret errands, and who had to wait for planes. The place was very closely guarded. A number of servicewomen kept the house in order, cooked the meals, and gave the boys some social life. . . . But if we asked the Fannies about our comrades who had gone out before us, they became dumb and knew nothing.

Eric Welsh knew quite a lot. He had had the place completely wired, with microphones in the bedrooms, dining room, library, and so on. Farm Hall was not only a staging area for foreign agents going out; it was an interrogation center for agents and their captives coming in. Loyalties were automatically questioned, and the wiring gave information sometimes not elicited through interrogation. A few years ago, the floorboards in Farm Hall were taken up for refinishing, exposing finely crafted containers, like pencil boxes, with wires in them. Some of the wires can still be seen leading to a room in the service wing that retains its special locks. This was the wartime listening post. On this occasion, Welsh's men had much to listen to, because the Gunnerside team was at Farm Hall for three months, an unusually long tenancy.

At the end of that time, the team took off from the nearby RAF Tempsford field. Group Captain K. S. Batchelor headed the field operations.

> In 1943, as a Wing Commander, I took command of No. 138 (Special Duty) Squadron of the RAF at Tempsford. . . . In the case of the "Gunnerside" operation I was, quite unusually, briefed on its importance. My friend Wing Commander John Cosby, in charge of air operations in SOE Baker Street, came down to Tempsford to brief me specially. Heavy water was not mentioned but John said the Germans were after an explosive a million times more powerful than anything yet known. In my disbelief I told him he ought to take more water with it!

Precisely at midnight the six men of the Gunnerside team landed thirty miles northwest of the Vemork plant and in a week met up with the four men of the Grouse team, renamed Swallow. Three of the combined team formed the demolition party and the others the covering party. Cutting the factory gates, the ten easily slipped by the German guards. Two of the demolition party entered the heavy-water concentration plant by the cable tunnel and another by a window. They placed explosive charges on the concentrating cells, lit the fuses, and departed as easily as they had entered. The operation, practiced an infinite number of times at Farm Hall, was entirely successful. The concentration cells were destroyed and the two teams escaped without a single loss.

The jubilation in Welsh's office was indescribable. And after Winston Churchill read the special force report, he scribbled across its face, "What is being done for these brave men in the way of decorations?" They were decorated by Norway and by England. Norway also wanted to bestow a decoration on Eric Welsh, but when they asked for a summary of his services on behalf of Norway, he stalled. Finn Nagell, his Norwegian intelligence contact in London, kept pestering. Finally, in October 1943, Welsh supplied his personal data, and he concluded with the wireless reporting networks he had built up after the exposure of Skylark. The station and the operators he knew best, of course, were in his home town of Bergen with the code name THETA, headed by Bjarne Thorsen. Welsh reported to Nagell:

> At the present moment, there are 21 stations actively working in Norway under the Anglo-Norwegian intelligence service. In addition, there are 12 stations established, but which — for one reason or another — are not working at the moment, but which are expected in the very near future. There are also two stations projected for service in the near future.

The "near future" saw the culmination of the task originally set for Eric Welsh and his radio reporting stations. Another station, under Torstein Raaby, provided the critical information. On Christmas of 1943, the 31,000-ton *Scharnhorst* was taken to sea at night from Lang Fjord by Captain Fritz Intze. The *Duke of York*, the *Jamaica*, and four other British craft intercepted her, and the *Scharnhorst* went down just a day after she had left her safe harborage on the North Cape of Norway. There were other ships to watch, other ships to sink, but the decline of the German navy had commenced.

The fates had not been so kind to the Gunnerside operation. Working frantically, the Germans restored the Vemork heavy-water concentration cells. At the time the cells were blown up, they had been producing five kilograms of heavy water per day. The attack resulted in a loss of a ton of the substance. Jomar Brun later said of the German restoration: "The production rose faster than anticipated by Tronstad and myself. . . . Thus in June 1943 the production achieved at Vemork was about 200 kilograms, corresponding to an average of about 6.6 kg. per day. This was the highest figure recorded during the war." That was achieved by rebuilding and enlarging the plant at a speed completely unforeseen by the British.

The gallant Gunnerside operation did not seriously retard heavy-water production, but in terms of Norwegian national pride, the dividends were enormous. In terms of Anglo-American relationships, however, the raid was damaging.

The raid occurred at a time when Major General Leslie R. Groves, the head of the Manhattan Project and a staunch anglophobe, was looking for any reason to decouple the American atomic project from the British. He believed he didn't need the English, though it had been their preliminary work and constant prodding that had led to the Manhattan Project. And, furthermore, he didn't trust them.

General Groves was quite certain that press reports of the action against the heavy-water plant came about because of a dereliction of British security, an opinion shared by his principal scientific advisers. Vannevar Bush shot off a note to Harry Hopkins, the President's close friend and adviser, with a clipping from the *New York Times*: "The attached clipping shows what can happen when control is loose and security insufficient. It gives sufficient basis in itself for insistence that knowledge be passed only to those who really need to know it. Perhaps you will wish to ask 'how come.' "

The article in the *Times* appeared on April 4, five weeks after the raid, and may have been the way that General Groves heard about it. As to "how come," it was the Germans who had announced the raid in the first instance, not the British. The German commander-in-chief in Norway, General Nikolaus von Falkenhorst, was filled with admiration for the precision of the sabotage affair. He considered it to be entirely a successful operation by men in British uniform, and he ordered no reprisals against the civilian population.

But for another general, the Gunnerside raid was cause for reprisal against the British. Groves determined to show them how one should *really* disable the Norwegian heavy-water production facilities.

TWENTY-EIGHT

The General Steps In

AFTER VANNEVAR BUSH met General Groves in September 1942, he wrote to Harvey Bundy, assistant to Secretary of War Henry Stimson, that, "having seen Col. Groves briefly, I doubted whether he had sufficient tact for such a job. . . . I fear we are in the soup." But as time went on, the two men found they had much in common, especially their dislike and suspicion of the British. Perhaps Groves inherited that from his father, an army chaplain. Descended from French Huguenots who had settled in America in the mid seventeenth century, the elder Groves nourished, for unknown reasons, a hatred of George III, something that his son was not reluctant to mention.

As Bush had noted, tact was not one of Groves's virtues, so he protested about the Norwegian heavy-water situation to General Sir John Dill, the British military representative in Washington, and he pressed for British approval for Americans to bomb the Rjukan area. The Norwegians disapproved, hoping that, despite vastly increased German security measures, the heavy-water equipment might somehow be sabotaged again. But Groves was persistent. Bombers of the Eighth Air Force had been attacking targets in southern Norway for some time.

General Groves did not realize that in July the bombing of the magnesium plant at Herøya had already appreciably diminished the heavy-water output of Vemork. The reasons were subtle and, in a way, connected with Beck's book.

A Herøya engineer, Kjell Nielsen, begins his story in the village

of Tretten, north of Lillehammer, during the evacuation of April
1940. General Ruge had promoted Nielsen, a corporal, to second
lieutenant.

> A car stopped and an English-speaking officer came out and asked if
> someone could help him with the engine. We proposed to give him
> another car, but he said he would prefer to keep his own. The license
> plates were hidden, but the right-side wheel indicated that it was an
> English car. As it would take a little time to find out what was wrong,
> I asked if he and his companion would like something to eat, and we
> went to a small café, where I discovered that the other man was French.
> They both used their own language.

It turned out that the Englishman was the British liaison with General Ruge. He was Frank Foley, and the Frenchman was Bertrand-
Vignes. Although Kjell Nielsen did not realize it, nor did Foley and
Bertrand-Vignes, the three were together at the beginning of Norway's heavy-water saga.

Nielsen was captured, released in July 1941, and asked by Norsk
Hydro to build a magnesium plant for the Germans at Herøya in
southern Norway. He was reluctant to be seen as collaborating with
the Germans, but he perceived some useful possibilities. Twice, he
was sent to Bitterfeld to consult with Adolf Beck and his team. He
read Beck's book and obtained reports on the magnesium process.
He photographed the reports and put the undeveloped film into
empty toothpaste tubes so that they would be destroyed if an unin-
formed person should open them. The information reached England,
supplementing the data in the Book of Beck that had come with the
Oslo Report.

In the spring of 1943, London asked about the progress of the
Herøya plant, wanting to know all possible means of sabotaging it.
The idea was not to destroy the plant but to erode the German progress. As Nielsen later said, "Great was my surprise, then, when Herøya
was bombed in July 1943. I was out of the shelter in between the
attacks to try to give first aid to wounded persons. . . . Many people
were killed."

On July 24, 1943, the Eighth Air Force pre-empted the British
plans by dropping 1639 500-pound bombs. Fifty-four of the bombs
—that is, a thirtieth—found the plant in the "precision bombing"
raid, but the raid achieved its purpose. Concluded Nielsen, "Evidently

this bombing was a good training for the American Air Force, although not necessary, and it brought an end to the plans for Herøya." But throughout the war, the parent plant in Germany, Beck's plant, was never touched by bombs.

Jomar Brun has described the effect of the bombing of Herøya on the heavy-water production at distant Vemork: "After the American bombing . . . the load on the hydrogen [cells] was reduced by about 50 percent, resulting in a corresponding reduction of heavy water."

Kjell Nielsen went from danger to danger. He took a job at the heavy-water plant at Vemork. Later, he said, "On November 15, 1943, Vemork was heavily bombed in the early afternoon. . . . The heavy-water plant itself was not hit. . . . In the following period . . . I had plenty of opportunities just to open the bottom valves in the heavy-water electrolysis and empty the heavy water of different concentrations into the sewers. It was not done. I have been thinking of this question many times afterwards and asked why? I simply cannot explain it: it was stupid."

Twenty-one Norwegian civilians were killed. The "pinpoint" bombing did not touch the heavy-water apparatus at all. However, the plant could not be operated because the electricity-generating facility was put out of commission. And the nitrate plant, vital for Norwegian food production, was destroyed.

In London, the Norwegian government-in-exile thought the bombing action not only stupid but criminal, and it protested vigorously to both the Americans and the British. Jomar Brun wept. Leif Tronstad and Eric Welsh were shaken. It was not the way they had wanted things done, and innocent lives had been lost. A few days later, Tronstad wrote, for no one in particular but himself, "Hagen [Brun] is now more relaxed after having been heavily shaken up. Have cleared up the conditions regarding the attacks on Rjukan and Vemork. Hope the sacrifices have not been wasted, but what has passed will secure us the victory over the Germans. The heavy water will have great consequences in the future. Theodor [Welsh] is also disappointed in the way things were tackled this time."

Groves himself took great satisfaction that the Germans now knew that the heavy-water facility would be subject to attack after attack. And he was correct. Preparations were made to move equipment and the remaining stocks of heavy water to the German heartland. Professor R. Kronig has recalled a conversation two decades later:

> At a dinner, as part of a scientific conference held at Copenhagen in 1963, my wife sat next to Professor P. M. S. Blackett and in conversation with him touched the subject of Rosbaud, who had recently died. Blackett said: "He was a very good friend of mine" and stressed the valuable services which Rosbaud had rendered to the Allied cause during the war, adding . . . "He was the person who told us when a ship was leaving Norway for Germany with a cargo of heavy water. It was a one-man show."

Actually, it was more than a one-man show. It was indeed Rosbaud who supplied Eric Welsh with the information about the intended removals. Tipped off, Welsh instructed his Norwegian agents to provide information about the means and date of transportation. The railway from Vemork and Rjukan runs eastward to Lake Tinnsjø, where a ferry takes cargo to the railroad line, which goes south to a port on the Skagerrak. At 10:45 A.M. on Sunday, February 20, 1944, the charges placed the night before on the ferry *Hydro* exploded, sending the entire Norwegian stock of heavy water to the bottom of the lake, taking twenty-six passengers and crew along.

Ever since, Norwegians have been troubled by the question of whether the sacrifices were worth it. They deplored the lives taken in the American bombing raid of the previous November, but that was not their decision. The sinking of the *Hydro* was an act that was carried out by Norwegians and killed Norwegians. Most have been consoled by the thought that the action prevented the Germans from building the atomic bomb.

A heavy-water reactor is a perfectly good machine for manufacturing a plutonium explosive; in fact, it is the best. The United States did not go that route because it could not obtain sufficient heavy water in time. Instead, the United States used graphite in its reactors. Fortunately, love may have intervened to put the Germans on the path of heavy water instead of graphite.

It began when Paul Rosbaud's forty-seven-year-old friend Walther Bothe met Ingeborg Moerschner, thirteen years younger than he, during passage to New York on the liner *Hamburg* in June of 1939. Ingeborg was going to San Francisco to work for Fritz Wiedemann, the German consul general, former adjutant to Adolf Hitler, and a spy. Walther was going to a meeting at the University of Chicago, as was Werner Heisenberg. Ingeborg and Walther saw the World's Fair in New York and the sights of San Francisco, and a warm relationship began to develop. With considerable sadness, Walther returned alone to Heidelberg to work on building his cyclotron and to measure the nuclear properties of graphite.

His diary records his agony. On the first anniversary of their meeting, he wrote, "Ingeborg, I must once again write you a letter. Tomorrow, it is a year that you came into my life . . . " and he spoke of moonlight and dreams, concluding that he felt "like a drunken teenager." Two weeks later, he confessed that "I have been speaking of physics the entire day, while thinking only of you." The "drunken teenager" was also at that time measuring graphite the entire day, and he made a grievous mistake. He concluded that graphite was unsuitable material for a nuclear reactor.

Bothe's erroneous measurements were the reason the Germans turned to heavy water. Heisenberg had correctly calculated in the spring of 1942 that about five tons of heavy water would sustain a chain reaction at essentially zero power. And after June 1942, when the Germans had abandoned the quest for the bomb, because Reichsminister Albert Speer had no faith in the understanding of the physicists, the Germans placed an order with Norsk Hydro for five tons of heavy water. Jomar Brun has stated that "without bombing or other destructive actions, the Germans . . . might have reached the preliminary [heavy-water] goal about June 1, 1944."

Brun has estimated that even without the sabotage operations and the American bombings, the Germans could not have had a single bomb until August 1945 — but the war ended in May. He is overly generous in estimating German technology. From the time the first United States experimental chain reaction was started until plutonium was turned out in usable quantities was a period of about thirty months. On a similar basis, plutonium for a German bomb would have been available about the end of 1947 if the production of heavy water had not been disrupted and if the Germans had ever learned how to make nuclear weapons.

Welsh knew in the middle of 1942 that the Germans were not embarked on a bomb program, but he became convinced of that only a year later. This is confirmed by the official SIS history:

The spring of 1943 was also the date from which Allied authorities
began to feel increasingly reassured in relation to Germany's nuclear
research programme, another problem [in addition to gas warfare] with
which they had experienced increasing anxiety, especially since the
spring of 1941.

That assessment had not been reached by the time of the Gunnerside sabotage raids against Vemork. But by the time General Groves
ordered the November 1943 bombing attack, and certainly by the
time Welsh ordered the sinking of the *Hydro* on Lake Tinnsjø, it was
quite certain that the Germans were going nowhere in making the
bomb. Welsh knew that if the Germans were to change direction
suddenly, it would take many years for them to produce a bomb. He
also knew that the Uran Verein, the Uranium Club—the group of
academic physicists who were doing government-sponsored research
on nuclear fission—had had to flee southward to Hechingen and that
conditions there for research were not at all satisfactory. Welsh also
appreciated that Allied bombings had sharply reduced the industrial
support for any push toward the bomb.

Such reasons—although he never asked for them nor would they
have been given—would not have swayed General Groves. But why
did Eric Welsh order the sinking of the *Hydro* for no apparent useful
purpose? No answers were ever given by Eric Welsh. But he did have
a purpose.

John Turner, Welsh's liaison with XU, has offered the answer: "The
Germans got into their head, and it was encouraged from the British
side, that heavy water was absolutely necessary to produce the atom
bomb. . . . [The British] encouraged this by blowing up the ferry."

In Welsh's mind, the Germans had to be kept on the track of the
scarce heavy water and away from graphite. But he was wrong in
that. Toward the end of the war Karl Wirtz—a member of the Uranium Club—experimented on the same batch of graphite that Walther
Bothe had found unsatisfactory four years earlier and found it perfectly acceptable. But then it was too late. High-grade graphite was
required for the V-2 rocket vanes and was in very short supply. The
graphite shortage forced the cancelation of production of a surface-
to-air missile, the Wasserfall, which might have successfully defended
the German cities and war machine. There was no possibility of Germany's having a working graphite reactor until 1948 or later and a

bomb a year or two after that. Thus, the bombing of Rjukan and the sinking of the *Hydro* had no meaning at all—but that is war.

The person most affected by the deaths was Leif Tronstad, who felt a personal responsibility. No longer was he willing to send Norwegians into Norway while he directed operations from the relative safety of London. Toward the end of 1944, the men of Operation Sunshine parachuted onto the Hardangervidda. Their mission was to protect industrial and strategic installations from being blown up by the retreating Germans, for victory in Europe seemed to be near. The leader was Leif Tronstad, with a new code name, Julius. Tronstad was prepared to stay in Norway until the war ended.

The following March, he and Gunnar Syverstad, code name Kaare, captured the treasonous magistrate from Rauland. While the two were interrogating the magistrate, the traitor's brother shot Julius and Kaare through a window and killed them. On the night of March 11–12, 1945, Norway lost two heroes, just weeks before the war ended. One of them, Leif Tronstad, was given a state funeral and became enshrined as a National Hero of Norway. A former Boy Scout, he might have wished it that way.

As for the spy who provided the information, he—and the general who would not have believed him—dined in New York in 1961. After the war, Eric Welsh had told General Groves something of Paul Rosbaud, and Groves wanted to see this spy for himself. In Groves's lexicon at that time, a spy was a Soviet spy, so he extended the invitation to Rosbaud with some suspicion.

The dinner at the Rockefeller Institute lasted six hours. Even Groves fell under the spell of the man, but he remained skeptical. Afterward, Groves noted in his private files:

> During the war he served as a British agent in Berlin and managed to maintain reasonable contact with Welsh. . . . He was aware of the atomic energy work of the Germans and was very much disturbed over the possibility of their success. However, from 1944 on, he knew they would not succeed. He was afraid however that they would continue their work after the war and would rise again in an attempt to dominate the world. For that reason he wanted the heavy water and uranium to be captured and carefully preserved. His wife was a Jewess. Despite his name he implied he was not. Just how much value his information was to us I do not know. It was of course confirmatory of all the other information we received during those years.

Until early 1945, the general had never received through his own operations any but trivial intelligence on the German program. Of course, Rosbaud's information was "confirmatory of all the other information" because much of the "other information" was Rosbaud's!

Groves supposed that Rosbaud was being devious about his religion, and he had other suspicions. "One never knew of course whether he might not be a double agent or even operating exclusively for the German intelligence," and, "I do not believe that he had a true appreciation of the Russian danger and was primarily worried about the possibility of German destruction."

Fortunately, Paul Rosbaud did not report to General Groves during the war.

TWENTY-NINE

Ex-filtration

THE OFFICIAL HISTORY of the British Secret Intelligence Service, as thus far written, has only the following acknowledgment of three of Welsh's most important agents:

> By the beginning of 1942 the SIS had established a young scientist in the University of Stockholm to report on his own work, on the whereabouts of German scientists and on the contacts of Swedish scientists with Germany, and he was still reporting in 1943. But his reports have not been retained in the files. The same applies to reports from a well-placed writer for a German scientific journal who was in touch with the SIS from spring 1942 and to those from a Norwegian scientist who provided information about German scientists from the same period.

Of course, the "well-placed writer for a German scientific journal" was Paul Rosbaud. Actually, he was reactivated in 1941, but not until a year later did Welsh begin to take seriously his reports, particularly the one on Peenemünde. The "Norwegian scientist" was Harald Wergeland, researching in Oslo and working with XU. The "young scientist" was Njål Hole, working with Lise Meitner in Stockholm.

Early in 1943, Hole reported to Welsh that Victor Goldschmidt, Lise Meitner, and Niels Bohr wished to be brought over to England. Part of the craft of the spy is infiltration. In extricating a spy or anyone important to the business of spying, the British Secret Intelligence Service employs the strange term "ex-filtration." Nineteen forty-three was the year of ex-filtration duties for Eric Welsh. Jomar Brun had been kept in Norway longer than he should have been in order to provide information on the heavy-water plant. On the other hand, he had been invited to Berlin in January 1942 to discuss heavy-water production, and Welsh was reluctant to lose a source like Brun. Only because of a direct order from Winston Churchill did Eric Welsh ex-filtrate Brun at the end of 1942. Now, there were several other cases, each of which presented problems.

Official records show that Victor Moritz Goldschmidt was ex-fil-trated from Stockholm to London on March 3, 1943, as related in an earlier chapter. Hilde Rosbaud had heard from Lise Meitner at New Year's that he was safe, for Meitner had written, "You may be inter-ested to learn that your friend in Oslo is well and out of danger." Before Welsh banished him to the English countryside, Goldschmidt was thoroughly interrogated, with Leif Tronstad participating in some of the sessions.

The shocker for Welsh came on March 15. It was a Monday, and Welsh had enough problems on his hands, having heard that on Friday the *Scharnhorst* had joined the *Tirpitz* in northern Norway. His wireless reporting network had successfully replaced the demolished Skylark network, but there was a limit to his resources. And in matters of atomic energy, technical cooperation with the Americans had reached a new low.

That Monday morning, Welsh and Tronstad wanted to focus on Rosbaud's visit to Oslo the previous June, and Goldschmidt provided more detailed information. It was, in fact, the morning that Welsh really began to feel more comfortable about Rosbaud's reliability and his extraordinary access to sources. V.M. told the two interrogators that Rosbaud had come to Oslo in uniform. Consequently, he did not want to visit too many professors in their offices or homes and had asked V.M. to arrange the meeting with Odd Hassel in an inconspic-uous place.

It was in speaking of Hassel that V.M. dropped his bombshell. The American naval attaché in Stockholm, Captain Walter Heiberg, had been asked to investigate, through Norwegian sources, the German interest in heavy water. If that was true, the Americans were infringing on Welsh's territory. They might disturb delicate channels and expose his agents to needless danger. Welsh was seething, and he fired off a signal to the new Norwegian intelligence chief in Stockholm, Major Ørnulf Dahl. (Churchill's intervention in 1941 had convinced the Norwegian government that Roscher Lund should remain in Stockholm during the delicate period of forming and consolidating intelligence operations in Norway and in Germany. After a year, those operations were working smoothly enough for Roscher Lund to take charge of Norwegian intelligence operations from London. In this, he was ably assisted by Major Finn Nagell, who saw Eric Welsh more often than did Roscher Lund. And Major Ørnulf Dahl assumed charge of general intelligence matters in the Norwegian legation. But about the time when Roscher Lund departed for London, a separate facility, exclusively for XU liaison, was established in Stockholm.)

Five days later, Goldschmidt told Tronstad alone something more astonishing. Hassel had told V.M. that the United States was willing to pay $1 million for further information. The Americans were pushing the British out of the atomic energy business by means of the enormous resources they were able to draw on, and now, Welsh thought, they were willing to put out big money to displace the British in the Norwegian intelligence theater. The Fox was becoming most uncomfortable; he wondered whether Goldschmidt himself had been courting the Americans, or vice versa. In one of his messages to Njål Hole in Stockholm, Tronstad affirmed that Goldschmidt had arrived in London, but added that "he likes to interfere in things that he doesn't understand."

Not long after, Welsh heard from Ørnulf Dahl that the Americans had *not* been in contact with the Norwegian legation in Stockholm about heavy water. But perhaps the American naval attaché was attempting to contact sources in Norway without going through the British or the Norwegian government-in-exile. That, in Welsh's view, was even more heinous.

If those approaches had been made, it would appear that the primary recruitment source was Odd Hassel, and that the Americans had decided at this critical moment to pay him $1 million for information. Or perhaps the Americans hoped that Hassel would agree to ex-filtrate himself to the United States in return for that sum. Welsh could not afford the loss of such a source.

As a result of the controversy in July and August over the Houtermans message, the British had been forced to reveal to the Americans that the Germans did not have a full-scale nuclear reactor operating, but they had added that "research was still in progress." Welsh certainly did not disclose the name of his primary source, Paul

Rosbaud, but apparently did give the Americans the name of the intermediary, Odd Hassel.

On August 31, Vannevar Bush wrote to the chief of army intelligence, General George V. Strong:

> I mentioned certain long-range developments in which the Germans are interested. I now have further information. A plant at Vemork is producing 120 kilograms per month of one of the essential materials and shipping it to Berlin, and then it goes into the hands of Dr. Heisenberg, the distinguished physicist. This information comes from the British in rather devious ways.

Devious indeed, for that describes Eric Welsh. Although the Arcadia conference between Winston Churchill and Franklin Roosevelt in early 1942 had established certain modes of intelligence cooperation between the two countries, a considerable number of those in the SIS were skeptical of the security standards of the newly created Office of Strategic Services. Welsh was among them. For the few, very few, contacts he had to make in Washington, he bypassed William Stephenson, who was the usual liaison in New York between the SIS and the OSS. Welsh relied on James Chadwick, who was keeping his eye open for British interests in the American atomic project.

In his August message to General Strong, Vannevar Bush expressed the desire that the United States not be dependent on the British for atomic intelligence: "I hope that the same sort of information is getting to you directly and more completely." But it was not, and Strong asked for the source. Replied Bush, "I will be glad to give you the information as to the particular Norwegian consultant if you would like to have it." The very proper New England scientist would never think of using the word *informer*, so he gave the name of the *consultant*, Odd Hassel, to General Strong.

The military attaché at the American embassy in Stockholm was Lieutenant Colonel Hugh B. Waddell, but he was due for transfer and was to be replaced by a novice in Scandinavian affairs, Colonel Charles E. Rayens. The naval attaché, Captain Heiberg, had been in Stockholm since July 1940 and was going to stay a while. He was the logical man to make the arrangements. If Goldschmidt was correct about the intent of the Americans, Heiberg must have gotten through to Hassel, but evidently was not able to persuade him to accept the American offer. General Strong's later reports on atomic energy were sparse, elementary, and erroneous. They could not have come from Odd Hassel; presumably, the United States saved $1 million.

The Americans also tried to enlist Victor Goldschmidt, but they couldn't find him. In May 1943, General Groves sent Colonel W. Ashbridge to the OSS to see what information the organization had on Goldschmidt. Ashbridge reported to Groves that the "OSS states that Dr. Goldschmidt, who is a Jew, was recently arrested in Norway but was later released and was permitted to resume his lectures as Professor of Mineralogy at the University of Oslo. Their latest news of him was November 20, 1942." The episode shows that the OSS did not have a good source in Oslo, for since the end of 1942 it had been common knowledge in that city that Goldschmidt had escaped to Sweden.

By the time General Groves became interested, Goldschmidt was in England, in the custody of Eric Welsh, and was telling him all about the American mischief. In his present mood, Welsh was not about to tell the OSS or General Groves where Goldschmidt was.

A master of dirty tricks, Welsh, on reflection, silently applauded the Americans for their attempted end-run but forever after was extra cautious about the identity of both his primary and secondary sources. Paul Rosbaud, the primary source for the information that caused the Anglo-American rift, remained innocent of what he had started. He was simply happy that his good friend Victor Goldschmidt had escaped death at Auschwitz.

Welsh also lost Hassel as a source. The professor was arrested in a roundup of students and faculty at Oslo University at the end of 1943 and imprisoned by the Germans until the beginning of 1945. In Stockholm, Lise Meitner was shielded from a similar fate, but she also wished to go to England. Eric Welsh was faced with the decision of whether to ex-filtrate her. Pragmatically, he decided not to.

One of eight children, Lise Meitner was born into a Viennese lawyer's family. Philipp and Hedwig Meitner were drawing away from the traditions of their own parents, ever more conscious of the growing anti-Semitism in the Austro-Hungarian Empire. They had stopped attending the Moorish-style Israelite Synagogue on Tempelgasse and had had all of their children baptized. Lise graduated from an all-girls' school in the year that Paul Rosbaud was born. Already fascinated by physics, she never wavered in the pursuit of understanding

the fundamental laws of nature, and she developed insights not paralleled by the eminent men of science with whom she later collaborated.

It is interesting that five contemporary women made the same decision at about the same time: to devote themselves to science rather
than *Kinder, Kirche, und Küche* (children, church, and kitchen). They
were Ellen Gleditsch in Oslo, Elizabeth Rona in Budapest, Clara von
Simson in Berlin, Berta Karlik and Lise Meitner in Vienna. Their
common decision drew them together, and they came to represent
the elite female scientific talent of that era. Ellen Gleditsch described
the choice they had to make:

> Now, does a career of research present many difficulties in itself? . . .
> There is a difficulty, one that is greater for women than for men, the
> difficulty involved in the fact that a woman's time is so often needed
> by a home, husband, and children. A woman who wants to do research
> must first reconcile her professional work, which is her means of living,
> with her research, and then she must co-ordinate with these her wom-
> an's interest.

Such was the intensity of Lise Meitner's involvement with her research that "her woman's interest" had the lower priority all of her
life. Men were quick to sense that. Otto Hahn, a few months younger
than she, felt compelled to say "There was no question of any closer
relationship. Lise Meitner had had a strict, ladylike upbringing. . . . For
many years I never had a meal with Lise Meitner except on official
business. Nor did we ever go for a walk together. . . . And yet we were
really close friends."

Closeness in the German-language culture is well defined. It arrives
when two people are comfortable enough to address each other with
the familiar *Du* instead of the formal *Sie*. After a long time, *Du* came
to Lise Meitner and Otto Hahn. But it rarely came for others; even
other women who worked in her field, rare as they were, were not
able to form close friendships with Lise Meitner, however they tried.
Elizabeth Rona, a versatile Hungarian physicist, chemist, and geo-
physicist, commented, "The temperaments and personalities of Meitner and Hahn complemented each other; Hahn was gay and self-
confident, with a pleasant sense of humor. It was a pleasure to work
with him. . . . Meitner was an introvert, shy and reserved. It was difficult to have a close personal relationship with her, but one had to

admire her devotion to her work and her critical search for just the right solution to scientific problems."

Hahn liked Meitner because he respected her as a person and as a scientist and had become dependent on her insight. A chemist, Hahn was scornful of most physicists, but through the years it was the physicist Meitner who kept Hahn on the right track in his investigations. No matter how good his chemistry was, it was meaningless without the interpretations and directions Lise Meitner usually gave. Many other physicists, especially the younger ones in Germany, did not understand the symbiosis between Hahn and Meitner. They also did not like her, because, just as Hahn distrusted physicists, they distrusted chemists. Whatever the relationship between Hahn and Meitner might have been, its peculiarity was compounded by the strange fusion of a really top-notch chemist and an exceptional physicist. Yet it was the fusion that brought discovery.

They began their collaboration in a carpenter's shop in Berlin at the back of the Kaiser Wilhelm Institute of Chemistry. They worked with radioactive substances and discovered new ones, like thorium D and protactinium. They were working toward the latter discovery when World War I arrived and both went to the front lines. Lise Meitner became a nurse in an Austrian field hospital, operating x-ray equipment. She tended the wounded. Hahn created wounded with unconventional warfare.

He became a gas pioneer with the 126th Infantry Regiment and applied his talents at Verdun and then was posted to the same Isonzo front where Paul Rosbaud was fighting. While Rosbaud was using a rifle, Otto Hahn was there to plan and observe a poison gas attack, and his unit used the insidious substance effectively on October 24, 1917, against the Italians. Hahn's unit was then transferred back to the Western Front to employ gas with equal effectiveness against the other Allies.

The senior scientific adviser for gas warfare was Fritz Haber, who with Carl Bosch had invented a new process for creating ammonia that made Germany independent of outside sources for fertilizers and explosives. Haber was convinced that the use of gas would bring a quick end to the war, and besides, he thought the French might use gas first. He explained all this to Hahn, who had been against the use of gas but later confessed, "You might say that Haber put my mind at rest." In a letter, Fritz Haber's son has observed about Hahn:

> I thought his observations about chemical warfare and his meetings with father as well as the "interviews" were unconvincing. Front-line observers [such as Hahn] "saw the effects of . . . weapons." If they didn't, they were useless observers. That's how it was with the British, and I am convinced that my father would not have put up with an "observer" whose reports were incomplete. I am satisfied that Hahn did his job competently and efficiently; later on, he may have been embarrassed by poison gas (other Germans felt like that too) and in his book attempted to exonerate himself. In my opinion, unnecessarily so.

Toward the end of the war, Haber, fearing that he might be regarded as a war criminal, went into hiding and grew a beard, but fate was kinder to him. In 1918, Haber won the Nobel Prize for chemistry. In 1945, his associate in gas warfare in World War I, Otto Hahn, was awarded the Nobel Prize for 1944 for the discovery that led to the atomic bomb. It should be remembered that Alfred Nobel had instituted his prizes "for the good of humanity."

Meitner did not share in that prize, and she was glad of it. She did not share it though she deserved as much credit as Otto Hahn. In general, the scientific community had no great liking for this older, rather antisocial woman, and few physicists in Germany or anywhere else felt disposed to help her—even in time of her great need. To be sure, Otto Hahn, Paul Rosbaud, and Dirk Coster had aided her in getting to Stockholm in 1938, but once there she was absolutely miserable. One of Meitner's non-Swedish colleagues believes that "the Swedes could have helped her much more. She knew more about nuclear physics [than they did]. They didn't want a foreigner to take the lead." The Royal Swedish Academy of Science awards the Nobel Prize for physics. Members of the academy were Meitner's co-workers. If they were unwilling to recognize Meitner's talents in the laboratory, it was not likely that they would announce them to the world by honoring her with the Nobel Prize.

Her host at Stockholm's Institute of Physics, Manne Siegbahn, had just built a cyclotron, but Meitner felt that he was more interested in doing experiments than interpreting them. C. D. Ellis, of King's College at the University of London, petitioned the highest echelons of the British scientific establishment to bring Meitner to Britain to join the other refugee scientists. Few of them could boast accomplishments approaching hers. But the final veto was imposed by no one less than Frederick Lindemann, Lord Cherwell, Churchill's friend and adviser and no admirer of any form of woman. On September 23, 1938, he rendered his judgment:

> Miss Meitner is certainly one of the most distinguished women physicists in Germany and I very much hope if she should have to leave that country [she had already left] that she will find a congenial post somewhere. But I should not be prepared to press very strongly that we should invite her to come to Oxford. . . . I hope you will not think me unsympathetic to Miss Meitner, whom I know and like, but whose plight appears to be more contingent than actual.

It is easy to understand Cherwell's position. His official biographer, Frederick Winston, the Earl of Birkenhead, has written, "Two of Lindemann's indefensible prejudices appeared early: his abhorrence of negroes [*sic*] and his aversion from Jews. . . . His dislike of coloured people was by far the stronger of the two. They filled him with a physical revulsion which he was unable to control."

Lindemann also had an aversion to his mother, brother, and animal protein. He never married. He kept cats. His attitude toward Meitner was not surprising.

Some other scientists tried to help Meitner. Sir James Chadwick, the discoverer of the neutron, was genuinely fond of her. The war caught Chadwick in Stockholm, where one day he patiently listened to Meitner's plea. He affirmed his invitation to come to Cambridge. He certainly had the power and prestige to invite her. That evening, still disturbed about the conversation, he penned Meitner a note from his room in the Hotel Stockholm:

> I have been thinking over your position during the day and I have come to the conclusion that it would be better to tell Professor Siegbahn how matters stand—that you have had an offer from Cambridge and that you would like to go there if it can be arranged. . . . From the conversations I have had with him I am sure that he is willing and anxious to do all he can to make your position in Stockholm comfortable but that owing to lack of funds and of assistants he cannot do more at present. . . . I am ready to do anything to help you.

But Sir James did not anticipate that John Cockcroft would not be entirely positive. In mid October, Cockcroft sent Meitner a thank-you-so-much letter, concluding, "I think you ought to think over very carefully the question as to whether you still wish to come to Cambridge." Cockcroft did not dislike Meitner, but for him it was both a budgetary and a security matter. Although Cockcroft later accepted the fact that Lise Meitner's nephew, Otto Frisch, was not a German spy, at the time Meitner herself was trying to come to England, Cockcroft was highly suspicious of Frisch. The following April, the Cambridge professor with excellent contacts in the SIS met privately with Jacques Allier and, in a "long discussion" about Otto Frisch, assured him that Frisch would be closely watched and that his correspondence would be monitored by the British intelligence services. If the nephew was suspect, so would be the aunt. Later in the war, Cockcroft and Eric Welsh had another reason to keep Meitner in Stockholm.

At the end of 1943, Cockcroft temporarily lost his nuclear scientists to America and had both space and money for Meitner. Frisch was sent with the British contingent to the supersecret Los Alamos weapons laboratory. He would not have been if there were still suspicions about his being a German spy. His aunt's knowledge also would have been an asset in the Anglo-American atomic bomb project. But Meitner was never ex-filtrated. It was a word that she would have abhorred, anyway.

Harald Wergeland, the "Norwegian scientist" mentioned anonymously in the official SIS history as a source, has written:

> Lise Meitner in Stockholm and I in Oslo were in 1942 summoned to join the English group working on nuclear fission. As physicists, we both tried not to take part in this project, but declared ourselves ready for other service. Lise Meitner — who discovered uranium fission and was a candidate for the Nobel Prize in 1947 [sic] — told me later that she was grateful for not having been awarded in this context.

"Other service" for Harald Wergeland was the supplying of information to cope with the threat of the German atomic bomb. Did Lise Meitner perform "other service"? Harald Wergeland replied: "About Lise Meitner's work I know only what you heard from Hole. When I was asked to join the group in England I declared myself ready to come as soldier, but not as nuclear physicist."

Brynulf Ottar, the witness to the transmittal of the Oslo Report and the XU representative in Stockholm, had this to add:

> With respect to Meitner, it is my impression that she, like Wergeland, was very religious and for moral reasons strongly against the devel-

opment of the atomic bomb. But she was equally opposed to Hitler. Therefore I think she, like Wergeland, would do everything to fight Hitler, but they would not participate in the development of the bomb. These two physicists and many others including Niels Bohr were afraid of the consequences of such a development, and this put them in a difficult position with respect to their conscience: Should we take a chance on destroying all mankind in order to get rid of Hitler?

As long as the war lasted, they were in a pinch, but as soon as the war was over, they could reveal their fears and views, and they certainly did. I think that Meitner helped the Allies as best she could, but she did not want to do the devil's work.

The question remains: Was Lise Meitner more than a passive and casual source of information for the British? Perhaps part of the answer lies in the saga of the young scientist who, as the history of the British Secret Service records, was established "in the University of Stockholm to report on his own work, on the whereabouts of German scientists and on the contacts of Swedish scientists in Germany." Njål Hole, who had received his degree in nuclear physics at the technical university in Trondheim in 1938, was very well acquainted with Professor Leif Tronstad, who would soon become the Fox in association with his work with Eric Welsh.

Tronstad had been ex-filtrated from Norway on September 21, 1941. Njål Hole decided to leave at the same time. The day after Hole arrived at a Swedish transit camp for Norwegians, Tronstad came up to him at breakfast and suggested that Hole get a job in a physics institute. And when Hole arrived in Stockholm there were more specific instructions awaiting him in the form of a letter at the Norwegian delegation. It was from Tronstad, who urged Hole to get a position where there was good contact with Swedish physicists. "Keep an eye open," instructed Tronstad, and he was very specific that the eye be cocked on atomic energy. Hole was instructed to report to the intelligence officer at the Norwegian delegation, Major Ørnulf Dahl. At the SIS in London, Hole's operation was labeled Epsilon.

Hole was very welcome in Manne Siegbahn's laboratory at the Nobel Institute because of his experience with the electrostatic nuclear particle accelerator at Trondheim. At Siegbahn's physics institute, they were using a cyclotron to accelerate particles.

Wartime was a productive period for Njål Hole, even if it was not for Lise Meitner. The two saw each other every day. Hole later said,

"I don't know if Meitner gave information to anybody else." After the war, Hole received a visitor one day in Trondheim. It was the local British consul, who handed Hole a decoration — the Order of the British Empire. Hole asked him what it was for. The consul replied, "It's not my job to know that. It's my job to deliver it." But Hole knew what it was for.

Hole reported to the Norwegians; if Meitner reported information to anyone, it would not have been through that channel, except for what she told Hole. As an Austrian in Sweden, her channel to Britain would have been through Eric Welsh's representatives in Stockholm.

One of those representatives was John Turner, who was born in Norway. In the earlier part of the war, he was an operational deputy to Eric Welsh. On September 15, 1943, he was posted to Stockholm to be Welsh's contact with XU under the code name Pettersen.

In Stockholm, Turner reported to the SIS head of station at the passport offices at 12 Birgir Jarlsgaten, a long wide avenue leading southward to the dock area and into the fashionable Strandvagen, where the British legation stood on a knoll at number 82. The Norwegians, too, kept their sensitive intelligence operation separate from their legation, at 37 Banérgaten, where Major Dahl handled intelligence matters, except those of XU. The XU headquarters were a few blocks west at 32 Skeppargatan, where Brynulf Ottar was in charge. This was central Stockholm, and all of the addresses were within walking distance of each other. And the city was a haven for spies from all countries.

The SIS chief of station was Cyril Cheshire. A former timber merchant, Cheshire was well built, a little over six feet tall, and with a sallow complexion. He was half Russian and spoke Russian, German, and French. The hard-working Cheshire was the archetype of the spymaster in a novel. He did not mix with the British legation staff, but was liked by his own. Eric Welsh had placed two men with Cheshire, John Whistondale to provide liaison with Norwegian agents passing between Germany and Sweden, and John Turner to be the liaison with the Norwegian XU. Turner has said that Meitner reported to Welsh directly through Cheshire. An associate of Meitner's also reported that she was in contact with Cheshire.

Thus, though there is no positive evidence that Meitner was a British agent, a conclusion that many scientists would find it most difficult to accept, the circumstantial evidence is very strong that she was. She was a magnet for German scientists, many of whom corresponded with her and sometimes visited her. Rosbaud's friends Otto Hahn, Max von Laue, and Josef Mattauch lectured in Stockholm, and through them Meitner and Hole gleaned much information. She was a channel for Rosbaud to his family and friends in England. Technical books from Rosbaud came to Welsh through Meitner, and that is another indication that she was in contact with Cheshire. Some of those books contained secret messages. It was her way of contributing to Hitler's defeat without working on the atomic bomb—which, in the final analysis, had nothing to do with his defeat. Hers was a meaningful contribution to the Allied victory over Germany.

In January 1949, Eric Welsh, known for his compassion for fellow professionals, made a gesture on behalf of Lise Meitner for the very great services she had performed for him. Meitner was still trapped in Stockholm, no longer because of the war, but because there were few choices for her. The spymaster wrote to Lord Cherwell:

> I do not know whether you are aware that some action has been taken in an endeavour to find some sort of employment for Lise Meitner in this country. . . . There has been some talk that she might be invited, either by the Royal Society or the Royal Institute, to come and spend the rest of her life [she was then seventy] in this country; but I under-stand from my connexion that it is difficult to find an appropriate means whereby this could be financed. . . . I would respectfully suggest that anything which might be done to alleviate these personal worries would be a good scientific investment for this country. . . . If there you see eye to eye with me in this matter, perhaps you could interest yourself in this affair?

Then Welsh suffered a massive heart attack. Lord Cherwell sent him a note, expressing concern about his welfare. Welsh worried that Cherwell did not mention Lise Meitner, so from his sickbed in the King Edward VII Memorial Hospital for Officers, he asked his secretary, Julia Alloway, to prod Cherwell. But Winston Churchill's friend remained silent on the subject of Meitner, even though he knew full well of her services to Britain.

THIRTY

"Nicholas Baker"

WELSH was not eager to ex-filtrate Lise Meitner, but there was one person whom he wanted very much to bring out. Niels Bohr, in occupied Denmark, was less important to Welsh as a source of intelligence than was Lise Meitner in neutral Sweden. But Bohr, in England, would be most useful as an adviser on the production of the atomic bomb. Several messages had come from Bohr to the Fox. It was Bohr, according to Jomar Brun, who advised Tronstad to sabotage the Vemork production plant. Although Bohr was reluctant to leave his own institute, feeling that his presence there helped to protect the staff, in one message to Tronstad, Bohr indicated that he would like to see him again. To the British, that seemed a hint that the Dane was ready to flee Denmark.

After hearing this, Welsh proposed to Sir Stewart Menzies that a letter of invitation, signed by James Chadwick, be sent to Bohr. On January 24, 1943, C informed SIS chief Cyril Cheshire in Stockholm that such a letter of invitation had been prepared. Could Cheshire suggest a safe means of delivery to Bohr? Cheshire replied that that would be simple; a microfilm of the letter, hidden in a bunch of keys, could be delivered to Bohr. Stockholm received the special set of keys on February 8. Thanks to the Danish underground, the keys arrived safely, with these instructions for Bohr:

> . . . keys A and A1 of the message which has to be extracted. Key A1 is the one with the number 229 on it and key A is the *long* key next to it. . . . A small hole to a depth of 4 mm has been bored in the two keys. The holes were plugged up and concealed after the message was inserted. Professor Bohr should gently file the keys at the point indicated

until the hole appears. The message can then be syringed or floated out on to a microscope slide. The message is a very, very small microfilm and is repeated in duplicate in each key. It should be handled very delicately.

The technique with the keys illustrates the versatility of Welsh's special equipment assets. One of his resources was the laboratory in the headquarters of the Special Operations Executive in Baker Street. Wilfrid Mann had worked with Bohr in Copenhagen and now he worked for Eric Welsh. The making of the keys was not his responsibility or talent. But one day Welsh came to him with a brainstorm. Could Mann develop a secret writing technique using radioactive materials? Mann tried, but the process proved messy, and he abandoned that idea when he found he was receiving massive doses of radiation.

Incidentally, Mann was later posted to Washington as Welsh's representative and, in the course of his official assignment, worked closely with Guy Burgess and Kim Philby, whose primary allegiances were with the Soviet government. Thus, the two would have known much about Welsh's operations. Coupled with the dual roles of Alan Nunn May, who also was at one time in contact with Welsh, it seems that the Soviets may well have known or deduced that Welsh had a good source in the Reich during the war.

Bohr took his time in replying to Chadwick's invitation. "Chasers" were sent, but Bohr merely answered that he would like to keep in touch. He knew the British wanted him to work on the atom bomb, and he began to give serious thought to questions of producing materials for the bomb and how the bomb itself could be assembled. After he was prodded again by Welsh, Bohr replied on June 4 by courier to Stockholm, "I do not think the matter about which there is so much talk is possible." Even by then, Bohr had not arrived at the fundamental insight that Rudolf Peierls and Otto Frisch had achieved over two years earlier. Bohr's mind was regarded as the most perceptive in the world of physics, but simple insights are often the most elusive.

London, of course, was interested in Bohr's negative opinion and asked him for amplification, which, on June 19, Bohr gave, in a long letter in English, showing precisely why an atomic bomb was not possible.

Regardless of that opinion, Welsh, Lord Cherwell, and James Chadwick wanted Bohr out of Denmark because of the danger to his personal safety. Chadwick and Cherwell got a cable to Bohr at the end of September: WAR CABINET PRIORITY HAS BEEN GRANTED FOR IMMEDIATE JOURNEY.

Finally convinced of the gravity of his situation, Bohr allowed the Danish Resistance to take him and his wife, Margrethe, to Limhamn, whose tall chimneys on the cement works announced from afar that this was Sweden. Their sons came over within a few days.

Sir John Anderson had considered Victor Goldschmidt "an old gas bag" and had wanted him removed from Stockholm as soon as possible. (Welsh had wanted to remove him permanently from anywhere.) Now Sir John and Welsh were faced with very much the same problem in the person of Bohr. Stockholm swarmed with Gestapo agents, and Bohr was the most recognizable scientist in Scandinavia. The Scandinavian public knew his face and his large head, out of proportion to the rest of his body. He put off going to England while he visited Lise Meitner and other scientists.

During one visit, Njål Hole spoke with Bohr about the 1941 visit of Werner Heisenberg and Carl von Weizsäcker to Copenhagen, and Bohr said he believed that Heisenberg had come to gather information. Coupled with all of the other evidence, there can be no doubt that the two German physicists were in Copenhagen on an intelligence mission. And that added to Lise Meitner's fears. She had said to Hole, "I am afraid that the Allies have no man such as Heisenberg."

Bohr also took on a mission to save the Jews of Denmark. He sought and received audiences with the Swedish foreign minister, Crown Prince Gustav Adolf, and King Gustav himself. He was not particularly receptive to the suggestion of his three armed Swedish security guards that he try to be a little less visible, for he considered his immediate mission of overriding importance.

The mission was successful. While Bohr was still in Stockholm, the Swedish government made a formal offer of asylum to Jews in transport, but the Nazis rejected the offer as soon as it was made. Welsh tolerated this good work, but with some impatience. When Bohr asked to stay another day or two so that he could be available to dine with the king, that was the last straw. Welsh got word of the delays while he was in a submarine surfaced in the rough waters of the North Sea just after he had supervised the landing of two clandestine agents.

Welsh was ever meticulous with details when the lives of his men were at risk, and whenever possible he would launch dangerous missions himself. He scribbled an order that a Mosquito be dispatched to Stockholm to bring Bohr out forthwith, and that further excuses by Bohr be ignored. The submarine commander asked Welsh, "Are you turning green because of the seas or because of the message you've just sent?"

Bohr himself was about to turn green or at least an unnatural color. On October 6, 1943, he was driven to an unarmed Mosquito at Stockholm's Bromma Airport and fitted with flying suit, parachute, and oxygen mask. The Mosquito had to fly high over Norway to avoid German aircraft and then dive rapidly toward Scotland. When the pilot ordered Bohr to turn on his oxygen supply, his ears and the earphones were at different locations. Regulation equipment had little relevance to Bohr's huge skull. The pilot thought his passenger was dead, but Bohr recovered on the way down, grateful for the nap. His son Aage was taken from Sweden to England the next week, but the entire family was not reunited·until the war ended in Europe.

Bohr was installed in a room at St. Ermin's Hotel in Caxton Street, near 54 Broadway, where the SIS operated under the cover name of Government Communications Bureau — someone's drollery. Bohr was given an office in the Old Queen Street headquarters of the British atomic energy project, operating under the code name of Tube Alloys. There was no problem with his security clearance nor with his son's. St. Ermin's was a convenient place to put people who had to be watched, and its fourth floor housed a section of the Special Operations Executive. A senior official or scientist was always with Bohr. The only place he was instructed not to be seen was the Athenæum, which was frequented by civil servants and scientists. The other favorite SIS hotel was the Savoy, where SIS and MI5 grilled double agents and then dined on some of the finest food in London. And it was there, on October 8, 1943, that one of the most extraordinary private dinners of the war was held. Never in history had so much secret information been discussed by so few.

Those dining that Friday evening were Lord Cherwell, Churchill's close adviser and paymaster general; Wallace Akers, the director of Tube Alloys; Michael Perrin, his deputy director and the man charged with atomic energy intelligence liaison with the SIS; Niels Bohr; and

Eric Welsh. Welsh briefed Bohr, giving him in detail the German story, most of which had been obtained through Paul Rosbaud, in part with the help of Sverre Bergh. Rosbaud had failed to bring Bohr the story in person, so in effect Welsh was serving as proxy. The last firm impression Bohr had had from Heisenberg was that the Germans were at work on the bomb, but in the past few months Bohr had concluded that the bomb was not possible for technical reasons. So he was not astonished at the negative news.

Then James Chadwick dropped his bombshell. The bomb *was* possible, and the Americans and the British were making it in the United States. The two Allies had healed their rift. At this point, Welsh cautioned Bohr to be discreet about the intelligence being divulged to him that evening. Akers and Perrin then gave the technical briefing. They told of the first successful chain reaction achieved by Enrico Fermi at Stagg Stadium in Chicago on December 2 of the previous year, of plutonium and the huge factories being constructed at Oak Ridge, Tennessee, and Hanford, Washington. And they explained that Bohr could not meet with many more British atomic scientists because the best of them were departing for the bomb design-and-construction site on an isolated mesa at Los Alamos in New Mexico.

Four days later, Bohr met with Cherwell in his office. "Niels," asked Cherwell, "is this bomb going to go off?" Bohr replied, "That is what I want to stop." And they spoke of other matters — of conditions in Denmark, of there being no grounds for anxiety about a German atomic bomb — and then went into a technical discussion of the critical mass of a bomb. Would Bohr like to go to Los Alamos? Indeed he would!

Meanwhile, Bohr was given a complete briefing about everything that was going on in Britain and was taken to see the atomic research facilities. No longer was there any doubt in Bohr's mind that the atomic bomb was possible. At the Birmingham facility, where Imperial Chemical Industries was looking into various methods of heavy-water production, a luncheon of honor was held for Bohr. Jomar Brun was seated at Bohr's left. Bohr spoke in Danish, and Brun spoke in Norwegian, and none of the ICI officials could understand either one. Brun asked Bohr whether heavy water would be useful. The Great Dane, as he was called, replied, "No, not during the war — but it may be of industrial importance after the war."

When Bohr came to England, General Groves's initial intelligence mission was preparing for its first beachhead in Italy. The mission had been named Alsos, Greek for *grove*, presumably providing deep cover. Led by the flamboyant Colonel Boris T. Pash, a veteran of combat in Russia against the Bolsheviks, the mission attempted to find out what progress the Germans had made toward an atomic weapon. They were singularly unsuccessful. A year later, then able to penetrate the Reich itself and fortified by the addition of very competent scientific advisers, headed by Samuel Goudsmit, the Alsos mission was most successful, but that was late in the game—in the wake of the British.

Much to the distress of General Groves, who was not consulted, Winston Churchill and Franklin Roosevelt had agreed in August 1943 to resume atomic cooperation and to exchange intelligence information on the subject. Making the most of what he considered to be an insidious arrangement, Groves dispatched Major Robert Furman, one of his brightest officers, to England. When Furman met Bohr, he asked him whether he knew anything about the uranium deposits in Czechoslovakia. Bohr replied that he did, for that was where Madame Curie, decades ago, had found some of the ore from which she extracted radium. Bohr was not being patronizing to Furman, but he was surprised by the vast difference between what the British knew about the German atomic project and what the Americans knew.

The British educated the major, and Furman reported to General Groves the British intelligence information about the German failure to build the bomb. But as late as May 1944, when the British gave General Groves a personal briefing on what they had learned from Paul Rosbaud and others, the general still refused to believe, or did not want to believe. He replied, "Well, you *may* be right, but you can't be sure. . . . Those Nazis know how to control their scientists much better than I can control ours."

Bohr, now, knew much more than Groves was willing to know. Yet he still wanted to participate in making the bomb. He never wanted it used, but he was beginning to view it, if properly controlled, as a force for peace in the postwar world.

Bohr and the British laid down the condition that Bohr would go to Los Alamos as an official adviser to Tube Alloys, not as an American employee. He would have full access to information, as he had had in England, and would not be "imprisoned" at Los Alamos. The condition was accepted, and at the end of November Bohr departed for the United States. Once at Los Alamos, he was given the name Nicholas Baker, and his son Aage became James Baker. But the pseudonyms fooled no one.

General Groves's memoirs mention Bohr's name only once, and then in a trivial context. But the official history of Los Alamos says:

> He came at the right moment. The exigencies of production, the innumerable small problems which confronted the physicists, had led them away from some of the fundamental problems of the bomb. The study of the fission process itself had been neglected, and this obstructed reliable predictions of important phenomena. . . . Here Bohr's interest gave rise to new theoretical and experimental activities which cleared up many questions that were left unanswered before.

Much of the success of the bomb program must be attributed to Niels Bohr, yet he never departed from the aim he had expressed to Lord Cherwell: "That is what I want to stop." In subsequent months he met with Roosevelt and Churchill in an attempt to persuade them, but in that he was unsuccessful.

Anna Rosbaud and Paul, 1896.

The Heinnisser family villa in Waltendorf.

Door to the apartment house at 8 Trauengauergasse, Graz, where the family lived during Paul's childhood.

Paul Rosbaud at 3 Quergasse, Graz, circa 1909.

Top: Johann Strajner, Paul's "father," as a spelunker.

Bottom: Karl Gaugl, Paul Rosbaud, and Anna Rosbaud.

Sketch of Paul Rosbaud as an Austrian soldier on the Isonzo, 1918.

Hans and Paul Rosbaud with Paul's daughter, Angela. Graz, 1936.

Ruth Lange and fellow athletes in training in the early 1930s. Ruth is in the right foreground.

"Red Hilde" Benjamin, Ruth Lange's sister; after World War II, Benjamin was minister of justice in the East German government.

Ruth Lange.

Major Frank Foley in Oslo, autumn 1939.

Margaret Reid.

General Otto Ruge in colonel's uniform before his promotion.

"The Griffin." Paul Rosbaud in wartime.

Beck's book.

Eric Welsh, at right, in uniform.

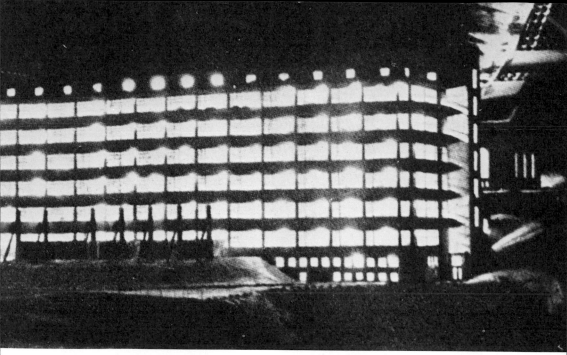

The hydroelectric plant at Rjukan at night.

The Vemork plant after the air raid on November 16, 1943. The
damage shown did not affect the heavy water production plant.

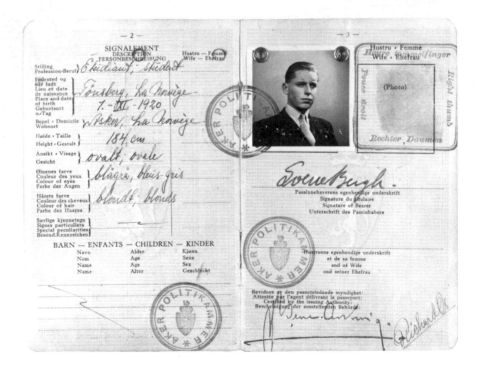

Dismantling the German atomic reactor at Haigerloch after the war. Commander Eric Welsh is at the top, second from the left.

OPPOSITE PAGE

Top: The entrance to Farm Hall *(left)*, and the door to the "listening room."

Bottom: Sverre Bergh's passport.

Max von Laue.

Otto Hahn.

The Kaiser Wilhelm Institute in Dahlem, where Hahn and Strassman split the uranium nucleus.

Victor Goldschmidt.

Lise Meitner.

Henri Piatier, 1959.

Leif Tronstad as a major.

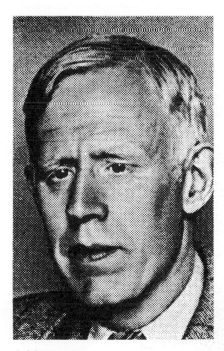

Odd Hassel.

Hilde Rosbaud, Samuel Goudsmit, and Paul Rosbaud on the occasion of the Tate Medal award to Paul Rosbaud by the American Institute of Physics.

Paul Rosbaud's body about to be buried at sea.

THIRTY-ONE

Double-Cross

WHETHER OR NOT General Groves cared to know that the Germans were out of the atomic race, it was common knowledge in Scandinavia. After the American bombings of Rjukan in November 1943, discussions in Swedish scientific circles—especially at the physics institute where Lise Meitner worked—had become animated, and Swedish physicists were incensed. British intelligence saw an opportunity in the situation.

On Sunday, December 26, 1943, the day the *Scharnhorst* was sunk, the major headline in the London *Sunday Express* was THE SECRET WEAPON MAY NOT COME OFF. Beneath it was a long and accurate feature article by Kai Siegbahn, the son of Lise Meitner's reluctant host, Manne Siegbahn. He explained the fundamentals of nuclear energy and described the prewar research. As for the bomb, Siegbahn concluded:

> Despite all the secretiveness about researching in the uranium problem,
> I venture to say that the uranium bomb is still non-existent, except as
> a research objective. . . . It is rather difficult to say if it is possible at all
> to construct such a bomb, but for the present it seems as if an essential
> link is missing for making the uranium bomb a reality.

Even more remarkable, the *Sunday Express* went beyond Siegbahn's opinion to assure its readers that "it may therefore be a source of consolation to know that able Swedish atoms-scientists believe that the Germans have not succeeded in creating atom explosives." The *Express* explained its sources for the information by saying, "Swedish scientists had close contacts with German scientists until the Germans recently arrested Norwegian professors and students." Among those recently arrested was, of course, Odd Hassel.

Press security on the atomic bomb was extremely tight in the United States and even tighter in Britain, so the article's appearance seemed at first a puzzle. The *Express* was owned by William Maxwell Aitken, Lord Beaverbrook, formerly minister of war production and now lord privy seal. Lord Beaverbrook was intimately familiar with the history of the atomic bomb project and its present course, and he was in constant touch with his editors about what they should print. It was quite clear, then, that Kai Siegbahn's article was no accident—but what was its purpose?

It was not hard to discern the reassuring purpose of the message to the British public. Rumors about Hitler's secret weapons had been rife, and the actions against Rjukan had focused attention on the bomb. But the Gestapo and the Abwehr also read the British papers.

From the exploit of Jacques Allier to the attacks on the Norwegian installations, the Germans had kept reading the lesson that heavy water was essential for atomic research and that the Allies would do anything to halt production. Now, an article by a distinguished neutral scientist—apparently published with official approval—carried the strong implication that the British were still in a research stage and without much hope of "making the uranium bomb a reality."

The article was, of course, a deliberate SIS plant, conceived in the Double-Cross Committee (the XX Committee), chaired by John Masterman of MI5. Since the 1930s, the Abwehr had been sending agents to Britain in the guise of refugees or businessmen. In wartime, they came by submarine or parachute. The XX Committee was formed to exploit captured German agents after they had been "turned." It had seven goals: to control Abwehr activity, to catch its spies, to learn its methods, to obtain its codes, to uncover its plans and deceptions, to influence those plans, and to deceive the enemy. The *Sunday Express* article fitted the last two objectives.

The top SIS expert on the Abwehr was Frank Foley of Section V, so he was recruited to the XX Committee as a senior adviser. In the early months, his work was interrupted by a special assignment, conducting the lengthy interrogation of Rudolf Hess. When he returned four months later, Foley took up the deception business once more. A close colleague in the SIS has said, "In Section V, he was the specialist in running double agents, working with J. C. Masterman in MI5. He was very much the elder statesman ... giving useful advice whenever called on."

Perhaps the most famous—and bizarre—deception was Operation Mincemeat. In the summer of 1942, when the invasion of Sicily was being planned, Churchill said, "Everyone but a bloody fool would know that it's Shishily." The problem was how to make the Germans into bloody fools. Ewen Montagu of Naval Intelligence had the brilliant idea of planting false information in the briefcase of a corpse in a staff officer's uniform. The body was placed in the Mediterranean, where it would float ashore in Spain, and the papers were sure to be shown to the Abwehr. The scheme worked, and the Germans were tricked into believing that the landings would take place in Sardinia.

At about the same time, Welsh was devising his own plan for misleading the Germans on atomic matters. It would have to involve a Norwegian already under his control who was also an atomic scientist. After searching through the files, he narrowed down the possibilities to a citizen of Bergen named Helmer Dahl, who probably had been first recommended by Sir Edward Appleton to the SIS. Dahl, then as now at the Christian Michelsens Institute in Bergen, had worked under Appleton at Cambridge before the war. (Appleton would later receive a Nobel Prize in physics.)

Welsh hoped that the plot would go something like this: Dahl would be "kidnapped" by the British and forced to work on the British atomic program. He would later be sent back to Norway on a secret mission concerned with heavy water. Dahl would then "defect" to the Germans with detailed but misleading information that the British were getting nowhere in their search for the atomic bomb. It would be a grand deception worthy of the XX Committee's goals.

Unfortunately, the Gestapo pounced first. Dahl was held for interrogation in late October 1941. The immediate danger was that Welsh's wireless reporting station THETA, of which Dahl was a member, would be compromised. Even if Dahl did not talk, there was someone else who might incriminate him—Willy Simonsen, a co-worker at the institute who was reported to be next on the Gestapo arrest list. Simonsen did not belong to THETA, but he was aware of Dahl's activities.

The Bergen Resistance quickly poisoned Simonsen—not seriously enough to kill him but badly enough to put him in the hospital. They then spirited him out of the hospital and over the border to Sweden.

Dahl was released in February 1942, but the Gestapo put him under strict surveillance. At two o'clock in the morning after he was freed, a Resistance member came to him with a message from Welsh, warning him that the Gestapo was still watching. Orders were not to contact THETA and to be prepared to leave for England. His family could go with him.

The "Shetland bus" was the usual means for transporting agents into or out of Norway. It was used, for the most part, by the SOE, and it consisted of some battered fishing boats. In contrast, Welsh's one-ship navy was the sturdy *Borghild*, skippered by Jacob Syltøy and armed with machine guns. On March 18, 1942, the *Borghild* carried Ellinor and Helmer Dahl and their sixteen-day-old daughter, Catherine, to Scotland.

By this time, Dahl had been exposed too much, and the "kidnapping" scheme had to be abandoned.

The one great failing of the XX Committee was that it did not have the German "shopping list"—that is, the kinds of information German agents were charged with obtaining. As Masterman put it, "A careful and intelligent study of all the traffic could . . . have given an accurate picture of all the more important German interests and intentions throughout the war. In retrospect it is clear that more use could have been made of this product of the double-cross agent's work."

So there was essentially no attempt to gather through Double-Cross the type of information Rosbaud was providing. The committee itself did not know the identity of SIS sources, but they did need information provided by the sources to concoct the replies to questions from the turned Abwehr agents. Ewen Montagu has written in a letter: " 'Scientific' deception/intelligence gathering was done by each service to meet its needs and we each consulted our own experts. That was also the way in which replies to questions were concocted—naturally with consultation if more than one service was involved (though such occasions were very rare)."

Atomic energy was one area where Rosbaud's information might have interacted with the XX Committee, but Montagu was "pretty sure that no other member of the Committee (other than I) knew of the atom bomb project . . . and I only at a latish date and . . . as something to keep clear of. [I was] merely to note any relevant German interest and, if I found any, to report it to the Director of Naval Intelligence *only*." Montagu was mistaken, of course, because the committee's senior adviser, Major Francis Foley, knew much about atomic matters.

Toward the end of 1941 and early 1942, the Abwehr (German military intelligence) put the bomb high on its agents' shopping list. There was, of course, the thwarted attempt by Heisenberg and von Weizsäcker to pick Niels Bohr's brains. Then, in 1941, the Abwehr sent a requirement via Alfredo to Tricycle. Some foreign firms had been searching South America for uranium deposits, and Berlin wanted to know how uranium was processed, the quantities, and the purities. These were reasonable questions for that time.

Alfredo was an Abwehr agent working under a business cover in Rio de Janeiro. Tricycle was the flamboyant Yugoslav Dusko Popov, a double agent working for the XX Committee (and supposedly the model for Ian Fleming's James Bond later on).

In February 1942, the Abwehr sent another atomic request to its British-controlled agents. It was fuller and more specific. This time, there were questions not only about raw materials but about the separation of the heavy component of uranium. Clearly, the Abwehr had acquired a technically knowledgeable consultant.

The XX Committee could not afford to ignore any questions. And so there must have been consultations with the Tube Alloy people; reasonable-sounding but essentially useless answers must have been composed and transmitted by the controlled agents. But none of this is verifiable; it is still buried in the classified records of the Secret Service.

There was also the other side of the matter to be considered. In the winter months of 1942–1943, Rosbaud was uneasy, and he stayed away from Berlin as much as possible. It was becoming apparent to Welsh and Foley that by not asking atomic energy questions of their German-controlled double agents, they might be signaling the Abwehr that the SIS had a reliable source in Germany quite unknown to the German service. It could be disastrous to get the Germans started—even by default—on a hunt for someone who had access to many German atomic physicists.

The British had had one reliable informant in the Abwehr and one very questionable one. The reliable man had been an officer named Paul Thümmel, who until the spring of 1942 supplied some valuable information. The dubious one was Johann Jebsen, recruited by Popov and given the cryptonym Artist. After the bombing of the Norwegian heavy-water plant in November 1943, it seemed essential to start a false trail leading away from Rosbaud. Accordingly, Tricycle was asked about a German atomic weapon, and he passed the request on to Artist on the assumption that the Abwehr would learn of it at once.

Artist reported that Otto Hahn had been approached directly and had stated that "research had not progressed enough to produce an atomic bomb." It was a perfectly honest answer, and there are several ways of interpreting its intent. Perhaps Artist was not a double agent but simply a man who was willing to spy for Britain. (He was later drugged, smuggled out of Lisbon and back to Germany, and grilled by the Gestapo about another matter.) Perhaps the Germans had been convinced that the British bomb was as remote as their own and thus did not mind telling the truth.

After the abortive attempt to assassinate Hitler in July 1944, the Abwehr was absorbed into Himmler's intelligence organization, the Sicherheitsdienst (SD), under Walter Schellenberg. From then on, the collection requirements sent to agents showed much less sophistication. In the purge of the Abwehr, some technical expertise seems to have been sacrificed.

On November 2, 1944, Friedle Gaertner, code name Gelatine — an Austrian woman expatriate — received this inquiry: "In which part of London is the Uranium Research Institute, in charge of Lise Meitner, a Jewish emigrant, in conjunction with Professor O. R. Frisch?"

There was no such institute in London, and, as every scientist in Germany knew, Meitner was working in Stockholm. Otto Frisch was at Los Alamos — but presumably the XX Committee did not reply as to his whereabouts.

Again, as late as February 1945, the SD asked a German agent under FBI control where heavy water was being produced in America and which laboratories were handling large quantities of uranium. Again, the question revealed that German intelligence had such slight knowledge that it could not manage to compose relevant questions.

Oddly enough, Rosbaud was the only person in Germany who had any sense of the progress of the Anglo-American effort to build the bomb—and he deduced that from the questions Eric Welsh asked him about the German effort.

There were many times when the British, even Eric Welsh, had doubts about Rosbaud. John Turner, one of Welsh's men in Stockholm, said that the Griffin's reports were so comprehensive and accurate that from time to time Welsh and C would suspect that he was a double agent. Each time that happened, Rosbaud would be cleared again by Frank Foley.

THIRTY-TWO

Cover

OCCASIONALLY it was within London's power to do some small thing to allay German suspicion of Paul Rosbaud, but it was a very limited kind of support. It was left to him to establish a fabric of cover made up of circumspect behavior in a Nazi society, close attention to security, and protectors in just the right places. Two of those right places were the Nazi Party and the Abwehr — and there is no doubt about the identity of one of Paul's protectors who held a position in both.

One of the most perplexing incongruities in Paul Rosbaud's life was his friendship with Friedrich Karl Drescher-Kaden — and it was without doubt a genuine friendship. Paul almost never had anything good to say about a Nazi, but he almost never had anything bad to say about Drescher-Kaden.

Some of this comes through in a letter Paul wrote to his brother a year after the end of the war. He said that his "hatred of the Nazis has not diminished during the past months and I realize with great anxiety that many came back. Only the really decent ones like Drescher-Kaden meet difficulty compounded with difficulty." He then added a most significant sentence: "And he was the one who saved many human lives probably better than even mine."

That remark hints at some strangely incongruous wartime actions that may have been lost to recorded history with the death of Rosbaud.

The paradox comes from the fact that Friedrich Karl Drescher-Kaden was an early convert to Nazism and participated in the most notorious Party activities from the 1920s on. The NSDAP was created by disgruntled veterans of the First World War who believed that

Germany had been given a stab in the back, a *Dolchstoss*, by anarchists, Bolsheviks, Jewish merchants, and all sorts of enemies invented by their embittered minds. And with the signing of the Treaty of Versailles, many German veterans became convinced of a global plot to deprive their nation of the God-given "German right."

Other political reactionaries formed their own armies — mercenaries, essentially — in several 100,000-strong *Freikorps* to regain disputed territories on Germany's eastern frontiers. In the early months of 1919, the Allies themselves encouraged the Free Corps to battle the Bolsheviks in Lithuania and Latvia. The most notorious and influential of the Free Corps was the brigade led by former navy Lieutenant Commander Hermann Ehrhard. His brigade was the first organization to flaunt the swastika in Germany, the emblem that Hitler adopted as the symbol of the Nazi Party.

Drescher-Kaden finished World War I as a first lieutenant and returned to his schooling in the physical sciences at the University of Breslau. He continued his studies at Göttingen and began to emerge as a most promising student of mineralogy and geology. He caught the attention of Victor Goldschmidt, then still at Oslo, and, inevitably, that of Paul Rosbaud, scientific adviser to *Metallwirtschaft*.

In 1929, the year of turmoil for Goldschmidt in Oslo, Drescher-Kaden gained more approval from V.M. by joining an expedition to Greenland to investigate deposits of Goldschmidt's favorite mineral, olivine. But when Goldschmidt came to Göttingen that year, Drescher-Kaden accepted a professorship at the Mining Academy of Clausthal in the mineral-rich Harz Mountains. During this time, Drescher-Kaden had been actively rallying students and faculties to the Nazi cause. He was finally accepted as a full member of the Party on the first of August 1932 and given membership number 1250567.

The young professor rose rapidly in the Nazi hierarchy that controlled the universities, becoming a Reichsreferent for the Nazi Party's Office for Technology just after Hitler came to power. At the same time, he was appointed to one of the most repugnant positions in German academic society. He became the Reichsvertrauensmann at the Clausthal Mining Academy. Since the First World War, German intelligence had placed their Vertrauensmänner, or V-men, as agents in key locations throughout the world. Literally, they were "trusted persons." Actually, they were spies, moles, and informers.

When the Nazis took control they placed V-men inside universities, factories, and wherever else subversion and anti-Nazi sentiment might arise.

In that position, Drescher-Kaden reported to the Party, but he was also serving the Abwehr. An interesting memorandum to the Ministry for Science, Education, and People's Culture from the Abwehr address at 72–76 Tirpitzufer shows how essential Drescher-Kaden's services were. On August 27, 1942, the German High Command politely regretted that Drescher-Kaden could not be posted for certain educational purposes, because "Captain Drescher-Kaden has been called to active service on the General Staff of the Army to undertake special tasks. For the moment, he is indispensable to the Wehrmacht." Thus, in addition to his technical services to the Reich, Drescher-Kaden had become indispensable to its military and intelligence arms, and he was a faithful servant of the Nazi Party as well. It may be significant that Rosbaud was in contact with Captain Drescher-Kaden at his Abwehr field post, number 12519.

Why Paul Rosbaud sought the friendship of a man like this may never be fully explained. Rosbaud saw compassionate qualities in Drescher-Kaden, but they could hardly balance the professor's fervent support for the Nazi state. Paradoxically, he probably did not support Hitler, and in that there was at least some common ground, for Drescher-Kaden knowingly backed Rosbaud in his activities against Hitler. Rosbaud did not "use" Drescher-Kaden as he used other Nazi scientists, like Pascual Jordan, for his own ends. And Drescher-Kaden used the expertise of Paul Rosbaud legitimately for special missions and for advice in his Raw Materials Working Group, which rendered valuable services to the Reich.

Although this complicated relationship is far from clear, there was an acknowledged synergism between the two men that promoted the goals of each.

When Victor Goldschmidt was forced to flee Göttingen in 1935, Drescher-Kaden, then at the Technische Hochschule in Berlin, and in frequent contact with Rosbaud, was called to take the directorship of V.M.'s institute. But first he had to undergo an investigation to establish quite firmly that he was a loyal Party member and of pure Aryan descent. And once more, Friedrich Karl Drescher-Kaden, close friend of the Jew Victor Goldschmidt and the Nazi-hater Paul Rosbaud, was certified as one of the most loyal of Nazis. The letter of "clearance," which was issued from the Nazi Party headquarters in Munich, dated April 8, 1936, read, in part:

> The Regional Criminal Justice Führer knows Drescher-Kaden from those times [before 1932] and knows that he later cooperated actively with the Office for Technique. In terms of National Socialism, there are no objections to Party Comrade Drescher-Kaden. Scientifically, he is considered very good. Drescher-Kaden's only disadvantage is that he tries to organize too much, with the result that his practical work suffers.

Paul Rosbaud had a very similar view. He said of Drescher-Kaden five years later, "As my friend he is the most unreliable in unimportant things but the most reliable in important things. An absolutely decent character, old Party member." There is the dichotomy, succinctly stated: "an absolutely decent character, old Party member." To interpret that is to understand much about Paul Rosbaud and how he survived during the war.

Drescher-Kaden had met Victor Goldschmidt and Paul Rosbaud in the 1920s, and through the years the three not only became good friends but began to call on one another for favors. When Goldschmidt was forced to leave Göttingen, it was fortunate that Drescher-Kaden was the man who took over his position. Paul Rosbaud was to write, "Much later, part of Goldschmidt's money was transferred to Oslo as a result of a very courageous and outspoken letter written by F. K. Drescher-Kaden . . . to the president of the German Reichsbank, Hjalmar Schacht." As noted earlier, it was an equally courageous letter from Drescher-Kaden that helped Paul Rosbaud return to Oslo in 1942 to pay a visit to V.M. — a visit that enabled him to report to the British on the German atomic program. And two years later, Drescher-Kaden's intervention would save Rosbaud's life.

Where did Drescher-Kaden gain his influence? After Hermann Ehrhard's Freikorps had been suppressed, Ehrhard formed the Viking League, of which Drescher-Kaden became a member. Many of the senior officers of the Abwehr had belonged to the Viking League, and Admiral Wilhelm Canaris, head of the Abwehr, was himself a long-time associate of Hermann Ehrhard's.

Drescher-Kaden, as a former member of the Viking League, was a favored member of the Abwehr, in which he seems to have been a reserve officer. What better safeguard could a spy have than a well-established friend in the intelligence service? That was undoubtedly one of the "important things" Rosbaud wanted to rely on.

Rosbaud, of course, had other contacts in the Abwehr; one was Major Professor Hans Mortensen, who occupied Room 326 at 82 Tirpitzufer, the address of Abteilung I of the Abwehr. Under Colonel Hans Piekenbrock until 1943 (and afterward under Colonel Georg Hansen), this section of the Abwehr ran spies and specialized in the collection of information about foreign powers. Rosbaud seems to have had fairly frequent contact with Mortensen at his office and at his apartment at 180 Kurfürstendamm.

Mortensen, a geomorphologist (one who studies the features of the earth's surface), came to Göttingen a year before Victor Goldschmidt left. He became one of V.M.'s close associates and later an associate of Drescher-Kaden as well. Thus, he entered the circle of Paul Rosbaud's acquaintances. What his precise functions were in the Abwehr are unclear; the important thing is that he was another of Rosbaud's contacts in Canaris's intelligence service.

Rosbaud was known less favorably to others within the Abwehr. One officer, Michael Graf Soltikow, described in his memoirs a conversation with Japanese Ambassador Saburo Kurusu in which the ambassador speculated about weapons of the future. Soltikow replied:

> I am informed about this problem not only from Heisenberg, but also because I have read the pertinent literature, especially the unfortunate article . . . in *Naturwissenschaften*, in which the editor, Dr. Rosbaud, disclosed Otto Hahn's discovery . . . to all nations. I compare this article to Pandora's Box.

Soltikow was director of Abteilung III/D, in charge of *Spielmaterial*, or disinformation. Obviously, he was bitter that Rosbaud had informed the world about the discovery of nuclear fission.

Thus, through Drescher-Kaden, Mortensen, and others, Rosbaud had excellent contacts. One can be sure he used them effectively both for information and to protect himself.

One of the people connected with the transaction to recover V.M.'s money in Göttingen later became Rosbaud's probable connection to the anti-Nazi underground. A native Stuttgarter, Fritz Elsas was born into a wealthy Jewish family. After graduating in economics and law from the University of Tübingen in 1914, Elsas became scientific assistant to the Stuttgart City Administration and in 1926 was vice president of the German and Prussian Association of Cities. The president was Carl Goerdeler, and the fates of the two men became entwined. Goerdeler became the chief mayor of Leipzig and Elsas became the deputy mayor of Berlin. After Hitler came to power, Elsas was dismissed. He returned to writing about political science, became V.M.'s financial adviser, and settled into as inconspicuous a life as he could manage.

As war neared, Goerdeler and Elsas tried to forestall the calamity and to warn the Allies. One of Goerdeler's more notable efforts was his meeting, in Ouchy, Switzerland, with Hjalmar Schacht, who had been fired by Hitler from his post as president of the Reichsbank. They felt that if London and Paris would be firmer with Hitler, the invasion of Poland might be averted. Their views were delivered to Edouard Daladier, the French premier, and to Prime Minister Neville Chamberlain but were ignored.

Elsas, Goerdeler, and Colonel General Walter von Reichenau met on November 6, 1939. Von Reichenau thought that Hitler's plan to attack the Low Countries was completely crazy, and it was agreed that Elsas would warn the British. He did so, but to no effect.

Somehow, Elsas managed to remain in Germany, and after the abortive plot of July 20, 1944, Goerdeler fled to Elsas's house. Both were later arrested and executed.

Just because Paul Rosbaud knew Carl Goerdeler and Fritz Elsas does not mean he was part of their underground group. In fact, John Turner recalls that Welsh had specifically warned his people to stay away from that group, which was thought to have been infiltrated by the Gestapo. But there can be no doubt that Rosbaud knew much of what was going on in the German underground.

The Kapitza fiasco prompted Paul to establish other covers. Almost instinctively, he seemed to grasp an ancient principle of deception, which is described in a modern Central Intelligence Agency manual: "It is generally easier to induce an opponent to maintain a pre-existing belief than to present notional evidence to change that belief. Thus, it may be more fruitful to examine how an opponent's existing beliefs can be turned to advantage than to attempt to alter these views." Rosbaud could have written that manual.

It was important to establish patterns to keep the Gestapo at ease and ward off suspicion. One of Rosbaud's most successful and enjoyable gambits was the creation of the Circle of Friends, the Freundeskreis. Composed of eleven good friends and their wives, the Freundeskreis met, usually on the first Friday evening of the month, in the elegant Bristol dining room on Unter den Linden, nestled between the Ministry of Culture and the building that was the Russian embassy until mid 1941. They took a large table and ate and drank well, even in wartime. "On March 1st [1943] the upper stories of the Hotel Bristol were damaged but the lower stories are still fully in use," Max von Laue wrote to Lise Meitner. Undaunted, the Freundeskreis continued to meet regularly. The conversation was lofty and uninhibited. Usually there was an invited guest from out of town, and if necessary the schedule would be shifted.

Otto Hahn was not a regular member of the Freundeskreis, but he was often invited. One evening he brought along a young colleague of Walther Bothe's, Arnold Flammersfeld. Flammersfeld has said, "The food was still fairly good there.... We dined in the large dining room at a reserved table. The room was full of other people, so it is not likely that any dangerous conversation was held." But at other times Paul had different conversations, more dangerous, with just one or two people in the same Bristol dining room.

Paul's friend and the confidant of his lesser secrets, Max von Laue, was a regular member of the Freundeskreis and reported most of the meetings to Meitner in Stockholm. Thus, not only the other patrons of the Bristol and the Gestapo knew of the Freundeskreis; the censors became used to it.

The only charter female member of the Freundeskreis was a remarkable feminist, Clara von Simson, whose views were akin to those of Ellen Gleditsch. Von Simson had done pioneering low-temperature physics with Franz Simon, but Simon was spirited out of Germany by Frederick Lindemann. After that, and with Clara's increasing apprehensions about the fate of Germany and German science in general, her scientific work began to decline, and it had ceased altogether by the start of the war. Friends became concerned and finally persuaded Clara to take a fairly dull position with a private patent office just down the avenue from the Bristol.

There was also Julius Springer, one of Rosbaud's bosses. Paul never spoke much of him later except to say that "he amazingly survived the twelve years [of Nazi rule] and helped to re-establish the old publishing house again." A Freundeskreis member who did not survive was Arnold Berliner, the Jewish editor of the Springer journal *Naturwissenschaften* until 1935, when he was dismissed. Many a scientist owed much to Berliner, who had encouraged talent by publication. Ferdinand Springer had hired Paul partly to fill the void left by the departure of Berliner.

Arnold Berliner was too eminent for the Gestapo to send him, in those years, to a concentration camp, but they killed him by other means. Paul Rosbaud mourned that "the rations for food, as for all of [Arnold Berliner's] necessities, were reduced. Finally the vegetables ended, then fruit, then meat, then coffee. . . . Fearing the coming of the Gestapo, he lost his resolve on the night of March 22, 1943." Always kept informed by Rosbaud and von Laue, Lise Meitner transmitted the news to Hilde Rosbaud, in London, that Berliner "died at the end of March. Being threatened to get deprived of his home, he preferred to die." Only the Freundeskreis had the courage to attend Arnold Berliner's funeral.

As innocent as it was, the Freundeskreis certainly directed Gestapo attention to Paul as did his attending the funeral of Arnold Berliner, his presence at the reception at the Soviet embassy in Berlin on behalf of Peter Kapitza, his fleeting contacts with Frank Foley, his assistance to refugees, and his association with Hilde and Georg Benjamin. Furthermore, clearance for each of Paul's trips abroad was required from Heinrich Himmler's Reichssicherheitshauptamt, or RSHA, the parent organization of the Gestapo and the SS. Certainly, the Gestapo files on Paul Rosbaud must have been very thick.

His Gestapo dossier can no longer be found, nor are Rosbaud's Graz police records any longer in the city archives, although those of his family remain. Possibly the British Secret Service, the Soviet NKVD, or perhaps Paul himself vetted all the records shortly after the war.

Whoever the searchers were, they missed two scraps of paper. One is a letter, dated November 7, 1940, recommending elevation of Paul Rosbaud from associate member to senior member of the Association of German Iron Workers of the National Socialist Union of German Technicians. Such a recommendation did not necessarily mean that a candidate was a Nazi Party member, but it implied that he was acceptable to the Party. And the fact that a copy of the letter was found in the Gestapo files meant that security clearance of the candidate also was required.

The second slip of paper is more specific. It is an RSHA approval, dated April 12, 1943, for Rosbaud to journey to occupied Holland later that year. The rubber stamp reads "Detrimental memoranda of a political nature not found." That the Griffin managed to remain "clean," at least until April 1943, was not the least of his remarkable achievements.

Paul never kept any piece of paper that might incriminate those with whom he engaged in illegal activities. He always put his address in his letters so that friends could keep track of his whereabouts, but he frequently destroyed address books lest they prove dangerous to those same friends. In a letter of August 8, 1941, to his brother, Paul confessed something that could have been incriminating had the letter been intercepted. Paul implored Hans to "please always, always write your address on your letters. I get rid of address books as a matter of principle." A rather elaborate address book from prewar days does exist, however, and it shows some continuity from prewar to wartime associates. It gives a few scant clues to the scientists who, without sensing Rosbaud's ultimate purpose, gave him much information.

Sometimes the danger was not always from the Gestapo. On each of two nights in January 1943, the RAF dumped 150 tons of high explosives and 200 tons of incendiaries on Berlin. Paul assured his brother:

> I am OK. I am healthy and have accepted the loss of my possessions quietly and without any bad psychological reaction. There was no doubt about the outcome from the first moment. I was in a neighbor's air raid shelter and heard the incendiary bombs hurtling down. I ran out and saw smoke coming from my house, ran inside, but quickly came out again, half suffocated. I could do nothing at all. The neighbors tried to help me with their ridiculous anti–air raid implements in a touching way, but nothing could help. When the fire department came with four or five hoses they first directed the water on those doing the helping. It was an auxiliary fire department. The regular fire department people who came later drank all the liquor, which was in the basement.

The liquor was one of Paul's more tragic losses of the war. He survived other air raids and took delight in foolish little risks to irk the Nazi authorities. When copper was called in for armaments, Paul cornered his own supply. He would ask visitors for their small change and then bury it in his garden. When traveling alone in a railroad compartment, he unscrewed the copper fixtures and threw them from the moving train. The post office instructed people to use the correct denominations of stamps to save paper. Paul would post letters not requiring a return address with blocks of the lowest denomination stamps he could find.

Perhaps Paul Rosbaud led a charmed life. Yet there is something still lacking in the explanation of how he survived and how he gleaned much of his information. It is clear that he received technical and military information from sources not named in his professional address files and from sources not connected with the Norwegian and French underground networks. Nor was he affiliated with the German group behind the attempts to assassinate Hitler, although he knew of them through his friend Karl Friedrich Bonhoeffer, whose father and brother were affiliated with Carl Goerdeler and died for it.

Two remarkable brothers were the Protestant theologian Dietrich Bonhoeffer and the physical chemist Karl Friedrich Bonhoeffer. Their sister Christine married Hans von Dohnanyi, a high officer in the Abwehr. Karl Friedrich, married to Greta, Hans's sister, was one of Rosbaud's sources on heavy water. As the war progressed, Karl Friedrich, for reasons of conscience, tried to minimize his work on heavy water but at all times knew precisely what the physicists were doing with the substance. Paul Rosbaud spoke of him as an "ally." The arrest of the Goerdeler group endangered the life of both, but both survived.

There may have been an underground group consisting of government officials, military officers, and professionals that funneled information through Rosbaud to the British and helped ensure his survival. And he may have been its only survivor. That is what he said to his brother in November 1946. "The last years have not passed without leaving marks upon me. There were too many in the underground who could not be saved and, at the end, only I slipped through by a hairsbreadth. My hatred of the Nazis has not diminished."

If such a group did exist, Rosbaud never spoke of it after the war except in such vague and guarded terms as these. It is quite likely that the SIS disapproved of any public mention. Rosbaud, always loyal to the SIS, would have remained silent.

THIRTY-THREE

The Tears of the Oppressed

PAUL ROSBAUD'S concern for himself was secondary to his concern for others. At moments of particular danger, when he thought he would not survive, he took consolation in what he was doing to help other people.

Except for some sporadic RAF raids, Berlin did not feel the full fury of the aftermath of Operation Overlord, the invasion of Normandy, until four minutes after ten on June 21, 1944. In one terrible half hour, 876 aircraft of the Eighth Air Force dropped the equivalent of a tenth of the force of the Hiroshima bomb on Berlin in the form of high explosive and incendiary bombs.

The thought that his family would never know of what he had been doing for Hitler's victims was disquieting to Paul, so he confessed in a letter to his brother as much as he would ever say of the matter during the war:

> The American attack was the heaviest and in its consequences can be compared with a catastrophe of nature. It made me think of the eruptions of Mount Pelée and of Krakatoa, when the sun remained darkened for many hours . . . . It has been impossible for a long time to do any positive work. There is always debris to clear away or a similar task. But it really does not disturb me, for I am working positively in other ways. For a long time now, I have been turning toward those to whom the first lines of the serious song refer. This is truly a beautiful activity and one that provides greatest satisfaction and helps to carry one through these times.

The "serious song" was no mystery to Hans, for nothing was more familiar to the brothers than the second of Brahms's "Four Serious Songs" (*Vier Ernste Gesänge*), with words from Ecclesiastes:

> So I returned, and considered all the oppressions that are done under the sun: and beheld the tears of such as were oppressed, and they had no comforter: and on the side of their oppressors there was power; but they had no comforter.

Brahms had written the music, his final masterpiece, for the dying Clara Schumann, who had once given Anna Rosbaud piano lessons and encouragement. Hans was born just months after Clara died, and Paul was born right after Brahms died. Anna would often remind the boys of that.

Paul kept a copy of the verse in a frame on his desk throughout his life. (The same verse was a symbol of the White Rose student group in Munich that vainly opposed Hitler.)

Paul's knowledge of "the tears of the oppressed" in Nazi prisons and concentration camps was first hand. Walter Brecht, Rosbaud's Darmstadt schoolmate, recounted a startling recollection:

> Later we met seldom; once in Berlin, when I learned about German concentration camps and their nature for the first time. This meeting could not have been long after his discharge from a concentration camp. For he was very reticent in his statements because of threats received at the time of the discharge.

When he was asked for more details, Brecht replied:

> It must have been about 1942 that Paul Rosbaud told me briefly about the concentration camp. It was the first time that I heard about the existence of the camps. I am not quite sure whether he said that he himself had been in the Oranienburg camp, or whether he talked about friends who had been held there and beaten with rods. On being dismissed from the camp, one was brutally threatened to keep secrecy, so he would not tell me more. This point is not clear and I regret that I cannot clear it up. If he himself was in the camp, it must have been for a few days only. Surely the reason for his imprisonment was an incautious remark. That is the best of my knowledge; I cannot tell you more.

But Paul's Gestapo record remained "clean" to the end of the war, showing that he probably had not been under arrest in a prison or concentration camp. He was, however, one of the handful of citizens of Hitler's Reich who actually tried to penetrate concentration camps of their own volition. And Paul sometimes succeeded. It was probably what Rosbaud told Brecht after one of those visits that remained indelible in Brecht's mind.

Fortunately, Paul's own family was out of reach of the Gestapo, though things were not very easy for Hilde and Angela in an austere wartime Britain. There were limits to the assistance Professor Hutton could provide, because he was assisting other refugees as well. After the start of the war, clients lost interest in gymnastics, and Hilde and Mrs. Atkinson were forced to abandon their school in Greenwich. Angela, like other London schoolchildren, was evacuated to the countryside. Hutton found a school for her in Hastings on the south coast and a position for Hilde teaching languages at a nearby school.

William the Conqueror had swept through Hastings in 1066, and Hitler might well sweep through there with his Operation Sea Lion after the June 1940 evacuation of Dunkirk. So, again with the help of R. S. Hutton, a place was found for Angela at a rather nice inland school near Worcester. Luckily, Hilde was able to obtain a position at a nearby school again — as a drill instructor. But some months after Eric Welsh became head of the Norwegian Section of SIS, he found it more convenient to have Hilde closer to him, in London, for communicating with Paul. Angela remained at Malvern.

Welsh found Hilde a flat in a small hotel on Prince's Square in Bayswater, where she remained for the duration. And he got her a position as a receptionist at a false teeth clinic. In wartime London, a salary of two pounds ten was not bad, and in a week with good commissions, Hilde was able to take home three pounds. Except for the air raids, the rationing, and worry about Paul, life once again was not too hard for her.

Angela's relationship with her mother was becoming ever more strained, so she did not at all mind being at Malvern. During term breaks at home she would listen to Dame Myra Hess's noontime concerts at the National Gallery, which went on uninterrupted during the air raids. Dame Myra took a liking to the teenager, and in an act reminiscent of Clara Schumann's kindness toward Anna Rosbaud, the English pianist taught Angela Rosbaud.

Hilde's mother had died many years earlier, but her father was still living. From Paul, via her uncle in Switzerland and via Lise Meitner, came disquieting news. At the end of 1941, Paul had gone to Mainz to see what he could do for the elderly man. The Nazis were turning him out of his house in the Kaiserstrasse. Paul thought he might make a deal with Gerster, the upstairs neighbor, to buy the house and promise Karl Frank a room for the rest of his life. But the city government returned the contract, with the remark "The Jew Karl Israel Frank has no right to insist on living in the house of Herr Gerster." Gerster let him stay anyway.

The house on Kaiserstrasse was destroyed by a direct hit in the big air raids of the summer of 1942, but miraculously Karl Frank survived. He found asylum at the Israelite Hospital, where Paul found him in August. The rumor was that everyone would be deported to Theresienstadt and Auschwitz. Paul hoped "that by some grace or mercy he might die" before being transported. And so hoped Hilde. On November 23 of that year, Hilde wrote to Lise Meitner that she "had very sad news about my father and only hope and pray that he is dead." She had learned that her father was in Theresienstadt, but did not know that he had died a week earlier and that the coroner at the camp had already issued death certificate number 50/12446.

Nor did Paul know that. The following year, he tried to go to Theresienstadt and got as far as Lobositz, five miles away, but even the Griffin could not get close to that concentration camp that time.

Paul's compassion for suffering people was so intense that he was willing to risk the pain that would surely be inflicted on him by the Gestapo if it ever discovered but a small fraction of his illegal activities. Even in times of personal danger from the war itself, Rosbaud was always eager to help friend and stranger. Although Ruth Lange was aware of many of Paul's activities, she did not know their details and would not have understood them. She never heard of his code name, the Griffin. But she was Paul's willing accessory in aiding Hitler's victims, and this is what Rosbaud had to say about her:

> Her active work against the Nazis began almost immediately after 1933, when she refused to do anything for the Nazis and their organizations. She . . . devoted all of her energies to helping people who were suppressed and persecuted, whether they were Jews, Communists, Social Democrats, prisoners of war, foreign slave workers. She was the only person who knew about my illegal activities right from the beginning, and she gave me every help and encouragement. Her brother-in-law

was a Jewish doctor, Georg Benjamin, a very great man and a leading figure in the underground fight against fascism. He was arrested in 1933 and sent to a concentration camp. When he was released in 1934 he at once resumed his political work, until his arrest in 1936, when he was sent to prison for six years. After these six years he was sent to one of the most dreadful camps, in Wuhlheide, near Berlin.

Thus it was that in 1942 Paul encountered at first hand the horrors of a concentration camp, although he had known of them long before. Not many would go to see for themselves what Ruth and Paul saw.

It was there that I saw for the first time in my life people with hunger edema. Through a secret message, Ruth's sister learned where her husband was working. Ruth and I went to this place disguised as working people, and Ruth succeeded in getting in touch with her brother-in-law under the eyes of the SS guards and giving him as much food as we could carry. Together with her sister she bribed watchmen to provide him with enough food to keep him from starving. After a few weeks Dr. Benjamin was sent to another concentration camp—Mauthausen —where he was killed by the Nazis.

Mauthausen coroner's certificate number 5348/1942 notes that Dr. Georg Benjamin perished on August 26, 1942, at one-thirty in the morning. He had killed himself on the electrified fence.

Their helping concentration camp inmates did not cease with the death of Ruth's brother-in-law. Paul recorded that

Ruth accompanied me when I went to see Jews deported and came with me to the Jewish hospital, which was run by Jewish doctors and watched by the Gestapo and SS—the last station of those wretched and poor people before they were sent to Auschwitz and other camps. In 1944 when I moved to Teltow she came and shared the house, which was something like an illegal HQ, with me, my old housemaid, and a French POW, and it was there that she led in organizing help for Russian, French, and Yugoslav people in concentration camps, the few still existing Jews, Dutch and Norwegian slave workers, and so on. Whether it was food for half-starved people, cigarettes, medicine for sick POWs, she arranged for it. It was there that she met all my "allies," Laue, Hahn, Mattauch, Bonhoeffer, and many others.

That was the most that Paul Rosbaud ever said about his illegal work. Grateful survivors were his witnesses. For example, right after the war, a woman named Elizabeth Arutinskaya, who had survived her three and a half years in a concentration camp, asked Hans Rosbaud for his brother's address in order to thank Paul "for his infinite kindness and much help before I was transported from Berlin."

Arnold Flammersfeld, the co-worker of Otto Hahn and Walther Bothe, recalls a specific incident:

> After the heavy bomb damage of Hahn's institute in Berlin-Dahlem on February 14, 1944, I participated in the cleaning-up work. One of the employees of the institute, Ludwig Gille, the head of the mechanical shop, was an influential and dangerous Nazi. He had brought four or five concentration camp prisoners to help. They were working in their striped prison clothing. By chance I saw Rosbaud distribute to them rolls he had brought. This courageous deed made a deep impression on the young people. We would not have dared to do it.

Although other scientists witnessed the same episode and the miseries of the concentration camp prisoners working outside and inside their institutes, after the war most claimed that they had no idea of the terrible truth. Even though a scientific colleague who had seen the "first cynical mass execution of Jews in Poland" reported the horror to Werner Heisenberg, Mrs. Heisenberg confessed, "We lacked the imagination to picture the organized crimes our people were capable of." This, about a physicist generally believed to have been a master at interpreting observable phenomena.

There are many other testimonials, most of them scanty. But each is compelling. Sometimes Rosbaud bought freedom for a family from the Gestapo. Other times he helped young people to escape being drafted, or if they were, to find them a factory assignment to save them from being sent to the front. And if they were sent to combat, Rosbaud would see that they received books, food, and clothing. "Paul Rosbaud was for us, for Fritz Laves and for me, who refused to support the Nazi regime; often he was *der Ritter in der Not* (the knight in [time of] need). This is the testimony of the physical chemist Helmut Witte, now at Rosbaud's old school in Darmstadt. But Rosbaud, wrote Witte, was not optimistic:

> At the beginning of the war I was immediately drafted into the military and as a soldier began to correspond with Paul Rosbaud. To make me cheerful, he sent me books at the front. After the French campaign, that is, in the autumn of 1940, Rosbaud had great fear that Hitler might win the war. After Easter of 1940, I was reassigned because of disability and went to Hamburg. I came regularly on furlough to visit Paul Ros-

baud, the last time a few weeks before the destruction of his house in Berlin. At this last conversation, he was deeply pessimistic about the war. He was certain that Hitler would eventually lose the war, but he feared that the war would demand many more sacrifices.

Fritz Laves's widow, whose husband also gained deferment from military service through Paul Rosbaud, recalls a more poignant episode. Having failed in 1942 to obtain release of his father-in-law from Theresienstadt, Paul Rosbaud returned to the concentration camp to try to rescue a family of five. Writes Malitta Laves:

> Rosbaud referred to the head of the family as a scientist. He got them out of Theresienstadt. He told me he went disguised as a *Beerenweib* [a woman searching for berries] in the woods near the camp, hiding and exchanging money with the SS guards. I remember the sum of 10,000 marks. He told us he had no guarantee at all that the five persons would be released after he had deposited the money. But he said literally "The SS guards honored their obligation as thieves might do honor among themselves." Tragically, one of the three children died while fleeing.

That was the beginning of 1943. The Russians were destroying the last German bastions in Stalingrad. Rommel was retreating westward after his defeat at El Alamein on November 2, and the Anglo-American armies landed in Algeria and Morocco six days later. Hitler's reversals were encouraging, but Rosbaud knew that victory was distant.

THIRTY-FOUR

The Code of Codes

As THE ALLIES were building up their forces for the invasion of Normandy, Paul Rosbaud was increasing the flow of information to Eric Welsh. The volume of reports was so vast that the intermediaries began to wonder about Rosbaud. How could one person have access to such a broad variety of information and be so audacious as to flood the London SIS with it? That was the question that John Turner heard being asked in the passport control office at 12 Birger Jarlsgatan in Stockholm. But every time there was doubt at that station, London simply replied, "Trust him."

Not so inclined were some of the Norwegians themselves. In mid 1944, the Griffin needed a special courier who would pass through Stockholm or Oslo. Sverre Bergh at the moment was carrying out another task, so Paul turned to Bergh's uncle Theo Findahl. Through his job as Berlin correspondent for Oslo's *Aftenposten*, Findahl himself passed many intelligence items by code in his telephone conversations with his editor, Niels Jörgen Mürer, in Oslo. But many of the Griffin's messages were technical in nature and not suitable for transmission by telephone.

The Norwegian Rowing Club at Hessenwinkel was a sort of clearing house for the intelligence operations expedited by Findahl and a Norwegian businessman, Camillo Holm. A colorful character, Holm was in the textile trade and a supplier of cloth to the German military and naval services. As such, he was able to judge with some accuracy the movements and general whereabouts of military units. He also had excellent contacts in the International Red Cross, which had access to the POW camps. Prisoners were assigned to civil and military construction projects, and the camps were prolific sources of information.

So Theo Findahl had a fair appreciation of which and how much intelligence was moving from the Reich through Norwegian channels. In the spring of 1944, he became worried about Rosbaud. Sverre Bergh, on the other hand, had no doubts at all about the Griffin.

The Norwegian students at the various Hochschulen would be returning soon to Norway for summer vacation. As it happened, Bergh had a number of very special papers, which several students at Dresden had obtained without the help of the Griffin. The papers were of such importance that it was thought better that Bergh not carry other information as well — the basket and eggs theory. Thus, when Rosbaud contacted Findahl, the journalist suggested another student at Dresden, Ragnar Winsnes. Findahl had two tasks for Winsnes, one of which was unknown to Rosbaud. Just as Findahl spoke in code to his editor in Oslo, he had a telephonic code arrangement with Rosbaud. Bergh, in fact, does not believe that Rosbaud and Findahl ever met.

Winsnes, who now lives in a manufacturing town in southern Norway, has given a detailed account of his meeting with Rosbaud, his memory vivid not only because of the man he met but because of the date: June 6, 1944. Perhaps Paul's elation over the Allied invasion of Normandy caused him to be a little less cautious than he usually was about revealing his code name to a stranger, even one recommended by Theo Findahl. But, in any case, he had a very important task for Winsnes and had to trust him. As Winsnes has put it:

I knew about Paul Rosbaud for about a year or a year and a half, but I met him only once, the day it was announced in Germany that the English and Americans had gone ashore in France. I saw him for an hour or two. He told me that he was known under the name of Der Greif — the Griffin.

Winsnes has described the circumstances of the meeting:

Einar Borch and I were in Berlin, where I had to pick up my transit visa at the Swedish legation. We spent the night there, and made an appointment with the former president of the University of Oslo, D. A. Seip. Having received my transit visa, we went to the meeting with Seip. As I had a task to attend to, I had to leave before the others. This task concerned Rosbaud. Over the phone I had made an appointment with him for a meeting at the Anhalter Bahnhof. We spent an hour together, exchanging information as we walked the streets. He wanted certain information communicated to certain persons in Oslo.

Anhalter Station was a favorite rendezvous point for Rosbaud, as was the elegant Hotel Excelsior, which was connected with the station by tunnel. The Excelsior had everything — a good restaurant, a post office, travel agency, and a fashionable lounge where the higher-class demimonde of Berlin displayed themselves. Altogether, it was the kind of atmosphere suited for spies. And only a block from Gestapo headquarters at that.

Winsnes and Rosbaud had a beer, and several highly incriminating pages were passed to Winsnes in a folded newspaper. Had they been seized, they would have meant little to a Gestapo agent — but they certainly would have been evidence of a conspiracy. Rosbaud gave Winsnes the name, author, and year of publication of a book published by Springer Verlag. The pages also contained a long message in some sort of code. Winsnes has described it:

> The page number, the first word in a paragraph on that page, and a code for the code. There were several such pages and several paragraphs and codes. He asked me to arrange for this information to be communicated to London. I asked him to explain this coding procedure, and he told me that the first word in a given paragraph was connected with another word, which marked the beginning of his report in the text [of the named Springer book]. Those in London had a list of this coupling of words. The code itself consisted, as far as I remember, of two letters, and the people in London knew which code applied to those two letters. He also told me that he occasionally inscribed clandestine information in other Springer publications, but he rarely could do anything with *first* editions of books, because the authors had too much control over the text. However, with later editions the publisher's editor had more freedom to rewrite and update the text. This freedom he took advantage of, with relish.

Thus, books were more than a means of livelihood for Rosbaud; they became weapons against the Nazi book-burners. Books and a book exhibition brought the 1939 report to Oslo. Books continued to transmit information from the Griffin to Welsh throughout the war.

The "code of codes" technique described by Winsnes is worth examining more fully.

Book coding is an ancient technique. The code used by Frank Foley and Margaret Reid during the retreat from Oslo was classic. An obscure book — in April 1940 the choice was *Sesame and Lilies* — is selected by the coders and decoders. Each letter of the message is described by three numbers that identify the page of the book, the line on that page, and the position of the enciphered letter in the line. Only if the book is known does the message become known.

The code devised by Welsh for the Griffin had an extra safety feature: if the coded message was compromised and the book known, the intercepting party still would not have been able to decipher the message. Rosbaud called this method the "code of codes." In any book on a given subject there were words galore to tell the tales Rosbaud wished to tell. His method was the following:

He would find a paragraph containing, for example, the word *uranium*. The page and the first word of the paragraph were the first two parts of the code. First words of a paragraph are usually words that appear frequently. Rosbaud and Welsh had a master list of couplings of frequent words. Identifying the first word of a paragraph would then identify *another* frequent word in the paragraph.

Thus, if the paragraph containing the word *uranium* began with the word *There*, and the master list in London had *there* coupled with *also*, the decoder would then look for the word *also* in the paragraph. Once it was found, the position of *uranium* would be given by a two-letter alphabetical code, the code of codes. If *uranium* was five words after *also*, a two-letter code, like AK, might represent *plus five*. If *uranium* was seven words before *also*, a code like RW might represent *minus seven*.

All coding and decoding is tedious. The advantage of the code-of-codes technique over the usual type of book code is that it is more secure and three code groups represent not just a single letter but an entire word. If finding a coupling word to correspond to the first word of a paragraph sounds implausible, it isn't, for both words are frequently used.

Most of Rosbaud's messages had a technical content, and he was the ultimate arbiter of which technical books Springer Verlag would publish. Winsnes related that "Rosbaud identified one book for me, but I do not remember the title. I asked him if I had to take the book with me. 'No,' he answered, 'the book can be bought in a bookstore in Stockholm.' This was the way the books came to London. It may also be that they were decoded in Stockholm."

Stockholm was not the only channel for the books. Rosbaud sent many books through his brother-in-law Rudolf Frank in Basle. Frank forwarded the packages to Hilde Rosbaud, who knew perfectly well that Eric Welsh was intercepting them. In regard to the Stockholm channel, Rosbaud was deceiving Winsnes only slightly.

Relying on the availability of bookstore copies was chancy at best. Shipments sometimes were delayed or sold out early. There was a reliable friend in Stockholm, Lise Meitner. About the time that Winsnes passed through Stockholm, Rosbaud had been displaying, in his messages to Meitner, a certain anxiety about books. On a postcard, dated June 27, 1944, he wrote, "Recently, very little has been published concerning physics and mathematics. I shall give you eight special books that perhaps are of interest to your work program." In all probability, one or more of the eight books contained special messages. Meitner would have passed the books to Njål Hole or given them directly to the SIS head of station in Stockholm, Cyril Cheshire.

In Stockholm, on his way to Oslo, Winsnes posted "a very important message" from Rosbaud to the Norwegian legation, but he no longer recalls what it was. He does recall very well, however, what happened in Oslo. The circumstances could not have been more mysterious. Winsnes had been instructed by Findahl to contact the Tobacco King, Johan H. Andresen, in his villa in Bygdøy. Andresen had spent his youth in Germany and Sweden studying the tobacco industry and now was the head of the large Tiedemanns Tobaksfabrik, his own bank, and a number of other enterprises. He and his wife, the former Eva Klaveness, who was related to Odd Hassel's mother, sometimes entertained as though a war were not going on, but Johan Andresen was very much in contact with the Resistance groups. According to Winsnes:

> I went there and was received by Andresen and his wife. There was a large party going on in the house. I explained that I brought best regards for them. They took me aside, and I gave my password. The Andresens looked at each other quickly, then said: "This is for Arvid." Mrs. Andresen spoke with me while her husband went to fetch Arvid

Brodersen. He was in the house and was wearing a tuxedo. When he came up to us, Mrs. Andresen suggested that we talk on a bench in the garden.

Winsnes handed Brodersen the message encrypted by the code of codes, but he had another mission, unknown to the Griffin. Findahl wanted reassurance that Paul Rosbaud was not a double agent. Winsnes gave Brodersen both Rosbaud's name and the code name the Griffin, for Findahl was not sure the two were one and the same. Brodersen later reported that he passed the information along to a close contact, who conveyed it by radio to London, probably to Welsh. And once again Welsh authenticated Rosbaud, passing the message back to Oslo. Then, probably via a coded telephone conversation with the *Aftenposten* editor, Findahl was reassured.

When Arvid Brodersen and Winsnes met again in 1984, almost precisely forty years to the date after the meeting in Andresen's garden, Brodersen wrote:

> The young men in Dresden were only ostensibly studying. In reality they were mostly concerned with their clandestine work. They were serious students, and impressed their teachers as such. But they were also most serious in their Norwegian patriotism, and eager to serve their country and its allies in the struggle for liberation and victory.
>
> Winsnes told me that the hardest part of their intelligence work was getting the information out of Germany. Whenever one of them went home for vacation, he carried the current reports with him. They occasionally got some help from Swedish diplomatic couriers, who would take an envelope with them in the bag, and then hand it to one of the student group who "happened" to travel north on the same train, as soon as they reached Swedish territory. But more often they had to carry the material all the way themselves. . . . Winsnes was very favorably impressed by Rosbaud as a person, at this one meeting with him.

Arvid Brodersen, an internationally known expert on anti-Hitler Resistance movements, had never met Rosbaud. But, reflecting recently on his indirect contacts with the Griffin through Sverre Bergh, Ragnar Winsnes, and others, he concluded that "Rosbaud was no spy in the sense of a controlled and paid agent of a foreign power, but an ethical person acting on his own deeply felt need: to do his best to prevent Hitler from winning the war."

Brodersen's judgment is entirely correct. Eric Welsh was not the absolute spymaster of Paul Rosbaud. He did send the Griffin intelligence-collection requirements, but Rosbaud was his own judge on how to respond. It was he who set the priorities on which information was worth collecting. Rosbaud's channels to London were not exclusively through networks controlled by Eric Welsh. If it was convenient to pass information through safe French or Dutch Resistance groups or through contacts in Switzerland, that was just fine. This sometimes exasperated Welsh.

But the two men had great respect for each other. Contrary to all rules of espionage, Rosbaud knew to whom he was reporting in London throughout the war. The degree of mutual trust was so great that it seems likely that the men must have met before the war and collaborated in intelligence operations. When Rosbaud worked with Frank Foley, the common bond was the compassion that both felt for human suffering. Eric Welsh was very different from Foley. Devious and forceful, but ever solicitous of the welfare of his agents, Eric Welsh was as motivated as Paul Rosbaud in the obsession to destroy Hitler. And both men were enthralled by the Great Game of Spying.

THIRTY-FIVE

Victory

ALMOST A YEAR before the invasion of Normandy, the British had in their hands the plans for a German defensive weapon that could have spelled catastrophe for the Allies. At least one German general and a handful of Norwegian students were fearful of that possibility and sought to forestall the calamity by getting the specifications for the weapon to the British.

There were about a hundred Norwegian students in Dresden, between five and ten of them Nazi collaborators. A similar number were active secret agents reporting to Eric Welsh through Norwegian contacts in Stockholm and Oslo. Belonging to neither group was Anders Vikoren. He was, however, aware of a major intelligence coup pulled off by Sverre Bergh, Einar Borch, and another student, and he has described it this way:

> The only thing I know is that a friend of mine [his name is known, but he declines to be identified] once acted as a guard outside a house while Borch entered a flat that was purposely left open while the owner, a German officer, was away. Borch thus gained access to drawings having to do with one of the two missiles, V-1 or V-2. No name was mentioned to my friend.

Ragnar Winsnes has added more details:

> My friend . . . copied the drawings and I typed the text. It was a night's work. We did it in my friend's place. Einar was with us. He slept because he had to bring the originals back the next day in the morning. I knew about the V-2 because I was one of those who brought out the message

that Peenemünde had to be bombed. At that time I thought it was the V-bomb. But Sverre Bergh knows better. He brought the drawings and the text from Dresden to Stockholm, where he had time to examine what it really was.

Bergh did know better. It was not a report on the V-1 or the V-2, but a description of a defensive missile, the Wasserfall (Waterfall), which Hitler completely ignored, much to his disadvantage. The Luftwaffe (Air Force) would have been responsible for deploying the Wasserfall, but the Army Weapons Command had a major role at Peenemünde. General Fritz Lindemann was a General of the Artillery who possibly had contact with the Wasserfall program. Lindemann's uncle Max and his Finnish wife Elsa, née Äström, had a flat on Haemelstrasse in Dresden. And Elsa, a fanatical anti-Nazi, knew Einar Borch well. The Wasserfall papers may have been Fritz Lindemann's futile contribution in his personal struggle against Hitler. After the July 1944 plot against Hitler, Fritz Lindemann was murdered by the Gestapo. His wife committed suicide.

Bergh placed the Wasserfall papers in his student notebooks and brought the lot to the Gestapo, explaining that they were school papers he had to study during Christmas vacation in Norway. The Gestapo placed its official seal on the package, enabling Bergh to carry it across the borders through Denmark to Sweden. By this time, Bergh had developed a keen sense of how to outwit the Gestapo, and one of those ways was to make it work on his behalf. Bergh delivered the documents to John Whistondale at the train station in Gothenburg about the time that Peenemünde was being bombed. With supreme confidence, which could have proved embarrassing, British intelligence ignored the Wasserfall papers.

Paul Rosbaud was generally informed of what the members of his "flock" were reporting independently and once in a while contributed to those reports. The Noah's Ark Resistance group had been broken by the Gestapo, but Henri and André Piatier continued to operate through the Martial-Albert-Armand network, with headquarters in Spain. They sent to London, by the end of 1943, the complete specifications of the V-1 and V-2. After the bombing of Peenemünde, the missile factories were transferred to underground sites in the Harz Mountains and elsewhere. Piatier's group continued to transmit detailed information on a number of the underground factories until the end of the war. The artist Käthe Kollwitz was living in Nordhausen, the site of the most important V-2 manufacturing plant, Mittelwerk. The slave laborers there were housed in a camp called Mittelbau, which history records as the notorious concentration camp Dora. Paul was close to the Kollwitz family and is known to have been in touch with Käthe in Nordhausen. Through Sverre Bergh, he sent particulars of the rocket component facilities in the salt mines at Stassfurt and the locations of firing sites on the Channel coast.

One of those sites—at Mimoyecques, near Calais—proved to be particularly odd to Allied photo interpreters. The official SIS history reports that "it was intended for a long-range multi-barrelled rocket firing gun of revolutionary design (the Hochdruckpumpe), though what this was remained unknown until the site was overrun." But Rosbaud had described the technique to Sverre Bergh, who passed the information on to London. This seems to be another instance where either the information was not sent along by Eric Welsh or came to him in some manner that did not suggest a reasonable degree of credibility.

Rosbaud's contacts in the navy remained good, especially through the office of Admiral Carl Witzell, the sometime patron of Fritz Houtermans. The German U-boats were almost useless because of the attacks against them when they surfaced for air. In 1944, German submarines were fitted with a Dutch invention, the *Schnorkel*, or breathing tube, which allowed the U-boats to remain submerged for longer periods and made them less vulnerable to radar detection. The British received a substantial amount of information about the Schnorkel from the interception of signals, and a technical description was supplied by Rosbaud, with the assistance of Sverre Bergh.

The catalogue of what Rosbaud sent to London through Sverre Bergh and Henri Piatier, through Holland and Switzerland, and through channels we shall never know about is vast. Through Bergh alone, the Griffin's transmissions averaged about one a month, each incorporating several kinds of information.

The Rosbaud family had strong ties to Croatia. In the fall of 1942, there came to Paul's home in Zehlendorf a relative from Yugoslavia, described to Hans Rosbaud as "a very healthy, handsome lad, who is starting to let his beard grow." "Anton" was with the Croatian delegation in Berlin, so Paul joked that his home was "nearly extraterritorial." From its chancery on Brahmsstrasse in the Grunewald suburb, a substantial staff facilitated coordination of Croatian units with the German army and the SS and was in possession of a considerable amount of information that might be of interest to Paul Rosbaud. Anton, as a junior assistant to the military attaché, Colonel von Dessović, and the police attaché, Branko Buzjak, often acted as a courier for the delegation.

Rosbaud also had dealings with a man named Radič and a Frau Saukič in the delegation, but nothing is known of the nature of those contacts. What is known is that one member of the delegation, Anton, rendered high service to the Allies.

Anton soon became part of the Rosbaud household, along with Ruth Lange, Henri Piatier, and the elderly housekeeper, Klara. If the Rosbaud domain was not legally "extraterritorial," it certainly was conspiratorial. Anton was considered completely trustworthy, and assisted the Griffin in some of his illegal ventures, although only one such operation has been uncovered.

In the middle of 1943, Dr. Mile Budak, the Croatian minister, sent Anton to Stockholm with a diplomatic bag. Anton sealed the bag, enclosing a small package of "flour" given him by Rosbaud. In Stockholm, he separated the package from the documents and called a contact. It probably was John Whistondale of the SIS. A man with a British accent soon appeared at the door of Anton's hotel room, gave the correct code word, and departed with the "flour."

Shortly afterward, two gentlemen without British accents appeared with a curvaceous blonde and suggested that perhaps Anton would be willing to accept a token of appreciation for the delivery of the package. Anton, though not one to avoid the fairer sex, thought it prudent to decline the gift. An hour later, the same two gentlemen appeared with a sensuous-looking youth and made similar gestures of gratitude. This time, Anton did not hesitate to slam the door.

The two unknown men may have been Swedes who monitored the foreign intelligence services. On the other hand, the generous fellows may have been with Himmler's intelligence arm, the SD.

Anton never did learn what the flour was, for Rosbaud never told him more than he needed to know. Possibly the whitish material was a uranium compound, which would have been one of Eric Welsh's priorities at the time. But as 1944 progressed, Welsh's priorities began to change from technical descriptions to information that would help smash the German war machine. And Rosbaud began to devote more of his energies toward helping others.

Paul had a particular empathy for Norwegians languishing in Bergen-Belsen, Auschwitz, Theresienstadt, Neuengamme, and elsewhere. Some Norwegians were detained in more pleasant circumstances, in a large mansion in Gross-Kreutz, a village just west of Berlin. Among the privileged were Professor Didrik Arup Seip, former rector of Oslo University, and the family of Dr. J. B. Hjort, both of them known to Thor.

In his 1946 memoirs, Seip wrote,

> Just about that time [mid August 1944] we heard rumors about plans for the liquidation of the concentration camp prisoners when the enemy troops were approaching. The first warning came to us from ... P. Rosbaud, who was working in a publishing house in Berlin. He earlier had been acquainted with several Norwegian scholars of the natural sciences and also tried to make things easier for Norwegian professors imprisoned in Norway. He asked me to inform the Swedish Legation [in Berlin] about the fact that he had given us this warning. This I did, and at the same time the engineer Einar Borch traveled to Stockholm, where he reported on Rosbaud's warning.

Hjort's daughter Wanda recently elaborated on the account:

> This was very important information [Rosbaud's], which we later got confirmed from other authorities. It helped us to do what we could to counter the plans of the Allied command, that all prisoners should "stay put" in the camps until the Allies came to liberate them *after* the capitulation. Thus Dr. Rosbaud made an important contribution to the later "Bernadotte expedition," which, with the help of the Danish Jyllandskorpset [Jutland Corps], got most of the Danish and Norwegian prisoners out of Germany before the final collapse of the German Reich.

In those months, Rosbaud also had to save his own life.

Adolf Hitler had built his command post in East Prussia at Rastenburg, near Weimar, the city that was the cradle of the republic Hitler had destroyed. On Thursday, July 20, 1944, Colonel Claus Schenck von Stauffenberg came to a conference at Hitler's Wolf's Lair, placed a yellow leather briefcase near Hitler, and excused himself "to make a telephone call." When the two pounds of plastic explosive in the briefcase detonated, von Stauffenberg was racing in an automobile toward a waiting He-111 to take him to Berlin to join other officers prepared to take over the government. He made it to Berlin but was unaware that a heavy oak table support had protected Hitler from the full force of the explosion.

Perhaps it is significant that Paul Rosbaud suddenly decided to leave Berlin the next day. The Normandy invasion in June had brought hope to him, as it had to others in Europe impatient for the Nazi yoke to lift. It was time to be pragmatic, to plan ahead. Rosbaud talked his boss into doing something about saving the Springer stock of books jeopardized by the bombings. And what better place to hide them than where Hermann Goering was hiding his pillaged paintings and other art objects? Earlier, Paul had started corresponding with Count Johann Otto Herberstein about the use of one of his castles. This was a good time to visit Graz and to see the count.

First, he would sample the delights of Vienna. If he were to be arrested, he might as well have one last fling. But within three hours of his arrival, he was found by the local Springer representative, Otto Lange. A telegram, worded in the strongest terms, was calling Rosbaud back to Berlin. Paul expected the worst—and was not disappointed.

Awaiting him was an induction notice from the Organization Todt. Paul had been conscripted to enforced labor. There were but a few hours before he had to report. It had to be coincidence. Had Rosbaud been implicated by the Gestapo in the Hitler assassination plot, his immediate fate would have been more harsh. But induction into O.T. eventually would have had the same consequence.

Todt—sounding like *Tod* (death)—was appropriate for the construction force created by Fritz Todt in 1938. Todt's organization was in charge of the major military construction projects, such as the Atlantic Wall, the railway lines into Russia, and, eventually, the building of the underground factories, such as the one at Nordhausen, to produce jet aircraft and the V-2 rockets. Todt had first priority on all forced labor assets, concentration camp inmates, political and criminal prisoners, and conscripted German citizens. After Todt's death in an air crash in February 1942, the Organization Todt had been assigned by Hitler to Armaments Minister Albert Speer. In May of 1944, Xaver Dorsch, the Nazi Party undercover man in Speer's ministry, managed to wrest control of all construction in the Third Reich.

The working conditions in the O.T. camps were bad enough before Dorsch took over, but his ruthless drive created conditions that the chief physician of O.T., Dr. A. Poschmann, reported to Speer as "Dante's Inferno." It was into that inferno that Paul was to be thrust, and he was in no condition for it. An infection that had brought his weight down to 125 pounds in 1942 had not completely left him. He had been weak ever since, and his vigor was never fully restored for the rest of his life. Even a brief period in the service of Organization Todt surely would have killed him. The person who saved Rosbaud from penal servitude and very probably from death was his Nazi friend Friedrich Karl Drescher-Kaden.

In January, Hans Rosbaud had been awarded a Nazi decoration, a Wreath for War Service, and Paul feared that this might render him a bit careless in the Strasbourg academic circle, which Rosbaud believed to be the most tainted in Germany. He warned Hans, "Be careful with your 'wreath.' My most urgent warning concerns . . . the chemist couple. There is a direct connection to certain places that often has been made use of in a quite unpleasant manner." The reference was to the Noddacks. Still, credit should be given where credit is due. Walter and Ida Noddack had discovered the element rhenium in 1925, and if her prewar suggestions about what to look for had been accepted by such as Joliot-Curie, Enrico Fermi, and Otto Hahn, the fission process might have been discovered much earlier.

But their behavior in the Nazi era had been reprehensible, and Paul wrote to Hans, "With both of them I had counted myself almost a good friend, but I have severed every connection and exchange of letters. I give you the same warning concerning the internist."

The internist was Dr. Hirt, director of the University Anatomical Institute. He had several joint research projects with Dr. Sigmund Rascher at Dachau. Rascher sent Hirt "specimens," and Hirt provided the results to Rascher for use in his work for the Ahnenerbe institute for "racial purity." Dr. Eugene von Haagen, a Hirt subordinate, was also doing some interesting research on biological warfare. Just the previous November, Haagen had complained to Hirt that his spotted fever tests were being hindered because of the hundred prisoners sent to him in the last shipment from Dachau, eighteen arrived dead and the rest were in "unusable" condition. He demanded another hundred in better condition. But if Rascher was unhappy, Hirt was not. He was collecting "Jewish-Bolshevik" skulls at Strasbourg for the Ahnenerbe skull collection.

Strasbourg was the most Nazified of all the universities, and such was the gruesome nature of its medical research. Some of that research was not on campus but at a nearby fort that had been part of the Maginot Line. Still, most of the university staff cannot have been unaware of the skeletal "specimens" being used by their medical colleagues for experiments.

As the reference to the "internist" shows, Rosbaud knew, and he felt compelled to extend his warning: "I do not know the other higher ups, but would like to warn you if there is any doubt. I had to deal with these people for twenty years and know them too well." The only one Paul would trust at the university, he told his brother, was Drescher-Kaden: "The mineralogist is the most distinguished and most superior of all of them, in spite of certain defects for which he cannot be blamed." Paul's trust was not misplaced.

Drescher-Kaden had never wavered in his friendship for Paul Rosbaud, although they had often argued long and bitterly about Nazism. Two days after the attempt on Hitler's life, when all suspects in the anti-Hitler plot were being brutally rounded up, Drescher-Kaden dropped everything he was doing to save his friend. He immediately made application to Organization Todt for a deferment of the call-up, claiming that Rosbaud's work was critical to the war effort. Drescher-Kaden had stronger ammunition. He was able to cajole the director of Goering's Reich Research Council, Walther Gerlach, into issuing a special order requiring Rosbaud's services.

Then Otto Hahn came to the fore, objecting to the Armaments Ministry that Rosbaud was a *Rüstungs Kommando*, one of a special category of essential armaments workers. Within a day's time, Rosbaud was declared a *Schlüsselkraft*, a worker essential to the conduct of the war.

There was no point in staying around Berlin and considerable merit in leaving the city for a while as long as the *Schlüsselkraft* certificate was safe in his pocket. So Paul went off to Vienna again for a revelry of a magnitude he had not intended when he was in Vienna a few days earlier. When he recovered, he took the train to Graz to complete his business with Count Johann Otto Herberstein. He took a room at the Wiesler overlooking the Mur and, as was his habit whenever he was in Graz, walked a few blocks to the neighborhood where he was born—always interviewing old people, still seeking the secret of his paternity.

He supped with Count Herberstein in the Eggenberg Palace. It was an irony that Paul relished thoroughly. As a boy, he could never have entered the Eggenberg Palace. Around 1625, Hans Ulrich von Eggenberg selected a fine piece of land west of Graz and constructed his own fantasy of harmony with the world. It had 24 halls of state with 52 windows, and the number of windows in the entire palace was 365. The decorations were planets and stars. In due course, the palace became the property of the Herberstein family and, inevitably, a part of Reichsjägermeister Hermann Goering's collection of palaces.

The music school of the province of Steier was relocated there during the war, and Count Herberstein and his wife, Baltimore-born Idella Scarborough, were allowed to reside in certain chambers. Paul discussed with the count the possibility of storing the Springer stocks in one of the other Herberstein palaces. Rosbaud thought the count "a little soft and a little decadent," but he was "a man of the world." Johann Otto was agreeable enough but thought that a palace owned by Hermann Goering was perhaps not appropriate. Would Springer like to store its stock at Hartberg, where the Herberstein family was depositing its own valuables? There were a few potential problems. For one thing, the Hitler Youth organization was thinking of taking over the castle. Also, there were twenty British prisoners of war being held there at the moment. Rosbaud replied, regarding the POWs, "To the contrary, they would not disturb us."

So Paul journeyed to Hartberg to look over the fairy-tale castle at the foot of the vine-covered Ringkogel. The wines were (and are) famed. They were not the least of Rosbaud's enjoyment there; he was in no hurry to return to Berlin. The place was ideal, with numerous dry underground caverns, and if the Hitler Youth did not confiscate it, Paul decided that would be the repository for the Springer stocks. Not knowing what the situation was in Berlin, he dawdled in Styria. Always on the prowl, he decided to look up an old girl friend of Hans's in Gleisdorf. But when he found that she had become the somewhat formidable Führer of the local farmers, an official position, he backed away.

Gleisdorf is not far from St. Marein, where Paul's sister, Martha, had grown up, married, and died in childbirth. Paul tried to find her son, Andreas, but to no avail. He wrote to Hans, "Maybe he lies in a grave somewhere in Russia." Paul had never seen his nephew, and he never again tried to find him. Actually, Andreas is still alive.

Survival had become increasingly hazardous for Sigurd and the Griffin, not because of the Gestapo, but because of the intensive Allied bombings. On the evening of February 13, 1945, Sigurd and his girl friend were dining at the elegant Europahof near the main train station in Dresden. The city had not yet experienced Allied retribution, but it did that night. The two miraculously escaped the British bombs and the St. Valentine's Day massacre by the American bombers the next day. The ever-resourceful Sverre Bergh took an abandoned car and drove northward the next day to resume his recent assignment of reporting the results of the Allied bombings, including that of Dresden — from the unique viewpoint of one who was there. His reports to London on the damage to industrial targets proved to be a valuable supplement to the photoreconnaissance assessments.

Two months later, Paul Rosbaud found himself facing the Soviet army. His house at Fritz Reuterstrasse 29 in Teltow stood precisely at the focal point of the southern portion of the Soviet pincer movement on Berlin. Just to the north of the house was the Teltow Canal, 150 feet wide and 7 feet deep. On its northern bank were ferroconcrete pillboxes and gun emplacements. Volkssturm battalions of adolescents, elderly, and sick men had been stationed to defend the canal. It was obvious that the Russians would concentrate on the Teltow strongpoint, so the Rosbaud ménage, including Ruth Lange, Hilde Benjamin, and the faithful Klara, prepared to flee.

It was Friday, April 20, 1945. Sverre Bergh, driving from Dresden to Count Folke Bernadotte's headquarters at Friedrichsruh, near Hamburg, in a truck with registration number P.K.W. II 10942, carried a pass issued by the Swedish church in Hamburg, one of a series of passes he had wangled during that period from the church, the International Red Cross, and the Swedish consulate in Hamburg. Skillfully evading the Russian army, which was executing its pincer movement on Berlin, he drove toward Potsdam. Rosbaud's house was on the way.

When Bergh entered, he found a grinning man in rags. It was Paul, who proudly displayed to Bergh the carpenter's box that he was about to strap to his back. It had to be the briefest of visits, and the "carpenter's" face took on the expression of an idiot as Bergh drove away. The Rosbaud household fled only a few minutes later to the country cottage of an elderly typographer, Georg Bergmann, a Communist friend of Hilde Benjamin's.

During the afternoon of April 22, 1945, the 7th Guards Tank Corps of Lieutenant General V. V. Novikov leveled Paul Rosbaud's empty house. On April 24 the Russians crossed the Teltow Canal and by evening were in Berlin. The Kaiser Wilhelm Institutes were occupied two days later, but the battle for central Berlin was bitter and bloody. Soviet troops presented Josef Stalin with a May Day gift of the Reichstag, and Adolf Hitler rewarded Paul Rosbaud and the rest of the world by committing suicide in his bunker.

Paul returned to Teltow a week later. He checked to see if his telephone worked. Curiously, it did, for during all the destruction, the telephone system was the only utility that did not seem to be affected. A Russian soldier burst into the room and, seeing Rosbaud speaking into the strange apparatus, thought he was a spy, a notion truer than others might have suspected! Rosbaud talked the Russian into sparing him. Not only that, but shortly after the episode Rosbaud wangled a series of passes from the Russian command and began to wander freely in the rubble that was Berlin.

Hilde Benjamin didn't have to hide from the Russians. She was charged by them to organize a system of criminal justice in Berlin. The Soviets requisitioned a nice house on Boltzmanstrasse in Dahlem for Hilde, Paul, and Ruth and issued a pass to Paul. In July, at the beginning of the Potsdam Conference, the Americans and British were allowed to enter Berlin. Ruth Lange has since joked about her sister's being picked up each morning by a black Russian staff car and Paul's being driven to the American and British headquarters by Jeep. Generous rations and liquor were provided the Rosbaud household from the canteens of all the occupying forces. Paul's domain, finally, had become truly "extraterritorial," and once again, in ruined Berlin, he was enjoying the good life.

But Rosbaud being Rosbaud, the Russians soon began to interrogate him, though under the most pleasant of circumstances. The chief interrogator was Colonel I. K. Kikoin, a leading scientist in the Soviet atomic energy program. After General Groves's Alsos mission arrived in July, Rosbaud would visit Kikoin in the morning and the scientific director of Alsos, Samuel Goudsmit, in the afternoon for several weeks, until Rosbaud decided that it would be safer to stick with the Americans. Goudsmit began to learn the precise nature of the Russian interests and formed a close friendship with Rosbaud that endured until Paul died.

In early autumn, a soldier delivered an invitation to Rosbaud from Kapitza. He recognized the handwriting but did not believe that Kapitza was in a hotel in Berlin and took the note to Goudsmit, who was equally skeptical. (Goudsmit remembered the hotel as the Adlon, but that could not be, since the Adlon had burned to the ground on April 30.) When Rosbaud arrived at the hotel, he was seized on the steps by two Russian officers. Fortunately, the two Jeeps filled with soldiers, supplied as escorts by Goudsmit, were able to wrest Rosbaud away. But Rosbaud's days in Berlin were numbered.

Sverre Bergh, in the British occupation zone, crossed over to Stockholm and, on instructions from Eric Welsh, on June 12, was issued a one-way visa to London. Welsh asked Bergh to think of a way to bring Rosbaud out, but no reasonable plan resulted. The Russians were not letting out anybody, dead or alive, except in an easterly direction.

THIRTY-SIX

Conspiracy at Farm Hall

PAUL ROSBAUD was free again, but the members of the Uranium Club were not. Max von Laue was not a member, but he worked where the others worked, in Dahlem, which had sustained very little damage throughout the war. On the night of February 15, the RAF carried out one of its heaviest raids on Berlin. The next day, von Laue wrote to Lise Meitner: "Yesterday's air attack did not leave any special damage to the Kaiser Wilhelm Institutes of Physics, Cellular Physiology, Biology, Biochemistry, Anthropology, and Physical Chemistry. The same is true of Hahn's house."

Slight as the damage was, the Uranium Club decided to move its work to a cave at the side of a Hohenzollern castle at Haigerloch, in the Swabian Jura, south of Stuttgart. While the Russians were consolidating their hold on Berlin, General Groves's Alsos mission was capturing the documents and the scientists in their redoubt. Eric Welsh attached himself to the mission to be sure he was not left out in the cold in the sharing of the booty. Ten of the scientists were remanded to the custody of Welsh at his personal redoubt, Farm Hall, from which, two years earlier, the Gunnerside team had departed to sabotage the Vemork heavy-water plant.

Welsh, the master of deception, did not anticipate that a grand deception would be conceived at the lovely Georgian country house. The river Ouse flows in front. On the far side stretches the largest lea in England, which William Cobbett described in 1822 as "by far the most beautiful meadows that I ever saw in my life." Cobbett's exuberance was captured a century and a half earlier by Samuel Pepys, who went beyond simply admiring "the country maids milking their cows there . . . and to see with what mirth they all came home together in pomp with their milk, and sometimes they have music go before them." Alas, the unwilling "guests" at this estate, Farm Hall, had no country maids with whom to frolic, but they had music aplenty and lacked for little else.

These ten members of the Uranium Club were men of some distinction: Eric Bagge, Kurt Diebner, Walther Gerlach, Otto Hahn, Paul Harteck, Werner Heisenberg, Horst Korsching, Carl von Weizsäcker, and Karl Wirtz. Because he happened to be around when the others were swept up, von Laue, a Nobel laureate, was also taken prisoner, though he had not been working on the uranium problem. He was also the closest in spirit to Paul Rosbaud.

At Farm Hall, the men had food and quarters that were sumptuous in comparison with what they would have had in immediate postwar Germany. And when they complained to their captors, which was often, their wardens just asked whether they would have preferred to be taken off to Russia, as many of their colleagues had been. Eric Welsh visited often in full and correct uniform, with all of his medals; he was rarely seen like that elsewhere. The internees began to refer to him, behind his back, as Goldfasan — Gold Pheasant. He was their captor, who on one occasion responded to their complaints by saying that if he had his own way, he would have them all shot.

Each scientist was assigned a prisoner-of-war batman to attend to his needs. The library and music room had all that could be desired, and the elegant dining room to the left of the entrance hall was witness to servings that belied the austerity of postwar England. Their upstairs bedrooms were handsomely paneled; some had fireplaces. The rose garden was carefully tended by Otto Hahn. And when the scientists desired a modicum of privacy, they could stroll among the poplar and lime trees, free of all insects except electronic bugs.

R. V. Jones has written that it was he who suggested to the chief of the SIS that Farm Hall be bugged to monitor the conversations of the German scientists. Maybe he did, but if C smiled, it was because he knew that Eric Welsh had bugged the estate, lime trees and all, years ago.

The thought crossed the mind of only one scientist, Kurt Diebner, who asked Werner Heisenberg, "Are there microphones installed here?" To which the amused Heisenberg replied, "Microphones installed? Oh, no, they're not as cute as all that. I don't think they know the

real Gestapo methods; they're a bit old-fashioned in that respect."
After all, Heinrich Himmler had been an old family friend of Heisenberg's, so he should have known whereof he spoke. But Heisenberg
failed to appreciate that Eric Welsh was every bit as "cute" as the
Gestapo. So the scientists spoke freely among themselves, displaying
the same naïveté they had fortunately displayed about worldly matters
throughout the war. In reality, the arrogance of his scientists had
saved the world from Hitler's atomic bomb.

Max von Laue, however, was the outcast, treating the pious conclusions of his fellow inmates with a certain degree of gentlemanly
scorn. As a result, the others soon behaved toward him with painful
rudeness, of which von Laue did not complain until the last year of
his life, and then only to Paul Rosbaud, to whom he wrote:

> In the captivity from the end of 1945 to the beginning of January 1946,
> I had to suffer from my co-prisoners, particularly from Weizsäcker. At
> that time he was already prejudiced against me. The prejudice became
> stronger during the interrogation about the heavy water . . . and became
> open hostility when I quoted Busch [Field Marshal Ernst Busch, a Hitler
> disciple]: "The biggest scoundrel always stays on top," in reference to
> the Röhm affair [the assassination in 1934 by Hitler's thugs of another
> thug, Ernst Röhm] and Hitler's victory. It happened in the first days
> that British Major Rittner guarded us. Right away, Weizsäcker became
> aggressive and said, among other things, that one does not even use
> such expressions, and so on.
>
> I attribute it to his influence, which he knows how to use with everybody who happens to be in power. Rittner, basically quite a friendly
> man, started to talk about German militarism. As you already know, I
> responded, using the original English, " 'My country, right or wrong'
> was not formulated in Germany." I said it rather excitedly and in a loud
> voice. Rittner never forgave me for that. Thus Weizsäcker had achieved
> his goal of creating trouble between me and Rittner. Others too turned
> against me. Dr Horst Korsching called me a "traitor" once. Korsching
> had become a prisoner as Heisenberg's assistant. The situation became
> really bad when the vociferous Gerlach joined us. It happened at Faqueval [in Belgium, on the way to Farm Hall].
>
> It seems he had brought some materials against me from German
> army files so that Rittner could use them. Gerlach was already furious
> with me because during wartime I had not responded to his statement
> "We must be victorious."
>
> Gerlach also incited our batmen against me. Once I gave a pair of
> trousers to one of them for ironing and received them back with large

burned spots so that I could not wear them anymore. It happened by "mistake."

In the letter to Paul Rosbaud about his persecution, von Laue added:

Please excuse this emotional outburst. I must think of what Einstein replied to an unknown person who told him her difficulties during her school years. He dissuaded her urgently from publishing, saying that everybody who complains about past sufferings gives a wrong impression. But you will understand me correctly.

A year before he died, in a car accident, the tormented Max von Laue was unable to contain a secret more terrible than just his persecution by some of the members of the Uranium Club. He had read a favorable review of Robert Jungk's new book, *Brighter Than a Thousand Suns*. Jungk, whose avowed aim was to "work toward the humanization of science," dehumanized the American and British scientists who had worked on the atomic bomb but humanized the scientists in Germany by saying not that they lacked the knowledge to make the bomb, but by explaining that they had had the moral fortitude to resist making the bomb. Jungk's book was an early example of the shameful fiction that has now been taken as gospel. Documentary evidence proves its falsity. But that the most important of the German scientists should actually have conspired at the end of the war to create and perpetuate that myth is the primary reason that the British Foreign Office will not decide until 1992 whether to release the transcripts of the Farm Hall conversations.

The tale is told in Max von Laue's letter to Rosbaud. Because it is a document of the highest historical importance and, like the Farm Hall transcripts, has been unavailable, it is quoted here in full, in translation:

Berlin-Dahlem
4·4·59

Dear Rosbaud!

Yesterday it happened that I read the newsletter of the Society for Social Responsibility in Science, December 19 (no. 80). I read it with greatest interest, and I should like to say something in connection with it, not for the public but with the request that you keep this letter secret until the appropriate time. It should not be read by a larger audience as long as I live.

In the reviews of Jungk's book *Brighter Than a Thousand Suns* which appear in this newsletter, all the reviewers treat the German atomic physicists who were active during the Second World War as a united group. Only once is an . . . attempted individual action by Heisenberg mentioned (by Edward Condon). In fact, each opinion was different, which is natural, of course. For this reason I wish to report here what I remember about the time of the Second World War and the captivity which followed. I am convinced that my memory is still pretty good.

Anyhow, I do not have much to report. I never had the ambition to be an atomic physicist, as you know. Only the Western Allies called me one, in 1945. Only once — I do not remember whether it was in 1941 or 1942 — was I invited to a meeting of the Uranium Club in Berlin, where I got the impression of a somewhat comical secret affair. (In the discussion, uranium was mentioned only as "metal.") It seemed to be a rather muddled business, without a real purpose. Much was changed after the Kaiser Wilhelm Institute for Physics was moved to Hechingen. Once I visited the cave in the rocks in Haigerloch, where the experimental pile of uranium was supposed to be protected from the bombs. But my previous impression was not changed by what I saw there.

After the occupation of Hechingen by the French and of the Kaiser Wilhelm Institute by the action group Alsos, members of the latter searched the institute for the assumed German development of the atomic bomb. But they did not find much; they only found the supply of heavy water that had been hidden in Haigerloch. But they did not tell that to us members of the institute, and commenced an interrogation, about the water, in which Otto Hahn, Weizsäcker, Wirtz, and, I believe, also Bagge had to participate. Heisenberg (who had previously gone to the Walchen Lake) had initiated only Wirtz and Weizsäcker into the secret of the hiding place, so the entire conversation was conducted between two Allied officers and those two. Then something very unpleasant happened. After an hour-long fencing and all sorts of subterfuges, they finally admitted to knowing where the hiding place was, whereupon the Allies responded, "That's correct; we found it several days ago."

Atomic physics and atomic bombs were hardly mentioned during the time of our captivity, at least not as far as I remember. We all believed that, as with us, nowhere had the production of the bomb been successfully achieved. We thought it was a propaganda trick when the BBC in London reported on August 6, 1945, that an atomic bomb had been dropped on Hiroshima. But in the evening we all assembled around the radio and heard Attlee's speech. He read a letter that was composed by Winston Churchill, and then there was no doubt that there was a true uranium bomb. Of course, our reaction was tremendous.

But it was very different with each person. Otto Hahn said with deep emotion, "I had nothing to do with that." The English Major Rittner, who together with Captain Brody guarded us and took care of us, called me in for a talk under four eyes and asked me to make sure that Hahn did not do any harm to himself. I responded that I had no fear in this respect at all, but that I thought it necessary to keep a check on Gerlach during the night. In the same sense, I spoke with Heisenberg and Weizsäcker, who shared a bedroom next to Gerlach. They judged Gerlach's mental condition more benign, though he had seemed to have a real nervous breakdown, with many tears. Fortunately, they were correct.

After that day we talked much about the conditions of an atomic explosion. Heisenberg gave a lecture on the subject in one of the colloquia which we prisoners had arranged for ourselves. Later, during our table conversation, the version [N.B.: Here the German word *Lesart* was used; it means an interpretation not necessarily corresponding to actuality] was developed that the German atomic physicists really had not wanted the atomic bomb, either because it was impossible to achieve it during the expected duration of the war or because they simply did not want to have it at all. The leader in these discussions was Weizsäcker. I did not hear the mention of any ethical point of view. *Heisenberg was mostly silent.* [Emphasis supplied by von Laue.]

That's my report. I read the book by Jungk only in parts and put it away because I found so much that could be proven incorrect, and thus I could not rely on the rest. I am surprised that the criticism by the Americans is so mild, as can be gathered by the newsletter.

Very cordial greetings,
Your,
M. v. Laue

"The version that the Germans really had not wanted the bomb" is what disturbed Paul Rosbaud from 1945 until the end of his life. He knew the truth, but in his review of Jungk's book for the journal *Discovery*, he could only go so far:

A more important factor is omitted [from the book]: the Germans knew in principle a bomb *could* be made; they had no idea *how*. A detailed theory of the A-bomb had never been developed in Germany. . . . Out of all of the theory emerges a strange picture in which it sometimes appears that the German physicists alone have no actual or moral guilt for the A-bomb.

Yet that myth came out of the conspiracy at Farm Hall. Rosbaud knew it to be a myth before the Uranium Club was interned at Farm Hall, and it is known that Eric Welsh consulted with him about the transcripts. So Rosbaud was bound not to reveal the full truth, just as he was bound not to reveal what services he had performed for His Majesty's Government during the war.

When he received Max von Laue's unsolicited letter, Paul saw a way out of his dilemma. He asked the Royal Society, of which von Laue was a member, "to take it [the letter] into safe custody for the information of future generations," for, he explained, the letter contradicted the commonly publicized German scientists' version that "we knew all about how to make a bomb, but of course we didn't tell the Nazis, so others must be blamed—we are guiltless."

On May 8, 1985, the president of the Federal Republic of Germany, Richard von Weizsäcker, the brother of Carl F. von Weizsäcker, declared before the Bundestag, "We need and we have the strength to look truth straight in the eye without embellishment and without distortion. . . . Anyone who closes his eyes to the past is blind to the present."

But even to those with open eyes, the Farm Hall transcripts are not available. Paul Rosbaud had hoped that his and von Laue's final legacy, the letter in the archives of the Royal Society, would present the truth to future generations. He did not reckon with those who did not wish the truth to be known. The von Laue letter and all of the correspondence related to it have been purged from the archives of the Royal Society on aristocratic Carlton House Terrace, once the location of Adolf Hitler's embassy to Great Britain.

Epilogue

A BRITISH OFFICER attached to the Churchill party at the Potsdam Conference brought Paul Rosbaud a letter from his wife. Hilde chided Paul for not having come to Britain during the war. He replied:

> Did you realize that people like me could not travel ten miles without special permission and without being questioned at least twice? Did you or the people who gave you the well-meant advice want me to be shot by the SS? After all, you can tell those people that I did more for the victory of the Allied nations here than I could have done in London.

That was all Hilde would ever be allowed to tell, for Paul Rosbaud was silenced by British law and by his own preference for never giving the details of his activities. He wanted no reward or recognition except from one person. Writing from Berlin to his daughter, Angela, in September, he poured out his inner feelings as he was unable to do with anyone else:

> When I saw you last time, you were twelve years old, and now you have joined the army. I am very proud of it and I am sure you will appreciate the great honour to serve in such a gallant and disciplined an army. I am perfectly sure that you will do your best to be worthy of this honour. . . .
> I never in my life pretended to know everything better as other people do and if I was sure that I really know better I did not let it know. I never felt superior to other people, I tried always to be modest and humble. But first of all I was never selfish, I always let other and poorer people have the same as I have and today after nearly fifty years of my life, when I look back I think that I was right. Especially during the

last twelve years it was like a permanent warning to look at other people—those people responsible for all the turmoil of the last six years, they always wanted to be superior to the rest of the world, they knew everything better as the best experts, they were selfish and never took into consideration others—and where are they today? You see, Angela, this was my great triumph. These people have disappeared or they will come before the tribunal and I, I am living and safe. It gave me all the time a wonderful feeling, especially in those awful moments when danger became greater as it ever has been before, to know that if something should happen to me that someone would say, "Thou art my beloved son in whom I am well pleased."

At the end of 1945, Paul was smuggled out of Berlin in military uniform by Eric Welsh. With the support of Welsh, Sir Charles Hambro, and Count Frederick van den Heuvel, Rosbaud helped to establish a Springer affiliate in London. The books hidden in the Herberstein castle supplied the initial stock. Paul moved on to another scientific publishing venture with a captain who had been press officer in Berlin for the Foreign Office. Rosbaud suggested the name of Pergamon Press. The two had a falling-out, and Robert Maxwell went on to become a British "press baron."

Paul held various consultancies with European scientific publishers. The American Institute of Physics awarded him its first Tate Medal for his services to scientific publishing. Sometimes he had his payments from German firms remitted directly to Ruth Lange. She lives today in Berlin in poverty, but is apparently content to have been with Paul during the most trying years of his life. Two of his other mistresses lament that Paul ruined their lives.

Ruth's sister, Hilde Benjamin, became the minister of justice for East Germany and authorized the building of the Berlin Wall. She dispensed harsh justice to those who attempted to cross it and became known as Rote Hilde, Red Hilde. It is she who was the model for the president of the tribunal that tried the spy who came in from the cold in John le Carré's novel of that name. The woman who had opposed the tyranny of Adolf Hitler sentenced 146 people to death, 356 to life imprisonment, and more than 24,000 to a total of 116,476 years of penal servitude. Hilde Benjamin also lives in Berlin—on the other side of the Wall.

After a series of operations for malignancies, Victor Moritz Goldschmidt died in 1947. Some days before his death, he had written to Paul that "the wise principles of Moses Katz are guiding and protecting me." In 1974, Norway honored V.M. with an eighty-five-ore memorial postage stamp.

Charles Peyrou and Henri Piatier became distinguished senior researchers at the European Center for Nuclear Research and the French Atomic Energy Commission. Sigurd — Sverre Bergh — is a successful, internationally known consulting marine engineer.

R. V. Jones and Eric Welsh fought bitterly for the control of postwar atomic intelligence. Welsh won.

After Eric Welsh died, on November 22, 1954, no public notice was taken in Britain, but a Norwegian newspaper carried an obituary by Welsh's Norwegian counterpart, Alfred Roscher Lund:

> He [Welsh] certainly could have written the world's most exciting book. . . . Everyone who worked with him, and especially those people whom he himself sent out, remember his great concern for his men. . . . We also remember how proud he was because of the duty he had and the honor he felt in serving his country and Norway at the same time. . . . We who were his good friends would like to send him a last message: His memory will live among us.

On October 5, 1945, Lieutenant Colonel A. R. Roscher Lund wrote a secret citation for Sverre Bergh, whose

> mission was to get information . . . in connection with the German experiments with the Atomic Bomb . . . and other experiments. . . . He carried out all of his tasks to the utmost of his ability.

Lund became a member of the United Nations Advance Party in Palestine. Drawing on his negotiating experiences with the British, Roscher Lund became an influential moderating force between the British authorities and the Haganah, according to Chaim Herzog, then a military officer and now president of Israel. Herzog emphasized to his colleagues that Roscher Lund "was speaking as a man who was chief of Norwegian intelligence during the war and in close liaison with British intelligence during all that period." Roscher Lund died in 1975.

Frank Foley died in 1958. The next year, a grove of trees was planted in his memory at Kibbutz Harel in Israel. At the 1961 trial of Adolf Eichmann, a witness for the prosecution named Benno Cohn, once an active Zionist in prewar Berlin, praised Frank Foley as "a man who in my opinion is one of the greatest among the nations of the world. . . . He rescued thousands of Jews from the jaws of death."

Held in high esteem by the American occupation forces in Germany, Hans Rosbaud conducted his orchestra in Munich until 1948. He then served as principal conductor of the Southwest Radio Symphony Orchestra at Baden-Baden and was guest conductor of major orchestras throughout the world. He became best known for conducting the première of Schoenberg's *Moses and Aaron*. Hans died a month before Paul; he had left his substantial fortune to the perpetuation of a nature reserve at the St. Gotthard Pass in Switzerland.

On the twenty-fifth of January 1963, Paul Rosbaud bequeathed his estate of £500, his gold watch, his gold Tate Medal from the American Institute of Physics, and two lithographs, one by Chagall and one by Toulouse-Lautrec, to his daughter, Angela. To his wife, Hilde, he left his scientific books, and to the woman he had been living with, his stamp collection.

Three days later, Paul Rosbaud died of leukemia at St. Mary's Hospital in London. As he had wished, he was buried at sea.

ACKNOWLEDGMENTS AND SOURCES

We are in a unique time, when the story of the Griffin can be told. Six years ago, before the first volume of the official *British Intelligence in the Second World War* was published, the secretary of state for foreign affairs "advised wartime intelligence staff on the limited extent to which they were absolved from their undertakings of reticence." That they were and are by nature reticent made those people ideal intelligence officers. They are cognizant that the information to which they were privy "remains subject to the undertakings and to the Official Secrets Acts and may not be disclosed." Although restrictions remain severe, few sources would have agreed to make any statements at all about Paul Rosbaud before the publication of the first volume of the official SIS history in 1979.

Toward the beginning of the Rosbaud project, the author of that history, F. H. (now Sir Harry) Hinsley graciously received me at St. John's College in Cambridge, of which he is the Master. He said, "I'm glad you found him." And that was all he told me during that visit and subsequent ones, when I filled him in on the progress of the investigations. But the sentence sustained me, as Hinsley probably sensed it would. Thank you, Sir Harry.

None of the people I corresponded with or interviewed in the course of researching this book can be said to have violated his or her trust, nor was anyone asked to do so. Many checked with the appropriate authorities before agreeing to be interviewed by me or to correspond with me. Everyone replied, but only a very few felt they were not in a position to contribute, nor were they pressed to do so. Moreover, the majority of sources were not British, for Paul Rosbaud was not a British citizen when he played the role of the Griffin, and none of his immediate contacts — or "cut-outs," in the parlance of the game of espionage — after 1939 were British. Consequently, the full story of the Griffin was never and is not now under official British control — or, indeed, under the control of any other nation.

The only person who knew the full story of the Griffin was his spymaster, Eric Welsh. I met Welsh when he came to consult with the U.S. Atomic Energy

Commission in mid September 1949, after the Soviets exploded their first atomic bomb. He soon had one of his recurring heart attacks and was hospitalized at Garfield Memorial Hospital, where we talked. He was a difficult patient, and the nurses were eager to get him discharged as soon as possible, so a U.S. Air Force plane flew him home. In the next two years I saw him three or four times in London and in Washington and came to like him and his tales. But none of the tales was of what he did during the war or of Paul Rosbaud. I did not know him that well. No one did.

The story of Rosbaud as a spy, then, has been pieced from correspondence, documents, interviews, and official records—none of which contains but a small fraction of the complete saga, often indirectly. Although they knew only a little of the full scope of Rosbaud's espionage activities, the few people really close to him generously told me about their lives with Paul. My meetings and correspondence with his wife, Hilde, and daughter, Angela, were delightful, and I am grateful to them for making available their memorabilia. The hours I spent in Berlin, recording the stories of Ruth Lange and seeing her lively demonstration of how to shot-put, were memorable moments, indeed. I am most grateful to these women, and to others who prefer to remain anonymous, for sharing their memories, some intimate, with me.

Paul Rosbaud himself never sought recognition for his wartime work toward the Allied victory, and he destroyed most of his personal papers before he died. Some of his papers were destroyed by others after he died. But he deposited a few documents, most not related to his specific acts but of historical importance, with close friends. Several of those archives have been located. Others are known to exist but are sealed until 1993.

Paul Rosbaud's papers in the archives of the British Secret Service officially do not exist. The open SIS history (of course, there is a closed one) seems to acknowledge the truth of Flaubert's dictum *Pas de monstres, et pas de héros.* Thus, in the official SIS history, Paul Rosbaud is identified only as "a well-placed writer for a German scientific journal who was in touch with the SIS from spring 1942." And the SIS deters further inquiry about Paul Rosbaud by firmly stating that "his reports have not been retained in the files."

When I asked the U.S. Central Intelligence Agency to search its files for materials on Paul Rosbaud, I was told that "no records responsive to your request were located."

I have found only a single declassified U.S. document attesting to the exceptional wartime services of Paul Wenzel Rosbaud. It was in connection with the estate of Victor Goldschmidt, and the strength of the statement is perhaps sufficient in itself to demonstrate the high esteem in which the British government, by informing the United States government, once held the services of Paul Rosbaud. The statement is contained in a memorandum of the U.S. Department of Justice, dated April 26, 1955, and reads:

> [Rosbaud] returned to Germany determined to assist England and its allies at all costs. This he accomplished. The records in this matter contain official cor-

roboration that Dr. Rosbaud remained in Berlin during World War II for the purpose of obtaining certain technical intelligence for the United States and the United Kingdom. This information was extremely useful and invaluable for the allied cause and involved great risk on the part of Dr. Rosbaud. His activities on behalf of the allied cause were successful and of such importance that even today they cannot be disclosed and are still highly classified. After the end of hostilities, Dr. Rosbaud, in November 1945, was invited by the United Kingdom to go to England and to work for that country. This invitation was in recognition of his significant contribution to the allied cause during the war years.

To reconstruct what has been "lost" from the official files, I have consulted approximately five hundred people and over a hundred archival sources in one way or another during the course of writing this book. Some people requested that their names not be acknowledged, and their request has been honored. Others did not object to acknowledgment but did not want specific attribution. All were told that the materials were being collected for a book. Perhaps when time has taken its full toll of the remaining living sources— anonymous or otherwise—all the names can be revealed, and connected to their contributions. But for the moment, all I can do is acknowledge most of the sources by name and a few by their specific contributions. But whether or not their names have been mentioned in this book, I wish to thank most sincerely every one of them and hope that those who have not been acknowl- edged below for quite substantial help will not take offense. The Rosbaud story has been well hidden, is exceptionally complex, and unfolds daily. There are bound to be errors, for which I apologize. To those who helped me with translations ranging from the Scandinavian languages to Slovenian, I express my appreciation.

To Robie Macauley, who nursed the project and manuscript through dif- ficult periods with his expert knowledge of the general subject, I shall be forever grateful.

One: Graz

The early background of the Zolchner side of Anna Rosbaud's family is in the 1804 *Zolchner Codex*, the original of which was examined in Yugoslavia. A transcription was made by Paul Rosbaud in 1933 and is presently in the possession of Dr. Vincent Frank-Steiner of Basel, Switzerland, who also has kindly provided other family information. The story of Judith Ginsburger is detailed in the *Zolchner Codex*.

The life of Wenzel Rosbaud, Paul Rosbaud's grandfather, has been recon- structed from official police and court records in Vienna and Graz. The Heinnisser family is chronicled in Anton Sender's 1900 history of the Graz cathedral choir and in Wolfgang Suppan's *Music Lexicon of Steier*. The inter- actions of the Heinnisser and Rosbaud families have been traced through the police records of Wies and Graz.

No archivist could have been more helpful than Gerhard Maurauschek of the Magistratsdirektion of Graz. My persistent probings in Graz, and my letters, as I tried to identify Paul Rosbaud's father, were met by Dr. Maurauschek with patience, understanding, and advice. That the search was successful is in no small measure due to him.

My learning of the brother Bruno Rosbaud came through the discovery of a document dated May 4, 1939, in the parish of Ormoz, Yugoslavia, signed by Pastor Remagi Jereb. Subsequently, Bruno's daughters were found to be still living in Yugoslavia. They and other family members have supplied abundant documentation on Bruno and other aspects of family history, and members of the Rosbaud family who had not known of one another were reunited. That was not the least of my satisfactions in writing the book.

Two: Metamorphosis

Paul Rosbaud was a prolific correspondent all of his life. After the war, he began to reflect, in communications with friends, on his past before 1933, but hinted little of his wartime activities. The papers of Samuel Goudsmit, in the possession of Irene Goudsmit, the Bohr Library of the American Institute of Physics, and elsewhere contain such observations. I have drawn on them in this and succeeding chapters.

Paul Rosbaud's complete military record in World War I can be found in the Military Archives of the Austrian State Archives in Vienna.

Three: Contacts

The 1960 and 1963 memoirs of Rosbaud's brother-in-law, Rudolf Frank, are rich in anecdotal materials used in this chapter. Also, I have been favored with correspondence from long-time personal friends of Rosbaud, especially from Hermann Mark and Walter Brecht. Rudolf Hess's impressions of Frank Foley are to be found in Hess's personal statement in Dicks et al., *The Case of Rudolf Hess*.

Four: The Strajner Deception

The Strajner documents are found in the Archives of Hans Rosbaud in the Moldenhauer Archives at Washington State University, Pullman, Washington. The collection is a rich source of information for both Hans and Paul Rosbaud. I am also deeply indebted to Hans Moldenhauer, a pupil of Hans Rosbaud and the inheritor of his papers. He is, of course, a foremost expert on Hans Rosbaud, as is Joan Evans, who has been a faithful correspondent.

The program for Hans Rosbaud's December 17, 1938, Winterhilfe concert in Graz and other materials were made available by Wilhelm Rosbaud of Graz, whose archival research and enthusiasm have been invaluable to me. I count him as a new and valued friend.

Five: Private Lives

Much on Frank Foley's assistance to Jews in prewar Germany is documented in Naomi Shepherd's *A Refuge from Darkness*. More details are found in the trial records of Adolf Eichmann, made available by Yad Vashem, Israel, where the staff was very responsive. Ms. Shepherd has provided valuable additional information, as have Walter Schwartz and several of Foley's former SIS associates.

Six: V.M.

There is much published biographical material on Victor Goldschmidt. Paul Rosbaud's personal reminiscences are to be found in his biography of Goldschmidt in Farber's *Great Chemists*. The quotation from Schcherbina was kindly provided by Denis Shaw. Torlein Kronen has been generous with information about Ellen Gleditsch, as has the International Federation of University Women. Aslak Kvalheim, who worked closely with V.M., provided many personal details.

Seven: The Man Who Wasn't There

Odd Hassel preferred not to be here or there to anyone. But his portrait has been pieced together from observations of former students and from Sir Derek Barton, who was jointly awarded the Nobel Prize in chemistry with Hassel in 1969.

Eight: Kapitza

The late Paul Ewald provided me with his personal recollections of the event at the Soviet legation in Berlin. The correspondence between Anna Kapitza and Paul Rosbaud is in the Meitner Archives of Churchill College, Cambridge. I am indebted to Mrs. Ulla Frisch and to the Master, Fellows, and Scholars of Churchill College, University of Cambridge, for permission to examine the Meitner Archives and to quote from them. Comprehensive background on the Kapitza case is given in Lawrence Badash's *Kapitza, Rutherford, and the Kremlin*.

Nine: The Exiles

The principal sources for this chapter were the published biographies of Max Born and Otto Hahn. The Meitner Archives at Churchill College provided additional materials. Professor Nicolas Kemmer and some people who wish to remain anonymous were very helpful. Dr. Esther Simpson gave background on the Academic Assistance Council. The correspondence between Peter Kapitza and Max Born is in the Maria Mayer Archives at the University of California at San Diego.

Ten: Midwife to Fission

The story of the discovery of fission is well known. It is very well detailed in David Irving's *The German Atomic Bomb*. Rosbaud's central role in communicating the basic papers is described in Fritz Krafft's biography of Fritz Strassmann and in Dietrich Hahn's books about his grandfather. R. S. Hutton described Rosbaud's disclosures to him in London in his autobiography. Rosbaud's meeting with John Cockcroft is noted in the latter's diary at Churchill College, Cambridge.

Eleven: Departures

The Margaret Reid diary is in the Brotherton Library at the University of Leeds, to which I am also deeply indebted for other Margaret Reid and Frank Foley materials. A good part of the Reid diary has been published in her *April 1940* (with General Rolstad), in Norwegian. Mrs. C. M. Charlton, a close friend of Margaret Reid's, greatly facilitated my access to her papers and memorabilia.

Rosbaud's use of Professor Lark-Horovitz is recounted in personal letters to Samuel Goudsmit. Hubert M. James, professor emeritus at Purdue University, was in Oslo at precisely the same time as Paul Rosbaud and Lark-Horovitz, visiting the same professors. He kept a diary, and his memory appears to be infallible.

Twelve: Beck's Book

Rosbaud mentioned his role in the transmission to Oslo of Beck's book in an autobiographical note submitted to the American Institute of Physics before he received the Tate Medal. Further information on Beck's book, its transmission, and its fate has been provided by Metallgesellschaft A.G. of Frankfurt, Magnesium Elektron Ltd. of Twickenham, and F. A. Hughes Marine Ltd. of Epsom.

Thirteen: The Oslo Report

Previously, the original and sole source of information on the Oslo Report was Dr. Reginald V. Jones. Other stories have elaborated on the saga beyond what Dr. Jones has stated, and they are cited in that context in the text of the book. Dr. Jones has proved to be a faithful and delightful correspondent during the research phase of this book, and I am most indebted to him. However, he has generally remained silent on questions regarding the Oslo Report. On that subject and many others, Jones's wartime chief, Group Captain F. W. Winterbotham, was most generous in his interview and correspondence, and, as the text indicates, I have drawn on his experiences. Sir Charles Frank, R. V. Jones's wartime associate, consented to a most worthwhile interview.

The witnesses and near-witnesses to the passing of the report had a special interest in the solution of the Oslo Report mystery. The testimony of Odd Hassel's student Brynulf Ottar was exceptional. And because he was a founder and an important member of the supersecret XU intelligence organization, I value immensely his contributions throughout the book. Also, for this chapter and others, Magne Skodvin, Bjarne Thorsen, and Kaleb Nytøren gave me hints that aided me in my detective work.

Fourteen: Author, Author?

The major published sources are R. V. Jones's works and the East German publications of Julius Mader. Teddy Lindstrom's article on the Oslo Report and an interview were very illuminating. Dr. Gertrud Asby, the widow of Erhard Tohmfor, provided many details about Hans Kummerow and others.

Fifteen: The Solution

Archives of Norwegian newspapers at the time of the event provided the important clue: the exhibition of German books in Oslo in November 1939. The Meitner Archives, other Rosbaud correspondence, particularly with Norwegian scientists who knew of Rosbaud's presence in Oslo at that time, provided further clues. And, of course, Brynulf Ottar was the most important witness.

Sixteen: Retreat

Most of the actions of Frank Foley are taken from the Margaret Reid diary in the Brotherton Library. Major General Leif C. Rolstad, who shared the experiences of April 1940 with Margaret Reid and Frank Foley, could not have been more helpful.

Jacques Allier's confidential notes are on microfilm in the collection of the papers of Hans von Halban at the Niels Bohr Library of the American Institute of Physics in New York.

Seventeen: Cut-off

The Lise Meitner letter to Otto Frisch is in the Trinity Library, Cambridge, and I thank the Master and Fellows of Trinity Colege as well as Ulla Frisch. The *Broompark* account is from Charles Weiner's 1969 interview with Kowarski, from the Niels Bohr Library. The intelligence affiliation of the Earl of Suffolk is given in Dusko Popov's autobiography. The 21st Earl of Suffolk, Michael Howard, provided me with encouragement in my investigation of his father's adventures. The presence of Frank Foley in Bordeaux and his flight from the Germans at the time is documented in his letter to Dr. Walter

Schwarz, dated March 19, 1957, and in statements made to neighbors in Stourbridge about the same time.

Eighteen: Theodor

Biographical information on Eric Welsh is found in the Archives of the Norwegian Home Front Museum in Oslo, from relatives, and in Nigel West's *MI6* (where the name is spelled "Welch"), and from former associates at the International Paint Company and in the SIS.

Gulbrand Lunde was a notorious collaborator, and information about his political career is abundant in Norwegian archives. His scientific career is chronicled at Oslo University, the Stavanger Library, and at the Research Laboratory of the Norwegian Canning Industry.

Nineteen: The Forest of the Griffin

Paul Rosbaud's 1941 visit to Greifswald is described in a contemporary letter to his brother Hans, now in the Moldenhauer Archives at Washington State University. Ernst Moritz University at Greifswald has provided information on the lore of the locality and on Professor Jander.

Twenty: Sigurd

Information on Sigurd (Sverre Bergh) was obtained in the course of several interviews with him and correspondence. He was the main link between Paul Rosbaud, XU, and Eric Welsh, and has been most generous with his time in helping me to tell the story of the Griffin. Official Norwegian documents confirmed Sigurd's activities. Other confirmations and supplementary information came from former colleagues of his in XU. The director of Norwegian intelligence was Alfred Roscher Lund, whose relatives have provided interviews and documentation, as have several of his associates.

Major General Reider Torp, director of the Norwegian Resistance Museum, has been most helpful, as have Olav Riste and Tore Gjelsvik, chroniclers of the Norwegian Resistance.

Tore Hytten and George Kachmar of the U. S. embassy in Oslo facilitated some of my visits and data gathering.

Anne-Sofie Strømnes, the widow of Sverre Bergh's XU "controller," Øivind Strømnes, and his alternate was exceptionally helpful, and I thank her and her son, Bjørn, for their Norwegian hospitality.

Twenty-one: The Visit

There are many tales concerning the visit of Werner Heisenberg and Carl F. von Weizsäcker to Copenhagen in 1941. Professor von Weizsäcker generously agreed to meet with me for a long and enjoyable exchange of views on the wartime German atomic project. The key intelligence documents are to be found in the archives of the Manhattan Project in the U.S. National Archives, also obtainable on microfilm from University Microfilms, Ann Arbor, Michigan. The Meitner and von Laue letters, reflecting their view of the visit, are at Churchill College, Cambridge.

Sir Rudolf Peierls, who with Otto Frisch had achieved the seminal understandings that made the atomic bomb possible, was most generous in interview and correspondence. In Oxford, he and Lady Peierls were gracious hosts, as was Lady Charlotte Simon.

Twenty-two: Return to Oslo

Material on the Houtermans intelligence mission to the USSR are in the archives of Samuel Goudsmit. The letter of Drescher-Kaden to Rosbaud, arranging the Oslo visit, is in the private archives of R. S. Hutton in Cambridge. Further details are in the correspondence of Tom Barth's brother and son with the author. Harald Wergeland and Werner Romberg have provided the details of the Rosbaud discussions in Oslo. Wergeland considers Paul Rosbaud to have been "one of the Bhodis for my generation." I am deeply indebted to Professor Wergeland for enlightening me.

Twenty-three: "The Heart of Your Enemies"

The Moses Katz story is told in Paul Rosbaud's biography of Victor Goldschmidt in *Great Chemists*. Many of Goldschmidt's reflections about Moses Katz are in his postwar letters to Rosbaud, copies of which have been made available by Hilde Rosbaud. Professor Magne Skodvin has been most generous in providing the details of Goldschmidt's arrest and subsequent interrogation by Norwegian authorities. The Ersta Hospital in Stockholm has provided information on Goldschmidt's stay there.

Twenty-four: "The House Is on the Hill"

The principal source for the first part of the chapter is Sverre Bergh. The wartime summary reports of R. V. Jones are located in the Public Records Office at Kew. The Technical University of Berlin has provided biographical information on Volmer and Stranski. Herbert Stifter's daughter and W. E. A. de Groot have been generous with the information on Stifter. Above all, I am immensely grateful for the efforts of M. D. Frank and H. B. G. Casimir in helping me to sort out the elements of the wartime Dutch intelligence networks.

Twenty-five: The French Connection

The main sources are Ruth Lange, Henri Piatier, Charles Peyrou, and André Piatier. Henri Piatier provided documents, reminiscences, and memorable Latin Quarter hospitality.

Marie-Madeleine Fourcade, head of the Noah's Ark French Resistance cell, has given important corroborative information.

The Berlin Document Center contains the Nazi Party and career records of Pascual Jordan.

Twenty-six: The Fox

I am very grateful for the hospitality of Edla Tronstad and her son Leif and for the limited access to some of Leif Tronstad's papers, and I thank them for inviting me into their homes. Bjørn Rørholt has been both a friend and guide through the more murky and unknown adventures of the wartime Norwegian intelligence activities from Skylark to the end of the war. He also was in frequent contact with Eric Welsh and knew of some of the Griffin's activities.

Twenty-seven: "Juice"

The heavy-water saga is the best-known wartime Norwegian exploit, but this chapter focuses on some of the unknown dimensions. For them, I am most indebted to knowledgeable Norwegians and, most particularly, to many interviews and voluminous correspondence with the wartime chief engineer of the heavy-water plant at Vemork, Jomar Brun. The reactions of General Groves and Vannevar Bush are to be found in the U.S. National Archives.

Twenty-eight: The General Steps In

The American bombing records of Rjukan are at Maxwell Air Force Base, Alabama. Kjell Nielsen was a witness to the Herøya and Rjukan raids. John Turner, Eric Welsh's personal aide, has provided important corroborative details. The Groves account of his dinner with Paul Rosbaud is in his personal file at the U.S. National Archives.

Twenty-nine: Ex-filtration

The interest of General Groves in Victor Goldschmidt is in the Ashbridge diary in the Manhattan Project Files in the U.S. National Archives. Meitner materials are at Churchill College, Cambridge, in the papers of Otto Frisch at Trinity College, Cambridge, and in the papers of Lord Cherwell at Nuffield College, Oxford. Archivists there and at many other institutions in the United States and in Western and Eastern Europe were most generous in providing requested materials.

Thirty: "Nicholas Baker"

Sources are interviews with Robert Furman, Sir Michael Perrin, and Njål Hole, as well as the published reminiscences of Aage Bohr and other wartime associates of Niels Bohr. Sir Michael, the wartime deputy director of the British atomic energy program and a close friend of Eric Welsh and Niels Bohr, has provided encouragement throughout the writing of this book, and I shall always remember the conversations with him in his home and in the pubs.

Thirty-one: Double-Cross

Interviews and correspondence with former members of Section V of SIS who declined to be identified helped me fit together pieces of a very intricate puzzle. Correspondence with the late Ewen Montagu, who conceived Operation Mincemeat, was also helpful.

Thirty-two: Cover

Nazi Party and professional career documents of Drescher-Kaden in the Berlin Document Center were bountiful sources. Professor Drescher-Kaden himself was graciously receptive to an interview but unfortunately fell gravely ill before it could be arranged. In the Goudsmit archives, postwar statements of Paul Rosbaud about Drescher-Kaden and other German scientists helped to illuminate contradictions between what people were and what they appeared to be. Georg von Simson kindly provided Paul Rosbaud's description of the Freundeskreis and biographical materials on Clara von Simson. The Technical University of Berlin also was very cooperative.

The relatives of those martyred in the July 20, 1944, plot against Hitler provided personal insights that are unobtainable in the literature. I wish to thank particularly Peter Elsas and Reinhard Goerdeler, as well as Eberhard Bethge of the remarkable Bonhoeffer family.

Thirty-three: The Tears of the Oppressed

Helmut Witte, Walter Brecht, Mellita Laves, Ruth Lange, Arnold Flammersfeld, Pincus Jaspert, and many others were witnesses and beneficiaries of Paul Rosbaud's compassionate activities on behalf of those arrested by the Gestapo and those in concentration camps. Their accounts and letters are poignant attestations that Paul Rosbaud was much more than a spy. He and Frank Foley spied not just to win a war, but in retribution for the victims of Adolf Hitler.

Thirty-four: The Code of Codes

The initial source for this aspect of the Griffin's techniques was the eminent Norwegian historian Arvid Brodersen, who mentioned Paul Rosbaud in his autobiography. Professor Brodersen has become a good friend and an indispensable adviser during the entire course of the writing of this book. With his help, I located Ragnar Winsnes, Paul Rosbaud's messenger for the code of codes. Winsnes, initially an anonymous source, has agreed to be named. His personal contact with the Griffin and the code of codes provided clues to other important incidents.

Thirty-five: Victory

Winsnes, Sverre Bergh, and Anders Vikoren are the sources for the Wasserfall incident. Wanda Hjort Heger, Arvid Brodersen, and the published memoirs of Didrik Seip are the sources for the Rosbaud tip-off about Scandinavian prisoners, which eventually activated the rescue mission of Count Folke Bernadotte. The Croatian connection was derived from information provided by Ruth Lange, Henri Piatier, and anonymous sources in Yugoslavia.

Rosbaud's rescue from the Organization Todt by Drescher-Kaden is described by Paul Rosbaud in a contemporary letter to his brother Hans, found in the Washington State University Archives. The mission to Count Herberstein is described in several letters in the same collection. Although the present Count Johann Otto Herberstein could not locate corroborating documents at his castle, I thank him for looking for them.

Thirty-six: Conspiracy at Farm Hall

A few quotations from the unreleased Farm Hall transcripts are to be found in the memoirs of General Groves. Another account is in the diaries of Eric Bagge in his book with Diebner and Jay. The "missing" von Laue letters and copies of Paul Rosbaud's correspondence with the Royal Society are in the privately held archives of R. S. Hutton in Cambridge. Mr. and Mrs. Eschenic graciously received me at Farm Hall.

Other Acknowledgments

I wish to thank the Rockefeller Foundation for a mid-research grant as a scholar-in-residence at Bellagio, Italy.

Finally, I salute that grand master Paul Rosbaud, who scattered the clues that posthumously guided me through the ultimate adventure.

BIBLIOGRAPHY

Adlon, Hedda. *Hotel Adlon: The Life and Times of a Great Hotel.* New York: Horizon Press, 1960.

Akademie der Wissenschaften. "Obituary: Hans Mortensen, 17 January 1894–27 May 1964," *Jahrbuch: 1964.* Göttingen.

Alexandrov, Victor. *OS 1: Services Secrets de Staline contre Hitler.* Paris: Culture, Art, Loisirs, 1968.

Amaldi, Edoardo. "The Bruno Touschek Legacy." *CERN* 81–19, December 23 1981. Geneva: European Organization for Nuclear Research.

American Institute of Physics. "Dr. Paul Rosbaud to Receive First John T. Tate Medal of American Institute of Physics," press release, September 28, 1961.

Andrew, Christopher. *Secret Service: The Making of the British Intelligence Community.* London: Heinemann, 1985.

Anger, Per. *With Raoul Wallenberg in Budapest.* New York: Holocaust Library, 1981.

Ardenne, Manfred von. *Ein glückliches Leben für Technik und Forschung.* Berlin, DDR: Verlag der Nation, 1980.

Armenteros, R., et al., eds. *Physics from Friends: Papers Dedicated to Charles Peyrou on his 60th Birthday.* Geneva: Multi-Office S.A., 1978.

Attorney General of the Government of Israel. "In the District Court of Jerusalem: Criminal Case No. 40/61. The Government of Israel vs. Adolf, the Son of Adolf Karl Eichmann. Minutes of Sessions Number 14 and 15," April 25, 1961.

Badash, Lawrence. *Kapitza, Rutherford, and the Kremlin.* New Haven: Yale University Press, 1985.

Bagge, Eric, Kurt Diebner, and Kenneth Jay. *Von der Uranspaltung bis Calder Hall.* Hamburg: Rowohlt, 1957.

Barth, Tom, and Gulbrand Lunde. "Lattice Constants of the Cuprous and Silver Halides." *Geol. Tidsskr. Bd.* 8. S. 281-92, 1926. Oslo.

Barwich, Heinz and Elfi. *Das Rote Atom.* Munich: Scherz Verlag, 1967.

Batchelor, G. K. *Geoffrey Ingram Taylor*. Biographical memoirs, vol. 22. London: Royal Society, 1976.

Beck, Adolf. *Magnesium und seine Legierungen*. Berlin: Verlag von Julius Springer, September 1939. British edition: *The Technology of Magnesium and Its Alloys*. Translated by F. A. Hughes & Co. Ltd. and Magnesium Elektron Ltd. London: F. A. Hughes & Co. Ltd., 1940.

Becker, Kurt A., and Jochen H. Block. "Iwan A. Stranski," in *Berichte u. Mitteilungen der Max-Planck-Gesellschaft*, March 1980.

Beesley, Patrick. *Very Special Intelligence*. Garden City: Doubleday, 1978.

Beevor, J. G. *SOE: Recollections and Reflections; 1940–1945*. London: The Bodley Head, 1981.

Bekker, Cajus. *Hitler's Naval War*. London: Macdonald and Jane's, 1974.

———. *The Luftwaffe War Diaries*. Garden City: Doubleday, 1964.

Benjamin, Hilde. *Aus Reden und Aufsätzen*. Berlin, DDR: Staatsverlag der Deutschen Demokratischen Republik, 1982.

———. *Georg Benjamin: Eine Biographie*. Leipzig, DDR: S. Hirzel Verlag, 1977.

Benjamin, Walter. *Briefe*, vols. 1 and 2. Edited by Gershom Scholem and Theodor Adorno. Frankfurt-am-Main: Edition Suhrkamp, 1978.

Bennett, Air Vice Marshal D. C. T. *Pathfinder*. Aylesbury: Frederick Muller Ltd., 1958.

Bergier, Jacques. *Secret Weapons–Secret Agents*. London: Hurst & Blackett, 1956.

Bernadotte, Count Folke. *Instead of Arms*. Stockholm: Bonniers, 1948.

———. *The Fall of the Curtain: The Last Days of the Third Reich*. London: Cassell, 1945.

Berninger, Ernst H., ed. *Otto Hahn in Selbstzeugnissen und Bilddokumenten*. Hamburg: Rowohlt, 1974.

Beyerchen, Alan D. *Scientists under Hitler: Politics and the Physics Community in the Third Reich*. New Haven: Yale University Press, 1977.

Biquard, Pierre. *Frédéric Joliot-Curie*. Greenwich, Connecticut: Fawcett Publications, 1966.

Birkenhead, The Earl of. *The Prof in Two Worlds: The Official Life of Professor F. A. Lindemann, Viscount Cherwell*. London: Collins, 1961.

Bjerg, Hans Christian. *Ligaen: Den Danske Militaere Efterretnings Tjeneste: 1940–1945*. Two vols. Copenhagen: Gyldendal, 1985.

Bjørnsen, Bjørn. *Det Utrolige Døgnet*. Oslo: Gyldendal Norsk Forlag, 1977.

Blackett, P. M. S. *Jean Frederick Joliot*. Biographical memoirs, vol. 6. London: Royal Society, 1960.

Blumtritt, Oskar. *Max Volmer 1885–1965: Eine Biographie*. Berlin: Technische Universitat, 1985.

Bøhn, Per. *IMI: Norsk innsats i kampen om atomkraften*. Trondheim: F. Bruns Bokhandels Forlag, 1946.

Born, Max. *My Life and My Views*. New York: Scribner's, 1968.

———. *My Life: Recollections of a Nobel Laureate*. New York: Scribner's, 1978.

———. *Physics and Politics*. New York: Basic Books, 1962.

————. *The Born-Einstein Letters*. New York: Walker & Co., 1971.

Bothe, Walther, and Siegfried Flügge (senior authors). "Nuclear Physics and Cosmic Rays," parts I and II: *FIAT Review of German Science 1939–1946*. Berlin: Office of the Military Government for Germany, 1948.

Boyle, Andrew. *The Fourth Man*. New York: Dial Press, 1979.

Brænne, Sverre B. "Aktototat vedr. Norsk Hydros jubileumsbok. Norsk Hydro 50 År, 1905–1955," internal document of Norsk Hydro, April 1952.

Brett-Smith, Richard. *Berlin '45: The Grey City*. London: Macmillan, 1966.

Bridges, Lord. *John Anderson, Viscount Waverly*. Biographical memoirs, vol. 4. London: Royal Society, 1958.

Brissaud, André. *The Nazi Secret Service*. New York: Norton, 1974.

British Science Museum. *The World of Two Atomic Scientists: Max Born and James Franck*. London, 1983.

Brodersen, Arvid. *Fra et Nomadeliv: Erindringer*. Oslo: Gyldendal Norsk Forlag, 1982.

————. *Mellom Frontene*. Oslo: J. W. Cappelens Forlag A.S., 1979.

Brown, Anthony Cave. *Bodyguard of Lies*. New York: Harper & Row, 1975.

————. *The Last Hero*. New York: Times Books, 1982.

Brun, Jomar. *Brennpunkt Vemork: 1940–1945*. Oslo: Universitetsforlaget AS, 1985.

Bush, Vannevar. *Pieces of the Action*. New York: Morrow, 1970.

Carlgren, Wilhelm M. *Svensk Underrättelsetjänst 1939–1945*. Stockholm: Liber/Allmänna Förlaget, 1985.

Calvocoressi, Peter. *Top Secret Ultra*. New York: Pantheon Books, 1980.

Casimir, Hendrik B. G. *Haphazard Reality. Half a Century of Science*. New York: Harper & Row, 1983.

Central Intelligence Agency. *The Rote Kapelle: The CIA's History of Soviet Intelligence and Espionage Networks in Western Europe, 1939–1945*. Washington, D.C.: University Publications of America, 1979.

Childs, Herbert. *An American Genius. The Life of Ernest Orlando Lawrence*. New York: Dutton, 1968.

Clark, Ronald W. *The Birth of the Bomb*. London: Scientific Book Club, 1961.

————. *The Greatest Power on Earth*. New York: Harper & Row, 1980.

Clayton, Aileen. *The Enemy Is Listening*. London: Hutchinson, 1980.

Cockburn, Stewart, and David Ellyard. *Oliphant*. Adelaide, South Australia: Axion Books, 1981.

Cockcroft, Sir John. *Niels Henrik David Bohr*. Biographical memoirs. vol. 9. London: Royal Society, 1963.

Collier, Basil. *The Battle of the V-2 Weapons*. London: Hodder & Stoughton, 1964.

Colvin, Ian. *Master Spy. Admiral Canaris*. New York: McGraw-Hill, 1952.

Compton, Arthur Holly. *Atomic Quest*. New York: Oxford University Press, 1956.

Conant, James B. *My Several Lives*. New York: Harper & Row, 1970.

Cookridge, E. H. (pseud. of Edward Spiro). *Set Europe Ablaze*. New York:

Crowell, 1967. Published in Great Britain as *Inside S.O.E.* London: Arthur Barker Ltd., 1966.

Coɾrens, Carl W. "Victor Moritz Goldschmidt," in *Naturwissenschaften*, vol. 34, no. 5, 1947.

David, L. R., and I. A. Warheit. *German Reports on Atomic Energy: Bibliography of ALSOS Technical Reports* (YID-3030). Oak Ridge, Tennessee: U.S. Atomic Energy Commission, June 6, 1952.

Deacon, Richard. *A History of the British Secret Service.* London: Panther Books, 1980.

Denham, Henry. *Inside the Nazi Ring. A Naval Attaché in Sweden 1940–1945.* London: John Murray, 1984.

Deutsch, Harold. *The Conspiracy Against Hitler in the Twilight Zone.* Minneapolis: University of Minnesota Press, 1968.

Dicks, Henry V., et al. *The Case of Rudolf Hess: A Problem in Diagnosis and Forensic Psychiatry.* London: Heinemann, 1946.

Dornberg, John. *Munich 1923.* New York: Harper & Row, 1982.

Dornberger, Walter. *V-2.* New York: Viking, 1954.

Douglas-Hamilton, James. *Motive for a Mission: The Story Behind Hess's Flight to Britain.* New York: Macmillan, 1971.

Dresden, Technisches Universität. *Geschichte der Technischen Universität Dresden.* Berlin, DDR: Deutscher Verlag der Wissenschaften, 1978.

Dulles, Allen W. *Germany's Underground.* New York: Macmillan, 1947.

Dunlop, Richard. *Donovan: America's Master Spy.* Chicago: Rand McNally, 1982.

Ehrman, John. *Grand Strategy*, vol. VI, October 1944–August 1945. London: Her Majesty's Stationery Office, 1956.

Erismann, Hans. "Professor Hans Rosbaud," in *Zuercher Chronik*, March 15 1985, Zürich.

Ewald, P. P. *Max von Laue. 1879–1960.* Biographical memoirs, vol. 6. London: Royal Society, 1960.

Ewald, P. P., ed. *Fifty Years of X-Ray Diffraction.* Utrecht: Oosthoek's Uitgeversmaatschappij, 1962.

Faligot, Roger, and Pascal Krop. *La Piscine. Les Services Secrets Français, 1944–1984.* Paris: Éditions du Seuil, 1985.

Farren, W. S. *Henry Thomas Tizard* (with a note by R. V. Jones). Biographical memoirs, vol. 7. London: Royal Society, 1961.

Findahl, Theo. *Undergand: Berlin 1939–1945.* Oslo: Forlagt A. V. H. Ascehoug & Co., 1945.

Flechtner, Hans-Joachim. *Atomzertrümmering.* Berlin: Wilhelm Limpert Verlag. 1942.

Flemming, Peter. *Operation Sea Lion.* New York: Simon & Schuster, 1957.

Fourcade, Marie-Madeleine. *Noah's Ark.* New York: Dutton, 1974.

Frank, Rudolf. *Spielzeit meines Lebens.* Heidelberg: Verlag Lambert Schneider, 1960.

——. "Errinerungen an Hans und Paul Rosbaud," in *Das Neue Mainz*, no. 4, April 1963.

Friedrich, Otto. *Before the Deluge: A Portrait of Berlin in the 1920's.* New York: Harper & Row, 1972.

Frisch, O. R. *Lise Meitner.* Biographical memoirs, vol. 16. London: Royal Society, 1970.

———. *What Little I Remember.* Cambridge: Cambridge University Press, 1979.

Frisch, O. R., Paul Rosbaud, et al. *Trends in Atomic Physics.* New York: Interscience Publishers, 1959.

Fuchs, Klaus Emil Julius. "Proceedings against, at Bow Street Magistrates' Court, London WC2, February 11, 1950." Washington, D.C.: Federal Bureau of Investigation.

Fuller, Jean Overton. *The German Penetration of SOE: France 1941–1944.* London: William Kimber, 1975.

Gallagher, Thomas. *Assault in Norway.* New York: Bantam Books. 1981.

Galm, Ulla. *Clara von Simson. Preussiche Köpfe.* Berlin: Stapp Verlag, 1984.

Gamow, George. *My World Line.* New York: Viking, 1970.

———. *Thirty Years That Shook Physics: The Story of Quantum Theory.* Garden City: Doubleday, 1966.

Garlinski, Jozef. *Hitler's Last Weapons: The Underground War Against the V-1 and V-2.* New York: Times Books, 1978.

Gentner, Wolfgang. *Entretiens avec Frédéric Joliot-Curie à Paris occupé 1940– 1942.* Heidelberg: Max Planck Institute für Kernphysik, 1980.

Gilbert, Martin. *Winston S. Churchill: Finest Hour: 1939–1941.* Boston: Houghton Mifflin, 1983.

Gisevius, Hans B. *To the Bitter End.* Boston: Houghton Mifflin, 1947.

Gjelsvik, Tore. *Norwegian Resistance.* London: Hurst & Co., 1979.

Goldberg, E. D. "Goldschmidt, Victor Moritz," in *Dictionary of Scientific Biography.* New York: Scribner's, 1972.

Goldschmidt, Maurice. *Sage: A Life of J. D. Bernal.* London: Hutchinson, 1980.

Goldschmidt, V. M. "Om super-uraner, grunnstoffer med større kjerneladning enn 92," in *Fra Fysikkens Verden. Argang 3, 1941–42.* Oslo: Norsk Fysik Tidsskrift., 1942.

Goudsmit, Samuel A. *ALSOS.* New York: Henry Schuman, 1947. Republished, Los Angeles: Tomash Publishers, 1983, with a special foreword by R. V. Jones, stating, "Our knowledge was, incidentally, largely due to Paul Rosbaud."

Gowing, Margaret. *Britain and Atomic Energy: 1939–1945.* London: Macmillan, 1964.

Grazer Stadtwerke A.G. *100 Jahre Grazer Tramway.* Graz, 1979.

Grazer Stadwerke A.G. *75 Jahre Elektrische Strassenbahn in Graz.* Graz, 1974.

Green, William. *Rocket Fighter.* New York: Random House, 1971.

Groves, Leslie R. *Now It Can Be Told.* New York: Harper & Row, 1962. London: André Deutsch Ltd., 1963.

Gunston, Bill. *World War II British Aircraft.* New York: Chartwell Books, 1985.

———. *World War II German Aircraft.* New York: Chartwell Books, 1985.

Gunter, Paul. "Clara v. Simson zum 65 Geburtstag," in *Berichte der Bunsengesellschaft für Physikalische Chemie, Zeitschrift für Elektrochemie*, vol. 66, no. 7, 1962.

Haber, L. F. *The Poisonous Cloud*. Oxford: Oxford University Press, 1986.

Haffner, Sebastian. "Secrets of the July 20 Plot: By 'A Student of Europe,'" in *The Observer*, July 21, 1946.

Hagg, Gunnar. *Arne Westgren*. Stockholm: Kungl. Vetenskapsakademien, July 1978.

Hahn, Dietrich. *Otto Hahn: Begrunder des Atomzeitalters*. Munich: List Verlag, 1979.

———. *Otto Hahn: Elebnisse und Erkenntnisse*. Düsseldorf: Econ Verlag, 1975.

Hahn, Fritz. *Deutsche Geheimwaffen 1939–1945*. Heidenheim: Eric Hoffmann Verlag. 1963.

Hahn, O., and F. Strassmann. "Über den Nachweis und das Verhalten der bei der Bestrahlung des Urans mittels Neutronen entstehenden Erdalkalimetalle," in *Naturwissenschaften*, vol. 27, 1939. Submitted December 22, 1938, to Springer Verlag; published 1939. (This is the classic paper, submitted through Paul Rosbaud, that marks the beginning of the nuclear age.)

Hahn, Otto. *A Scientific Autobiography*. New York: Scribner's, 1966.

———. *My Life*. New York: Herder and Herder, 1970.

Haigerloch Stadtverwaltung. *Atom Museum Haigerloch*. Haigerloch: Drukerei ST Elser, 1982.

Hancock, W. K., and M. M. Gowing. *British War Economy*. London: His Majesty's Stationery Office, 1949.

Harms, Norman. *Waffen SS in Action*. Carrollton, Texas: Squadron/Signal Publications, 1973.

Harrod, Roy Forbes. *The Prof: A Personal Memoir of Lord Cherwell*. London: Macmillan, 1959.

Hartcup, Guy, and T. E. Allibone. *Cockcroft and the Atom*. Bristol: Adam Hilger Ltd., 1984.

Hartmann, Peter. "Grabstein für eine Million," in *Weltwoche Magazin*, Zürich, September 2, 1981 (the Hans Rosbaud Alpine Reserve).

Hastings, Max. *Bomber Command*. New York: Dial Press, 1979.

Haukelid, Knut. *Skis Against the Atom*. London: William Kimber, 1954.

Haushoffer, Albrecht. *Moabit Sonnets*. Translated by Arvid Brodersen. New York: Norton, 1978.

Hawkins, David. *Project Y: The Los Alamos Story. Part I. Toward Trinity*. Los Angeles: Tomash Publishers, 1983.

Hayes, Paul M. Quisling. *The Career and Political Ideas of Vidkun Quisling 1887–1945*. Devonshire: David & Charles, 1971.

Heger, Wanda. *Hver fredag foran porten*. Oslo: Gyldendal Norsk Forlag, 1984.

Heider, Max. "Erinnerungen an Hans Rosbaud," in *Neue Zeit*. Graz, December 29, 1963.

Heisenberg, Elisabeth. *Inner Exile: Recollections of a Life with Werner Heisenberg*.

Translated by S. Cappallari and C. Morris. Boston: Birkhauser, 1984. Published in West Germany as *Das politische Leben eines Unpolitischen*. Munich: R. Piper Verlag, 1980.

Heisenberg, W. "Research in Germany on the Technical Application of Atomic Energy," in *Nature*, vol. 160, no. 409, August 16, 1947.

———. *Der Teil und das Ganze. Gespräche im Umkreis der Atomphysik*. Munich: R. Piper Verlag, 1969. Translated, with changes, as *Physics and Beyond: Encounters and Conversations*. New York: Harper & Row, 1971.

———. "Gott Sei Dank, Wir Könnten Sie Nicht Bauen," interview, in *Der Spiegel*, no. 28, 1967.

Heisenberg, W., W. Känzig, J. Burckhardt, H. Staub, P. Huber, and W. Albrecht. "Zur Erinnerung an Paul Scherrer-Sonderegger." Zürich, private printing, 1969.

Heitler, W. "Dr. Paul Rosbaud," obituary, in *Nature*, no. 4872, March 16, 1963.

Henderson, Sir Neville. *Failure of a Mission*. London: Hodder & Stoughton, 1940.

———. *Final Report*. London: His Majesty's Stationery Office. September 20, 1939.

———. *Water Under the Bridges*. London: Hodder & Stoughton, 1945.

Henshall, Phillip. *Hitler's Rocket Sites*. London: Robert Hale, 1985.

Hermann, Hauptmann (pseud.). *The Luftwaffe: Its Rise and Fall*. New York: Putnam's, 1943.

Hewins, Ralph. *Quisling*. London: W. H. Allen, 1965.

Hewlett, R. G., and O. E. Anderson. *The New World. 1939/1946*. Vol. 1: *A History of the United States Atomic Energy Commission*. University Park: Pennsylvania State University Press, 1962.

Hill, A. V. *The Ethical Dilemma of Science and Other Writings*. New York: Rockefeller Institute Press, 1960. (Initiated by Paul Rosbaud.)

Hinsley, F. H. *British Intelligence in the Second World War*. Vol. 1, 1979; Vol. 2, 1981; Vol. 3, part I, 1984 (all published). London: Her Majesty's Stationery Office.

Höhne, Heinz. *Canaris*. Garden City: Doubleday, 1979.

———. *Code Word Direktor: The Story of the Red Orchestra*. New York: Ballantine Books, 1982.

———. *The Order of the Death's Head: The Story of Hitler's S.S.* New York: Ballantine Books, 1981.

Howarth, David. *The Shetland Bus*. London: Thomas Nelson & Sons, 1951.

Howarth, Patrick. *Undercover: The Men and Women of the Special Operations Executive*. London: Routledge & Kegan Paul, 1980.

Huebner, Paul. "Philosopher Who Writes with a Common Touch" [Carl F. von Weizsäcker], in *German Tribune*, no. 1113, December 25, 1983. Translated from the *Rheinische Post*, December 8, 1983.

Hutton, R. S. *Recollections of a Technologist*. London: Sir Isaac Pittman & Sons, 1964.

Huzel, Dieter K. *Peenemünde to Canaveral.* Englewood Cliffs, New Jersey: Prentice-Hall, 1962.

International Paint Ltd. "International Paints: Its Origin and Growth, 1881–1918," unpublished archives document. London, 1982.

Irving, David (pseud. of John Cawdell). *Source Materials for the German Atomic Bomb* (U.K.: *The Virus House*). DJ Ref. 29–32. Four microfilm reels. East Ardsley: Microform Academic Publishers.

——. *The German Atomic Bomb.* New York: Simon & Schuster, 1967. Also published as *The Virus House.* London: William Kimber, 1967.

——. *The Mare's Nest.* Boston: Little, Brown, 1964.

——. *The Rise and Fall of the Luftwaffe. The Life of Field Marshall Erhard Milch.* Boston: Little, Brown, 1973.

Janouch. F. "Lev D. Landau: His Life and Work," *CERN* 79–03, March 28, 1979. Geneva: European Organization for Nuclear Research.

Johnson, Brian. *The Secret War* (first published by the BBC). New York: Methuen, 1978.

Johnson, Vivian Annabelle. *Karl Lark-Horovitz, Pioneer in Solid State Physics.* Oxford: Pergamon Press, 1969

Joint Committee on Atomic Energy, U.S. Congress. *Soviet Atomic Espionage.* Washington, D.C.: Government Printing Office, 1951.

Jones, R. V. "Lord Cherwell's Judgement in World War II," in *Oxford* magazine, May 9, 1963.

——. "Scientific Intelligence: Some Aspects of Its Development from 1939–1945," lecture at the Royal United Services Institution, February 19, 1947. (It was this lecture that revealed the Oslo Report to the public.)

——. "Sir Henry Tizard," in *Nature*, vol. 205, no. 4975, March 6, 1965.

——. "The Glare of the Rocket," in *Chemistry and Industry*, March 27, 1965.

——. "Thicker Than Heavy Water," in *Chemistry and Industry*, August 26, 1967.

——. *The Wizard War: British Scientific Intelligence, 1939–1945.* New York: Coward, McCann & Geohegan, 1978. Also published as *Most Secret War.* Sevenoaks: Coronet Books of Hodder & Stoughton, 1979.

——. *Winston Leonard Spencer Churchill.* Biographical memoirs, vol. 12. London: Royal Society, 1966.

Jones, Vincent C. *Manhattan: The Army and the Atomic Bomb.* Washington, D.C., Center of Military History: United States Army, U.S. Government Printing Office, 1985.

Joubert, Air Chief Marshal Sir Philip. *Rocket.* London: Hutchinson, 1957.

Jungk, Robert. *Brighter Than a Thousand Suns: A Personal History of the Atomic Scientists.* New York: Harcourt, Brace & World, 1958. Published in Switzerland as *Heller als tausend Sonner.* Bern: Alfred Scherz Verlag, 1956.

Junkes, Giuseppi, S.J., "P. Luigi Gatterer, S.J.," in *Memorie della Societa Astronomica Italiana*, vol. XXIV, no. 3, 1953.

Kahn, David. *Hitler's Spies: German Military Intelligence in World War II.* New York: Macmillan, 1978.

——. *The Codebreakers.* New York: Macmillan, 1967.

Kapitza, P. L. "Plasma and the Controlled Thermonuclear Reaction." Nobel lecture, December 8, 1978, Stockholm.

Kaufman, Louis, Barbara Fitzgerald, and Tom Sewell. *Moe Berg.* Boston: Little, Brown, 1975.

Kemmer, N., and R. Schlapp. *Max Born.* Biographical memoirs, vol. 17. London: Royal Society, 1971.

Kennedy, Ludovic. *Pursuit. The Chase and Sinking of the Bismarck.* New York: Viking, 1974.

Klee, Ernst, and Otto Merk. *The Birth of the Missile: The Secrets of Peenemünde.* London: George G. Harrop & Co., 1965.

Klein, Alexander. *The Counterfeit Traitor.* New York: Henry Holt, 1958.

Krafft, Fritz. *Im Schatten der Sensation. Leben und Wirken von Fritz Strassmann.* Weinheim: Verlag Chemie, 1981.

Kramish, Arnold. *Atomic Energy in the Soviet Union.* Stanford: Stanford University Press; Oxford: Oxford University Press, 1959.

———. *The Nuclear Motive: In the Beginning.* Washington, D.C.: Wilson Center, Smithsonian Institution, 1982.

Kraushaar, Luise. *Berliner Kommunisten im Kampf gegen den Faschismus. 1936–1942.* Berlin, DDR: Dietz Verlag, 1981.

Laqueur, Walter, and Richard Breitman. *Breaking the Silence.* New York: Simon and Schuster, 1986.

Lasby, Clarence G. *Project Paperclip. German Scientists and the Cold War.* New York: Atheneum, 1971.

Leibholz-Bonhoeffer, Sabine. *The Bonhoeffers. Portrait of a Family.* London: Sidgwick & Jackson, 1971.

Leverkuehn, Paul. *German Military Intelligence.* London: Weidenfeld & Nicolson, 1954.

Lewin, Ronald. *Ultra Goes to War.* New York: McGraw-Hill, 1978.

Ley, Willy. *Rockets, Missiles & Space Travel,* revised and enlarged edition. New York: Viking, 1958.

Lifschitz, E. M. *Lev Davydovitch Landau.* Biographical memoirs, vol. 15. London: Royal Society, 1969.

Lindstrom, Teddy. " 'Oslo-rapporten' kunne ha forkortet krigen med to ar." Oslo: Vi-Menn, 1980.

Lovell, Sir Bernard. *Patrick Maynard Stuart Blackett, Baron Blackett of Chelsea.* Biographical memoirs, vol. 21. London: Royal Society, 1975.

Lunde, Gulbrand. *Kampen for Norge.* Oslo: Gunnar Stenersens Forlag, 1941.

———. "The Research Laboratory of the Norwegian Canning Industry," in *Tidsskrift for Hermetikindustri,* vol. XVI, no. 6, 1931.

———. *Vitamine in Frischen und Konservierten Nahrungsmitteln.* Berlin: Julius Springer, December 1939.

Maass, Walter B. *Country Without a Name: Austria under Nazi Rule, 1938–1945.* New York: Frederick Ungar, 1979.

Mackset, Kenneth. *Kesselring: The Making of the Luftwaffe.* New York: David McKay, 1978.

Macmillan, Captain Norman. *The Royal Air Force in the World War.* London:

George G. Harrop & Co., 1950. (Vol. IV has reference to the Oslo Report.)

Mader, Julius. *Geheimnis von Huntsville*. Berlin, DDR: Deutscher Militaerverlag, 1963.

Mahoney, Leo James. *A History of the War Department Scientific Intelligence Mission (ALSOS), 1943–1945*. Ann Arbor: University Microfilms, 1981.

Mann, Wilfrid B. "Professor Leif Tronstad," in *Fra Fysikens Verden*, vol. 27, no. 1, 1965.

———. *Was There a Fifth Man?* Oxford: Pergamon Press, 1982.

Martelli, George. *The Man Who Saved London: The Story of Michel Hollard*. London: Companion Book Club, 1960.

Mason, Herbert M. *Hitler Must Die!* New York: Norton, 1978.

Masterman, J. C. *The Double-Cross System*. New Haven: Yale University Press, 1972.

McGovern, James. *Crossbow and Overcast*. New York: Morrow, 1964.

Mehra, Jagdish. "The Birth of Quantum Mechanics." Werner Heisenberg Memorial Lecture, *CERN 76–10*, March 30, 1976. Geneva: European Organization for Nuclear Research.

Meitner, Lise, and Otto Hahn. *Atomenergie und Frieden*. Paris: UNESCO, 1954.

Mendelssohn, Prof. K. *The World of Walther Nernst*. Pittsburgh: University of Pittsburgh Press, 1973.

Metallwirtschaft: Wissenschaft und Technik. Berlin: Georg Lüttke, 1921–1947.

Michel, Jean. *Dora*. New York: Holt, Rinehart & Winston, 1980.

Middlebrook, Martin. *The Peenemünde Raid: The Night of 17–18 August 1943*. London: Allen Lane, 1982.

———. *The Schweinfurt-Regensburg Mission*. New York: Scribner's, 1983.

Mitcham, Samuel W., Jr. *Hitler's Legions: The German Army Order of Battle, World War II*. New York: Stein and Day, 1985.

Moldenhauer, Hans. *The Death of Anton Webern*. New York: Philosophical Library, 1961.

Montagu, Ewen. *The Man Who Never Was*. Philadelphia: Lippincott, 1953.

Moore, Ruth. *Niels Bohr*. New York: Knopf, 1966.

Mott, Sir Nevill. *Werner Heisenberg*. Biographical memoirs, vol. 23. London: Royal Society, 1977.

Murray, Williamson. *Strategy for Defeat. The Luftwaffe 1933–1945*. Maxwell Air Force Base, Alabama: Air University Press, 1963.

Naval Intelligence Division. *Denmark*, January 1944, London.

Naval Intelligence Division. *Netherlands*, October 1944, London.

Naval Intelligence Division. *Norway*, vols. I and II, October 1941 and January 1943, London.

Newman, Bernard. *They Saved London*. London: Werner Laurie, 1952.

Nielsen, Kjell. "The Bombings of Herøya and Rjukan," unpublished manuscript, Sandvika, Norway, 1970.

Norges Hjemmefrontmuseum. "Lieutenant Commander Eric Welsh, R.N.V.R.," unpublished archives document, Oslo, 1943.

Oberdeutsche Provinz, S.J. "P. Joseph Junkes, S.J.," memorial note, Munich, April 1984.

Oliphant, M. L. E., and Lord Penney. *John Douglas Cockcroft.* Biographical memoirs, vol. 14. London: Royal Society, 1968.

Olsen, Oluf Reed. *Two Eggs on My Plate.* Chicago: Rand McNally, 1953.

Ottosen, Kristan. *Theta: Et blad fra motstandskampens historie 1940–1945.* Bergen: Universitetsforlaget, 1983.

Parry, Albert. *Peter Kapitza on Life and Science.* New York: Macmillan, 1968.

Pash, Boris T. *The Alsos Mission.* New York: Award House, 1969.

Peierls, Sir Rudolf. *Bird of Passage: Recollections of a Physicist.* Princeton: Princeton University Press, 1985.

———. "Atomic Germans," in *New York Review of Books,* July 1, 1971.

———. *Otto Robert Frisch.* Biographical memoirs, vol. 27. London: Royal Society, 1981.

Perrault, Gilles. *The Red Orchestra.* New York: Simon & Schuster, 1969.

Perutz, Sir Max. "That Was the War: Enemy Alien," in *The New Yorker,* August 12, 1985.

Petrow, Richard. *The Bitter Years: The Invasion and Occupation of Denmark and Norway, April 1940–May 1945.* New York: Morrow, 1974.

Philby, Kim. *My Silent War.* London: Macgibbon & Kee, 1968.

Pickalkicwicz, Jausz. *Secret Agents, Spies and Saboteurs.* New York. Morrow, 1973.

Piskari, Margot, and Günter Übel. *Die KPD Lebt!* Berlin, DDR: Dietz Verlag, 1980.

Popov, Dusko. *Spy Counter Spy.* New York: Grosset & Dunlap, 1974.

Powys-Lybbe, Ursula. *The Eye of Intelligence.* London: William Kimber, 1983.

Read, Anthony, and David Fisher. *Colonel Z. The Secret Life of a Master of Spies.* London: Hodder & Stoughton, 1984.

Reich, Willi. *Schoenberg. A Critical Biography.* New York: Praeger Publishers, 1971.

Reid, Margaret G. "Norway—1940. A Diary of the War in the Gudbrandsdalen Seen through the Eyes of British Cypher Clerk Margaret G. Reid," manuscript. Leeds: Brotherton Library, University of Leeds.

Reid, Margaret, and Leif C. Rolstad. *April 1940: En krigsdagbok.* Oslo: Gyldendal Norsk Forlag, 1980.

Rideal, E. K., and U. R. Evans. "Professor Leif Tronstad," obituary, in *Nature,* vol. 156, July 21, 1945.

Rife, Patricia Elizabeth. *Lise Meitner: The Life and Times of a Jewish Woman Physicist.* Ann Arbor: University Microfilms, 1983.

Riste, Olav, and Bertt Nökleby. *Norway 1940–45: The Resistance Movement.* Oslo: Tanum-Norli, 1984.

Rona, Elizabeth. *How It Came About.* Oak Ridge, Tennessee: Oak Ridge Associated Universities, 1978.

Rørholt, Bjørn. *Amatorspionen "Lerken."* Oslo: Hjemens Forlag, 1985.

Rosbaud, Paul. "Secret Mission," review of *ALSOS* by Samuel Goudsmit, in (London) *Times Literary Supplement*, June 5, 1948.

———. "Das Royal Society Mond Laboratory in Cambridge," in *Metallwirtschaft*. February 17, 1933.

———. "International Exchange of Scientists," in *Research*. London: Butterworths Scientific Publications Ltd., 1949.

———. "Prof. Max von Laue. For. Mem. R.S.," obituary, in *Nature*, vol. 187, no. 4739, April 27, 1960.

———. "Victor Moritz Goldschmidt," in *Great Chemists*. Ed. Eduard Farber. New York: Interscience, 1961.

———. Review of *Brighter Than a Thousand Suns, Discovery*, March 1959.

Royal Norwegian Government Information Office. *The Gestapo at Work in Norway*. London, 1942.

Rozental, S., ed. *Niels Bohr: His life and work as seen by his friends and colleagues*. Amsterdam: North Holland Publishing Company, 1967.

Salpeter, P. E., S.J. "P. Alois Gatterer, S.J.," in *Microchemica Acta*. Vienna: Springer Verlag, vol. 1–2, 1953.

Schmid, Erich. *Erinnerungen an Hans Rosbaud*. Zürich, privately printed, 1972.

Schweigert, Horst. *Dehio Graz*. Vienna: Verlag Anton Schroll & Co., 1979.

Seip, D. A. *Hjemme og i fiendeland*. Oslo: Gyldendal Norsk Forlag, 1946.

Sender, Anton. "Geschichte des Domchors in Graz. Von den Zeiten Erzherzogs Karl II bis auf unsere Tage," in *Kirchenmusikalisches Jahrbuch*, Graz, 1900.

Sevruk, V., ed. *How Wars End: Eye-Witness Accounts of the Fall of Berlin*. Moscow: Progress Publishers, 1969.

Shachtman, Tom. *The Phony War: 1939–1940*. New York: Harper & Row, 1982.

Shepherd, Naomi. *A Refuge from Darkness: Wilfrid Israel and the Rescue of the Jews*. New York: Pantheon Books, 1984.

Shirer, William L. *Berlin Diary*. New York: Knopf, 1942.

———. *End of a Berlin Diary*. New York: Knopf, 1947.

———. *The Rise and Fall of the Third Reich*. New York: Simon & Schuster, 1959.

Showell, Jak P. M. *The German Navy in World War II*. Annapolis: Naval Institute Press, 1979.

Simon, Leslie E. *Secret Weapons of the Third Reich*. Old Greenwich, Connecticut: WE, Inc., 1971.

Skelton, Geoffrey. *Paul Hindemith*. New York: Crescendo Publishing, 1975.

Smyth, Henry D. *Atomic Energy for Military Purposes*. Princeton: Princeton University Press, 1945.

Snow, C. P. *Science and Government*. Cambridge: Harvard University Press, 1960.

Soltikow, Michael Graf. *Meine Leben bei Canaris*. Vienna: Moewig, Paul Neff Verlag, 1980.

Sonsteby, Gunnar. *Report from No. 24*. New York: Lyle Stuart, 1965.

Speer, Albert. *Infiltration*. New York: Macmillan, 1981.

————. *Inside the Third Reich*. New York: Macmillan, 1970.

————. *Speer Collection*. Microfilm reel 119. BA-RL 3/332–33) London: Imperial War Museum, 1985.

Spence, R. *Otto Hahn*. Biographical memoirs, vol. 16. London: Royal Society, 1970.

Spruch, Grace Marmor. "Pyotr Kapitza: Octogenarian Dissident," in *Physics Today*, September 1979.

St. George Sanders, Hilary. *The Left Handshake: The Boy Scout Movement During the War, 1939–1945*. London: Collins, 1948.

Stafford, David. *Britain and European Resistance 1940–1945: A Survey of the Special Operations Executive, with Documents*. London: Macmillan, 1980. Reprinted, with alterations, 1983.

Steiermaerkischen Musikvereines. *Schul- und Konzertbericht. Für das Schuljahre 1904–1911*. Graz: Verlage des Steirmaerkischen Musikvereines, 1903–1911.

Stevenson, William. *A Man Called Intrepid*. New York: Harcourt Brace Jovanovich, 1976.

————. *Intrepid's Last Case*. New York: Villard Books, 1984.

Strassmann, Irmgard and Martin. "In Memoriam Fritz Strassmann," Mainz, private printing, 1980.

Suess, Hans E. "Virus House. Comments and Reminiscences," in *Bulletin of Atomic Scientists*, June 1968.

Suppan, Wolfgang. *Steierisches Musiklexikon*. Graz: Akademische Druck u. Verlagsanstalt, 1962–1966.

Szilard, Leo. *His Version of the Facts*, vol. II. Ed. Spencer Weart and Gertrud Weiss Szilard. Cambridge: MIT Press, 1978.

————. "Reminiscences," in *The Intellectual Migration*. Ed. D. Fleming and B. Bailyn. Cambridge: Harvard University Press, 1969.

Tautorius, Werner (pseud. of Dr. Kurt Diebner). "Die Deutschen Geheimarbeiten zur Kernenergieverwertung waehrend des zweiten Weltkrieges 1939–1945," in *Atomkernenergie*, vol. 1, 1956.

Taylor, Fred, ed. *The Goebbels Diaries: 1939–1941*. New York: Putnam's, 1983.

Thomas, John Oram. *The Giant Killers: The Danish Resistance Movement, 1940–45*. New York: Taplinger, 1976.

Thomson, G. P. *Frederick Alexander Lindemann, Viscount Cherwell*. Biographical memoirs, vol. 4. London: Royal Society, 1958.

Tilley, C. E. *Victor Moritz Goldschmidt*. Biographical memoirs, vol. 6. London: Royal Society, 1948.

Trepper, Leopold. *The Great Game*. New York: McGraw-Hill, 1977.

Truslow, Edith C., and Ralph Carlisle Smith. *Project Y: The Los Alamos Story*. Part II: *Beyond Trinity*. Los Angeles: Tomash Publishers, 1983.

Tuck, James L. "Lord Cherwell and His Part in World War II." Unpublished manuscript, 1961. Archives, Los Alamos Scientific Laboratory, Los Alamos, New Mexico.

U.S. Air Force. "Peenemünde East Through the Eyes of 500 Detained at

Garmisch." Microfilm A5734. Index 1595. 519.652.1 through 519.6541-4, 1945. Maxwell Air Force Base, Alabama.

U.S. Eighth Bomber Command Headquarters. "Bomber Command Narrative of Operations. 131st Operation. November 16, 1943. Mission no. 1 — Rjukan." Maxwell Air Force Base, Alabama.

United States Strategic Bombing Survey. *A Brief Study of the Effects of Area Bombing on Berlin*. Washington, D.C.: U.S. Air Force, 1945.

United States Strategic Bombing Survey. *Light Metals Industry of Germany*. Part II: *Magnesium*. Washington, D.C.: U.S. Air Force, November 1945.

Verwey, E. J. W. *Jan Hendrik de Boer*. Biographical memoirs. Amsterdam: Royal Academy of Sciences of the Netherlands.

Vineta, fnu. *Der Vogel Greif. Segen und Märchen vom Ostseestrand*. Rostock, DDR, 1965.

von Braun, Wernher. "Survey of Development of Liquid Rockets in Germany and Their Future Prospects." Peenemünde, unpublished document, May 1945.

von Laue, M. "A Report on the State of Physics in Germany," in *American Journal of Physics*, vol, 17, no. 3, March 1949.

———. "Arnold Berliner (26.12.1862 – 22.3.42)," in *Naturwissenschaften*, vol. 33, no. 9, November 15, 1946.

von Schlabrendorff, Fabian. *The Secret War Against Hitler*. London: Hodder & Stoughton, 1966.

Wassermann, Günter, and Peter Wincierz. *Das Metall-Laboratorium der Metallgesellschaft A.G., 1918 – 1981*. Frankfurt-am-Main: Metallgesellschaft A.G., 1981.

Waverly, Lord (Sir John Anderson), and Sir Alexander Fleck. *Wallace Alan Akers*. Biographical memoirs, vol. 1. London: Royal Society, 1955.

Weart, Spenser. *Scientists in Power*. Cambridge: Harvard University Press, 1979.

Werrell, Kenneth. *The Evolution of the Cruise Missile*. Maxwell Air Force Base, Alabama: Air University Press, 1985.

West, Nigel (pseud. of Rupert Allason). *A Matter of Trust. MI5: 1945 – 72*. London: Weidenfeld & Nicolson, 1982.

———. *A Thread of Deceit: Espionage Myths of World War II*. New York: Random House, 1985.

———. *MI5: British Security Service Operations, 1909 – 1945*. London: The Bodley Head, 1981.

———. *MI6: British Secret Intelligence Service Operations, 1909 – 45*. New York: Random House, 1983.

Wheeler-Bennett, John W. *John Anderson. Viscount Waverly*. New York: St. Martin's Press, 1962.

Whiting, Charles. *The Spymasters*. New York: Saturday Review Press/Dutton, 1976.

Williams, Elvet. *Arbeitskommando*. London: Victor Gollancz, 1975.

Wilson, John Skinner. *Scouting Around the World*. London: Blandford Press, 1959.

————. "The 'Heavy Water' Operations in Norway, 1942–1944." Privately printed for the participants in the operations. London, December 1945.

Winnacker, Karl, and Karl Wirtz. *Nuclear Energy in Germany*. La Grange Park, Illinois: American Nuclear Society, 1979.

Winter, Frank H. *Prelude to the Space Age: The Rocket Societies: 1924–1940*. Washington, D.C.: National Air and Space Museum, 1983.

Winterbotham, F. W. *The Nazi Connection*. New York: Harper & Row, 1978.

————. *The Ultra Secret*. New York: Harper & Row, 1974.

Young, A. P. *The "X" Documents*. Ed. Sidney Aster. London: André Deutsch, 1974.

Zanetti, J. Enrique. *Fire from the Air: The ABC's of Incendiaries*. New York: Columbia University Press, 1942.

Zuckerman, Sir Solly. *From Apes to Warlords*. New York: Harper & Row, 1978.

zu Putlitz, Wolfgang. *The Putlitz Dossier*. London: Allan Wingate, 1957.

INDEX

Aas, Oddvar, 151
Abwehr, 203, 209, 215; XX Committee vs., 200, 201; purged, 204; Paul and, 206, 208, 210
Academic Assistance Council (England), 46, 47
Aerograd (film), 36, 41
Aftenposten (Oslo newspaper), 106, 223, 228
"Agent R.34," *see* Andreasen, Aage C. Holger
Agrenov, Dimitri, 10
Aircraft, British (RAF), *see* Britain
Aircraft, German: production, 66, 151, 235; pilotless, 67; Me-262, 150, 151. *See also* Luftwaffe; "Secret weapons"
Aircraft, U.S., *see* Eighth Air Force
Aitken, William Maxwell (Lord Beaverbrook), 200
Akers, Wallace, 196
Alexander Friedrich, Landgrave of Hesse, 13
"Alfredo" (German agent), 203
Allied Supreme Command, 108
Allier, Jacques, 83, 84, 87–88, 147, 188, 200
Alloway, Julia, 191
Alsos mission, 197, 240, 241, 242, 246
American Institute of Physics, 78, 250, 252
"Amniarix," *see* Rousseau, Jeannie
Anderson, Sir John, 135–36, 194
Andreasen, Aage C. Holger ("Agent R.34"), 138, 140–41
Andresen, Johan H., 227–28

Andresen, Mrs. Johan H. (Eva Klaveness), 227, 228
Anglo-Norwegian Intelligence Service, 91, 169
"Anton" (Rosbaud relative), 232, 33
Appleton, Sir Edward, 201
Arcadia conference, 182
"Artist," *see* Jebsen, Johann
Arutinskaya, Elizabeth, 220
Ashbridge, Col. W., 183
Äström, Elsa, *see* Lindemann, Mrs. Max
Atkinson, Robert d'Escourt, 26, 122
Atkinson, Mrs. Robert d'Escourt (Irmin), 26, 122, 218
Atomic research/bomb, 16, 34; Germany, 29, 43, 50–55, 109–32 *passim*, 143, 156, 160, 188, 189, 196, 197, (heavy water and) 83, 161, 174, 199, 201, 204, 246, ("Der Tag") 99, (abandoned) 99, 104, 128, 162, 175–76, 180, 197, 199, 244, 245, 247, (Paul's reports on) 129, 202, 208, (U.S. beliefs regarding) 163, 164, 197; Britain, 36, 46–48, 74, 84, 103–4, 109, 113, 114, 137, 156, 180, 188, 193, (code name "Tube Alloys") 195, 196, 198, 203, (XX Committee deceptions) 200, 201–203, 204, 205; Paul's reports, 52, 53–54, 129, 202, 209; France, 53, 84, 88, 251; U.S. experiments/use, 114, 118–19, 120, 124, 131, 156, 163–64, 174, 175, (Hiroshima) 53, 127, 216, 246, (Nagasaki) 124, (Manhattan Project) 128, 170, (vs. and with Britain) 162, 164, 170, 180–83 *passim*, 196,

Atomic research/bomb (*cont.*)
    197, 204, (Los Alamos) 188, 196, 198,
    204, (press security) 200; "refusal" to
    work on, 115, 120, 121, 129, 188–89,
    191, 245, 247, 248; "impossibility" of
    bomb, 127, 129, 194, 196, 199–204
    passim; cyclotrons, 147, 175, 186, 189;
    political importance, 156; Soviet, 240.
    See also Heavy water; "Secret weap-
    ons"
Attlee, Clement, 246
Aubert, Axel, 84
Auschwitz, *see* Concentration camps
Austrian Anschluss, 25, 48, 76
Austro-Hungarian Empire, 141, 183

Bagge, Eric, 127, 243, 246
Baker, Josephine, 22
Baldur (British battleship), 96
Baldwin, Stanley, 38
"Balloon" (Dickie Metcalfe), 88
Banque de Paris et de Pays Bas, 83
Barth, Tom, 56, 76–77, 125, 126, 130,
    131
Bartók, Béla, 23
Barton, Sir Derek, 34
Batchelor, Capt. K. S., 168
Battle of the Atlantic, 90, 91, 96, 113
BBC (British Broadcasting Corporation),
    65–66, 97, 137, 143, 149, 246. *See also*
    Coded messages; Radio stations
Beaverbrook, Lord, 200
Beck, Adolf, 60, 62, 78, 80, 171, 172
Becker, Karl Emil, 101
Belgium: uranium supplies in, 84, 143;
    German occupation of, 87
Belz, Annemarie, 111
Benjamin, Georg, 24, 40, 141, 213, 220
Benjamin, Mrs. Georg (Hilde Lange),
    141, 213, 220, 239, 240, 250; in Horst
    Wessel case, 24, 40
Benjamin, Walter, 24
Berg, *see* Concentration camps
Bergen-Belsen, *see* Concentration camps
Bergh, Sverre ("Sigurd"), 150, 151, 160,
    196, 223, 224, 228, 251; joins Resist-
    ance, 98, 106–7, 108; meetings with
    Paul, 110–13, 137–38, 143; and
    rocket information, 138, 140–41, 154,
    230–31, 232; leaves Germany, 239–
    40, 241
Bergmann, Georg, 240
Berlin, University of, 46, 49, 104, 138,
    208
Berliner, Arnold, 213

Berlin Wall, 250
Bernadotte, Count Folke, 239
"Bernadotte expedition," 234
Bernal, John Desmond, 17
Bertrand-Vignes, Maj. (French military
    attaché in Oslo), 83, 172
Bethe, Hans, 123
Biological warfare, *see* Chemical warfare
Birmingham University, 47, 48, 84
Bismarck (German battleship), 91
Blackett, P. M. S., 173–74
Blohm and Voss (Hamburg shipbuild-
    ers), 92
Blunt, Anthony, 38
Bodelschwingh family, 117
Bodyguard of Lies (Brown), 72
Bohr, Aage, 120, 195
Bohr Institute, 86, 119, 192
Bohr, Niels, 16, 36, 39–40, 41, 47–48,
    51, 188; in occupied Denmark, 86–87,
    129, (German physicists visit) 115,
    116, 119–20, 203, (Paul's letter to)
    130–31; "ex-filtration" of, 179, 192–
    98
Bohr, Mrs. Niels (Margrethe), 86, 87, 194
Bonhoeffer, Dietrich, 215, 220
Bonhoeffer, Karl Friedrich, 215
"Book code," *see* Coded messages
Borbely, Samu, 142
Borch, Einar, 109, 224, 230, 234
Borghild (Welsh's "navy"), 202
Born, Max, 43, 44–45, 104, 118, 153
Born, Mrs. Max, 44, 118
Bosch, Carl, 185
Bothe, Walther, 30, 147, 174–75, 212,
    221
Boyes, Adm. Hector, 57, 64–65, 74
Boy Scouts Association, 166
Brænne, Sverre Bernhard, 158–59
Brahms, Johannes, 217
Bräuer, Kurt, 78, 81
Braun, Wernher von, 22, 98–99, 101,
    154, 155
Brecht, Bertolt, 14, 22, 24
Brecht, Walter, 14, 24, 217–18
Brendigen, Frøken Marie, 30, 56, 76,
    125, 130
Brighter Than a Thousand Suns (Jungk),
    245, 247
Briske, Hans, 139
Britain: Paul's unit surrenders to (World
    War I), 11–12; Paul's feeling for, 12,
    45; Paul warns of German atomic pro-
    gram, 54, 55 (*see also* Oslo Report); re-
    fuses visa for Paul, 57–58; and

occupied Norway, 82–83, 85; evacuates Dunkirk, 87, 218; shipyard strike in, 90; RAF bombing raids, 100–101, 112, 155, 214, 216, 242; and chemical warfare, 142; -U.S. rift, 162, 164, 170, 180, 183, (healed) 196, 197, 204. See also Atomic research/bomb; Secret Intelligence Service (SIS or MI6)
British High Command, 108
British Intelligence in the Second World War (Hinsley), 73
British Naval Intelligence, 91, 92, 201, 203
British Secret Service, see Secret Intelligence Service (SIS or MI6)
Brodersen, Arvid, 107, 227–28
Brody, [British] Captain, 247
Broompark (Scottish collier), 88, 147
Brown, Anthony Cave, 71
Brown Shirts, 24, 31. See also Nazi Party (NSDAP)
Bruining, Hajo, 143
Brun, Christopher, 93
Brun, Jomar ("Master"), 94, 157, 170, 175, 179–80, 196–97; and sabotage, 161, 167, 192; as "Sverre Hagen," 167, 173
Budak, Mile (Croatian minister), 233
Bukharin, Nikolai, 36–37
Bundy, Harvey, 171
Burgess, Guy, 38, 193
Busch, Field Marshal Ernst, 244
Bush, Vannevar, 128, 170, 171, 182
Buzjak, Branko, 233

"C," see Secret Intelligence Service (SIS or MI6)
Cabinet of Dr. Caligari, The (film), 22
Cadorna, Gen. Luigi, 11
Cahan, Samuel Borisovich ("Sammy"), 38–39, 41, 52, 105
Cambridge University, 36, 37, 38, 54, 73, 84 (see also Mond Laboratory)
Canada: produces heavy water, 84
Canaris, Adm. Wilhelm, 209, 210
Carlsberg Brewery (Copenhagen), 119
Carnegie Institution (Washington, D.C.), 51, 56
Casimir, Hendrik B. G., 118, 142, 143
Catholic Church, 142; Rosbaud family as members of, 4, 25, 145
Cavendish Laboratory (Cambridge University), 36, 84
Central Intelligence Agency, U.S., 144, 211

Cermet (ceramic), 150–51
Chadwick, Sir James, 87, 164, 182, 187, 192, 193, 194, 196
Chamberlain, Neville, 59, 211
Chemical warfare, 142, 143, 175, 185–86, 236
Cherwell, Lord (Frederick Lindemann), 16, 122, 187, 191–98 passim, 212
Cheshire, Cyril, 190, 191, 192, 227
Chicago, University of, 162, 174
Churchill, Winston, 113, 139, 154, 249; scientific adviser to, see Cherwell, Lord; contact with Norway, 82, 109–10, 180; and Greece, 90; and Battle of the Atlantic, 90, 91; and coded messages, 90–91; and Hess, 105; and atomic bomb/heavy water, 109, 167, 180, 198, 246, (-FDR agreements) 164, 182, 197; Privy Council of, 135; and SOE, 165, 169
Circle of Friends, see Freundeskreis
Clarendon Laboratory (Oxford), 46
Cobbett, William, 242
Cockcroft, John Douglas, 52, 53, 54, 84, 87, 162, 187–88
Coded messages, 224, 232; via BBC, 65–66, 137, 143; interception by "Ultra," 73, 75, 113; "book code," 82, 225–28; Enigma, Churchill and, 90–91; from POW camps, 149
Code names: for Paul, 2, 111; and code numbers, 97; for heavy water (IMI, XY, Soup, Juice), 166–67; for British atomic energy project, 195. See also individual names
Cohn, Benno, 251
Columbia University, 128
Colville, John, 90
Communist Party (KPD), 24, 38, 104, 105, 164
Compton, Arthur, 163
Conant, James, 162
Concentration camps, 40, 121, 141, 213, 217–18, 220–21, 234, 235; Mauthausen, 25, 220; Berg, 133, 135; Auschwitz, 134, 135, 183, 219, 220, 234; Oranienburg, 149–50, 217; Theresienstadt, 219, 234; Wuhlheide, 220; Mittelbau ("Dora"), 232; Bergen-Belsen, 234; Neuengamme, 234; Dachau, 236. See also Prisoners of war
Condon, Edward, 246
Cosby, Capt. John, 168
Coster, Dirk, 49, 186
Courant, Richard, 30

Curie, Marie, 29, 197
Cyclotrons, *see* Atomic research/bomb
Czechoslovakia: uranium in, 197

Dachau, *see* Concentration camps
Dahl, Helmer, 201–202
Dahl, Maj. Ørnulf, 180, 181, 189, 190
Daladier, Edouard, 211
Dale, Sir Henry, 46
Dames (German physicist), 54
Danish-German Society (Copenhagen), 120
de Boer, Jan Hendrik, 142, 143
Debye, Peter, 48–49
De Groot, W. E. A., 144
Denmark: invaded, 86; Bohr in, *see* Bohr, Niels
"Der Tag," 99, 100
Dessovič, Colonel (German military attaché), 233
Diebner, Kurt, 243
Dietrich, Marlene, 22
Dill, Gen. Sir John, 171
Discovery (journal), 247
Dohnanyi, Greta von (Mrs. Karl Friedrich Bonhoeffer), 215
Dohnanyi, Hans von, 215
Dohnanyi, Mrs. Hans von (Christine Bonhoeffer), 215
Donau (German vessel transporting Jews), 134, 135
Döpel, R., 129
"Dora" (Mittelbau), *see* Concentration camps
Dornberger, Gen. Walter, 99, 101, 154
Dorsch, Xaver, 235–36
Double-Cross (XX) Committee, *see* Secret Intelligence Service (SIS or MI6)
Dovzhenko, Alexander, 36, 41
Drescher-Kaden, Friedrich Karl, 31, 125–26, 206–10, 236, 237
Dresden bombed, 239
Dresden University, 106, 109
Druid network, 148, 149, 154
Duke of York (British battleship), 169
Dulles, Allen, 144

Eberlein, Gustav, 26
Eden, Anthony, 90
Eggenberg, Hans Ulrich von, 238
Ehrhard, Lt. Comm. Hermann, 207, 209
Eichmann, Adolf, 251
Eighth Air Force (U.S.), 171, 172, 216

Einstein, Albert, 16, 128, 139, 245; letter to FDR, 54, 162
Eisenhut (at I. G. Farben), 143
Elizabeth, Princess (palatine), 19
Ellis, C. D., 186
Elsas, Fritz, 210–11
Enigma, *see* Coded messages
"Epsilon" operation, 189
Ettinghausen, Walter, *see* Eytan, Walter
European Center for Nuclear Research, 251
Evening on Karl Johannsgade (Munch painting), 33
Ewald, Paul, 35, 41
"Ex-filtration," *see* Welsh, Lt. Comm. Eric ("Theodor")
Eytan, Walter, 108

Falkenhorst, Gen. Nikolaus von, 170
Farben, I. G. (industrial complex), 60, 83, 143, 157
Farm Hall (near Cambridge), 167–68, 169, 242–43, 245, 247
"Fauner," *see* Volmer, Max
Faye, Comm. Leon, 154
FBI, 204
Fearnly, Thomas, 63
Feinsilber, Sissy, 135, 136
Fermi, Enrico, 30, 51, 129, 196, 236
Findahl, Theo, 106, 112, 223–25, 227, 228
Finland-USSR pact, 78
Flammersfeld, Arnold, 212
Fleming, Ian, 203
Flügge, Siegfried, 52
Foley, Maj. Francis Edward (Frank), 90; aids Jews, 17–18, 25, 26, 251–52; relationship with Paul, 18, 25–26, 56, 57–58, 205, 213, 229; leaves Berlin, 56–57; and Oslo Report, 67, 69, 74–76, 105, 113; leaves Norway, 75, 81–82, 85, 96, 172, 226; and heavy water, 82–83, 84, 88, 172; awarded Order of St. Olav, 84; returns to England, 89, 97–98; and Hess, 105, 113, 200; and XX Committee, 200, 203, 205. *See also* Secret Intelligence Service (SIS or MI6)
Foley, Mrs. Francis Edward (Katherine), 56, 96
Foley, Ursular, 56
Foucarde, Marie-Madeleine, 147, 153, 154
Fowler, Vaughan, 153

"Fox," see Tronstad, Leif Hans Larsen
France: in World War I and postwar, 14, 146, 185; nuclear research in, 53, 84, 88, 251; secret service (Deuxième Bureau) of, 83; fall of, 87–89, 218; Resistance movement ("Noah's Ark") in, 148, 149, 150, 154, 155, 229, 231; Vichy government of, 149; occupies Hechingen, 246
Franck, James, 30
Frank, Carl Theodor (Karl Israel Frank), 13, 219
Frank, Sir Charles, 74, 75
Frank, Dr. Edward, 14
Frank family, 14
Frank, Hildegard (Hilde) Martha, see Rosbaud, Mrs. Paul Wenzel Matteus
Frank, Rudolph, 13, 15, 227
Franz Ferdinand, Archduke, 1, 9, 10
Freese-Pennefather, Harold, 63–64, 75
Freikorps, 207, 209
Freundeskreis (Circle of Friends), 212, 213
Frisch, Otto Robert, 47–48, 104, 114, 190, 198, 188; interprets Hahn's work, 51, 52, 127, 193; at Los Alamos, 204
Fromm, Gen. Ernst, 126, 128
Fuchs, Klaus, 103–4, 114, 115, 164, 193
Fugger family, 3
Furman, Maj. Robert, 197

Gaertner, Friedle ("Gelatine"), 204
Gatterer, Fr. Alois, S.J., 145
Gaugl, Karl, 9
Gentner, Wolfgang, 147
George Washington University, 51; research at, 53
Gerlach, Walther, 237, 243, 244, 247
German-Russian Society of Culture and Technique, 40–41
Germany: World War I and postwar, 14, 146, 185; economic recovery, 22; in Norway (World War II), see Norway; scientists leave, 32, 43–49 passim, 123; tests armaments in Russia, 40; -USSR pact, 56, 70, 76, 78, 123, (broken) 100, 114, 115; and "secret weapons," 59–60, 66–67, 87 (see also Atomic research/bomb; Rocket projectiles); U-boats and navy, 61, 91, 96, 158, 160, 169, 180, 199, (and Schnorkel) 232; aircraft, see Aircraft, German; Luftwaffe; occupies Low

Countries, France, 87, 144; and "Der Tag," 99, 100; air raids on, 100–101, 155, 214, 216, 219, 242; Federal Republic of, 117, 248; and chemical warfare, 143; V-men of, 207–8. See also Hitler, Adolf; Nazi Party (NSDAP); Resistance movements; Secret police
Gerster, Herr (Paul's father-in-law in house of), 219
Gestapo, 32, 40, 86, 89, 211, 244; established, 18; and Paul, 20, 21, 26, 42, 58, 221, 225, 235, (dossier) 213–14; arrests by, 50, 139, 140, 141, 201–202, 204, 220; and Oslo Report, 70–71; in Scandinavia, 119, 158, 160, 194; and atomic research, 129, 200; and Freundeskreis, 212, 213; vs. Resistance groups, 231
Gestapo Ahnentafel (Ancestry Register), 18
Gille, Ludwig, 221
Ginsburger, Judith (later Marie Augusta), 4, 18, 19, 145
Ginsburger, Moysis, 19
Glasgow (British cruiser), 85
Gleditsch, Ellen, 29, 34, 93, 184, 212
Gneisenau (German battleship), 91
Göckel, Herr (headmaster of private school), 28
Goebbels, Josef, 76, 80, 118, 119, 125; and Hans Rosbaud, 23–24
Goerdeler, Carl, 211, 215
Goering, Hermann, 31, 126, 151, 235, 238
Goldschmidt, Heinrich Jacob, 28, 30, 31, 32
Goldschmidt, Mrs. Heinrich Jacob (Amelie), 28, 30
Goldschmidt, Victor Moritz ("V.M."), 28, 33, 207, 211, 250–51; vs. Gleditsch, 29, 34, 93; at Göttingen, 30–32, 125, 207, 208, 209, 210; after return to Norway, 32, 34, 43, 56, 57, 63, 76–80 passim, 94, (during occupation) 87, 122, 124–26, 130, 133–35, (escapes) 135–36, 182, 194; and research, 34, 60–61, 76, 123, 124, 126, 131; "ex-filtration" of, 179–81, 182, 183
Göttingen, University of, 30–34 passim, 44, 101, 207
Goudsmit, Samuel, 197, 241
Government Communications Bureau, see Secret Intelligence Service (SIS or MI6)

Graphite, *see* Heavy water
Graz: as "hero city," 25
Greece: in World War II, 90
Greene, Sir Hugh, 66
"Greif, Der," *see* "Griffin"
Grieg, Edvard, 93
Grieg, Nordahl, 93
"Griffin" ("Der Greif"): Paul assumes
    name, 2, 111; as name of Hitler's dog,
    61–62; mythical tale of, 100. *See also*
    Rosbaud, Paul Wenzel Matteus: AS SPY
Gropius, Walter, 22, 24
Grosz, Georg, 22
Groth, Wilhelm, 52
"Grouse" team, 167, 168
Groves, Gen. Leslie R., 170–78 *passim*,
    183, 198, 199; Alsos mission of, 197,
    240, 242
"Gunnerside" team, 167–70, 176, 242
Gustav II (Gustavus Adolphus), king of
    Sweden, 116
Gustav V, king, and Gustav Adolf,
    crown prince, of Sweden, 193
Gyroscopes, 140. *See also* Rocket projec-
    tiles

Haagen, Dr. Eugene von, 236
Haakon VII, king of Norway, 82, 85, 86
Haber, Fritz, 185–86
"Hagen, Sverre," *see* Brun, Jomar
Hahn, Otto (Hanle), 16, 191, 212, 220,
    242; at Göttingen, 30, 101; Meitner
    and, 48–52 *passim*, 87, 184–86; and
    nuclear fission, 50–54 *passim*, 83, 128,
    186, 210, 236, (quoted on research)
    204, (institute bombed) 221, (in Ura-
    nium Club) 243, 246, 247; and Paul's
    rescue, 237
Hambro, Sir Charles, 165–66, 250
Hamburg (German liner), 174
Hamburg, University of, 47, 53, 132
Hampton, Victor, 140
Hansen, Col. Georg, 210
Hapsburg tradition, 116, 141–42
Harbison-Walker Company (Pittsburgh),
    61
Harteck, Paul, 52, 54, 243
Hassel, Odd, 33–34, 57, 63, 131, 227;
    and Oslo Report, 74–80 *passim*, 108;
    and heavy water, U.S. and, 157, 180,
    181–83; imprisoned, 183, 200
Haukelid, Knut, 168
Hauser, Ernst August, 15
Haus Mexico, 24

Haydn, Josef, 9, 21
Heavy water, 81–82, 131, 156–61, 179–
    80, 181, 196–97, 215; saved from
    Germans, 83, 84, 87–88, 147; Norsk
    Hydro produces, 83–84, 94, 143, 157;
    "blood thicker than," 159–60; sabo-
    tage/destruction of plant, 160–62,
    165–70, 171–76, 242; code names for
    (IMI, XY, Soup, Juice), 166–67;
    graphite vs., 174, 175, 176; German
    intelligence regarding, 200, 201, 204,
    246. *See also* Atomic research/bomb
Hedberg, Kenneth, 33–34
Heiberg, Capt. Walter, 180, 182
Heinnisser family, 4, 5, 6
Heinnisser, Franz, 5, 6, 7, 8, 20
Heinnisser, Josef (and son Josef), 5
Heisenberg, Werner, 30, 43, 174, 221;
    and Max Born, 44, 117–18; and
    atomic research, 104, 111, 115, 119–
    29 *passim*, 162, 175, 182, 194, 196,
    203, 210, 243, 246; Paul's attitude to-
    ward, 116, 117–18, 121; Leipzig insti-
    tute destroyed, 129, 160; interned,
    243–44, 246, 247
Heisenberg, Mrs. Werner (Elisabeth),
    119, 120, 221
Herberstein, Count Johann Otto, 235,
    237, 238, 250
Herberstein, Countess (Idella Scarbor-
    ough), 238
Herzog, Chaim, 251
Hess, Dame Myra, 218
Hess, Rudolf, 17, 105, 113, 200
Hicher, Walter, 143
Hilbert, David, 30
Hill, A. V., 46
Himmler, Heinrich, 75, 130, 144, 204,
    213, 233, 244
Hindemith, Paul, 10, 23, 24
Hindenburg, Paul von, 38
Hinsley, F. H. (Sir Harry), 69, 73, 108
Hipper (German battleship), 91
Hirt, Dr. (director of medical "re-
    search"), 236–37
Hitler, Adolf, 4, 9, 21, 38, 167, 174,
    248; "Griffin" as antagonist to, 1, 2,
    17, 27, 44, 52, 116–17, 150, 219, 228,
    229; assumes power, 16, 19, 24, 38,
    43, 46, 153, 207, 211; annexes Aus-
    tria, 25; and "secret weapon," 54, 59–
    60, 61, 68, 123, 129, 200, 231 (*see also*
    Atomic research/bomb; Rocket projec-
    tiles); dog owned by, 61–62; -Stalin

pact, *see* Germany; and invasion of Norway, Denmark, France, 79, 81, 86, 87, 89, 218; and sea power, 91; *Mein Kampf*, 101, 125; German opposition to/activities against, 144, 189, 208, 211, 217, 250, (assassination plot, 1944) 204, 211, 215, 234–35, 236 (*see also* "Griffin" as antagonist to, *above*); defeat of, 191, 222, 240

Hitler, Alois, 4

Hitler Youth, 36, 146, 238

Hjort, J. B., 224, 234

Hjort, Wanda, 224, 234

Hoel, Adolf, 134

Hoffmann, E. T. A., 15

Höhler, Ali, 24

Hole, Njål, 179, 181, 188, 189–90, 191, 194, 227

Holland, 92; German occupation of, 86, 144, 211; Paul visits (1942), 142–44; Resistance movement in, 144–45, 229

Holm, Camillo, 223

Holzapfel, Max, and Holzapfel firm, 92–93, 96

Hopkins, Harry, 170

Horst Wessel song, 24

Houtermans, Fritz, 122–24, 162, 163, 181, 232

Hutton, Robert Salmon, 26, 46, 54, 55, 84, 218

Hydro (Norwegian ferry): explodes, 174, 177

Hylleras, Professor (at Oslo "colloquium," 1942), 131

Iceland: British naval base in, 96

Imperial Chemical Industries (ICI), 99, 158–59, 160, 161, 196

Institute(s): for Physical Chemistry (Berlin), 23; of Theoretical Physics (Copenhagen), 48; for Advanced Study (Princeton), 51; for Radioactivity (Vienna), 52; of Inorganic Chemistry (Munich), 143; of Physics (Stockholm), 186

International Federation of University Women, 29

International Paints Ltd., 93, 157

International Red Cross, 223, 239

"Intrepid," *see* Stephenson, Sir William

Intze, Capt. Fritz, 169

Ioffe, Abram, 37

Israel, State of, 251

Jaeneke, Erna, 24

Jamaica (British battleship), 169

Jander, Gerhard, 100, 101, 102

Jebsen, Johann ("Artist"), 204

Jensen, J. Hans D., 132

Jentschke, Willibald, 52

Jervell, Dr. (prison camp physician), 133

Jews: and Jewish ancestry, 4, 16–20 *passim*, 25, 31, 48, 177, 210; aid to, 18, 25–26, 139, 194, 220–21, 251–52, (Lisa Meitner) 48–49, 50, 186; discrimination against/persecution of, 25, 30, 31, 44, 139, 153, 183, 187, (in Norway) 28, 125, 129, 133–34 (*see also* Concentration camps); in Germany, immunity for, 31; fantasies of, about return of Hapsburgs, 141–42

Joliot-Curie, Frédéric and Irène, 146–47, 236

Jones, Reginald V., 60, 61, 142, 144, 251; and Oslo Report, 65–68, 69–75 *passim*, 98, 103; and Peenemünde report, 138; quoted on Welsh, 156; and heavy water, 159–60, 161

Jordan, Pascual, 43, 117, 152–54, 208

"Julius," *see* Tronstad, Leif Hans Larsen

Jung, Carl, 152

Jungk, Robert, 245, 247

Junkes, Fr. Joseph, S.J., 145

"Kaare," *see* Syverstad, Gunnar

Kaiser Wilhelm Institute(s), 35, 48–49, 101, 240, 242; Paul at, 14, 36; atomic research at, 50, 52, 126, 185, 246

Kapitza, Peter, 16, 47, 52, 84, 105; Paul and, 36–37, 39–42, 211, 213, 241; in Soviet Union, 39–42, 43, 44–45

Kapitza, Mrs. Peter (Anna), 38, 39–40, 41, 44

Karl VI, Emperor (palatine), 19

Karlik, Berta, 184

Karl Philip, Prince (palatine), 19

Katz, Moses, 133–34, 135, 251

KGB, *see* Secret police

Kikoin, Col. I. K., 240–41

Klara (Paul's housekeeper), 233, 239

Klaveness, Eva, *see* Andresen, Mrs. Johan H.

Kockl, Ida, *see* Rosbaud, Mrs. Wenzel

Kollwitz, Kathe, 232

Korsching, Horst, 243, 244

Kowarski, Lew, 88

Kremer, Simon, 105

Kronig, R., 143, 174

Kummerow, Hans, 70, 115, 139–40
Kurchatov, Igor, 114
Kurzweg, Hermann, 99, 153
Kusuru, Saburo, 210

Lambers, Hille Ris, 142–43
Lange, Hilde, see Benjamin, Mrs. Georg
Lange, Otto, 235
Lange, Ruth, 23–27 passim, 40, 139–42
  passim, 148–53 passim, 239, 240, 250;
  anti-Nazi activities, 219–20
Laquer, Walter, 69, 70
Lark-Horovitz, Karl, 57–58
Latey, Maurice, 66
Laue, Max von, 30, 120–21, 191, 212,
  213, 220, 242, 243; postwar letters to
  Paul, 244–48
Laves, Fritz, 221
Laves, Melitta, 222
Lawrence, Ernest, 147
le Carré, John, 250
Leipzig experimental assembly de-
  stroyed, 129, 160
Lenin, V. I., 37
LePrince-Ringuet, Louis, 147
LFA (Goering's research establishment),
  151. See also Luftwaffe
Lie, Trygve, 109
Lindemann, Frederick, see Cherwell,
  Lord
Lindemann, Gen. Fritz, 231
Lindemann, Max, 231
Lindemann, Mrs. Max (Elsa Äström),
  231
London Sunday Express, 199–200, 202
London Times, 87
Lonna, Bodil, 133
Los Alamos, see Atomic research/bomb
Luftwaffe, 60, 62, 78, 123; research for,
  31, 150, 151; bombing by, 85, 142;
  cost of, 128; Paul in uniform of, 130,
  180. See also Aircraft, German
Lunde, Gulbrand, 76, 77, 93–94, 105,
  125, 126, 133
Lunde, Mrs. Gulbrand (Maria), 133
Lüttke, Georg, 16
Lüttke, Mrs. Georg (Gertrud), 16

Macauley Institute for Soil Research,
  136
MacDonald, Alexander, 1
Maclean, Donald, 38, 164
Maginot Line, 146, 237
Magnesium, see Technology of Magnesium
  and Its Alloys

Man Called Intrepid, A (Stevenson), 161
Manhattan Project, 128, 170. See also
  Atomic research/bomb
Mann, Wilfrid Basil, 87, 193
Mark, Hermann, 15, 17, 23
Marthinsen (chief of Norwegian state
  police), 134
Martial-Albert-Armand network, 231
Marxism, 24, 38, 45
"Master," see Brun, Jomar
Masterman, John, 200, 201, 202
Mattauch, Josef, 53, 54, 191, 220
MAUD Committee, 87, 99; reports on
  atomic bomb, 104, 114, 115, 164
Mauthausen, see Concentration camps
Maxwell, Robert, 250
May, Alan Nunn, 38, 163, 164, 193
May, Karl, 9
Meier-Leibnitz (physicist), 147
Mein Kampf (Hitler), 101, 125
Meitner, Lise, 16, 23, 35–36, 121–22,
  135, 194, 199, 204, 212, 242; corre-
  spondence with Paul and Hilde Ros-
  baud, 37, 39–40, 49, 78–79, 86–87,
  97, 98, 125, 180, 213, 218, 219, 227;
  works with Hahn, 48, 50–51, 52, 184–
  86, (discovers new element) 48, 185,
  (and nuclear research) 127, 128; es-
  capes from Germany, later from Den-
  mark, 49, 50, 53, 86; "ex-filtration" of
  (refused), 179, 183, 186–91, 192
Meitner, Philipp and Hedwig, 183
Mendeleev, Dimitri, 38
Mentzel, Rudolf, 124
Menzies, Sir Graham Stewart: as "C,"
  65, 66, 90–91, 96, 103–4, 109, 192,
  205, 243
Metallgesellschaft A.G. (Frankfurt), 15,
  78
Metallwirtschaft (weekly magazine),
  15, 16, 19, 36, 38, 61, 76,
  157, 207
MI5, 97, 104, 195, 200, 201
MI6, see Secret Intelligence Service
Miall, Leonard, 65–66
Michels, A. M. J., 143–44
Midtsku, Sverre, 157
"Mikkel," see Tronstad, Leif Hans
  Larsen
Milch, Field Marshal Erhard, 126, 127,
  128, 231
MILORG (Militaerorganisasjonen), 108
Missile, see Wasserfall
Mitchell, Maj. Leslie H., 75
Mittelbau, see Concentration camps

Moerschner, Ingeborg, 174–75
Møller, Christian, 120
Molotov, Vyacheslav, 56
Mond Laboratory (Cambridge), 37–38, 39, 52; shipped to Moscow, 41–42, 52
Mond, Ludwig, 37
Montagu, Ewen, 201, 202–3
Moon, Philip, 84
Mortensen, Maj. Hans, 210
Munch, Edvard, 33
Mürer, Niels Jörgen, 223

Nagell, Maj. Finn, 91, 169, 181
National Defense Research Council (U.S.), 163
Naturwissenschaften (periodical), 50, 125, 210, 213
Nazi Party (NSDAP): opposition to, 5, 20, 21, 27, 144, 147; members of, 16, 31, 43, 153, 206–7, 208; rise of, 16, 17, 24; anthem (Horst Wessel song) of, 24; vs. the Jews, *see* Jews; Paul and, 27, 101, 125, 144, 147, 206–9 *passim*, 213–14, 225; collaboration with, 31, 44, 45, 94, 146, 172, 230; vs. Bolsheviks, 36, 44, 76, 207 (*see also* Soviet Union), and nuclear research, 51, scientist members of, 101; swastika symbol of, 207; decorates Hans Rosbaud, 236
Neuengamme, *see* Concentration camps
New Gulliver, The (film), 36
Newill, Comm. J. B., 75, 81, 91
New York Times, 170
Nielsen, Kjell, 171, 172–73
NKVD, *see* Secret police
Noack, Ulrich, 76–77
"Noah's Ark" (French Resistance movement), *see* France
Nobel, Alfred, 186
Nobel Peace Institute, 63, 189
Nobel Prize and laureates, 30, 51, 75, 118, 124, 153, 243; for physics, 34, 38, 43, 123, 131, 188, 201; for chemistry, 146, 186
Noddack, Walter and Ida, 236
Nøkleby, Berit, 166
Norman, Frederick (Bimbo), 60
Normandy invasion, 216, 223, 224, 230, 235
Norsk Hydro, 83–84, 94, 143, 157, 158, 160, 172, 175. *See also* Heavy water
Norway: Jews barred from, ban lifted, 28, (ban returned) 125, 129, 133; World War I, 29, 92–93; invaded, oc-

cupied, World War II, 29, 75–87 *passim*, 91, 94, 106, 108, 122–34 *passim*, 171–72; Goldschmidt returns to, 32 (*see also* Goldschmidt, Victor Moritz ["V.M."]; olivine deposits in, 60; Resistance movement, 79, 106–11 *passim*, 130, 135, 150, 201–2 (*see also* Welsh, Lt. Comm. Eric); government-in-exile, 106, 108, 109–10, 157, 173; produces heavy water, 156, 167 (*see also* Heavy water; Norsk Hydro); bombed by U.S., 170, 172–74, 175–76, 199, 200, 204
Norwegian Academy of Sciences, 63, 76
Norwegian Canning Industry, 93
Norwegian Defense Research Establishment, 80
Norwegian Institute for Air Research, 79
Norwegian Raw Materials Commission, 126
Norwegian Rowing Club, 223
Novikov, Gen. V. V., 240
NSDAP, *see* Nazi Party
Nuclear research, *see* Atomic research/bomb; Heavy water
Nuremberg Laws (1935), 25, 31

Office of Strategic Services (OSS), U.S., 144, 182, 183
OGPU, *see* Secret police
Oliphant, Mark, 84
Olivine, 60–61, 207
Ollen, Olle, 150–51
Olsen, Comm. Just, 95
Opel, Fritz von, 22
Operation(s) (Allied and German): Barbarossa, 100, 114; Dürer, 154; Freshman, 167; Sunshine, 176–77; Mincemeat, 201; Overlord, *see* Normandy invasion; Sea Lion, 218
Oranienburg, *see* Concentration camps
Oregon State University, 33
Organization Todt, 235–36, 237
Ortner, Karl, 7, 8
Oslo Report, 172; delivery of, 63–64, 69–81 *passim*, 108, 125, 188; ignored, 65, 67–68, 113, 138; authors of, 66, 69–70, 71, 73, 105, 139; details described in, 66–67, 114, 123, 141; and Peenemünde report, 98, 100, 102; Welsh and, 103, 105
Oslo University, 28–29, 33, 34, 77, 107, 126, 183, 224, 234
OSS, *see* Office of Strategic Services

Ottar, Brynulf, 79–80, 107, 131, 188, 190
Otto Hahn Institute (Berlin), 23
Oxford University, 46, 60

Pash, Col. Boris T., 197
Pauli, Wolfgang, 43
Pavlov, Ivan, 40
Peenemünde, 116; rocket experiments at, 67, 68, 98–100, 101–2, 112, 138, 140, 152, 153–54; report ignored, 113–14, 138, 140–41, 179; bombed, 155, 231
Peierls, Rudolf, 47, 48, 103, 104–5, 114, 193
Pepys, Samuel, 242
Pergamon Press, 250
Perrin, Michael, 196
Pétain, Marshal Henri, 146
"Pettersen," see Turner, John
Peyrou, Charles, 146, 148, 150, 151, 152, 251
Philby, Kim, 38, 97, 193
Philips Eindhoven, 142, 143, 144
Piatier, André, 148–49, 231
Piatier, Henri ("Rhein-1202"), 139, 146–54 passim, 231, 232, 233, 251
Piatier, Juliette Grenier, 146
Piekenbrock, Col. Hans, 210
Piel, Harry, 61
Pihl-Johannessen, Conrad, 93, 94–95
Pihl-Johannessen, Lars, 93, 95
Pius XII (pope), 145
Plutonium, 174, 175, 196; German knowledge of, 29, 122, 123, 124, 127. See also Atomic research/bomb
Poland, 56, 59, 61, 78, 211
Polanyi, Magda, 139
Polanyi, Michael, 23, 139, 148
Popov, Dusko ("Tricycle"), 203, 204
Poschmann, Dr. A., 236
Potsdam Conference, 240, 249
Powys-Libbe, Ursula, 138
Prankl, Friedrich, 52
Prien, Lt. Comm. Gunther, 61, 91
Prisoners of war, 139, 146–52 passim, 220, 224, 238; Paul as World War I POW, 12; Uranium Club as, 242–48. See also Concentration camps
Ptushko, Alexander, 36
Purdue University, 57
Pyke, Geoffrey, 17

Quisling, Vidkun, 76, 78, 125, 126, 224

Raaby, Torstein, 169
Radar, 57, 67, 232. See also "Secret weapons"
Radetsky March, The (Roth), 142
Radič (Croatian contact), 233
Radio stations, 109, 113, 157, 169; THETA, 201, 202. See also BBC (British Broadcasting Corporation); Coded messages
Raeder, Adm. Eric, 79
RAF, see Britain
Rascher, Dr. Sigmund, 236
Ravens, Col. Charles E., 182
Ray, Maud, 87
"Red Hilde," see Benjamin, Mrs. Georg (Hilde Lange)
Reichenau, Gen. Walter von, 211
Reich Research Council, 123, 124, 126, 237
Reich War Office, 148–49
Reid, Margaret, 56–57, 74, 75, 81–82, 85, 96, 105, 226
Reilly, Sidney, 92
Reinhard (Gestapo agent), 70
Reksten, Egil, 158, 159, 160
Resistance movements, 165, 227, 229, 231. See also France; Holland; Norway
Reynaud, Paul, 87
"Rhein-1202," see Piatier, Henri
RSHA (Reichssicherheitshauptamt), see Secret police
Ribbentrop, Joachim von, 56, 117
Rideal, Eric, 17
Riste, Olav, 166
Rittner, [British] Major, 244, 246
Rockefeller grant, 79
Rockefeller Institute, 177
Rocket projectiles, 61, 66–67, 68; V-1 and V-2, 99, 101–2, 112, 128, 140, 154, 155, 176, 230–31, 232, 235. See also Peenemünde; "Secret weapons"
Röhm, Ernst, 244
Rolstad, Gen. Leif, 74–75
Romberg (at Oslo "colloquium," 1942), 131
Rommel, Field Marshal Erwin, 222
Rona, Elizabeth, 184
Roosevelt, Franklin D.: and atomic bomb, 54, 128, 162, 170, 198; -Churchill agreements, 164, 182, 197
Rørholt, Bjørn, 158–60
Rosbaud, Angelika Anna Maria Mathilde ("Angela," "Anka"), 15, 21, 25, 252; in England, 26, 27, 86, 109, 122, 218; Paul's letter to, 249–50

Rosbaud, Anna Aloisia, 4, 8–9, 10, 19, 21, 217, 218; children born to, 3, 5, 6–7, 20
Rosbaud, Bruno, 5, 6–7
Rosbaud family, 3–7, 9, 18, 232
Rosbaud, Hans (Johann), 220–21, 232, 238; as child/young man, 6, 8, 9, 10, 13–14, 116; as conductor, 7, 19, 21, 23, 115, 252; ancestry, 19, 20–21; Paul's letters to, 98, 102, 116, 141, 145, 206, 214–17 passim, 236, 237, 239; awarded Nazi medal, 236
Rosbaud, Mrs. Hans (Edeltraud Shäfer), 14
Rosbaud, Martha, 6, 7, 238–39; son of (Andreas), 239
Rosbaud, Paul Wenzel Matteus ("Bobby"): FAMILY, PRIVATE LIFE, PERSONALITY childhood/adolescence, 6, 8–10, 116; arrest, 10–11; in World War I, 11–12, 185; as British POW, 12; at universities, 13, 14–15, 45, 99; marries, daughter born, 13–14, 15; described, 14, 46, 148; takes job in Berlin, moves to Springer Verlag, 15–16, 17, 61; affair with Ruth Lange, 22–27 (see also Lange, Ruth); darker side of, 24; Catholicism, 25, 145, 177; moves wife and daughter to England, 26–27; postwar career, 250, (awarded Tate Medal) 78, 250, (meets Gen. Groves) 177–78, (von Laue letters to) 244–48; death, 252
  AS SPY   hatred of Hitler/Nazis, 1, 2, 17, 27, 44, 52, 116–17, 150, 206, 208–9, 221, 225, 228, 229, 237, (and Nazi friends) 101, 125, 206, 209, (cleared by Nazi Party) 213–14, 217, code name for, 2, 111; paternity/ancestry, 7, 8, 18, 19–21; aids Jews, war victims, 18, 219–21, 234, (Lise Meitner) 48–49, 50, 186; cover for, 18, 206, 211, (job as) 17, 36, 38, 41–42, 77, 78, 111, 143, 151, 160 (see also Springer Verlag [publishers]); as German citizen/"officer," 25, 57, 131, 180; as host to scientific gathering (Berlin, 1935), 35–36, 41–42; letters, (to Lise Meitner) , 37, 40, 79, 97, 125, 213, 227, (to Hans) 98, 102, 116, 141, 145, 206, 214–17 passim, 236, 237, 239, (to Bohr) 131–32, (to Hilde) 218–19, 249, (to Angela) 249–50; visits Soviet Union, 37, 38; risks exposure, 41–42; and atomic research/heavy water, 50–

55, 84, 121, 123, 124, 161–62, 174, 181–82, 196, 197, 204, (reports on German knowledge of) 111, 129, 131, 202, 209, 210; British visa refused, 57–58; co-editor of book, 60–62, 78; and strategic materials, 61, 76, 124, 143; radio messages to, 66, 97, 137; and Oslo Report, 71, 74, 77–80, 98, 100, 105, 113, 125, 225; visits Oslo, (1939) 77–80, (1942) 125–26, 129–31, 180, 209; contacts, 77, 78, 95, 109, 131, 140, 143, 207–11 passim, 215, ("V.M.") 29–32 passim, 43, 56, 60, 77–79, 124–35 passim, 180, 209, 251, (Houtermans) 122–23, (Vatican) 145, (French Resistance) 148–52 (see also France), (Tronstad) 156–57 (see also Bergh, Sverre ["Sigurd"]; Foley, Maj. Francis Edward [Frank]; Kapitza, Peter; Meitner, Lise; Secret Intelligence Service [SIS]; Welsh, Lt. Comm. Eric ["Theodor"]); warns of invasion of Norway, 79–80; living conditions (Berlin), 86–87, 101, 139, 151, (houses destroyed) 148, 214, 222, 240, "reactivated" (1941), 98, 109, 179; and Peenemünde, 100, 102, 112–13, 138, 140–41, 152–55, 179; Hapsburg tradition revered by, 116, 141–42; suspected, cleared, 141, 180, 205, 214, 217, 223, 224, 228, 240; European travels (late 1942), 141–44; and SOE, 166; conscripted to Organization Todt, 235–37; escapes Soviet army, 239–41, 250
Rosbaud, Mrs. Paul Wenzel Matteus (Hildegard [Hilde] Martha Frank), 13–14, 15, 21, 22, 31, 32, 227, 252; Jewish ancestry, 16, 25, 177; as gymnast, 23, 48, 218; in England, 26, 27, 56, 58, 97, 98, 122, 180, 213, 218, (letters from) 78–79, 86–87, 108, 219, 249
Rosbaud, Richard, 4
Rosbaud, Wenzel, 4, 5, 6
Rosbaud, Mrs. Wenzel (Ida Kockl), 4, 5, 144
Rosbaud, Wilhelmina, 4, 11
Roscher Lund, Capt. Alfred R., 108–9, 110, 111, 112, 140, 158, 160, 180–81; quoted on Welsh, 251
Rosenblum, Lesser, 133–34, 135
Rosenqvist, Ivan, 108
Rote Kapelle (Red Orchestra; spy ring), 70, 115, 140, 141. See also Soviet Union

Roth, Josef, 142
Rousseau, Jeannie ("Amniarix"), 154, 155
Royal Institute, 191
Royal Oak (British battleship), 61, 64, 91
Royal Society, 84, 191, 248
Royal Swedish Academy of Science, 186
Royal United Services Institution, 69
Ruester, Emil, 139
Ruge, Gen. Otto, 82, 85, 108, 172
Ruskin, John, 82
Rust, Bernhard, 53, 118, 119
Rutherford, (Lord) Ernest, 16, 36, 39, 41, 46, 47, 48, 52

Sabotage, 152, 161, 167–76 *passim*, 242
Sarajevo, 1, 10
Saturday Evening Post, The, 127
Saukič, Frau (Croatian contact), 233
Scandinavia, 92. *See also* Norway
Scarborough, Idella, *see* Herberstein, Countess
Schacht, Hjalmar, 209, 211
Scharnhorst (German battleship), 91, 169, 180, 199
Schcherbina, V. V., 31
Scheer (German battleship), 91, 113
Schellenberg, Walter, 204
Schickelgruber, Alois, 4
Schiller, Johann von, 116
Schmidt, Ernst, 151
Schnorkel, 232. *See also* Germany (U-boats and navy of)
Schoenberg, Arnold, 22, 23, 252
Schön, Michael, 148, 150, 151–52, 153
Schorsch, Liselotte, 23
Schulhof, Erika, 135
Schumann, Clara, 5, 217, 218
Schumann, Gen. Eric, 147
Seaborg, Glenn, 124
Secret Intelligence Service (SIS or MI6), 149, 160, 188, 195; Foley with, 17–18, 25, 57, 75, 84, 91; and scientific research, 25, 51–52, 60, 84; Paul and, 46, 49, 213, 215, 223; "C" as head of, 59, 65, 90, 91, 96, 103, 109, 192, 205, 243; and Oslo Report, 64–69 *passim*, 74, 75, 98; and "Balloon," 88; and Battle of the Atlantic, 91; Welsh with, 91–98, 103, 105, 110, 112, 131, 156, 165, 218; and "V.M." 's escape, 135, 136; Paul's direct contact with, 143; and ICI, 159; in Norway, 166, 167; official history, 175, 179, 188, 189, 232; and OSS, 182; in Stockholm,

190, 192, 227, 233 (*see also* XU); as "Government Communications Bureau," 195; liaison with atomic energy intelligence, 196; story planted by, 200; XX Committee of, 200–203, 204; ignores Wasserfall papers, 231
Secret police, 77; SS (Germany), 36, 76, 110, 213, 220, (SD intelligence arm of) 131, 204, 233; NKVD, OGPU, KGB (Soviet Union), 38, 92, 123, 213; RSHA (Germany), 213, 214. *See also* Gestapo
"Secret weapons," 59–60, 64, 66–67, 68, 87, 101, 199–200. *See also* Atomic research/bomb; Chemical warfare; Rocket projectiles
Seip, Didrik Arup, 224–25, 234
Seckles, Bernhard, 13
Sesame and Lilies (Ruskin), 82, 226
Shäfer, Edeltraud, *see* Rosbaud, Mrs. Hans (Johann)
Shape of Things to Come, The (Wells), 47
"Shetland bus," 202
Sicily invasion, 201
Siegbahn, Kai, 199, 200
Siegbahn, Manne, 186, 187, 189, 199
Signal interception, *see* Coded messages
"Sigurd," *see* Bergh, Sverre
Simonsen, Willy, 201
Simpson, Esther, 46, 47
Simson, Clara von, 184, 212
Sinclair, Adm. Hugh, 59, 65
SIS, *see* Secret Intelligence Service
"Skylark" operation, 157–60, 169, 180
Snow, C. P., 121
Society for Social Responsibility in Science, 245
SOE, *see* Special Operations Executive
Solberg, Halvor, 134
Soltikow, Michael Graf, 210
Sophie, Archduchess, 10
Soviet Union: Bolsheviks vs. Nazis, 36, 44, 76, 207; technology in, 36, 37, (Mond Laboratory shipped to) 41–42, 52, (atomic research) 114–15, 240; Paul visits, 37, 38; espionage by, 38, 40, 41, 70, 97, 105, 114, 115, 140, 141, 164, 192; purge (1934) in, 38; -German pact, *see* Germany; and Poland, 59; -Finland pact, 78; and citizen approval of system, 124; Commerce and Trade Delegation (Berlin), 141; Stalingrad, 222; enters Berlin, 239–41, 242; Paul escapes army of, 239–41. *See also* Secret police

Special Operations Executive (SOE), 165–66, 168, 193, 195, 202
Speer, Albert, 126, 127–28, 129, 175, 235–36
Spitz, Leo, see Szilard, Leo
Sporberg, Harry, 165–66
Springer, Ferdinand, 17, 213
Springer, Julius, 17, 212
Springer Verlag (publishers), 26, 41, 50, 61, 76, 79, 111, 143, 213, 235, 238; as Paul's cover, 17–18, 143, 151; and book shipments, book code, 77, 225, 256; London branch, 250
SS, see Secret police
Stalin, Josef, 36, 38, 240; -Hitler pact, see Germany
Stauffenberg, Col. Claus Schenk von, 234–35
Steinhoff, Eric, 99
Steltzer, Lt. Col. Theodor, 107
Stephenson, Sir William ("Intrepid"), 161, 182
Stifter, Herbert, 144–45
Stifter, Susanne, 144
Stimson, Henry, 171
Stockholm, University of, 179, 189
Storm troopers (Sturm Abteilung), 16
Storsveen, Arvid, 108
Strajner, Johann, 6, 8, 20–21
Strajner, Frau Johann (Theresia Wesiak), 6, 20, 21
Stranski, Iwan A., 138–39, 140, 141
Strasbourg University, 115–16, 237
Strassmann, Fritz, 50, 51, 128
Stravinsky, Igor, 23
Strømnes, Øivind ("Øle"), 107, 112
Strømnes, Mrs. Øivind (Anne-Sofie), 107, 112
Strong, Gen. George V., 107, 182
Suess, Hans, 132, 135
Suffert, Fritz, 50
Suffolk, Lord, 87–89
Suritz, Jacob, 35, 40, 41
Svendsen, Johanne Brun, see Welsh, Mrs. Eric
Syltøy, Jacob, 202
Syverstad, Gunnar ("Kaare"), 177
"Szenassy, Stephan," see Stranski, Iwan A.
Szilard, Leo (Leo Spitz), 16, 45–47, 54, 128, 162–63

Tass (Soviet news agency), 56
Tate Medal, 78, 250, 252

Taylor, Geoffrey I., 38, 41
Technology of Magnesium and Its Alloys (Beck and Rosbaud, eds.), 60, 62, 78, 80, 172
Teller, Edward, 51
"Theodor," see Welsh, Lt. Comm. Eric
Theresienstadt, see Concentration camps
THETA, see Radio stations
Thompson, George, 84
Thorsen, Bjarne, 169
Threepenny Opera, The, 24
Thum, Professor (at Darmstadt), 99
Thümmel, Paul, 204
Timofeev-Ressovsky (physicist), 148
Tirpitz (German battleship), 91, 160, 180
Todt, Fritz, 235
Tohmfor, Erhard, 139–40
Tohmfor, Mrs. Erhard (Gertrud Zimmerman), 139–40
Trettler, A., 40–41
Treusch, Br. Karl, S.J., 145
"Tricycle," see Popov, Dusko
Tronstad, Leif Hans Larsen ("Mikkel" ["Fox"], "Julius"), 156–57, 173, 176–77, 180; "ex-filtrated," 160, 189; and sabotage of heavy-water plant, 160–62, 166, 167, 192
"Tube Alloys," see Atomic research/bomb
Turner, John ("Pettersen"), 160, 174, 190, 205, 211, 223

U-boats, see Germany
Uhlir, Ottokar, 9
Ulster Prince (Irish ferry), 85
"Ultra," see Coded messages
United Nations, 251
United States: nuclear research in, 53, 54–55 (and heavy-water production) 84, 174 (see also Atomic research/bomb); seizes Goldschmidt's royalties, 61; and West Indies naval bases, 90; intelligence services (Army, OSS, CIA), 107, 114, 144; -Britain rift, 162, 164, 170, 180, 183, (healed) 196, 197, 204; bombs Norway, see Norway; bombs Dresden, 239
Uranium, 52, 233; stocks of, 53, 84, 143, 246; German program, 53, 123, 129, 162; and "uranium bomb," 119, 127, 128, 199, 200, 204, 246; deposits, 197, 203. See also Atomic research/bomb
Uranium Club (Germany), 176, 242–48
Urey, Harold, 83

V-1, V-2 rockets, see Rocket projectiles
van Arkel, Anton Eduard, 142
van den Heuvel, Frederick (Fanny), 149,
    250
Vereinigte Kuggellagerfabriken A.G.,
    106
Versailles, Treaty of, 40, 101, 207
Viking League, 209
Vikoren, Anders, 230
V-men (Germany), 207–8
Volmer, Max, 138, 139–40, 141
Volmer, Mrs. Max (Lotte), 139
Vorley, Norman, 57
Vossische Zeitung, 31

Wachtel, Col. Max, 154
Waddell, Lt. Col. Hugh B., 182
Wagner, Carl, 99
Wagner, Richard, 26
Wallenberg, Raoul, 17
Walther, A., 99
Walton, Ernest, 52
Wasserfall (missile), 176, 231
Weill, Kurt, 24
Weizsäcker, Carl Friedrich Freiherr von,
    115–20 *passim*, 123, 127, 194, 203,
    243–48 *passim*
Weizsäcker, Ernst von, 116, 117, 119
Weizsäcker, Richard von, 117, 248
Welle-Strand, Erik, 157
Wells, H. G., 46, 47
Welsh, Lt. Comm. Eric ("Theodor"),
    125, 211, 232; and Norwegian Intelli-
    gence/Resistance/XU, 91–96, 107–11
    passim, 137, 151, 189, 190, 201, 202,
    218, 230, 251, (decorated by Norway)
    169; and Paul, 94, 96, 98, 103–13 *pas-
    sim*, 131–37 *passim*, 142, 152, 157,
    177–83 *passim*, 196, 223–29 *passim*,
    247, 250, (doubts, authenticates) 180,
    205, 228; and Peenemünde, 102, 112,
    113, 140, 141, 152; and Oslo Report,
    103, 105; and atomic research/heavy
    water, 104, 132, 156–62 *passim*, 165–
    69, 173–76 *passim*, 201–205 *passim*,
    233, (Uranium Club) 242, 243, 244,
    247; and "V.M.," 135–36; and "ex-fil-
    tration," 179–82, 183, 188–96 *passim*,
    241, 250; Soviet knowledge of, 193
Welsh, Mrs. Eric (Johanne Brun Svend-
    sen), 93, 95
Wergeland, Harald, 132, 179, 188–89
Wergeland, Henrik Arnold, 28, 125

Werke, Askania, 140
Wesiak, Theresia, see Strajner, Mrs.
    Johann
Wessel, Horst, 24, 40
West Indies: U.S. bases in, 90
Whistondale, John, 110–11, 113, 151,
    160, 190, 231, 233
White Rose student group (Munich),
    217
Wiedemann, Fritz, 119, 174
Wigner, Eugene, 51, 54, 162
Willstätter, Richard, 30
Wilson, John Skinner, 166
Winkler, Johannes, 101
Winsnes, Ragnar, 224–25, 226, 227–28,
    230, 234
Winston, Frederick (Earl of Birken-
    head), 187
Winterbotham, Group Capt. Frederick
    W., 25, 60, 65, 66, 73, 75
Wirtz, Karl, 127, 176, 243, 246
Witte, Helmut, 221
Witzell, Adm. Carl, 123, 124, 126, 232
*Wizard War, The: British Scientific Intelli-
    gence, 1939–1945* (Jones), 69, 144
Wolverine (British battleship), 91
World of Yesterday, The (Zweig), 142
World Set Free, The (Wells), 46
World War I, 11, 45, 91, 92, 146; Nor-
    way in, 29, 92–93; chemical warfare,
    185–86; German veterans of (and
    NSDAP), 206–7
World War II, 55, 57; Norway in, see
    Norway; Hitler's peace bid (1939), 59;
    strategic materials, 61 (see also Atomic
    research/bomb); *British Intelligence in*
    (Hinsley), 73
Wuhlheide, see Concentration camps

XU (Resistance intelligence organ-
    ization), 132, 135, 140, 176; orga-
    nized, 79, 107–8; SIS and, 165, 179;
    in Stockholm, 181, 188, 190. See also
    Norway
XX Committee, see Secret Intelligence
    Service (SIS)

Yagoda, Genrikh Grigorievich, 39
Yale University, 29
Yugoslav partisans, 5

Zolchner family, 3–4, 18
Zweig, Stefan, 142